This Dummy Pulls His Own Strings

DWIGHT E. KNUTH

Copyright © 2016 Dwight E. Knuth.

All rights reserved. No part of this book may be used or reproduced by any means, graphic, electronic, or mechanical, including photocopying, recording, taping or by any information storage retrieval system without the written permission of the author except in the case of brief quotations embodied in critical articles and reviews.

All scriptures are from the KING JAMES VERSION
(KJV): KING JAMES VERSION, public domain

LifeRich Publishing is a registered trademark of
The Reader's Digest Association, Inc.

LifeRich Publishing books may be ordered through booksellers or by contacting:

LifeRich Publishing
1663 Liberty Drive
Bloomington, IN 47403
www.liferichpublishing.com
1 (888) 238-8637

Because of the dynamic nature of the Internet, any web addresses or links contained in this book may have changed since publication and may no longer be valid. The views expressed in this work are solely those of the author and do not necessarily reflect the views of the publisher, and the publisher hereby disclaims any responsibility for them.

Any people depicted in stock imagery provided by Thinkstock are models, and such images are being used for illustrative purposes only.
Certain stock imagery © Thinkstock.

ISBN: 978-1-4897-0989-9 (sc)
ISBN: 978-1-4897-0988-2 (hc)
ISBN: 978-1-489-70987-5 (e)

Library of Congress Control Number: 2016916685

Print information available on the last page.

LifeRich Publishing rev. date: 11/17/2016

To Reverend Erin,

My favorite I. Falls minister.

Thanks to you and to God for your service to our church and community.

My prayer for you is that you enjoy preaching the gospel as much as I enjoy hearing it from you.
May God Bless you and continue to make you a blessing.
Love
Dwight Knuth

Contents

Dedication..vii
Epigraph..ix
Preface...xi
Acknowledgements.......................................xiii
Introduction...xvii

   1. Closer to the Tuscan Sun - Italy....................1
   2. Lost in the Badlands...............................32
   3. Love of my Life, My Happiness......................43
   4. Philosophy and Love of Life........................68
   5. Army & Navy..82
   6. Crushes, Love, Romance & Foolishness..............126
   7. Boxing, Bar fights & other sports.................168
   8. My Hometown.......................................185
   9. Family - Heritage.................................225
  10. Health..334
  11. Work..354
  12. Friends...392
  13. On the Road – Hitchhiking & Riding the rails in the 1950's.....412
  14. Education...442
  15. Retirement..452
  16. I Believe...466
  17. Religion..474
  18. Last Chapter......................................503

Epilogue - One Dummy pulling his own strings.............531
Afterword..537
About the Author...539

Dedication

Happiness is like a kiss, you must share it to enjoy it.
Bernard Meltzer

This book is dedicated to my wonderful wife, Kathleen, who not only put up with my faults but loved me in spite of them. She, like her parents before her, was a wonderful person with many attributes I wish I shared. I love to use quotes in my writing because I find the people I quote are much wiser than I and have said what I think, much more eloquently. The following quote is from Victor Hugo who said, "The supreme happiness in life is the conviction that we are loved for ourselves, or rather, loved in spite of ourselves". Kathy has given me this conviction and happiness. I hope I have returned it.

With Love and Dedication, Always

Epigraph

Love Story of Life

Preface

My intent for this book was to record my life as a historical account of the times I lived, my accomplishments, my failures, my joys, my sorrows and my struggles. I wanted my kids, grandkids, great grandkids and descendants to have a record of their heritage. I wanted to record some of the stories of our ancestors and their struggles in creating a better life for their children, grandchildren and descendants.

I also wanted to convey my thoughts on life and living, not to hope for agreement but to show that I think for myself and so should the reader. Thus the name, this dummy pulls his own strings.

There is a book written about this very subject that I would recommend reading and as use for a guide in life. It is a short book, 7 short chapters and it is an old book written in 1903 by James Allen. It is titled, "As A Man Thinketh". It comes from a Bible passage in Proverbs, chapter 23, verse 7, For as a man thinketh in his heart, so is he. KJV James Allen's book is as valid today as it was when it was written but because it was derived from a Bible verse it refers to a Man rather than a person, male or female. It is good advice for anyone, regardless of gender. The seven chapters of this book are titled as follows:

Chapter One – Thought and Character
Chapter Two – Effect of Thought on Circumstances
Chapter Three – Effect of Thought on Health and Body
Chapter Four – Thought and Purpose
Chapter Five – The Thought-Factor in Achievement

Chapter Six – Visions and Ideals
Chapter Seven – Serenity

I highly recommend it as a guide to enhance your life and living. Say unto your heart, "Peace, be still".

My prayer for you, is that in your life, you will think for yourself and thus be the unique individual God created you to be. That you will share Love with someone special to you because that is the meaning of life, Sharing Love. That you will have faith and trust in a supreme being we refer to as God and will receive his gift of eternal life. That God will Bless you and make you a blessing to others. Peace be with you.

Acknowledgements

First and foremost, I thank God for allowing me to take up space on planet earth long enough to finish this book. I also thank Him for the strength, health and fortitude to accomplish this. I have much to be thankful to God for in this life, especially for answering my parents prayers for my well-being and faith during much of my life when it must have seemed to them that they had failed to lead me in the paths of righteousness. There is much about religion I am confused about but I have faith in God and his gift of salvation and eternal life for mankind.

I would like to acknowledge Aunt Elsie Kofstad and my sister Verla Kummer for creating the history of Aunt Elsie's family, her nine siblings and parents and her grandparents and their lives. Aunt Elsie wrote the original history and Verla copied it in her handwriting but word for word as Aunt Elsie wrote it. She did this so everyone could have a copy in Aunt Elsie's unique way of telling a story. Any spelling errors or other errors are strictly mine and not those of Aunt Elsie or Verla. Without their dedication and hard work, much of our family history would be lost. I am grateful to them and would like to thank them each personally but they are both deceased so it will have to wait. That is assuming I get my act cleaned up and am allowed to join them.

I would be remiss not to mention Viola Knuth for her creation of the family tree that took a lot of research, time, effort and dedication. She did such a nice job and graciously shared it with the entire family and anyone that had an interest. It was a great source for my own research and helped me connect the dots many times.

I would like to thank my lifetime friend, hitchhiking and rail riding buddy, fellow Golden Glove Boxer and Vietnam Veteran Charles Toy for pre-reading several chapters and helping jog my memory of some of our ill-spent youth. My memory of some events are not always clear or the same as his. Generally, I've found, when someone's memory of an event differs from mine, theirs is closer to reality than mine.

DavidTraiser, classmate, friend and fellow Vietnam veteran who spent an evening with me in his home going down memory lane, Thank you for a wonderful evening of laughs and conversation. To his gracious wife, Suzie, thank you for sharing your husbands' time and cooking and providing beverages and good company, the perfect hostess.

My wife, Kathleen, who was an avid reader who has read and owns more books than anyone I know and was an excellent literary critic as well as a language expert. She made many suggestions and helped reveal and correct many errors. More than likely, any errors that still exist were written after she died so she didn't have the opportunity to edit and correct them.

My daughter Kimberly who like her mother is an avid reader. She also found many language and spelling errors and made many suggestions as to layout and content.

My son Eric, who is a fanatic about correct English, spelling and facts. He also contributed to the layout and content and provided enthusiasm.

My sister-in-law, Kathy's sister, Vivian Larson who pre-read several chapters and made corrections, suggestions and jogged my memory.

Wikipedia has been a real friend to me and provided me with knowledge, understanding and clarification on many subjects.

My appreciation and gratitude to Christoffer the Count Knuth of Denmark who allowed me to use information about Knuthenborg, Denmark and his family in the chapter of Family Heritage. I'm sure we are related somehow and someday we may make the connection.

To Jen Rosel Juenger, former resident of Drake and author of the story of Dr. Hordinsky, I thank you for letting me use it in my book. I copied it word for word because she did such an excellent job of telling about this wonderful man, I couldn't improve it.

To Arlo Blumhagen, my classmate, friend and fellow Vietnam Veteran who allowed me to share one of his experiences in Vietnam.

To my sister, Fern Rau, who provided many stories of my childhood and family connections and memories. She also pre-read the chapter on family heritage and made corrections and added tips and knowledge that helped me in my research.

To my brother Dorel's children, Linda, Bill and Jeannie for allowing me to print their fathers autobiography and to Bill's wife Debra for her family research on the Ancestor and Heritage web sites and also to their children, Mathew and Michael.

To my cousins Carolyn Knuth Gupta, Roger Roth and Merideth Notbohm Peterson for helping me identify relatives on a photo dating prior to 1918. It was fun and enlightening.

To my Navy buddy, friend and fellow Vietnam veteran, Bill Allen and his wife Diane for their help in the design of the book cover.

Also to my Army/Navy buddies, classmates, friends and relatives who provided much of the material for my life stories and for shaping my life into the story of my Love of life and Love of the people surrounding me. I would be remiss not to mention my lifetime friend, Michael Toy who has taken up residence in eternity in a place we refer to as heaven. I'm sure God used him to answer some of my parents' prayers for my safety, to continue to breath and therefore to continue my life and arrive here. What a trip.

Thank you one and all.

Introduction

Whatever Lies behind us and whatever lies in front of us are but tiny matters in comparison to what lies within us.
                                      Ralph Waldo Emerson

This is the Autobiography of Dwight Eldon Knuth. Autobiographies are somewhat egotistical in nature. Perhaps it is our attempt to live forever or at the very least be remembered past our physical demise. The Author, of course, is trying to make him/her self look good, if only in their own alleged mind. The authors' memory of events and how they played out in real life is often different and unrecognizable compared to the readers' memory of those same events.

David Halberstam of the New York Times said, " Memory is often less about the truth than about what we want it to be."

P. D. James says, " Memory is a device for forgetting as well as remembering. To that extent, every autobiography is a work of fiction and every fiction an autobiography."

Having said that, If your memory of these events is different from mine, write your own Damn book.

It has been said about me that I march to my own drum, not a different drummer but my own drum. Said another way, this dummy is pulling his own strings. I guess I could be called an individualist which is a kinder way of saying egotistical. I am what I am and that's all what I am. No less, no more.

Mary Pettibone Poole said, "The next best thing to being clever is being able to quote someone who is." I am not clever so I will settle for the next best thing and use someone else's cleverness.

The quote I have lived by most of my life has been attributed to Abraham Lincoln because he said it so often. The quote actually belongs to Maurice Switzer. My maternal great grandfather was a Switzer so perhaps Maurice is a relative, which is why we think alike. His quote is, "It is better to remain silent and be thought a fool, than to speak up and remove all doubt." Anyone who knows me, knows that ship has sailed and me remaining silent is a joke in and of itself, so it behooves me to find a new quote to live by and for the time being I will go with Ms Pooles'.

Plato said, "The life which is unexamined is not worth living." This is my attempt at examining my life and I can tell you, to me, it certainly was worth living.

> **Be ashamed to die until you have won some victory for humanity.**
> **Horace Mann (1796-1859)**

1
Closer to the Tuscan Sun - Italy

It was a dream of my wife, Kathy, to someday travel to Italy. I think she wanted to look for a replacement for me. Someone tall dark and handsome instead of short fat and unattractive. We decided it would be educational and interesting and when we mentioned it to her sister, Vivian. She said, "wouldn't it be fun" and "I get to come along". How can you say no to that. Actually, we had invited all of Kathy's siblings along, including her sister, Vivian, at their own expense. Vivian was the only one that honored our offer. Kimberly, our daughter was included in the plan from the get go. Not only do we enjoy her company but she is a seasoned traveler and could probably keep us out of trouble. I took it upon myself to do research on the internet and the four of us decided to bypass the "old people's tours" and do Italy on our own. Vivian had been there previously with her daughter and cousins and they were their own tour guide. They survived and seemed to enjoy themselves. Although, one of them was robbed on the train while she slept. They traveled around Italy and Europe to many of the tourist areas and cities.

    We thought we would approach it a bit different and avoid the tourist areas and cities. It's not so much that we hate people but more we enjoy our own company. What's not to like? Instead, we thought we would settle in an area and drink and breathe the culture of the area. With the drinking in mind, we settled on an area in Tuscany that provided a bottle of wine daily with the accommodations. We thought it would be a good place to drink and breathe. As it turned out, the wine was not all that great but the air was exhilarating. I don't drink but the ladies mentioned something about the wine not being very strong and you could drink it like water with no ill effects. In fact, I witnessed many Italians doing just that. It wasn't unusual to see them drinking it with their lunch. Wine and pizza? I guess it's not that much different than soda and pizza. If you're going to drink wine you want some ill effects to go with it. Something to counteract the happy glow. At the very least, a little numbing of the brain.

    We wanted to be in an area where we could catch the train to other areas of Italy or Europe if we felt like travel or sightseeing. We also wanted to be in an area where we could settle in and enjoy the culture and slow paced daily life and get a feel for daily living in Italy. From past experiences, we found that we try to cram too much activity into each day and don't enjoy the simple pleasures of sitting on a bench and talking to a native of the area. With all these goals in mind, I selected the city of Lucca in Tuscany. It is a walled city with cobblestone streets built before the first Christmas. They originally started building the wall for protection but by the time it was completed, it was not necessary. It took them 300 years. I can see why, everyone takes an hour or two break every afternoon. I looked for a hotel in the city and in the process found there were many villas in the area that allowed you to do your own cooking, laundry etc. or you could hire a cook and eat Italian cooking. The villa sounded more economical and would provide more of a feeling of living there than a hotel so we selected a villa outside of Lucca close to the little village of Cappella. The internet is a great tool but can be misleading. The information we had was that it was on a hill with a slight incline. That was the biggest understatement I've encountered in my 70 plus years. It in fact was on top of a mountain with a one lane switchback donkey trail leading up the mountain to it. Not being aware of this, we elected to rent the top floor of this ancient stone villa which was three stories high. Our floor had three bedrooms, two baths, a kitchen and dining/living room. Off the master bedroom was a walkout rooftop (of the second story) patio that had a chest high wall to prevent someone falling off if they were drinking something other than Italian wine. On the first floor, there was a common area with couches and chairs and there were laundry accommodations. Across the stone drive was an old stone barn that had a ping pong table in it. On ground level was a full size swimming pool and patio area for laying/sitting in the sun. Behind the villa was another patio area with a rock built barbeque area and garden (courtyard).

For transportation, I rented the largest car I could get to transport us and our luggage. In my research, I learned there is an international driver's license you can get for traveling in Europe. My information said you can probably get by without one but different countries and even different areas have different rules so it probably is a good idea to have one to cover all the bases. Kim and I applied for one and received one so we were the designated drivers.

Our villa was run by an English speaking Italian lady by the name of Gill (pronounced Jill). I spoke with her on the phone several times and part of the package was she would do a grocery shopping for us prior to our arrival so we had groceries when we arrived. The English she spoke was the "Queens English" but living on the Canadian border, we're used to that, eh? She was much easier to understand and clearer than many of the telemarketers that think they speak English. We could buy train passes in advance for travel all over Europe but we elected to wait until we arrived to see if we really wanted to travel or just stay put.

With all the arrangements made and our airline tickets, passports and driver's license in hand we were ready for departure. You may have noticed, we didn't use a travel agency but did all the arrangements ourselves. This was no accident but by design. We don't like to be tied into specific arranged activities but rather go with the flow and do what we feel like doing and are up to at any given time. We selected late winter in Minnesota, I think February or March which was early spring in Italy. We wanted to avoid the summer crowds and the rates are more reasonable. The flowers were blooming in Italy but our swimming pool had not been filled at the villa. None of us cared about that and Gill was in fact cleaning it and filling it while we were there. I would sit by the pool and watch her work or gaze out at the Italian landscape of olive groves and grape vineyards from the top of our mountain. She was interesting to talk to and told me that the swimming pool was slowly sliding down the mountain. She would also identify the different local birds for me. The one I enjoyed most was the cuckoo bird. What does that say about me?

We flew from International Falls, MN to Minneapolis where Kathy's sister Vivian met up with us. From Minneapolis we flew to Amsterdam and then on to Pisa our final destination by air. At Amsterdam, we had some problems with security checks. Kathy is a smoker and had nicotine patches along to survive the long flights without smoking and also so the rest of us would survive. She had a little kids scissors in her purse so she could cut open the nicotine package to get at the patch and apply it. When her purse went through the x-ray in Amsterdam they noticed the scissors but it was so small they couldn't find it. She finally asked them what was taking so long and what they were having trouble with. They would run her purse through x-ray, look through it then run it through again. They finally showed her on the x-ray the scissors and she explained what it was and what it was for and got it out of her purse so they could see. They confiscated it and sent us on our way.

I had acquired passport holders that hung around our neck so we would have them handy and not lose them or have them stolen. When we went thru security checks, we had to put them in the basket to pass through x-ray. We also used them to carry our airline tickets in and a few hundred Euros. Because of all the commotion with the scissors, Kathy forgot to get hers out of the basket and put it back around her neck. We were a long ways from our gate and our plane was due to leave for Pisa and we were hurrying along trying to get to our plane before it took off. I got my boarding pass out so I was all set and told Kathy to get hers out and ready also as we hurried to our gate. She was frantically searching everywhere for it with no luck but a lot of panic. We finally concluded she must have left it at security because she didn't remember getting it from the basket. We told Kim and Vivian to go on to the plane while Kathy and I ran back to security to see if we could find her airline ticket, passport and Euros. As we approached security, one of the people that had been involved with the scissor search was running toward us with Kathy's holder which had everything in it, including the Euros. We did a quick thank you and turned around and ran back for the gate. We made it in time to catch our flight but not with any time to spare. Already we were having fun.

When we arrived in Pisa, we went to baggage claim to get our checked baggage. Par for the course, my bag didn't arrive. I had anticipated this and before leaving home had taken pictures of all our baggage and had them with my passport, airline tickets, and Euros. I found the lost baggage check counter just by guess, not being able to read any of the airport signs in Italian. I spoke to the person at the counter in English and she didn't speak English or understand it but she got another lady that worked at the counter that spoke a little and also understood a little. Since I couldn't speak Italian, she must have assumed I couldn't write Italian either because she asked me questions and filled out the forms for me and made copies of the pictures of the lost luggage. The next day, they delivered my bag to the Villa we were staying at, which was a couple hours from the airport.

The next hurdle was getting the rental car I had reserved. Again, the rental people were Italian and spoke Italian. What a surprise. There were a few that could communicate enough to figure out what we wanted and fill out the proper forms. I was supposed to call Gill from the airport so she could meet us at the villa but I couldn't get her on her cell. Turns out I had written down the wrong number for her cell. One of the rental counter guys somehow found her correct cell phone number and called her on his cell and let me talk to her. She spoke English, what a relief.

The public telephones at the airport were multilingual and would ask what language you wanted instructions in. English was one of the choices. Also the Automatic Teller Machines (ATM) that we used to get Euros from were multilingual. Many people in Europe speak more than one language and even those that don't can communicate enough to do business. It was both a challenge and interesting to shop in Italy. From the food stands in the airports, the sidewalk cafes, pizza shops, the bars and grocery stores, the leather and shoe shops and hardware stores to the tourist souvenirs, we were all able to communicate reasonably well and at least enough to acquire the services we required. Along the way we even learned a few Italian words. Some conversations would contain pointing, head shaking, English and Italian with possibly some Spanish and some of my own language my wife and daughter refer to as Drakeonian, derived from the village of my birth, Drake, ND. The language in Drake is spoken mostly by people of German heritage and involves phrases like, "throw me down the stairs, my hat" or "throw the bull over the fence, some hay". My wife and daughter were amazed at how well I communicated with the non-English speaking Italians when I spoke no Italian except for a couple basic words such as Bon Jour, Aqua, Nord and Sud. When I got us lost in Lucca and tried to find our way to the road that took us to our villa, I stopped a young couple that were speaking to each other in Italian and laughing and appeared to be in Love. People in love are generally happy and accommodating so I thought this would be a safe bet to ask directions from them. I knew that the city had a wall around it with a road along the outside of the wall and the road I wanted branched off that road. If I could find the wall, I could find my road. The problem was the city was built up outside the wall considerably and I couldn't find the wall. The conversation went kind of like this. Buongiorno, you speaka English. Negative shaking of the head and shrug of the shoulders by them. City wall, where? Shrugging of my shoulders to signify question. Them pointing in direction I assumed I should go if they understood what I was asking and them saying wall, wall. They also pointed to the road I should take and the direction I should drive on that road. An exchange of Buongiorno by all and they continued walking arm in arm, talking and laughing, probably at me. Happy to bring a smile to their face.

I could usually figure out what I needed to know if there was a non-English speaking person I could speak sign language with. It was when I had to communicate with a non-English speaking machine that frustrated and defeated me. For example, the parking lot gates with the arms you had to pay to exit or the Autobahn toll gate. Of course, my traveling companions all had ideas on how they should work and what I should try which helped so much. "I tried that already". Actually, it did help and we would eventually be released from the confines of the parking lot.

The Italians are great communicators when it comes to sign language especially when driving. Some roads converged at intersections where five or more roads came together. They would usually have signal lights but not always. An intersection of four converging roads with signal lights was no problem, pretty straight forward like I'm used to. More than four with signal lights, difficult but not impossible to figure out. More than four with stop signs, who has the right of way and who and what designates the order of right of way. I found the best way to establish the right of way at these intersections was to ignore the advice from the drivers in the back seat who didn't have an international drivers license. My daughter, Kim, who rode shotgun and had an international drivers license, had better advice but I didn't always heed it. Sometimes, it was best just to sit at the stop sign until the other drivers would wave at you in an unusual manner. They would place the left hand and arm horizontal, then with the right hand and arm, raise it perpendicular to the left arm and hand with the thumb and fingers coming together in some form of a salute to you and your courteous driving. I would acknowledge their salute by returning it, in kind and wait. When they started exiting their cars, I could be assured that this signified I had the right of way and could drive away with all my new friends waving and shouting at me in Italian.

Driving on the mountain roads is not for the timid. The Italians seem to think the mountain roads are to challenge their cars and driving abilities at high speed. Damn the torpedoes, full speed ahead. Of course if you get in their way, they lose some of their friendliness. They not only will tailgate but try to help you get up to speed. If your family sedan isn't capable of the speeds of their sport cars, they will pass you wherever and whenever they get the urge, left of you or right of you, on hills and curves, wherever there is a window of opportunity, be it legal or not, safe or not. They describe a window of opportunity as my patience has expired.

After we had what luggage arrived in our rental car and were armed with instructions how to get out of the rental parking lot and onto the road, we climbed in the car to begin our journey. Vivian and Kathy, the sisters and non-drivers in the back and Kim, my co-pilot riding shotgun. Of course, back seat drivers will always be back seat drivers so I could count on them for their suggestions and help. I gave them maps I had printed at home prior to leaving to keep them occupied trying to figure out where we were and where we needed to go. None of us could read the highway signs in Italian but we soon surmised that Nord was north and Sud was south which wasn't a big help if you don't know if you want to go Nord or Sud. The cities are the same in any language or at least close so Lucca was still Lucca and Rome or Pisa still Rome or Pisa. We were looking for the Autobahn and I thought I knew how to get there but was wrong. It seemed to me we were going the wrong direction but we finally spotted a sign that said Lucca. Being sure we were going the wrong direction and the sign that said Lucca was for a street named Lucca in Pisa, I pulled over by the sign and we studied the sign and map and the majority in the car, three women, convinced me I was wrong and if I wanted to co-exist with them, I should probably humor them and try their idea. I figured we could always spend the night in the car and wander around the next day until we happened across the autobahn and I could say, "I told you so". It turned out they were right and by slowing down, as they suggested so they could read the signs they didn't understand, they could make better choices of where to go and not to go. This whole process involved a lot of alternating swearing and praying in the back seat.

Once on the autobahn, a four lane road, with cars speeding along, either not being able to read the speed limit or ignoring it, we just had to watch for the exit to Lucca. We easily found the exit to Lucca but there were several of them and Gill had warned me about some construction going on. My instructions were to take a specific exit and drive until you run into the wall around Lucca. You can't miss it because it goes all around Lucca. Our first obstacle was a toll booth to exit the autobahn with instructions in Italian. After 15 minutes of trying to get the arm to rise with no success, I noticed a slot for a credit card or at least I hoped it was for that and that it wouldn't capture my credit card and keep it. I tried it, hoping I was pushing the right buttons, the arm lifted and even returned my credit card. Later when checking my credit card statement, it only charged me once.

Now we were closing in on our destination but it didn't get any easier. We found Lucca and missed most of the construction but couldn't find that elusive wall that was only about two to three stories tall and circled the city. After driving around aimlessly for a while with stomachs growling in hunger and in protest of the anxiety, I received another helpful tip from the not so silent majority. Why don't you call Gill and get instructions. What I wanted to reply was, why don't you call Gill on a pay phone that is not multi-lingual, but of course it made sense for me to call her because I was the only one she had communicated with and was driving so should be the one to get the instructions. So I found a pay phone and proceeded to try to figure out how to make it work and feed it the right coins and dial Gill. I was successful and Gill couldn't quite figure out where exactly we were from my description. She had some good advice though, just find the wall and follow the road around until you come to this road that will take you to Cappella. OK A little more driving around and more advice from the majority, stop and ask directions. Well, everyone knows men don't ask directions because they never get lost. We just take alternate routes. I surrendered my manhood and stopped to ask directions. I previously described that conversation or lack of one. At this point it was beginning to get dark and my eyes don't like to function at night. As long as I had already surrendered my manhood, I asked Kim to take over driving and I would take over co-pilot and shotgun. Now things started to come together. I attribute it to my abilities as co-pilot. We found the wall, followed it around until we found the road we were to take that even had a sign pointing to Cappella. We arrived at Cappella and found the road leading to the villa (Quaranta). Kim was doing a great job of driving due to my excellent skills as co-pilot. It was still light enough to see the road was leading directly to the mountain in the near distance. Along the road were vineyards and olive orchards. As we started up the mountain the road turned into a one lane switchback with no guard rails and the only place for vehicles to pass one another was where there was a driveway into a private home, church, vineyard or olive orchard. The switchbacks were less than U turns and were more like V turns. Kim did OK on the first ones but didn't quite make the turn on one so had to back up a couple feet at a time and go forward until she could make the turn. All the while the back end of the car would be hanging over the downslope of the mountain with nothing to keep you from rolling off the road down the mountain. She did great but there were a lot of prayers and swearing coming from the back seat but not a lot of advice. We passed a huge stone church built into the side of the mountain that Gill had told me about so we knew we were on the right road and about half way to our villa up the mountain. The practice was to honk your horn when you came to the switchback so a car going the opposite direction would know you were there. If and when you met a car, one of you had to back up until you found a spot wide enough to pass by one another. This didn't happen often but it did happen. Obviously, not a well-traveled thoroughfare.

    Eventually we arrived at the villa with the sign, Quaranta. Kim stopped the car on the road because the drive up to the villa was a steep incline and I don't think she wanted to try going up it. Gill walked down to the road to greet us and affirm that this was the right place. We all got out of the car and the former Hoffman sisters were emulating their father and grumbling and complaining with a little cursing and perhaps praying thrown in. Gill picked up on this and said in perfect Queen's English, " A bit daunting, eh?". Without missing a beat, Kathy replied in perfect Queen's English, "A bit Daunting? Holy Mother, Sweet Jesus". Now Kathy is neither Catholic nor Southern Baptist so I was a little concerned that she had switched from praying mode to swearing mode. I quickly whisked Gill out of earshot before Kathy switched to North Dakota farm girl cussing with perhaps a few drunken sailor phrases thrown in, she may have picked up from me. After the Hoffman ladies had settled down and became the ladies we know and love, Gill and I wandered back over to rejoin them so Gill could show us our quarters and explain things to us. Things like where the main circuit breaker box is in case of an electrical storm that causes the main circuit to kick off. After all we are at the top of a mountain and a lot closer to the source of the lightning as well as God. Perhaps this is what they had in mind when the song, Nearer my God to Thee, was written.

Our Villa "Quaranta" in Tuscanny, Italy

Because we are on the third floor, there were three flights of stone steps. I can't imagine how that happened. I guess it was just brilliant engineering. The entire villa was built of stone back when horses and donkeys and slaves were used for heavy work. Vivian was having hip and leg problems so having three flights of stone steps was not a happy maker for her. Now we have both sisters not too happy with the location or accommodations. I think both of them would have left if they wouldn't have had to go back down the mountain and by this time it was full dark so that wasn't going to happen. We lugged all of our luggage up the three flights of stone steps and assigned the bedrooms. Kathy and I being the only married couple present, got the choice bedroom with the skylight and the walk out stone third story patio. This was ideal for Kathy because she could walk out the bedroom door to smoke a cigarette in the clean fresh Italian mountain air. It's always nice to have fresh clean air to counteract the cigarette pollution. The others had access to this patio from a separate door in a hall way. There was patio furniture on the patio, what an unusual choice, so we could congregate and sit and observe the Italian country side from our mountain top. Many days we were above the clouds and could watch the clouds below us drift up the mountain and envelope us as they made their way up the mountain side. Often times they would deposit a fine mist on our faces on their way by. It was pleasant to sit and visit and observe the Italians in their daily rituals and lives. There was also some wildlife to observe such as the lizard like geckos and cuckoo birds. The geckos would crawl up the rock walls of the villa and visit us on the patio and the cuckoo birds would sing to us. I would generally wake up to their call, cuckoo, cuckoo. They may have been taunting me.

We settled into our Villa and planned some menus so we could go grocery shopping. Grocery shopping in Italy is much like grocery shopping the world over. There were some differences that we were unaware of, such as weighing and marking your produce when and where you select it rather than the clerk weighing it for you. Maybe Italians don't trust the clerk and think perhaps they have a heavy hand. At any rate, I didn't do this weighing and marking so the clerk couldn't find the tag on the produce and asked me about it in Italian. I just looked confused which isn't hard for me to pull off and shrugged my shoulders. She called for help and sent the person back to the produce with my selections to weigh and tag them. She was quite pleasant about it and even the people behind me in line were pleasant and patient with the damn tourist's spending money in their country. Many products that we consider staples, such as peanut butter, are difficult to find and obviously not that popular. The meat and fish section was a new experience for us. There was a lot of lamb which my wife and I love but my daughter, not so much.

The fish was plentiful, not fresh water fish but rather ocean fish which was unfamiliar to us. We finally picked one that we thought we would bake rather than fry as we usually do. We weren't aware that it was fresh from the Dead Sea. Most of the meats, other than fish, I would cook on the grill in the courtyard. It was a big grill built out of rock and was probably a hundred years old or more. It was a charcoal grill which I hadn't cooked on for 20 to 30 years. Most meals turned out edible and even sometimes good but not memorable.

The fish was very memorable. The girls, after some discussion, cussing and experimenting, thought they had the Italian stoves and appliances figured out. There were manuals for all of them, however, their Italian reading skills were no better than mine and unlike our manuals were not printed in five languages. They put the fish in to bake with all the seasonings, spices and whatever they thought would improve the taste. The smell of fish permeated the entire villa and probably the entire mountain. Cats came from miles around to sit on the doorstep and meow. This is no exaggeration, cats we had never seen before, suddenly appeared. The fish was actually very tasty and I would even venture quite good. However we couldn't get rid of the smell or the cats. We had put the bones and leftovers in the garbage so I decided to take the garbage outside to the barn. In this part of Italy, they don't have door to door garbage pickup. Everyone is responsible for their own garbage and must take it to a large dumpster about half way down the mountain where it is picked up weekly. Not having any outside garbage cans, I just took the sack of garbage out to the barn and set it there until we would go down the mountain and I could deposit it in the dumpster. The cats were having a field day with the fishy garbage and were fighting over it and making so much noise I had to go investigate. When I discovered the garbage all over the barn and cats everywhere, I set about cleaning up the mess and finding a suitable storage area for the remaining garbage. It turns out there was an enclosed area with propane tanks in it and an unlocked padlock on it. I put the remaining garbage in this area which kept the cats out of it. Now they only sat by it and wistfully meowed. We didn't buy any more fish.

Gill came daily to clean and replenish towels and anything we were in need of. Usually we were gone on our daily excursions by the time she arrived but some days we stayed around for a while. We could then inquire how to use the washer and dryer and other things that didn't work quite the way we expected, like the dishwasher. Sometimes, even after her explanations they didn't work the way we thought they should. Maybe we're slow learners.

We generally made it a point to be back to the villa by dark so we wouldn't have to drive up the mountain in the dark. One evening we were going to go out for a nice Italian dinner, probably after the fish episode. There was a little bar in Cappella at the foot of the mountain and we thought the girls could get a glass or two of courage there for the trip up the mountain. The drive up and down the mountain didn't bother me. It was the traffic on the roads and the uncertainty of where to go and how to get there that laid waste to me. Kim usually drove once we were down the mountain. She was very good at finding places and remembering how we got there and how to get back as well as interpreting Italian road signs. That college education at Cornell College was paying off. We looked around for a nice family dining establishment, one that perhaps had table cloths and napkins. There weren't a lot and those we found weren't open. We found that the nicer dinner establishments didn't open until 8:00PM. That was a little late for me with my diabetes. My blood sugar would plummet more than likely and the girls weren't that keen on going up the mountain after dinner even with a glass or two of courage. I believe we gave up on the idea, stopped for the courage and went up the mountain and ate at the villa. The little bar/bistro in Cappella became a daily stop prior to going up the mountain at the end of our daily excursions. It was situated right along a two way paved road with a sidewalk between it and the road, much like a village street. They had tables and chairs on the sidewalk so you could sit outside just feet away from the road and watch cars and trucks speeding toward you. These are Italian drivers so they do what they want. They might slow down if they see something that catches their interest or they plan to stop in or they might not. When the traffic speeding at us didn't bother the ladies anymore, I knew it was OK to attempt the ride up the mountain.

    We spent evenings enjoying the villa, the courtyard, the pool area, the patio and playing ping pong. We read, played cards and poker, visited and planned the next day. Sometimes we would go for walks along the mountain road. It was pleasant to sit and look out at the landscape of a mountain with a walled city in the distance and let your mind wander to the days when Jesus was walking the roads and visiting the villages educating the masses.

    One night a thunder and lightning storm literally came up the mountain and enveloped us. I mentioned that sometimes the clouds drifted up the mountainside and you could feel the mist on your face as it drifted over you and up the mountain. That's kind of what this thunderstorm did but this one had electricity in it. We had a sky light in our bedroom right above the bed so we were lying in bed looking through the skylight as the lightning flashed directly over the skylight and our heads. We had the lights on when it started and were reading books in bed, as is our habit, but one flash of lightning took out all the electricity in the villa. Gill had warned us that this often happens. It was a rock building and had been standing here for probably three hundred years so I wasn't too worried about a fire. However, on one of the subsequent flashes of lightning, fire shot out of the electric outlets on the walls of the bedroom. This was an awesome spectacle of electricity. The only other time I was that close to lightning was one time in an airplane when we flew through an electrical storm. This was a better view through the skylight with the lightning directly above it. Once the storm traveled up the mountain and was by us, I found a flashlight and descended to the cellar to reset the main circuit breaker to restore electricity to the villa. A flip of the switch and we were in business, no ill effects. I imagine before circuit breakers they had a lot of blown fuses they needed to replace. There was of course some heavy rain with the electrical storm but no ill effects from that either. The next morning, the cuckoos were still waking us with their unique call to a freshly washed earth.

Lucca, Italy

Most days we would go down the mountain and explore Lucca. Because it was around before the birth of Christ, it had a lot of interesting architecture, churches, towers and even the homes. They had many very tall towers that I imagine were used as lookout towers in the days when the city needed to be defended from attackers. The wall around the city was tall enough and wide enough to drive a semi-truck in it and in fact there was a road inside the wall as well as on top of the wall. We walked the road on top of the wall and could look down into people's courtyards and see all the red tiled roofs at eye level. Because the wall goes all around the city, you can walk around the city on top of the wall. There are ramps or steps to get up and down the wall.

Dwight in Lucca, Italy at sidewalk café waiting for the girls and their purchases of leather goods and jewelry.

They have benches for resting, visiting and observing. I spent much time on these benches, partly because I'm a people watcher and partly because I didn't have the energy of the younger ladies. Maybe it had something to do with their shopping and using me for a pack mule for their purchases. I was sitting on one of these benches, waiting for the ladies to bring me more packages to carry, when an elderly gentleman came and sat down beside me. He said Bon Jour and I replied in kind. He was well dressed and looked quite dignified. Soon he started speaking to me in what I assumed was Italian. I shook my head in a negative response and shrugged my shoulders. He then began speaking in another language that sounded French to me and I gave him the same body language response. This was a determined gentleman because he started speaking another language which might have been Spanish but he got the same response from me. This fellow must have been lonesome and really wanting a conversation because he wasn't giving up. He started speaking German. Having grown up in a German community and having my grandparents emigrate from Germany, I could understand some German but other than cursing, couldn't speak it. I mumbled something to the effect of no sprecken de duetsch. It must have been my American accent trying to speak German that gave me away and he immediately switched to English. We had a nice conversation. He wanted to know where I was from and when I told him USA wanted to know what state and city. When I informed him it was International Falls, MN he got a little excited and told me he knew MN and had been to the Mayo clinic there. Of course, I am very familiar with the Mayo clinic and many of the Drs. there, having doctored there on an annual basis for more years than I care to remember. So this was common ground for us and we were off discussing Mayo, Rochester, MN and the doctors and care. We had a pleasant conversation. When the ladies came with their abundance of packages, I introduced everyone to my new friend. Kathy's sister, Vivian, is an artist and she thought he would make an interesting portrait. She asked to take his picture but he for some reason didn't want her to. Perhaps he is a wanted man. She employed her persuasive charms and he relented and let her photograph him. It was a pleasant experience and conversation.

This Dummy Pulls His Own Strings

Street Musicians in Lucca, Italy

    Most of the streets were of cobble stone and very narrow. The small Italian delivery trucks and mini cars drove these streets, usually one way but most of the traffic was on foot or bicycle. One lady was riding her bike and her tire blew out which made a noise like a gun shot. I was just about to hit the deck when I saw what happened and saved myself some embarrassment. Dogs would sleep in the street and the traffic would go around them. Clothes would hang on balconies, drying in the sun. Sometimes there were clotheslines that extended from one side of the street to the other with clothes drying in the Tuscan sun. It brought back memories of a much simpler time. People would stop in the street to have a conversation and say goodbye in the typical Italian manner with a kiss on each cheek. There were a few musicians playing music in the street, an accordion, guitars and perhaps a saxophone, trombone and/or tuba. They were playing good dance music which always makes me want to dance. I wanted Kathy to dance with me but she is still my shy North Dakota farm girl and declined. In her defense, I think I'm a much better dancer than I actually am so can understand her hesitation. I dance like no one is watching when actually I'm creating a spectacle, which of course she becomes a part of. I have fun but at what cost to her?

Lucca, One of the many towers, presumably used for a lookout tower

In the center of the city is an area like a large courtyard where they hold an open air market selling all manner of goods. I found a cute homemade scarecrow for my garden that looked like it might fit in my suitcase. There was an older couple selling them. I asked the price in English because that's the only language I speak. My wife might dispute that I speak that fluently. Anyway, they answered in German. I might have said a word or two in German in response. They got all excited like we were long lost friends and started telling me they made them and how. I can understand a limited amount of German but can't speak it. I had to interrupt them and go back to my standard no sprecken de duetsch. That kind of killed the conversation and their enthusiasm. I handed them some Euros, they took what I assumed they were charging and gave the rest back and I was on my way with my scarecrow.

Sometimes while the ladies shopped for jewelry, leather, shoes and other feminine purchases, I would wander about on my own. I wandered into a hardware store because hardware and the stores that sell it interest me. This was a very small store with only two or three aisles but a very high ceiling. There were shelves that went up about ten feet high and above them was another five or more feet of space with things hanging on the walls and from the ceiling. They didn't waste any space. The shop owner came and greeted me with the usual Bon Jour and asked if he could help. I replied in English that I was just looking around and he replied in a broken English, much like I speak. He had poles with hooks to get things down and a ladder if it was needed. I found a nice brass bell, with 1911 engraved on it, hanging from a flat anchor to attach it to the wall. It reminded me of the Navy symbol. It had a nice tone and was quite loud and caught my interest. He explained it was a door bell that hung on the outside of the home next to the door and guests would pull the rope to tell you someone was at the door. It was supposedly more effective than knocking, especially if you lived in a two or three story apartment and the door was on street level. He said he sold a lot of them. It is not something I see in the states or Canada so it was unique to Italy and was even stamped made in Italy. It was a reasonable price, I thought, for brass, so purchased it. I wasn't sure how I was going to get it home but I managed and it now hangs by my back door. No one but my grandkids use it. Everyone reaches for the doorbell button but if I removed the doorbell button, maybe the brass bell would get more use. Either that or I would answer the door less. Perhaps if I removed the doorbell, I would be eligible for the no-bell prize. At the time I bought this brass bell, I wasn't giving the purchase careful thought. I live in northern Minnesota on the Canadian border. Every winter it gets at least 20 below zero a time or two and often reaches into the forty below range. When it gets that cold it is said to be a brass monkey night which translated into our native language means it's cold enough to freeze the balls off a brass monkey so you should bring in the brass monkeys. Now I also have a brass bell to bring in on those cold nights.

I observed that around noon, most of the shops close for several hours for a mid-day break or siesta. We think of siesta as an afternoon break or nap but originally it was taken at noon. Siesta is Spanish from the Latin sexta, meaning "the sixth hour." For Romans, noon was the sixth hour after sunrise, a hot time of day in the Mediterranean and a good time to stop working and get in the shade. This practice has obviously continued, even though the shop owners were already in the shade. It's a good practice, especially when you are with three ladies that love to shop for Italian leather and jewelry. It not only preserves the body and soul but also the bank account. It allowed us to take a lengthy lunch break at a sidewalk café, eat gelato, walk about the village, check out the architecture, rest weary legs on benches and people watch.

Lucca architecture

On one of the trips to visit Lucca, I was driving and found the main gate going into the city. There are many gates in the wall all around the city to allow entrance and exit at different physical

This Dummy Pulls His Own Strings

locations. I had been on the internet getting information for our trip to Italy and read an article written by people who were doing what we were doing, exploring Italy on their own without a guide. They mentioned there were parking passes for parking in Lucca but they were so confusing that you probably should park outside the city in a parking lot. I had used these parking lots which had gates on them that wouldn't let me out until I paid the proper parking fee for the time I had parked. I could never understand what that was and would get frustrated trying to exit the parking lot. I thought perhaps I would drive inside the gates and see if parking in there was any less frustrating. We drove in and immediately in front of us was a children's playground. In front of the children's playground was parking spaces, unoccupied. Of course we couldn't read any of the signs in Italian. Available parking right inside the gate, made me a bit suspicious but the ladies were encouraging me to go ahead and park there. What could it hurt? I kind of went along with their thinking. What's the worst that can happen, a parking ticket? Just ignore it and don't pay it. I know that works, I've done that in New York city when I was in the Navy. So I pulled into the parking space. We spent the day in Lucca, shopping, eating lunch in a sidewalk café, eating Gelato and doing tourist things.

We headed for the car with all our purchases only to not find it. Well, I left it right here, someone must have stolen it. On the other side of the playground I could see a police car setting with a policeman in it. I went over to report our car stolen. Again, not speaking Italian, a difficult job but with sign language and some English that he understood and some Italian I understood, by this time, he pointed me to the police station he was parked in front of. We collectively went inside because we had nowhere else to go and no way to get there. There was a receptionist police man behind a grated window inside the door that we tried to communicate with, with little or no success. I'm sure the window was grated because he was afraid some irate female would try to ring his neck. He went to get one of the police ladies that spoke some English. They invited us in to the room behind the grated window, probably so we couldn't escape if we became unruly and they wanted to detain us. We told her our story of how our car was stolen. She informed us that, no, the car was not stolen but they had it towed for parking in a no parking area without the proper parking permit.

Of course the ladies were incensed, especially Kathy who was telling her what an improper way to treat tourists who were spending money in your city. I was trying to calm the ladies so we wouldn't get thrown in jail for the night or the rest of our lives. I can see the headlines. They went to Lucca, Italy and were never heard from again. The lady policeman (shouldn't that be policelady or policeperson?) agreed with Kathy and said that they were stupid and apologized for their stupidity. A sigh of relief, no jail time in Italy. She informed us the fine and towing was over two hundred Euros. At the time the exchange rate, dollar to Euro, was pretty close to even so it was close to a two hundred dollar parking ticket. I paid the fine before the ladies succeeded in getting us thrown in the slammer.

We still didn't have any transportation and the car was miles away, outside the gates where it was towed. The policelady got a taxi for us which arrived promptly. Probably one of the policemen/ladies relatives waiting outback knowing we would need a taxi to recover our vehicle. On the way out of the police station to the waiting taxi, we passed a young couple who were speaking English and really not happy. Kathy was exhausted, needing a cigarette and crabby and made a passing remark saying, "what a trip". The young lady replied, "what a trap". They were there obviously for the same reason we were.

We rode across town to the fenced in area where they confiscated cars, not sure if we would also be robbed there again or what manner of outlaws existed where the taxi driver was taking us. We arrived and I advised the ladies to stay in the taxi until I returned. If they heard gunfire or smelled blood they should flee the scene. I paid the towing charges, returned to the taxi and paid the taxi driver while they retrieved our rental car. I believe Kim drove us back to Cappella because I was completely lost and

This Dummy Pulls His Own Strings

she seemed to know where to go and how to get there. I took over at Cappella after our stop for several glasses of courage and an extra one to calm the nerves. I don't imbibe in alcohol, for health reasons, so am the designated driver after the alcohol begins to flow.

Some days we just stayed at the villa and hung out. There was a ping pong table in the barn and Kathy and I played ping pong. We have a table at home and played daily for a summer when we had it set up in the garage. We became quite good at it, worthy opponents, enjoyed it and it was good exercise for us. This wasn't the ordinary barn used for horses and cattle but was more like a story and a half garage built of stone about 300 years ago. I'm sure at one time it was used for donkeys and/or horses but now it just housed a ping pong table and some stray cats.

We would also walk the mountain road enjoying the spring wild flowers, vines and shrubs as well as the architecture of the neighbors. Most of the buildings were ancient and built on the slope of the mountain with rocks from the mountain. There were many olive groves which seemed to do well in the mountain soil on the mountain side. Closer to the base of the mountain there were vineyards on the mountain slope. At the very top of the mountain where the road ended and there was a turnaround, was a group of bee hives with some bee activity. I was surprised that there were bees in them because it was early spring so they must have wintered over in the hives living off the honey. I don't believe winter is too severe here although they do get snow sometimes. There were spring flowers blooming on the mountain side so they had nectar to gather for making more honey.

I would spend time in the courtyard just observing the wildlife. Mostly the little lizards and the wild cats. I enjoyed the different birds and tried to identify them. My favorite was the cuck-coo. When I tired of the court yard I would go to the pool area to soak up some sun rays and read and look over the country side. The patio off our bedroom was another favorite area to spend time and contemplate. It's amazing that they could build something like this out of rock, most of it big rock, 300 years ago before the advent of mighty machines. I guess they had their methods and horse power.

Some evenings we would play cards or poker, drink wine, read, visit and plan. There was a TV in the common area on the first floor but I don't think any of us made use of it. Why would you go to Italy to watch TV? One day when the girls didn't want to go down the mountain, I took the car and went on an excursion to the surrounding country side. Lots of mountain roads and Italian drivers in sports cars. One day Kim went with me on one of these excursions. We stopped at a road side restaurant for a cup of coffee. The waitress wanted to know how I wanted my coffee and what kind. I tried to explain the best I could I just wanted an ordinary cup of coffee. She said you want Americano Coffee and brought me an espresso with a cup of hot water to pour the espresso in and dilute it.

When out and about we generally ate lunch at a sidewalk café or local pizza place. At a sidewalk café we would generally eat outside rather than going inside. One such place had Red Rooster on a Red Brick on the menu. I had read about it in one of our cookbooks and I decided to try it. Our waiter could speak some broken English well enough to have a conversation and to order. He told us he was from Sri Lanka and when I ordered the Red Rooster on a Red Brick said to me, "you better have a good Doctor".

Another day we ordered pizza slices at a local pizza place. You ordered at the counter which had glass display cases of different pizza slices and some other choices kind of like a deli. The girls there didn't speak English but I pointed to the pizza I wanted and they asked me in Italian what I wanted to drink. Somehow I knew what they were asking but didn't know how to say water in Italian so pointed to a bottle of water in the display case. They informed me it was Aqua which made sense because I associated it with the aqueducts they built in biblical times. The pizza wasn't as good as American pizza, I didn't think. It was plain cheese pizza but I suppose they omit all the chemicals from their cheese. While eating my pizza, I noticed other Italians coming in, ordering pizza and wine and aqua. They would pour some wine in a glass and then pour some water in the same glass. Why you would want to water down your wine is beyond my comprehension but I noticed more than one person at more than one table doing this so it must have been a normal habit for them. Perhaps it was their lunch break and they had to go back to work and didn't want to be under the influence. However, we got a bottle of wine a day with the villa when we rented it. The girls said it was very weak wine that was impossible to get even a glow from. Perhaps there is different strengths of wine in Italy and we got the weak, cheap stuff with the villa and the pizza place has the strong stuff.

When it was time to return to the good old US of A, we needed to find the Autobahn, Pisa and the airport there. Our flight was quite early, relatively speaking so we didn't have a lot of time to wonder around the countryside of Italy trying to figure out where we were going and where we had been. Vivian also had something she needed to be back for and could not afford to miss her flight. We decided to go to Pisa the day prior to our flight so we would be there in time and not miss it.

As it turned out, we found the Autobahn with no trouble. We even found the airport exit off the Autobahn and there was even a lady at the toll booth who we asked how to get to the airport and she pointed us in the right direction. We drove right up to the airport with no problem at all in record time. Our flight wasn't until the next morning so we had plenty of time to kill. Everyone was reluctant to leave the airport because we were afraid that we would get lost and not be able to find our way back again. We scouted out the airport and decided that we would just find a secluded area with comfortable seating and sleep right there. It wouldn't be the first airport I slept in. We decided not to turn the car into the rental people until the next day just in case we needed it for some reason. It turned out that was a wise decision.

We found a secluded area of the airport where there was no one but cleaning people and settled in the best one can for a peaceful nights doze. I don't remember exactly the hour, but some airport official rousted us up and told us we had to exit the airport terminal. They close it down for several hours during the night for cleaning or whatever. So we were hustled out the door. We weren't the only ones that had planned to stay in the airport overnight. There were others that exited the airport terminal only to sit on the hard cement benches outside the terminal for the night. It was quite chilly out there. We hustled to our rental car and settled in there with all of our luggage. We probably should have left the airport and found a hotel but that might have kept us occupied all night without success and then would have had to find our way back. So we just stayed put in the confines of the rental car all crowded together and uncomfortable but not cold. In the early morning light and fog we re-entered the terminal, checked in, turned in the car and were ready for our journey home. I was glad we had spent the night at the airport because I didn't have to drive in the fog and try to find the airport. When we checked our luggage, we had to check it to Amsterdam, pick it up at the airport there and then check it the rest of the way home. Something to do with two different airlines and they couldn't check it all the way for us.

When we arrived at Amsterdam, we were short one piece of luggage, my Wife's. No surprise here. A direct flight, Pisa to Amsterdam, no plane changes and yet they could lose a piece of luggage. We picked up the rest of the luggage, checked it and filed a lost luggage claim. I was old friends with lost baggage and cars in Europe. They told us it would more than likely show up on the next flight from Pisa and that I should call them in an hour and see if it had arrived. At least that's what I got out of the conversation, Italian from them and English from me. We had a few hour layover and had plenty of time to kill.

The baggage claim area was in a secure area of the airport as was the lost baggage claim area. This area was only for local airlines like the one we arrived on from Pisa. To get to our connecting flight we had to leave this secure area and go through a security check again. Also, to get to the area that food was available we had to leave the secure area. We were hungry and had time to kill so went to the food area, bought gross sandwiches of undetermined contents and attempted to eat them. Kathy and I went back to the area where the Pisa baggage claim was. Because it was in a secure area and we were not, I found a phone and called to see if Kathy's bag had arrived. In the good old US of A I would have just ignored the lost baggage and let it find me but I was told things didn't work that way here. If I didn't get the baggage and get it rechecked, we might never see it again. This bag had a lot of the shopping purchases in it. The leather goods, purses, shoes, brass bell and other treasures from Italy. To my astonishment and great joy, the baggage claim girl told me, over the phone, that our bag had arrived and was setting right in front of the claim counter as we spoke. She went through some lengthy explanation of how to get to the baggage claim area from where I was calling from. Not being familiar with the airport or the language, I told her we would find it and get the bag, not having a clue as to how to get there.

Kathy and I started to walk around and could see the big double doors we came out of when we left the secure area. We could also see and even read the baggage claim signs but couldn't find a way to get there. There was no security check point we could find to get to baggage claim and all the doors leading to the baggage claim were exit doors. We stood by the big double doors we had exited for a while and watched. The doors were closed but were swinging doors that would swing open when a flight arrived and people came out with their baggage. When the doors opened we could see the baggage lost and found claim counter and Kathy's bag setting in front of the counter. It was a little frustrating to see it and not be able to go get it.

Kathy came up with a fool proof plan. Just act like we don't know what we're doing. How hard could that be? She said, when the double doors open and people start walking out, she and I could just walk in, go to the lost baggage counter, grab the suitcase, sign for it or whatever the procedure was and exit through the same doors. I argued against it because I knew it was a secure area and we were coming from an unsecured area and it didn't seem right. It appeared that there were no security people around guarding the exit and it should be an uncomplicated endeavor. Things aren't always what they seem. We couldn't see the office with the one way windows that looked like mirrors from our side, just to the right of the doors. Of course, we couldn't see the armed security guard looking out that window with a big German Shepard dog by his side, watching the flow of people exit.

    Kathy asked me if I had a better plan and what we should do? Not having a better plan and thinking the shortest distance between two points were through those doors, I opted for entering the exit. The next time the doors swung open and people started exiting, we boldly entered the exit against traffic like we were supposed to be doing this. We probably got 10 steps inside the door when the armed guard came out of his office with his German Shepard by his side, his hand on his pistol in his holster. He was telling us to halt and I'm not sure of all the other gibberish he was saying in Italian. We stopped immediately, there was no place to hide and it was obvious he was speaking to us, even if we couldn't understand him. He somehow conveyed to us that he wanted to know what we were doing. I told him in English that we were going to the lost baggage claim to get our lost bag that was setting right there in plain sight. I also told him I had spoken to the lost baggage people on the phone and they were the ones that told me to come get the bag. He was very animated and excited and slapped himself on the forehead and said "Mama Mia". He obviously understood some English and could speak "almost English" which is a combination of Italian and English. He proceeded to tell us with hand gestures and some English that this was a secured area and you can't enter an exit door. I responded in a calm voice with a lot of "Sirs" thrown in that we didn't know how to get into this secure area and get our lost baggage that they told us to come and claim and that it was setting right there and we saw it and came to claim it. I also asked him to tell us how to accomplish that feat. I don't know if he understood any or all of what I was saying or if he in fact did not know how to get to our lost luggage another way either or thought I was too dumb to understand but he responded with a wave of his hands like "I give up". He told us, "I did not tell you this. Go get your lost luggage and leave". With that, we proceeded to the lost luggage counter, retrieved our suitcase and walked out the exit doors. He stood there with his German Shepard and watched us and I thanked him as we walked by. Rin Tin Tin, the German Shepard never uttered a growl or bark but then I never made eye contact with him either.

We found Kim and Vivian, checked our bags, went through security and boarded our flight home with no further complications. It was a long flight but went smoothly and we arrived back in Minneapolis and didn't encounter any problems going through customs.

We were in Pisa, twice and never went to the leaning tower of Pisa. It just didn't intrigue us, I guess. What is the big attraction to a faulty engineered building that isn't straight or probably not square either. Italy has many towers, some of which we climbed and they were perfectly straight and upright. You could see for miles from the top and didn't feel like you were tipping or falling off. That's my kind of tower. One we climbed, even had a tree growing on it's top. Why would you point out your faulty buildings? Sounds like bad planning to me, both the building of it and the pointing out of your failings.

The trip to Italy was great, fun and exciting. If I do it again, I probably will do the tourist trip where someone else does the planning, driving, cooking, shopping and speaking Italian. I might even do the art and architecture tours. As in all my travels, to wherever I went, I found people are pretty much the same. There are friendly and unfriendly, sweet and sour, happy and grumpy, fun and sad, funny and those that lack a sense of humor. I found that most of them respond in kind to how you treat them. If you want anger, be angry, if you want happy, be happy, if you want friendly, be friendly. Even when you can't communicate with language, you can communicate with emotions and attitude. Be Happy, Don't Worry.

2
Lost in the Badlands

The second year Kathy and I were married, I convinced her that a hunting trip to Williston, ND for mule deer with my sisters husbands and my nephews would be fun. Kathy liked the outdoors, hiking and communing with nature. She wasn't a big fan of camping but did it and enjoyed herself most of the time. She wasn't fond of sharing space and sleeping quarters with spiders and natures insects. She did like her creature comforts as she described them.

    I had an old British 303 I used for deer hunting but Kathy didn't have a rifle. Her brother Vince and I ran across a sale of 30-06 rifles for twenty five dollars so I bought one and gave it to Kathy for her Birthday in August just before deer season. Just what every young bride wants for a Birthday present from her new husband. I was just following her direction. She told me never to buy her household items for gifts. That takes you directly to sporting goods. What did I know, I was new to this. I think she was a bit disappointed but she was a good sport about it. I might add, I had encouragement from her brother who was a good friend, companion, hunting buddy and beer drinking buddy.

    Her younger brother Mike wanted to go along with us so I cleared it with my sisters and they said it would be fine and the first weekend of deer season we headed for Williston from Grand Forks where we lived. The guys had the hunt all planned and the area we would hunt in was south west of Williston along the Montana border near the little town of Cartwright. Much of this country is wild and uninhabited except by a few ranchers that leased land form the state or federal government depending on who owned it. Some of these ranchers had thousands of acres they used to raise cattle that roamed the hills. Much of the land was unfenced and there were few roads. This was the late 60's before God invented four wheelers or all-terrain vehicles. Many of these ranchers still rode horses to round up the cattle or take care of them. This was country where the deer and antelope played and the buffalo roamed. Much of this country was part of the North Dakota badlands just north of the Teddy Roosevelt national park. It was wild country but take your breath away beautiful. There was a lot of petrified wood just lying there, small cactus growing, rattlesnakes, burning coal deposits at ground surface and deep crevices that seemed endless in depth. There may even have been vicious Pumas in those deep crevices but we didn't see any. The scenery was a bigger attraction than the hunting although there was some nice whitetail and mule deer living and playing there.

We headed out on Saturday morning and hunted several areas. We had taken two cars and we split up thinking we could cover more ground by doing so. Kathy, Kathy's brother Mike, and I were in one group. Mike had borrowed a gun from Vince. We parked the car by a grove of trees in a valley and started to walk toward a likely area where we hoped deer might be. As we walked along the grove of trees we were talking and discussing how we should go about the hunt. I would look back occasionally as was my custom so on the return trip I would know what the landscape looked like so I could find my way back. It always appears different on the return trip. Imagine that.

After we had passed the grove of trees, I looked back and there were three or four deer coming out of the grove right where I had parked the car. We couldn't shoot at them for fear of hitting the car so we had to wait until they passed the car. We all started to shoot at the deer. None of us had scopes and I think all the rifles were shooting high because none of us hit any of them. I or we had neglected to sight in the rifles prior to this hunting trip. Of course the deer took off running up a hill and we kept shooting and missing. The deer disappeared over the top of the hill and we ran up the hill and got a couple more shots off but of course didn't hit any of them. Had we all gotten our deer with this opportunity, our hunting would have been over within the first hour. Maybe it was good planning not sighting in our rifles prior to the hunt. We hunted all day but didn't see any more deer. We had our chance and blew it.

The rest of the party, my nephews, Dean and Doug Kummer and my brother in law, Clarence Rau weren't having any better luck. In fact, I don't believe they even saw any deer. They were all better hunters and I'm sure had sighted in their rifles. Had they seen a deer, it would be providing sustenance all winter long.

Doug and Dean had hunted the area previously and also scouted out the area so were familiar with the area and terrain. They took us to several areas, all rugged, beautiful, but with no visible deer. We knew they lived there because there were signs but they were better at hide and seek than we were. It was getting towards late afternoon when Doug and Dean decided to take us to an exceptionally rugged area they had previously been to. We parked the vehicles at an approach and started walking. The start of the trek was not terribly rugged and relatively easy walking. There was even a prairie trail where I assumed the rancher had driven over and over leaving two tracks where the wheels met the prairie. As we were walking, I would periodically turn around to see what the landscape would look like on our return. I also tried to make mental notes of the general direction we were headed and landmarks along the way. This was probably my Army training playing out. If I had a compass with me I would have been checking that but minus the compass, I was navigating by where the sun was when I could see it and landmarks when I couldn't.

I specifically remember crossing the two track prairie trail and thinking we need to re-cross this on the return. We were walking apart but within sight of each other except when the landscape would occasionally remove someone from view. I was pretty vigilante about making sure they came back into view when we passed the obstacle for two reasons. One, if we saw some deer, I wanted to be sure no one was in my line of fire or I in theirs and B, I didn't want to be lost so it was important to keep Doug or Dean in view because they were the ones that were familiar with the area.

    We walked several miles this way and were in some really rough badlands terrain. It kept getting rougher and more spectacular as we kept going. At this point, I was enjoying the beauty more than the hunting but time was running out. It was getting close to sunset and time to turn around and go back. We all must have been thinking the same thing because we started drifting together until we were all in one group. At this point we had a view of some really spectacular badland scenery with the sun shining on the painted canyons and cliffs and making the different colors of the earth brilliantly stand out. We all stopped and just looked and inhaled the beauty with few words between us because there were not words strong enough to describe the beauty of the moment. As the sun set the colors were constantly changing so we took a moment to breath it all in.

    In North Dakota when the sun sets, it doesn't get dark for several more hours and depending on if you have clear skies can stay quite light out just from the celestial lights. We thought we had enough time and light left to make it back to our vehicles but thought we should get started. We started walking back as a group but as we came to less rugged terrain started to drift apart. I imagine we thought we had a better chance of flushing out some deer the more ground we covered. We walked along for several miles this way and the daylight was fading but it appeared that we were getting much closer to our destination just by the lay of the land. We had drifted farther apart than I liked but we, Kathy, her brother Mike and I were always in view of one another and we had Doug in our site. Dean and Clarence had disappeared from my view.

    I knew we had to cross the two wheeled trail to get back to our vehicles. From my bearings and observations, I thought we were drifting too far left and needed to bear right but we were following Doug so I put my trust in him as did the rest of us. Doug was on the far left of all of us and he came to a big rise (hill) and veered left to go around it rather than climbing it and going over it. At this point, I called Kathy and Mike over to me and told them we needed to go right to get back to the vehicles. Doug was out of sight at this point and Mike was adamant that he had gone left and we needed to follow Doug and go left. I didn't know why Doug had gone left but I knew Mike was right about where Doug had gone. Kathy was not going to let Mike go in one direction while she went with me in another direction and I agreed we should all stick together weather we got lost or not. So off to the left we went and by this time Doug was far enough ahead of us that we never caught a glimpse of him again. We kept bearing left because that was the last direction we saw Doug going. The terrain was getting rougher and rougher the farther we went and I could see we were not coming out but going deeper into the badlands.

The daylight was almost gone and it was overcast and a few snow flakes had begun to fall. At this point I knew we were not going to walk out before dark and it was getting harder to traverse the rough terrain without falling and getting hurt. I think it was Kathy that suggested we find a protected area with fuel for a fire and settle in for the night and try to find our way out in the morning before we broke our fool necks, stumbling around in the dark. I don't remember anyone opposing that strategy as much as we would have liked something to eat, a warm bed and cigarettes. We came across a small valley at the top of the hills we were in that had some cedar trees growing which provided some cover from the wind and some fuel for a fire. All three of us smoked and after a hard day of hunting we were all almost out of cigarettes and matches.

We selected a campsite on the edge of the cedars in a relatively flat area free of combustible material where we could start a campfire without setting the whole area ablaze. We were quite high up and we could see a cliff about a half mile or more across from our site. It was a pretty high cliff and from our vantage point couldn't see the bottom of it. There was probably about fifty feet of it that was visible to us. As we stood there, still awed by the beauty of the area, a big buck was standing on the cliff, sky lighted showing off his nice rack. Our first instinct was to take a shot at it. It was a clear shot from where we were. From my Army training, I knew it was a shot I could make if my rifle was on but I had not sighted in my rifle prior to the hunt and having missed several shots earlier and still not sighted in the rifle, wasn't sure I could make a killing shot from there. Even if I did hit it, we couldn't get to it to gut it and we probably would have just wounded it and couldn't track it down. So we decided not to shoot at it but just enjoy the majestic beauty of it until it got tired of looking at us and walked away.

    We gathered all the dead and burnable material we could find while it was still light. We were down to our last match to start the fire so we were very careful about getting it burning with paper we had in our pockets and dry tinder. We didn't resort to burning paper money, probably because we didn't have any. We were successful at getting the fire started. My Boy Scout training paid off. The next step was to be sure that someone stayed awake at all times to keep the fire burning and that we had enough fuel to keep it going. By this time it was completely dark and snowing lightly with a little breeze. I didn't think we had enough fuel for the fire so I set off into the extremely dark cedars to find more. It was so dark I couldn't see the trees for the forest, literally. I would bump into a tree and feel my way around looking for branches on the ground. After a few trips, I couldn't find any more dead branches and started breaking live branches and cutting them off with my hunting knife. I must have neglected to snap my knife in the sheath when I was finished gathering because when I got home my hunting knife was missing. I was a little upset by this because it was one I had borrowed from my Dad. While gathering firewood, I also found a piece of cedar branch or root that was shaped with a right angle and was about three to four feet long. I thought it was unusual and thought at the time, if I didn't need to burn it to stay warm I would take it home with me. Now that we had a supply of fuel, I thought I would either get some sleep or let the others sleep.

Kathy said she couldn't sleep anyway so she would keep the fire going and wake one of us if she got tired. We were all having nicotine withdrawal so we decided to share a cigarette before we went to sleep. Lighting it was no problem anymore now that we had a fire, even though we were out of matches. We also had some hard candy in our pockets so we shared some of that to stave off the hunger.

I had no trouble getting to sleep but staying asleep was the problem. Besides the rock hard ground there was the problem of roasting on the side facing the fire and freezing on the side that wasn't. There was a lot of waking up and rolling over to roast and freeze alternate sides. This went on for several rolls and in one of them I asked Kathy if she wanted to participate in the roast and freeze roll. She said she wasn't tired yet and would just as soon keep watch over the fire, listen to the night sounds and watch the falling snow sizzling in the fire. I assumed with the fire, we didn't have to worry about wild animals such as mountain lions, cougar, vicious pumas, wolf, fox, badgers, skunks and whatever else might be lurking in the night.

None of us knew if the others in our hunting party had made it out or if they had become lost also. Clarence had recently quit smoking so I was concerned that if he didn't make it out and got separated from Doug and Dean, he wouldn't have matches to start a fire. I wasn't too concerned about Doug and Dean. They were young and resourceful so unless they fell and broke a bone, I thought they would be ok with or without matches. They had hunted with their Dad, Cliff Kummer, for years, as had I and he was the best teacher any of us could have for hunting and survival skills.

Unbeknownst to us, at this time, was that Clarence had been separated from everyone else and gotten lost also. He kept walking until he finally came out at a road. Where he came out at was a long ways from the car and he had no clue which way the car was. He also didn't know what had happened to the rest of us. He started walking one way up the road for several miles and then second guessed which way he should be going and would turn around and go the other way. Out in the wilderness, there was no traffic on the road so he kept walking for hours. At least the walking kept him warm. Back and forth on the lonely country road that seemingly led to nowhere, not even sure it was the same road we had parked the car on.

Doug and Dean both had made it out and back to the vehicles. When no one else showed up and it was dark, they drove to a ranch house and put out the alert that we were lost. The ranchers in the area communicated by radio and they alerted all the ranchers in the area. This was not something new to them. Hunters were always getting lost in the area and they would search for them. In fact, the previous year, some hunters had gotten lost in the same general area and a snow storm came up and before they were found, one of them froze to death. I don't know the particulars, but I assume they didn't have the means to start a fire. Because of this the ranchers alerted the Sheriff in Williston and the search and rescue unit. They wanted to bring in a search plane but the darkness and snow prevented that until morning.

In the meantime the ranchers of the area drove around in their pickups and trucks in the dark and snow looking for any sign of us. They came across Clarence walking on the road and picked him up and that gave them a general idea of the area we were lost in. The owner of the land, who knew the terrain in this area best but who said he often got temporarily lost driving around, took another rancher with him and they drove around the prairie trails that could take them into the wilderness.

Meanwhile, back in Williston, my sisters, Fern and Verla and my brother in law, Clifford and Fern's kids, Melody, Cindy, Tammy, Wayne and friends, Dale and Marsha Volenchenko gathered at Verla and Cliff's home to wait for news and offer support to one another along with prayers.

Back at our campfire, it was approaching midnight and Kathy was keeping the fire going and I'm sure contemplating our situation and possibly offering a prayer or two herself. Now understand, she comes from a family that believes in God and prayer but does it in their own quiet way, never telling anyone what or who they are praying for but in touch with God, whenever his help is needed and in thanksgiving when it is not. Her Mother lost her first baby that was stillborn. After that, her mother prayed for another healthy baby. She was blessed with, not one but two, a pair of twins, Vivian and Vincent. When she became pregnant again, she delivered another set of twins, Lynn and Larry. Now she had four babies under two years old. Her prayers were answered and I'm sure she was telling God, enough now. So it was probably Kathy's prayers and my sisters and friends prayers that had God's protecting, guiding hand watching over us, keeping us from harm and making dumb decisions.

While Kathy is keeping watch by night, she is scanning the horizon and looking behind her where we had seen the big buck on the cliff across a chasm. She couldn't see anything there but for some reason, she was looking in that direction, not the direction she was facing. Perhaps she got tired staring into the fire or God directed her to turn around and look. When she did, she thought she saw headlights on the cliff. She immediately woke Mike and I up and asked what was over on the cliff. We concurred with her that they were headlights and not a figment of her imagination. I said we should fire three shots into the air, the universal sign of distress, and perhaps we could get their attention. We had no idea they were looking for us. They were parked and we couldn't see any movement. For all we knew, it could be teenagers, parking and drinking beer. That was naturally the first thing that entered my alleged mind because I had lots of experience with that.

Mike, grabbed his rifle and went a few steps up the hill behind the fire and fired three shots in succession into the air. From across the chasm we hear a bull horn and someone saying, OK we see you. Stay where you are, don't try to come to us, we will come and get you.

It took quite a while for them to reach us. While we were waiting we gathered our things and got dirt to put out the fire when we were ready to leave. We watched their progress as their flashlights came bobbing along first down the cliff side of the chasm and then up our side. When they got there, they took their flashlight and shined it down just a few feet from where our campfire was burning and directly behind where Kathy was sitting. You couldn't see the bottom with the flashlight beam. They then took a rock and dropped it. It seemed like it took forever before you could hear it hit bottom. It was their way of telling us how dangerous the terrain was and emphasizing the importance of following in their footsteps back. One wrong step in the dark could be fatal.

One took the lead with the flashlight and one the rear with another flashlight, lighting the path that was probably a wildlife trail and indiscernible to us. It took us a while to navigate our way back to the pickup. They told us they were about to leave when Mike fired the shots. They had originally stopped because they saw our campfire but they were trying to determine if it was a burning coal deposit or a campfire. They couldn't see any movement so they were thinking, burning coal deposit.

I guess in the badlands, there are many coal deposits that actually stick out of the earth's surface. If lighting strikes them, they start burning and some smolder for years. I believe there was divine intervention which led them to that spot, caused them to stop to look it over rather than dismiss it as burning coal. It was probably an answer to Kathy's prayers that caused her to turn around to look and see them.

It was quite a long ride back to the ranch and when we arrived, we were reunited with Clarence, Doug and Dean. Of course the news was relayed to Williston where my sisters, friends and family's were keeping watch. The ranchers wife had us all sit down around a huge table with room for 10 to 15 people. It could have been a scene from Bonanza. She gave us all coffee and commenced to prepare a huge meal of fried potatoes, eggs, bacon and coffee. What a feast and we all ate until we were full. I would guess it was probably about two in the morning by now. These were kind, generous people that put their lives and sleep on hold and answered the call when we were in trouble and needed help. It's possible they saved our lives. Upon returning to my sister's home in Williston, we found them all up, waiting for us and celebrating our safe return. Thanks be to God.

For several years after, my sister kept in touch with the ranchers that rescued us and fed us. I'm ashamed to say that I have forgotten their name. The name Melon comes to mind but I am not sure that is correct. We were not the only ones that they helped or rescued. It was probably an annual event every hunting season, yet they continued to answer the call for help. I probably would have been posting the land and trying to keep hunters out and telling them they were not welcome but these were extraordinary, wonderful, kind and forgiving people. They never once chastised us for our stupidity and careless behavior but in fact tried to make us feel better by telling us they lived there most or all of their life and still got lost on their own land. North Dakota is full of people just like them and the majority are farmers or ranchers. Always ready to help a friend, neighbor or complete stranger, putting their own lives on hold.

That year at Christmas, which was just a few months after this experience, there was a strange looking package under the Christmas tree from Doug and Dean, my nephews that had been with us hunting. We were all gathered together for the celebration of the birth of Jesus. The Williston bunch seemed mysterious and anxious for me to open this strange shaped and wrapped gift. When I did, I found the piece of wood that was in the shape of a right angle that was from a cedar root or branch that I had planned to save and take with me if I didn't have to burn it in the campfire for fuel. In the excitement of being found, I forgot about it and left it by the campfire. After we were rescued and at home talking about the experience I mentioned that I had forgotten to bring that with me. Doug and Dean were able to go back and find our campfire site and found the piece of wood and retrieved it. I still have that piece of wood in one of my flower gardens. As I write this, I calculate that was forty four years ago.

3
Love of my Life, My Happiness

Kathy – 1965

To know love is what life is all about.
To be in love is to possess something that is beyond the reach of age or time.
To give love is to be rich in the joys that give color to each day.
To share love with someone is to know the fullest meaning of what happiness can be.
Author unknown

The realities of faith, hope and love can make every day an exciting adventure.
Norman Vincent Peale

There is no remedy for Love but to Love more.
Henry David Thoreau

Love is an irresistible desire to be irresistibly desired.
Robert Frost

You can only learn to Love by Loving.
Iris Murdoch

Remember to laugh often and Love much.
Ralph Waldo Emerson

Love looks not with the eyes, but with the mind.
William Shakespeare

No one's perfect until you fall in love with them.
Andy Rooney

Don't be critical of your mates faults. It was those very defects that kept her or him from getting a better mate.

This Dummy Pulls His Own Strings

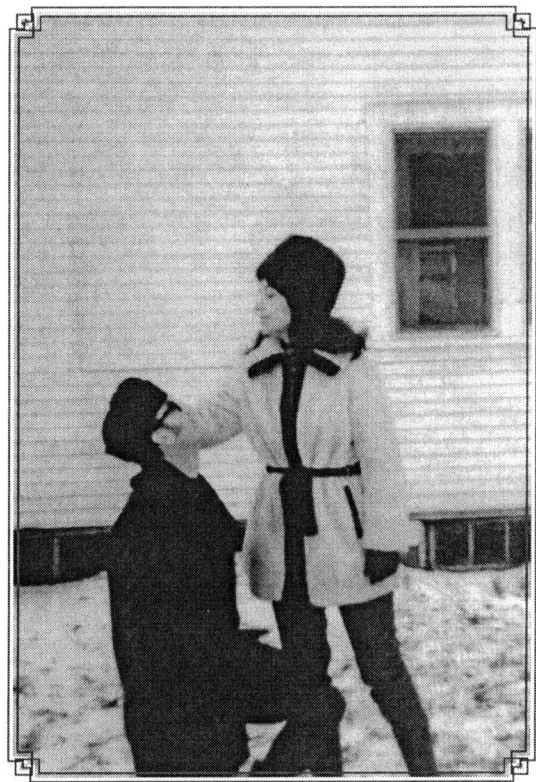

Proposal or Begging 1966

Kathy makes my heart smile. Kathy is the definition of Love, for me. Her smile brings the summer sunshine, her tears bring the rain, the touch of her lips are that magic moment, her eyes envelope you and make your mind a blank.

We are enough alike to agree on the important things in life but different enough to keep from being bored with each other.

She's my best friend, my confidant, my companion, my lover and my Love. As it is with most divine actions, I'm not sure why God blessed me with her but I am forever grateful. I have not put her on a pedestal, she was born on one, in my alleged mind. I have started to clean up my act because one lifetime with her is not enough, I want to spend eternity with her.

Her family is also wonderful. No surprise there, she came from good stock.

Dwight E. Knuth

I met Kathy for the first time in Kief, ND one spring evening in May of 1962, when a young man's fancy turns to Love . I was 20 years old and she was 15. She and some girlfriends were parked on Main Street of Kief, ND. Some of my friends and I had come to Kief to buy some beer at the local bar, Earls'. I could make the bar in Kief or in other words, they would sell me beer even if I wasn't 21. Lucky for me, I was a lush back then. I had just purchased a case of beer, it was Friday evening and the driver decided to drag main to see if there were any girls around. We all laughed at him because this was Kief with a population in the single digits. Main street was about two blocks long. Yet he drove down the street and on the next block in front of the post office was a car with four girls in it. He pulled in next to the car (diagonal parking) and we all got out. This was a time when most cars didn't have temperature control. The temperature was controlled by rolling down the window or leaving it up. This was a spring evening so windows were rolled down. Kathy was sitting just opposite of me so I got out and started talking to her. She was wearing that smile that makes you forget everything else around you. When she smiles, her eyes smile too and just envelope you. The driver of our car was a neighbor to Kathy, on the farm, so he came up to her and was asking her for a kiss.

Two lips must insist on two more to be kissed or you'll never know what love can do. So, on impulse, I stuck my head in the window, found my lips close to hers so I introduced my lips to her and I kissed her, before the other guy could, or before she could even respond to his request. This, in fact, was literally stealing a kiss.

She was the most beautiful girl I had ever seen and I thought she must be at least 17 if not older. That kiss was a magic moment. Fireworks, euphoria, floating on air, weak in the knees, higher than a kite can fly. There was a feeling like we were old friends though we had never met. It was instant happiness, no stirring required. There was a connection made with that first kiss and I knew immediately I wanted to get to know this lovely, shy, beautiful girl with the smile that lit up the earth. She still wears that smile and it still sends me floating on air.

This Dummy Pulls His Own Strings

Scientifically there was a 2010 study that shows that Love is like a drug. It sparks the same euphoric feeling as cocaine, in the same part of the brain. The brain is flooded with dopamine and norepinephrine, triggering euphoria. Falling in love also triggers adrenaline, which may make your heart race and your knees shake when you're near your lover. Weak in the knees is an old expression used for an adrenaline rush.

Being in Love is like being addicted. The same brain areas light up in people who are madly in love as those who use cocaine or opioids. Lovers also show the classic symptoms of addiction.

So it is with new love but over time new love becomes steadfast love. Again scientifically, at orgasm, the hormones vasopressin in men and oxytocin in women rise. These "cuddle hormones" can flood you with loving feelings for your partner. Scientists believe these chemicals help cement emotional bonds between lovers. The chemicals of romance may wane at the same time, so ecstasy gets replaced with devotion.

Back to the girls in the car on main street of Kief. The girls said they knew where there was a party in Kief and we could attend if we wanted. We returned to our car and followed them. I don't remember a lot about the party except that the evening was over before I was ready for it to end. Kathy was going home with her big brother, Vince. I was afraid I would never see her again. I didn't know where she lived, she didn't have a phone and I didn't want the night to end. We were standing in the middle of a mud puddle kissing good night and I asked if I could take her home. She said if her brother agreed to it, she would agree but he might kill me if I asked. I was willing to take that chance. I believe she was testing my resolve and courage or else she thought Vince would never agree so she was safe.

He was sitting in his car waiting for Kathy, drinking a beer and watching us in his rear view mirror. Kathy took me over to him and introduced me. I asked or maybe I begged him to let me take Kathy home. We said he could follow us. After bribing him with a beer or two, he agreed to it and he didn't kill me. He probably could have, especially at that point with my weak knees. Vince worked construction and physically was in very good shape. He was also very good looking, for a guy. No surprise, he's Kathy's brother. He was often likened to Paul Newman, physically. In fact this was the start of a great friendship between Vince and I that lasted the rest of his life. I was best man at his wedding. We drove Kathy home and said our goodbyes but not before I made a date with her.

Probably because I had been drinking and concentrating on Kathy on the way to her place, I couldn't remember how to get to her place for our first date. She didn't have a phone so I couldn't call her for instructions. It was either appear on her doorstep or forget about it. I decided to go to Kief to Earls' bar to ask for directions. Problem was, I didn't know her father's name so I had to ask them how to get to the Hoffman farm. Lucky for me, I was sober when the drunks at Earl's gave me instructions because it was not easy to find. Everyone had a different idea about the easiest way to find it. I relied on Earl for the final word because I thought he might be the most sober of the lot. For Earl's trouble, I bought a case of beer from him. I did find the farm and we went out and enjoyed each other's company. At least she agreed to a second date and then a third and so it went.

I remember one night, some of my friends and I were out drinking and had stopped at the bar in Butte to get some beer and we ran into some girls there. One of them knew Kathy. Her brother was a drummer in a dance band and had been dating Kathy. Somehow, I convinced her to show us the way to Kathy's farm from Butte and then to go inside to get Kathy out of her house. It turns out Kathy and her parents were already in bed.

This girl went right in the dark house without knocking, went upstairs to Kathy's room and drug her out to the car in her robe with her hair in curlers. Back then girls generally put their hair in curlers before going to bed and slept with curlers in their hair. We sat in the car and talked for a while until Kathy had to go in.

I had joined the Navy and had about a month before leaving for prior service boot camp at the Great Lakes Naval station in IL. I made the most of that time, dating Kathy several times and getting to know her a little better. The more time I spent with her the more I admired and liked her. She lived on a farm and her parents were hardworking, honest people, much like my own parents.

The hard part of dating Kathy was they didn't have a telephone so I couldn't call to make or break a date or change the time or let her know I may be late or just visit. This actually worked to my advantage because no one else could call to make a date with her either and we did all our visiting face to face. She was easy to talk to, not like a lot of girls I had dated who had limited interests, mostly themselves. She was unpretentious with a great sense of humor who liked to laugh and laughed often, sincerely and easily.

She was well mannered and very much a lady much like her mother who was a very classy lady. She could be shy but knew her own mind and was not afraid to speak it. She was very intelligent with common sense and good thought processes. She was mature beyond her years both mentally and physically. I don't really know if it was love at first sight but it was absolutely love at first kiss. I don't know how else to describe the feeling after that first kiss. I was smitten, to say the very least. The thought crossed my mind that she was a bit young for my advanced years but I dismissed it immediately.

The first sight of her was very easy on the eyes which made me want to taste her luscious lips but it was the taste of those lips that sent me into a tailspin. She seemed wise to me beyond her years but in reality, I knew she was too young for a serious relationship. When it was time for me to leave for the Navy, we parted friends with the understanding that we would keep in touch. This was not her strong suit. She was not a letter writer. I interpreted her lack of correspondence to mean she didn't have the desire to keep in touch. I thought the desire was mostly coming from me and perhaps I needed to give her space and time to explore the dating scenario. This I did.

In fact when I would come home on leave unannounced because of the lack of communication, I would sometimes find her all dressed up for a date with another guy. On one occasion, it was a fellow who was in the air force and I was still there when he came to pick her up. I met him and Kathy and he went on their way and I stuck around a while and visited with her mother. Her father was there also but like Kathy, until he got to know you and like you, he was a bit shy. I believe that was her last date with that fella, not because I said anything about it but because I took her out just about every night I was home on leave.

So it went. We would date as if we were going steady while I was home on leave and when I went back to base, she would go back to dating others and I would do the same. This seemed to work well for both of us and there was no guilt or betrayal, no accusations, arguing or fighting. I remember after some of those leaves, going back to base on the airplane feeling so lonesome for her it was close to unbearable and thoughts of AWOL occurred on several occasions. It was the hardest thing I have ever done in my lifetime, leaving her, going back to base and not knowing if she would still want to see me when I next returned or if she would be going with someone else. After getting back into the daily routine at base, the pain would ease and I would be left with pleasant memories and hopefulness. We did this through the entire four plus years I was in the Navy. I say four plus years because just before I was to be discharged, the Vietnam War heated up and everyone's enlistment was extended six months.

When my extended enlistment was up and I was about to be discharged, Johns' Hopkins medical facility in Baltimore, MD called me and offered me a job. I told them I wasn't interested but they insisted I should meet with them and see their facility and hear their offer. I thought, well I am going to be unemployed, what can it hurt? At least I will get the experience of an interview.

They took me out to lunch with their whole data processing (now referred to as IT) department, gave me a tour of the facility and made me an offer they thought I couldn't refuse. I told them I would consider it and get back to them and they tried to pressure me by saying there were other candidates for the position but I was the top one so if they didn't hear from me soon, they would have to go with another candidate. It had no effect on me since I was going to turn them down anyway. It seemed strange to me that I was the top candidate when I hadn't even applied for the position. I waited a few days and called them back and told them I had other interests. They immediately raised the offer and I again said I would consider it. It seems as though I'm lucky when it comes to taking tests. Not only had I graduated number one in my data processing class in the Navy, I had scored very high on the tests Johns' Hopkins gave me for employment.

My Chief and my commanding officer had also given me very complimentary recommendations. Before I got around to calling them back they called me and I again declined their offer. They immediately raised the offer and in order to get them off my back, I told them I would consider it. They then called my Chief and asked him what he thought it would take to get me to accept their offer. I was in the room with the Chief when he took their call. He told them he didn't know but money was always a good incentive.

I finally told them I was smitten by a girl back home in ND and was going to return to ND to see if I had a chance with her. I also told them that if that didn't work out I was probably going to Australia to seek employment so they should probably go with one of their other candidates. They thanked me for being honest with them and told me if my plans didn't work out they could probably find a home for me with them.

I loaded my boat with all my earthly possessions that the Navy had not already shipped home for me, hooked up the boat and headed west to the plains of ND. As I remember it, there was an advertisement on a bulletin board on base for someone that wanted a ride to ND the same time I was going and was willing to share expenses. I got in touch with her and it was agreed she would accompany me. She was the wife of a sailor stationed at Bainbridge and they were both from Grand Forks, ND. I have since forgotten her name but remember she was going home for her sister's wedding.

I was driving a 1965 Mercury Comet with a 289 engine. It was a light car and had a lot of get up and go and was a straight stick. A straight stick, for those of you too young to recognize the term, meant there was a clutch and you physically shifted through the gears, first, second, third as opposed to the automatic transmission that does the shifting for you. It also meant you could rev the engine, pop the clutch and squeal the tires as you accelerated. Great fun and hard on the tires. I had purchased it new in 1965. This was July of 1966. Because there were two of us to drive and because she was from ND and all ND girls knew how to shift and drive a straight stick, we drove all the way from the East Coast to ND only stopping for gas, sandwiches/drinks and potty breaks. There wasn't a whole lot of conversation because while one drove, the other slept.

I don't remember how many hours it took us but I remember it being late evening (bedtime) when we reached Grand Forks. ND. She invited me to spend the night at her parents' home to rest up before the last leg of my trip but I declined. I dropped her off and continued on my way.

There was a lot of road construction and detours and back then road construction wasn't using smooth paved bypasses around the construction. At least ND road construction wasn't. It was more like driving in a plowed field around the construction which was difficult pulling a boat. It slowed me down considerably but served to keep me awake. I was approaching Harvey, ND from the north on a smooth paved road and thought I had it made because Harvey is only 25 miles from home. I remember dozing off periodically and taking a lot of no-doz pills. As I was coming into Harvey I neglected to notice I had to cross a railroad crossing and that there was a freight train bearing down on it. The train blew the whistle at the crossing which was the only indication I had it was there. There were no flashing lights or arms and I was almost on the track before I came to a stop, slamming on the brakes and jumping out of my skin. Now I was wide awake.

On the other side of the tracks was a city park which I pulled into and tried to sleep. It took some time to get to sleep after the train scare but I slept for a few hours until the sun came up. I continued on home and I think everyone was still sleeping when I got there. I went right to bed and slept all day.

This Dummy Pulls His Own Strings

I got up in time for one of my Mothers' good dinners then got back in the car and headed out to see Kathy. I remember Kathy and her family giving me a very warm greeting which made me quite hopeful for our future. Actually, Kathy came flying out of the house and physically jumped into my waiting and eager arms and planted a big kiss on my lips. That will sure make you feel like you were missed.

Kathy had graduated from high school that spring, I was out of the Navy and unemployed and had some money from mustering out pay and leave pay so was footloose and fancy free and in Love. Kathy and I went out just about every night except when I was out of town at one of my relatives.

On one of these occasions, my sister, Verla had talked me into going back to Williston to her home to spend some time with her family. I don't remember the circumstances or details but I must have rode to Williston with Verla because I didn't have my car there. I was only going to spend a short time there because I had a date on Sat. night with Kathy. Something happened to prevent me from leaving when I was planning to go back home. Probably one of my sisters' home cooked meals delayed me. I was unable to call Kathy because they didn't have a phone so I had Verla take me to the airport so I could buy a plane ticket and fly to Minot. When I got to Minot, I found the bus had already left and I was unable to get any public transportation to Drake. I walked to the highway and started hitchhiking. I eventually got a ride but got back too late to go on my date with Kathy.

One of my friends, Danny Schafer, and I proceeded to drink a few cold ones and I talked him into driving me back to Minot so I could buy Kathy some flowers to make up for standing her up. We got there just before the florist closed and I bought a dozen long stemmed roses for her. I went to see her the following night and presented the roses to her which did the trick, especially after I explained that I had tried to make it and had even purchased airline tickets to try and make it. It was the first time she had received long stemmed roses. The middle of the prairie in ND isn't conducive for entertainment so most nights consisted of a couple six packs of beer and watching submarine races.

On Friday or Saturday nights there was usually a dance to go to and some nights we would get together with Kathy's brother Vince and his girl Connie and go to the bar in Drake, play some pool and drink a few cold ones. It was the life, party all night and sleep all day, get up wash the car, eat my Moms' wonderful cooking and do it all over again. One night I took Kathy out to a restaurant in Minot for dinner. After dinner we went to the Air Force base to the NCO (Non Commissioned Officers) club to do some dancing and have a few drinks. It didn't matter where we went or what we did, we always had a good time. We enjoyed each others company and liked being together.

When I visited my brother Dorel and his family in Bismarck, I went to the ND job service to apply for a job because the money was running out. It didn't look too hopeful for a computer career in ND in the mid-sixties. Not too many businesses were using computers then. It seemed mostly state or federal government were the only computerized jobs. I figured I would have to go to the twin cities of Minneapolis/St. Paul to find a job in my area of expertise. I really wanted to stay around home to pursue this young, beautiful, sexy, classy, teenager so I told them I would take anything available. Several weeks later I got a phone call from job service for an interview in Grand Forks, ND for a computer programmer with First National Bank. I thought this would be doable because I could at least come home on weekends to see Kathy.

So off I went to Grand Forks for the interview. I passed all the employment tests with flying colors and even though I wasn't qualified for the position and had no experience in what the job entailed, they were willing to hire me and train me. I guess there weren't many computer geeks in ND at that time. My experience was with IBM computers in personnel accounting and the bank was using Boroughs computers in the banking industry. Also, the pay was lousy, about one hundred dollars a week, not enough for a beer budget. The banks thought it was a privilege to work

This Dummy Pulls His Own Strings

for them and that you got a lot of prestige when you worked at a bank. Prestige doesn't buy much beer. I didn't buy into that philosophy but I thought it was a place to start and accumulate some experience and they were willing to educate me and train me as a computer programmer using assembler language for Boroughs which is close to the IBM assembler language and 1401 auto coder the Navy was using. When they made me an offer of employment, I accepted and started almost immediately. I rented a room at the YMCA and ate most my meals there at the little café. They had great cooks and it was almost like home cooking.

On weekends, I would go home to see my honey. Sunday evenings would find us sitting on her parents couch cuddled up and watching Lassie on a black and white TV and saying good-by for two hours. I would stick around until the last possible moment that would allow me to get back to Grand Forks just before midnight. Some week-ends in the winter, it would be storming so bad I couldn't see the road and would have to open the door and look down and follow the painted line in the middle of the road until the wind died down and I could proceed again with the door closed. Luckily, I was the only car on the road because if I had met a car, they wouldn't be able to see me and would have run into my open door. Talk about blind Love, this was the epitome of it.

So it went. Work five days, spend the weekends with Kathy and pine for her the rest of the week. Week nights I would write to her, pay bills, listen to records on my stereo, drink a beer or two and occasionally bowl or go snowmobiling with one of the single guys from work. Not much of a life compared to the Navy where I was working three to four jobs most of the time. I guess you could say I was a little bored or not so much bored as lonesome. I wanted to be with Kathy every day not just on weekends. The room at the Y was about 6 feet by10 feet. It was big enough for a single bed, a chair, desk and my stereo. It was quite cramped, to say the least. There was a black and white TV in a common lounge area but you had to watch whatever everyone else was watching. This was much like the Navy so it didn't bother me that much. I just didn't watch TV.

I found a room for rent in a large house that rented out rooms to several people. You could say it was a rooming house. The owner was a 97 yr. old widow of a dentist, Mrs. Moscow. She was a sweet old lady who was kind and did all her own house work. When I went to look at the room to rent, I discovered that there was no shower, only a bathtub. I loved my showers and took one daily ever since I was in the military. When I told her I wasn't going to rent the room she asked me why and if there was anything she could do to change my mind. I told her I liked the room but there wasn't a shower and I showered daily. She told me she would run my bath for me daily if I would rent the room. I also told her that I got called into work in the middle of the night and the phone ringing would disturb her and her other renters. She said she didn't mind getting up to answer the phone and the other renters wouldn't hear it. She was so sweet and convincing I couldn't turn her down and I rented the room and told her I could draw my own bath.

My room was on the second floor and at the bottom of the stairs was a phone for use by all who lived there. Of course the renters upstairs couldn't hear the phone ring so Mrs. Moscow would answer it and come upstairs and knock on the door of whoever the call was for. The bank computer center was a 24 hour operation and if they had trouble with the processing, they would call me to come in and fix it, regardless what time it was. Generally it would be 4 AM when they would call. I stayed there until I moved to an apartment shortly before I was married. When I moved out there was a library table that her husband had made that I really liked. I asked her if she would be interested in selling it. She told me no, she wouldn't sell it to me but that I could have it. It was about 80 years old at the time and I still have it and it must be about 130 years old or more by now. When Kathy and I became engaged, I took Kathy to meet Mrs. Moscow.

Being five years older than Kathy, I was 24 and she was 19, I was ready to settle into marital bliss before she was. It took me some begging, bribing, cajoling, brainwashing and possibly some bullying to talk her into it. I am very persistent and I finally wore her down. I never did get complete agreement from her but she didn't tell me to hit the road either. I finally thought that if I bought her an engagement ring and presented it to her, it might do the job.

It was getting close to Christmas so I visited the jewelry store in Grand Forks across from the bank. I told the owner the price range I was looking at and he brought out some choices, some which were above the range I was looking at. I thought it should be paid for before we actually got married. I found what I thought Kathy would like and what the jeweler was pushing and he came down in price and I went up in my range and made the purchase. I sold my boat to my brother-in-law, Clifford Kummer to help pay for the ring. After the fact, I learned I was following in my brothers' footsteps as he sold his motorcycle to buy a ring for his bride.

One of the guys I worked with was managing 3 apartment buildings with 4 two bedroom apartments in each building, a total of 12 apartments. I thought I would do the math for you. He got to live in one of the apartments at a reduced rate for managing them. The owner was an older Jewish fellow from Minneapolis who used to live in Grand Forks and had a photography business there by the bank. My co-worker was going to buy a house and move so they needed a new live in manager. They asked me if I would be interested in moving into one of the apartments and managing the rest. This consisted of mowing the grass, shoveling the walks, renting the apartments, collecting the rent and hiring repair people when necessary. I accepted the job and moved into the apartment. So I was prepared for marital bliss with a ring for my bride and an apartment to live in.

Christmas Eve I was at Kathy's parent's farm with her family, brothers, sister, nieces, nephews and parents. After the presents were opened I asked Kathy to come out to the car with me to get one present I had left out there. In the privacy and warmth of my car, I presented her with the rings and asked her to marry me. She said yes without any hesitation and we went inside and made the announcement. There was much merriment and celebration and a few toasts. I let Kathy pick the wedding date and she picked Sept. 2.

One of my good friends, Danny Schafer had just returned from Viet Nam and was helping his father in the wholesale business in Drake. His father had a stroke and was in the hospital in Grand Forks. Danny, his sister and mom were coming to Grand Forks from Drake to visit his dad on a Friday. I made arrangements for Kathy to ride along and spend the weekend with my boss, his wife and family. This gave Kathy and I the opportunity to go furniture shopping for our apartment. We went to the furniture store and picked out a sofa sleeper, a couple living room chairs, a dinette set and a bedroom set. My parents had given me a bed and dresser for the other bedroom and I had brought a recliner home with me from the Navy which needed recovering. My brother-in-law, Clarence Rau, who was my best man at my wedding, was an upholsterer and said he would recover it for me for a wedding present, which he did. So we were pretty much set up for housekeeping. It's a long, long time from Dec. to Sept. so a friend and neighbor to Kathy at the farm, Albert Krueger, asked if he could live with me and occupy the other bedroom until I got married. He was working as an appliance salesman in Grand Forks and was dating a college girl from Karlsruhe and asked if she could also live there. He said she would do the cooking and cleaning. I agreed to both requests.

Several weeks before the wedding, a couple of my friends from high school, who were also on the Golden Gloves boxing team with me, Emery Suckert and Danny Schafer and Kathy and I drove to McClusky to get the marriage license. When we returned we thought it would be proper to celebrate, especially because they were not invited to the wedding. I believe our goal was to drink Drake dry and possibly Balfour also. I remember the bar tender at Balfour, getting on my case because I came from a fine Christian family in Drake and my Dad was even a preacher and here I was consuming alcohol and proceeding to get drunk. I also remember Kathy coming to my defense and giving her what for and saying she shouldn't be so self-righteous because she was the one selling us the alcohol. We had a good time, in spite of the alcohol.

This Dummy Pulls His Own Strings

Kathy & Dwight, wedding, you may kiss the bride

    We agreed to have a small church wedding with only immediate family, siblings and their families and our parents. No aunts, uncles, cousins or friends would be invited. Many of my friends were very unhappy with our decision to have a small ceremony. Because they were not invited to the wedding or reception, they decided to have a keg party at the nursery which was just a grove of trees in the country. I believe it took place the eve of the wedding. I also think I drank enough to pass out and later heard that Kathy's brother Vince and Danny Schafer were arguing which of them was my best friend and who got to carry me to the car. I believe, Kathy was also at the party but I don't recall how either of us got home. I must have slept some and come to eventually because I remember trying to crawl into my bed. My nephews, Doug and Dean Kummer, I'm sure with the help of their parents and aunt and uncle Rau had put onions in my pillow and rocks in my bed and who knows what else. I just threw everything on the floor and passed out on the mattress. I was relatively un-hungover the next morning or maybe not completely sober yet. I recall getting up and singing, get me to the church on time. I remember waking up and saying a prayer of thanks for Kathy and asking God's blessing on our marriage and life. I don't think I sobered up all day or I was just high on life and my good fortune.

Cutting the cake, Sept. 2, 1967

We got married in the small country Scandia Lutheran church that Kathy's family belonged to and attended. It shared a minister with the Lutheran church in McClusky . The minister also worked at the job service in Bismarck. We elected to have one attendant each. I asked my brother, Dorel to be my best man but he was having some health problems and wasn't sure he could make it to the wedding. It turned out he didn't. So I asked my brother-in-law, Clarence Rau to be my best man. Kathy's Matron of honor was her only sister, Vivian. We had the rehearsal dinner at my parents' home the night prior to the wedding after the rehearsal. The reception was held at Kathy's parents' farm home. Kathy spent most of the summer, cleaning, painting and getting everything shipshape for the wedding.

Married

The wedding was small and quick and very nice, just the way we wanted it. Kathy wore a beautiful white dress just below the knee length. She was the most beautiful bride and for that matter, girl, my eyes had ever witnessed, coming down the aisle on her handsome daddy's arm. What a vision to behold, especially from my perspective. My prayers were being answered and my dreams coming true. I can tell you, after 45 years of marital bliss with her, I still can't believe I could have the good fortune to meet her and convince (brainwash) her to spend her life with me. This was the most important and memorable day of my life and the reason for my continuing happiness.

After the wedding we went to the farm for the reception and opening of the wedding presents. My sisters, Fern and Verla had asked me what we wanted for a wedding present. Being the smart ass that I am, I made a list of everything I could think of. They being equal or greater smart asses, made a huge box of all I had asked for either in miniature or in gag format. It took us a long time to open it and go through everything and it provided many laughs. I still have some of the things that were in that box. Some of the items were, a pole lamp that was made from a small tree branch with a miniature lantern hanging from it. Pole lamps were popular in the late 60's. There was a wall plaque that said, "Never question your wife's judgment. Look whom she married". A miniature set of pots and pans and many, probably around 20 items, too many to remember and list but it provided us hours of entertainment and laughs and conversation allowing my family to get to know her family and realize that none of us can be labeled normal. Of course, there were the normal wedding presents also from everyone.

Kathy's mom and sister had prepared food and we had purchased a wedding cake so we all dined bountifully. Nothing was catered but provided and served by Kathy's family. A very relaxed yet festive celebration. My nephews and Kathy's brothers decorated the car tastefully and we headed to Drake to stop at my parent's before heading off to New Rockford for the night on our way to Grand Forks, our apartment and marital bliss.

At Drake, my nephews, Douglas and Dean Kummer took Kathy's purse and she was not leaving without it because she had her birth control pills in it. No one else was aware of this but Kathy said she wasn't leaving without it. It was great fun for them but not so much for us. Eventually they returned it and we were on our way. We stopped at a motel in New Rockford for the night. We thought it was too far for anyone to follow us there and do anything to the car like put limburger cheese on the manifold or jack it up and put blocks under it. These were things they did in those days as a way to harass the bride and groom.

The wedding bliss continued. We went home to our apt. in Grand Forks and then went to International Falls to see my Navy buddy, Jim Gulbranson and his wife Kay. Not the ideal destination for a honeymoon but probably all we could afford. Because of the paper mill in International Falls which gave off a strong odor of Boise Breath, we said we would never live there. Never say never. We returned home to Grand Forks and I went back to work at the bank. The marital bliss continued and the Love, admiration, respect and adoration for the love of my life grew with each passing day.

I was not alone in my elevated opinion of Kathy. Even the children thought she literally was an angel.

After we were married and living in International Falls not far from the elementary school, one of our friends' kids would walk by our house on the way to school. It was his first year of school, probably kindergarten, so as all mothers do, his mother was concerned about his wellbeing. She knew his route to school would take him right by our house so she asked Kathy to keep an eye out for him and make sure he was safe and not getting into mischief. We had what we referred to as a sun porch in front of our house which was an oversized entrance with windows on two sides that allowed the morning sun to shine brightly in it. Kathy liked to drink a cup of coffee in the sun porch with the entrance door open, listen to the birds and observe the world coming to life in the morning. On one particular sunny, happy morning she was drinking her coffee when she observed our friends son, Sean, happily skipping down the middle of the road in front of our house, not on the sidewalk where a five or six year old should be. She got up, went to the screen door and said in a voice loud enough for Sean to hear, "Sean, get off the road". Sean stopped dead in his tracks, looked around, searching for the source of the voice but not finding it. He hurriedly went up on the sidewalk and continued his journey to school, periodically looking around to see if anyone was watching him. Kathy of course called his mom to tell her what had happened. When he returned home from school his mom asked him about his day and if there was anything special about his day. He said to his mom that an angel had spoken to him on the way to school and told him to get off the road. Indeed she had and I agree whole heartedly with you Sean that she is an angel.

This is the same little boy that had some ping pong balls in his back pocket that he carried around to have something to play with when life got boring. He was out and about with his mom in some public setting, I'm not sure where. It could have even been church because his mom was a Sunday School teacher.

Sean was in some way not behaving properly and after repeated reprimands from his mother, she grabbed him by the shoulders, lifted him up and sat him down on a chair or bench with some force. Sean looked up at her and said, "now you've done it mom, you've busted my balls".

How do you describe the emotion of Love. Poets and songwriters have been trying for centuries and they still can't pin it down. Probably because it is different for everyone and has different degrees of emotion. Some people need to hear that they are loved over and over probably because of their level of self-confidence, trust and other variables. Some are happy with expressing or hearing it once and letting you know if it changes. For me, I wanted to share my thoughts, time and experiences with Kathy. Communication was a large part of building our relationship. Not necessarily agreeing on all our thoughts but sharing them and learning the values of each other and respecting them. I guess you could say Love is like Magic, it sometimes can't be explained. There is a song that describes Love as Magic and is called "It's Magic". It is one of my favorites because it kind of explains how I feel. I believe it was first recorded by Doris Day, who started singing in the "big band" era. She was also a movie star. The Platters and several others also did versions of it. A few lines follow:

It's Magic

You sigh, the song begins;
You speak, and I hear violins
It's Magic

Why do I tell myself
These things that happened are all really true?
When, in my heart, I know, the magic is
My love for you

Nothing can compare to falling or being in Love. Nothing can be as painful as love that is not returned or shared. To live life

This Dummy Pulls His Own Strings

completely to its' fullest, you must experience both. If you have experienced unrequited love, you can love more deeply and value it. You can appreciate it just as you appreciate your health more if you have suffered through illness.

I am not a romantic that believes there is only one love for you. I believe you can be in love many times with many people but only in romantic love with one person at a time. In my world, you should love with all your heart and mind to the fullest of your capability. If you're not "all in", the chances of things going bad are much greater. If you are completely committed, you will have a much better relationship and therefore be happier and satisfied. In my alleged mind, many marriages end in divorce, not because they are incompatible, but because they are not accepting and forgiving. They think, because I am a perfect human being, you should be too, when in reality, neither of us are. It is not a selfless love. True romantic Love is one way traffic. It's a pure flow of giving to the one you love, expecting nothing in return. When you give love in this manner, you are happy and excited that the person you love accepts it and that is all you want in return. If you expect anything more, you will experience resentment and disappointment when you don't get it. You can't define another person's love for you. You can only define your love for someone else. If we gave more thought and effort to our relationship on a regular and constant level, we could improve the quality of it, our lives and our happiness. Too often, once the vows are spoken and the honeymoon is over, making a living and living life, take most of our thought and effort and the marriage becomes secondary. You fall in Love by chance but you stay in Love by working at it. Working at it, is probably not the correct wording. It is more like being aware of the others feelings, thoughts and emotions and caring about them. It is about communicating these things to one another. I guess you could call this "working at it".

In the Bible, Paul defines Love in what is referred to as the "love chapter", 1 Corinthians 13: 1-13 where he writes a letter to the people of the church in Corinth, guiding them in their new found faith. He tells them that love is the foundation of life and without love, everything else is meaningless. If you speak without love, it is meaningless words. It doesn't matter how much knowledge or faith you have, if you don't share it with love, it's meaningless. Love doesn't insist on its own way, is not irritable or resentful. Love is patient and kind, bears all things, believes all things, hopes all things, endures all things. Love never ends. There are three things that we should build our life around. They are faith, hope and love but the most important is love.

My parents were married for over 60 years and Kathy's for over 50. We have been married for 45 years and if the good Lord doesn't issue a recall on either of us, we hope to make it to at least 50 and hopefully more.

My greatest regret is that I didn't have this knowledge in my youth and am afraid I didn't treat my wife as kindly and loving as she deserved to be treated. However, she was a lot smarter than I and she put up with me and educated me. Hopefully, it was worth the time and effort for her.

If I had it in my power to give one gift to my kids, grandkids and descendants, it would be Love as I have experienced it. I'm talking about the giddy, higher than a kite can fly, makes you feel like dancing, puts a song in your heart kind of Love. The kind of Love where you want to share everything with your partner, your time, thoughts, experiences and all of your life and afterlife. The kind that is addictive and makes you want more. When you are separated, you wish you could share the time, space and experience with the one you love.

> For here you are, standing there, Loving me
> Whether or not you should
> So somewhere in my youth or childhood
> I must have done something good
> From "The Sound of Music".

> Love is the light and sunshine of life.
> We cannot fully enjoy ourselves, or
> anything else, unless someone we love
> enjoys it with us.
> Lord Avebury

This Dummy Pulls His Own Strings

I call this "sharing love"

Following are some descriptions of Love by children ages 4 to 8. From the mouths of babes............

"When someone loves you, the way they say your name is different. You just know that your name is safe in their mouth."

Billy age 4

"Love is what makes you smile when you're tired."

Terri age 4

"Love is what's in the room with you at Christmas if you stop opening presents and listen."

Bobby age 7

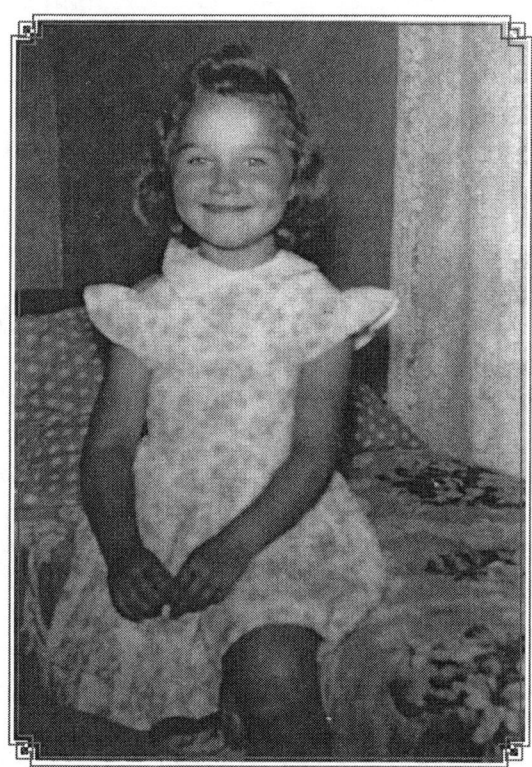

Kathy, age 6

4
Philosophy and Love of Life

"Life is what happens to you while you're busy making other plans"
John Lennon

Go forward in life with a twinkle in your eye and a smile on your face, but with great purpose in heart.
Gordon B. Hinckley

The greatest discovery of my generation is that a human being can alter his life by altering his attitude of mind.
William James (1842 – 1910)

To have joy one must share it. Happiness was born a twin.
Lord Byron

It's not how much we give but how much love we put into giving.
Mother Teresa

Those who bring sunshine to the lives of others cannot keep it from themselves.
Sir James M. Barrie

**There is so much good in the worst of us,
and so much bad in the best of us,
that it behooves all of us
not to talk about the rest of us.**
Robert Louis Stevenson

As a man thinketh in his heart, so is he.
Proverbs 23; 7, the Bible

Your character is the sum of your thoughts.
Anonymous

It is the mind that maketh good or ill, that maketh wretch or happy, rich or poor.
Edmund Spenser

Nothing can bring you peace but yourself.
Ralph Waldo Emerson

Much of what follows is just my opinion. I'm entitled to my stupid opinion. I'm not asking for agreement or trying to create disagreement. It's my view of life, love and the pursuit of happiness. Agree or disagree, it doesn't matter. I'm not trying to anger you or impress you. Just stating my philosophy of life.

- Live simply, speak kindly, care deeply, love generously.
- Love and be Loved.
    - There is no greater and powerful emotion.
    - Love is the basis of life, the meaning of life.
    - Don't be afraid of it but embrace it.
        - If you get hurt, have your pity party and try again because Love, not time, heals all wounds.
- Be Honest in all you say and do, in all your relationships and especially with yourself. As Thomas Jefferson said, " Honesty is the first chapter in the book of Wisdom".
- Don't procrastinate
- Anything worth doing is worth doing well. If you can't put your heart into it, take yourself out of it.

- Build character
- Mark Twain said, Courage is resistance to fear, mastery of fear, not absence of fear.
- Common Sense
- In our fast paced, multi-tasking world where we act and react before the thought process is even begun, common sense has become a rare commodity. I would say so few possess it that it has now become uncommon sense.
- Don't blame others or make excuses
- Excuses are lies confirming that you are not being true to your heart. When I was in basic training in the Army, our drill instructor (DI) would not accept any excuse for any shortcoming whether it was inspection, tardiness or any other shortcoming. The only answer he would accept from us was, "No Excuse, Sir". I've tried to continue that in my life. Instead of wasting time and effort making excuses or explaining the situation, correct the problem and move on.
- The only actions you are responsible for are your own. Own them. Take the credit or the blame, when necessary.
- The only thing constant is change, get used to it and don't fret about it.
- Life is too ironic to fully understand.
- You can't control anyone but yourself and sometimes not even yourself. Many people think that is what life is all about, control. They may be right. From the beginning of time, in the garden of Eden, God said, "Don't eat the apple", Adam and Eve rejected control by God and ever since someone has been trying to control someone else. Just like Adam and Eve, most people don't like to be controlled and reject it. Perhaps when God made us in his own image, he should have eliminated the control DNA. Of course this observation is in retrospect and I'm not qualified to second guess God's purpose or wisdom. It must be part of his plan for us.
- Don't put yourself down. There are a multitude of people that relish that, so it is covered.

- Don't criticize or be judgmental. We don't know all the facts or circumstances of a given situation and all of us are different and handle things differently.
- Mistakes are the growing pains of Wisdom. If you never make a mistake, you aren't doing anything. Some mistakes are too much fun to only make once, a repeat performance may be required. Don't let fear of making a mistake stop you. A life spent making mistakes is not only more enjoyable but more useful than a life spent doing nothing.
- Keep a positive attitude. Negative attitudes along with complaining and voicing gloom and doom, cause people to shy away from you. So unless you are trying to live in seclusion, you may not want to push people away. Positive things happen to people with positive attitudes. Kind of like a self-fulfilling prophecy. Perception is reality. Mark Twain's definition of an optimist is "A person who travels on nothing from nowhere to happiness."
- Don't avoid or run from problems or fears, face them head on and resolve them. It will make you feel good about yourself, your accomplishments and make you proud of yourself.
- Live in the moment, not in the future or past. Learn from the past, prepare for the future but live in the present. Notice and appreciate the beauty around you.
- Be yourself. Don't try to be someone else, there is only one of you. Celebrate being who you are and love being you. Be authentic and true to yourself. "Pull your own strings". If you like yourself, don't change for anyone. Let others take you as you are and who you are or not at all. How others see you is not important. How you see yourself means everything. You define your own life. Don't let other people write your life's story for you.
- Be grateful, count your blessings, name them one by one. Even in adversity you have something to be grateful for. Adversity and failures are great learning experiences which add to your knowledge. Focus on what you have, not on what you don't have.

- Care about people. Be kind. It generally makes someone else feel good and also makes you feel good about yourself.
- Live by choice, not by chance Be motivated, not manipulated. Work to excel not to compete. Anything worth doing is worth doing well. Listen to your own inner voice, not the jumbled opinions of everyone else.
- Choose to be around the right people; positive, respectful people. Surround yourself with people that support you and who make you happy to be in their company. Weed the people out of your life that depress you or bring you down. It's great to be supportive and helpful to others but some people just suck the life out of you. Learn who they are and weed them out. Surround yourself with people you like and enjoy being with.
    - People who stimulate positive thinking and attitudes.
    - People who laugh and make you laugh.
    - People who are kind in thought, word and deed.
- Don't pursue an education to become wealthy. Pursue an education to make yourself happy. If you love doing what you're doing, it's not work.
- Subscribe to the philosophy of the slow talkers of America because the trouble with talking too fast is, you may say something you haven't thought of yet.
- Don't swear or use profanity, especially in conversation. It makes you look like you don't have a sufficient vocabulary to express yourself. It not only reflects poorly on you but on your parents and your upbringing. That may be old school but I'm of the old school generation where if you had bad manners, it more than likely was because you weren't taught proper manners. My Father was a man who seldom swore and never "took the Lords' name in vain". One time we were working on some farm machine and he went to pound a bolt out with a hammer and hit his thumb instead of the bolt and he said "shit". That was probably the only time I heard him swear, if indeed that is swearing .

This Dummy Pulls His Own Strings

I'm not a stranger to swearing. As a youth and drunken sailor, I was an expert and prolific curser. Many of my friends are prolific swearers and it doesn't bother me that much when it is a group of friends hanging out. I will not avoid you or judge you if you swear. That's not my job or responsibility. I may analyze, in my private thoughts, why you find it necessary to use profanity and what you are trying to accomplish by doing that but it doesn't change my opinion of you. But in polite society, to my way of thinking, swearing should be avoided. I find myself distracted from the actual content of what's being said by the profanity. It is becoming more common and like my three year old grandson replied when he used the word "hell" and was asked where he heard it. He said, "only the whole planet". So I may be fighting a losing battle. Most of it is used for shock value but few are shocked anymore. When that happens, perhaps we will clean up our act. Either that or it will be accepted in polite society, which seems to be the trend. I found in my youth, when I could swear with the best of them and would to impress my friends and peers, that I would have to speak cautiously when in polite society to avoid letting some profanity escape my lips. Being a lazy youth, I found that was way too much work. I soon concluded that if I eliminated profanity from my thoughts and therefore my speech, I didn't have to worry about profanity slipping out in polite society. So it was my laziness, not a moral decision, that made me try to eliminate profanity from my thoughts and speech.

Delving further into it and over analyzing it, what is swearing and why do we do it? To me swearing is using the name of God in vain. Most of the rest is just bad language or improper use of it. We do have many adjectives that can be used to describe a person, place, thing or situation. We don't need sexual acts to describe something or someone. Most often those descriptions are inaccurate and confusing anyway. Are we swearing to impress others. It doesn't impress me, but in fact makes me think the swearer is uneducated or chooses not to use his/her education. The general public must not think what some refer to as swearing is proper because we make up words to use in place of the actual swear word. An example is frickin. To me that says you can't spell or you don't have the adjectives, verbs or nouns at your disposal to use the one that fits the situation. The Urban Dictionary says Fricken or Frickin is an adultered way to say Fucking. So why not say what you mean? If one is offensive, than the other is probably also offensive to some if not all who take offense to the original. I personally have no problem with either, other than it doesn't accurately describe anything unless you're talking about sex, in which case use the right words. I have been accused of Pontificating about this subject but I'm not sure the Pope agrees with me. Somebody posted on Facebook today that the Pope said the "F" word over the weekend. I doubt it is true but if it is true that he did, I would ask, why? He certainly shouldn't be an expert about it. If I was in his position and celibate, I might say it quite frequently but as an invitation or inquiry. If the Pope is using it in his everyday conversation, I guess I may as well shut up or shut the front door.

One substitute that does offend me is "gosh darn". The Urban Dictionary says it is a nice way of saying "God Damn". How can you ever say "God Damn" nicely? This, to me, is breaking a commandment. I don't claim to never break commandments but why do it in everyday conversation? This is the same God we pray to and attend church to worship, honor and then take his name in vain. I don't often quote the Bible because I am not an expert on the Bible or a Bible scholar but verses that I think apply are found in Philippians 2: 9-11. " At the name of Jesus, every knee should bow, in heaven and earth and every tongue confess that Jesus Christ is the Lord, to the glory of God the father." This is in a letter, Paul & Timothy sent to the people at Philippi instructing them in their relatively new faith. Paul thinks we should honor and worship Jesus at the very sound of his name. Perhaps he didn't mean we should literally get on our knees but at the very least, respect and honor his name. As I've said before, there are many interpretations of the Bible which is why we have so many religions. My point? Using the name of God to swear, is not honoring him, is breaking a commandment and serves no purpose in daily conversation. Other phrases that have nothing to do with God but are considered swearing, don't serve a purpose that I can determine. I say use other adjectives that describe the sentence. Maybe I'm nitpicking and not living in the real world but I have a right to my stupid opinion just as you do to yours.

- What do I want from Life?

I can describe it by a few lines from a song named, "This is all I ask".

> Beautiful girls, walk a little slower when you walk by me
> Lingering sunsets, stay a little longer with the lonely sea
> Children everywhere, when you shoot at bad men shoot at me
> Take me to that strange enchanted land
> Grown-ups seldom understand
>
> Wandering rainbows, leave a bit of color for my heart to own
> Stars in the sky, make my wish come true before the night has flown
> And let the music play as long as there's a song to sing

- When sadness enters your life as it most certainly does and will, when your heart is sad, look for joy and you will

- find it. Be grateful, do something to brighten someone else's day. Be the sunshine for someone else rather than a dark cloud that hides the sunshine. Remember this bible verse from Psalm 118:24 This is the day the Lord has made. Let us rejoice and be glad in it.
- It takes sadness to know what happiness is, noise to appreciate silence and absence to value presence. In some cases, "absence makes the heart grow fonder".
- Some things that make my life better and that makes my heart smile.
  - My Children
  - My Grandchildren
  - A sense of humor
  - An appreciation of beauty in all things
  - Service to and love of our country
  - Moderation in all things
  - Gratitude for one's blessings
  - Making the most of what one has
  - Having good friends
  - Making learning a lifetime pursuit
  - Making family a priority
  - My religion and relationship with God
  - Always having a book that I am reading
    - I always end the day reading a chapter or two in bed.

I have found that if you love life, life will love you back.
Arthur Rubinstein

Laugh as much as you breath and Love as long as you live.
Author unkown

If we are cheerful and contented, all nature smiles.... The flowers are more fragrant, the birds sing more sweetly, and the sun, moon and stars all appear more beautiful and seem to rejoice with us.
Orion S. Marden

> I have been driven many times to my knees by the overwhelming conviction that I had nowhere else to go.
>
> **Abraham Lincoln**

> To live is so startling, it leaves little time for anything else.
>
> **Emily Dickinson**

> To succeed in Life, you need three things: A wish bone, A back bone and a funny bone.
>
> **Reba McEntire**

> You must be the change you wish to see in the world.
>
> **Mahatma Gandhi**

The change I would like to see is Happiness.

Happiness

Do something every day to make someone happy, even if it's to let them alone.

Don't worry, be Happy. Don't borrow trouble or make it a self-fulfilling prophecy. To quote Mark Twain, "I have been through some terrible things in my life, some of which actually happened".

Everyone has their own definition of happiness and it seems everyone is searching for their own version of it. To me happiness is being comfortable in my own skin. Liking, Loving or at least not hating the person I am and the person I am becoming.

Happiness is not the result of getting something you don't have, but rather of recognizing and appreciating what you do have. You create happiness with your attitude, your behavior and your actions. It's all up to you.

These truths should be self-evident but yet many of us need to be reminded of them.

I've found that you need to maintain self-respect in order to like yourself and live with yourself. To maintain self-respect you need to be respectful of others and treat everyone with decency, respect and courtesy. That doesn't mean you have to like or agree with everyone, just treat them decent even if they are not decent themselves. Don't lower yourself to their standards.

There is a poem by Edgar A. Guest titled "Myself". My father gave this poem to me when I was in the Navy, probably because he thought, as an independent young person, I was straying from the straight and narrow and the teachings I had been raised on. I thought at the time and still do that it was very good advice. This poem has been with me since my father gave it to me and I value it as a guide for everyday life and living.

Along with the poem, The Golden Rule pretty much covers all situations and relationships. Try not to judge people. Accept them for what and who they are and if they irritate you, stay away from them. Just because someone hasn't had a formal education, doesn't make them stupid and even if they are not very intelligent, it is the way God made them so try not to judge them. Some of us were lucky and God gave us good brains as well as good looks and nice personalities. ☺ Not everyone was that lucky. In spite of what you may have heard, we are not all created equal. If we were all equal and the same, some of us would be unnecessary. Some of us have to work harder to be acceptable to society and some of us just don't care if we are. Anyone is capable of anything given the right circumstances, be it good or evil. We all make choices in our lives. Sometimes they are not always the right choice or the wise choice or even the best choice. Whenever possible, I choose Love over hate, forgiveness over retribution, a kind word over a judgment, a smile over a frown, humor over sadness, gratefulness over ungratefulness. People may not remember much about you but they will always remember how you make them feel, especially about themselves. Try to make someone happy and feel good about themselves.

- Be grateful, count your blessings.
- You are the only person responsible for your emotions. Don't wait for someone else to "Make" you happy. That's your job.

> Happiness is having a large, loving, caring, close-knit family, in another city.
> George Burns, comedian

Relationships

Require time and effort. They thrive when the parties involved make the effort and take the risk of sharing their honest thoughts and belief's. Open communications and honesty is the key.

You get out of life what you put into it. If you want love, show love. If you want friends, be friendly. If you'd like to feel understood, try being understanding. If you want honesty, be honest. It's a simple practice that works.

There is a purpose for everyone you meet. Some people will test you, some will teach you; but most importantly, some will bring out the best in you. Learn to see and accept the differences between these people and treat them accordingly.

Everyone changes. Our needs change over time. When someone says, you've changed, it is not necessarily a bad thing. Sometimes what they are trying to tell you is that you stopped living your life the way they would like you to. Guess what? It's your life, you get to make the choices of how you live it.

I don't have a lot of regrets but the ones I hold onto and can't dismiss are the ones where I hurt someone, regardless of the reason. Having said, I told you so or I warned you, doesn't ease their pain. If I could have do overs on these, I would hope I would try to ease the pain more and not be so self-righteous and judgmental about it. It's not that important to be right, if you are causing someone else pain. Do you want to be right or happy? If you can't be kind, at least be vague.

Outside a dog, a book is Man's best friend. Inside a dog, it's too dark to read. Groucho Marx

This being A chapter on the philosophy of Love and Life, it seemed proper to include a philosophy of one of our great leaders of our times that inspired us to change through peace and love. I think this speech he gave at Cornell College in Mt Vernon, Iowa in 1962 explains his concept and philosophy of love. This is the college my daughter, Kimberly, attended and received her degree from. Here then is a portion of the speech given by Dr. Martin Luther King Jr.

Now when I talk about love, I'm not talking about emotional bosh; I'm not talking about some weak, sentimental something; I'm talking about something strong and powerful. I'm talking about something that is active good will, not just a passive, dead something. People always raise the question, how can you love those who are oppressing you, those who are seeking to defeat you, those who are trampling over you with the iron feet of oppression—how can you love such people? And I always have to answer that question by going back to the Greek language, there I think it helps us in dealing with this question. There are three words in the Greek language for love. One is the word *eros*. *Eros* is a sort of aesthetic love. Plato used to talk about it a great deal in his *Dialogues*, "the yearning of the soul for the realm of the divine." It has come to us to be in a sense, romantic love, and so we all know about *eros*. In this sense, we have experienced it and read about it in all of the beauties of literature. In a sense, Edgar Allen Poe was talking about *eros* when he talked about his beautiful Annabel Lee, "with a love surrounded by the halo of eternity." In a sense, Shakespeare was talking about *eros* when he said, "Love is not love which alters when it alteration finds, or bends with the remover to remove. It is an ever fixed mark that looks on tempests and is never shaken. It is a star to every wandering bark?" You know, I can remember that because I used to quote it to my wife when we were courting. That's *eros*.

Then the Greek language talks about *philio*, which is another level of love. It is a sort of intimate affection between personal friends. On this level, you love because you are loved. You love those people that you like to be with, to talk with, that you have things in common with. In other words, this is friendship.

The Greek language comes out with another word. It is the word *agape*. *Agape* is more than aesthetic or romantic love. *Agape* is more than friendship. *Agape* is creative, redemptive good for all men. It is an overflowing love which seeks nothing in return. Theologians would say that it is the love of God operating in the human heart, and when one rises to love on this level, he loves every man, not because he likes that particular person, but because God loves him, and he rises to the level of loving the person who does the evil deed, while hating the deed that the person does. And I think that this is what Jesus meant when he said, "Love your enemies," and I'm happy that he didn't say "Like you enemies," because it's pretty difficult to like some people.

End of Dr. Martin Luther King Jr's speech.

5

Army & Navy

I joined the Army National Guard when I was 17 and A junior in High School. Unlike my brother, Dorel, who joined the Navy when he was 17 while we were at war, I wasn't motivated by honor and duty. It was 1958 and you could join under the delayed entry whereby you didn't start active duty until you graduated from high school. We had meetings once a week on Tuesday evenings for a couple hours. The meetings were in Harvey, ND, about twenty five miles from Drake. One of my teachers was in the guards and I rode to the guard meetings with him. He told me that we were not student/teacher while in or traveling with the guard. He knew I smoked and he said I could smoke around him without any consequences. This was during the time when students who smoked and were seen smoking by A teacher or school board member, could be expelled from school. One of my classmates was smoking at home with his parents' knowledge and approval and a teacher observed him through a picture window. He was expelled for three days. So this was a big deal to me at the time.

You might ask, why would you join the National Guard when you're still in high school? Looking back, I wonder the same thing. The teacher who was in the Guards kind of talked me into it. I was not interested in going to college, probably because the teachers kept preaching that if we didn't work harder in college than we were in high school we would fail in college. I believed them and I wasn't ready to work any harder. My motto was, the

This Dummy Pulls His Own Strings

less I learn, the less I have to remember. I loved school but not the learning part, only the social aspect. I kind of thought the teachers might be right and I would be partying and socializing and fail the classes. Why pay money to do that when I could go into the service and party and socialize and travel and get paid. It seemed like a better fit for me. Then when I got out of the service, the government would pay me to go to school if I chose to and was ready to learn. They would also guarantee a loan for me to buy a house at a low interest rate. If I had enough time in service when I got out, I could get free medical service. Sounded like a much better deal than wasting money on college, at least for me but not for everyone.

I only had to serve six months active duty but if I liked it, I could go on active duty in any branch of the service I wanted. Kind of like a trial run. I would be paid for attending meetings so I would be getting a pay check while in high school which was appealing to me. I needed beer and cigarette money. Every summer we would play soldier for two weeks, which to a teenager sounded like fun. Then there was the honor and respect thing, the uniform and the possibility that it could equate to better luck with the ladies. This didn't pan out so well in the Army uniform but in the Navy uniform, it was a real help. Especially in ND in a sailor uniform, on leave. Girls who had never given me a second look or thought, when I was a civilian, when they saw me in my dress whites would run to me and wrap their arms around me, like we were long lost lovers. At airport bars, people would buy you a drink and start a conversation with you. This was before the Viet Nam war began. After we entered that war, it was best not to wear your uniform when not on base. All these factors lead me to join the Army National Guard at 17. A high school teen ager is not well schooled in reality, regardless of their GPA.

The 2 week summer camp was like a vacation or a big beer bash. The officers would take an army truck to the nearest town after evening chow. They would take orders for whatever alcoholic beverage you preferred and of course you would pay for it. They would fill the truck with alcohol and bring it to us for our evening of drinking pleasure. It didn't matter that you were under the legal drinking age. Usually a big bonfire would be started and some evenings they would wrap whole chickens in tin foil after putting barbeque sauce on them and put them around the edge of the bonfire. The chickens were compliments of the Army or your tax dollars at work.

    For someone that was used to hard work on a farm, it was like a picnic. I didn't even mind the guard duty in the middle of the night, except when I was hung over. One night I had a little too much to drink and was supposed to relieve another fellow at sentry duty at 2:00 AM. He was going to be leaving for Officer Candidate training after summer camp and he was all about doing everything by the book. We were on bivouac and I went to sleep or should I say, passed out, in my pup tent about midnight. Just before 2:00 AM, he came to my tent to wake me up. Of course I was still drunk and I just rolled over and went back to sleep. He came to wake me several times with no better results. I had been sleeping in my work uniform because that was what I had on when I made it back to my tent at midnight. He grabbed me by my boots and started dragging me out of the tent. Now, I am wide awake and I stumble to my feet, swearing and cussing and threatening to beat him to within an inch of his life, if I can only find him. He made a few threats also but his were more to the effect that I would spend the rest of the time in the stockade if I hit him. I didn't think that sounded like fun and it was probably something he could pull off with his connections, so I put down my guard, picked up my rifle and relieved him on guard duty. He never reported me or at least there were no repercussions from it. Some of the guys must have witnessed the scene because there were some comments made that I should have decked him. I probably would have but had trouble finding the deck. He was not a very popular guy among the enlisted men which is why he probably wanted to become an officer.

    Our company was part of a Combat Engineer Battalion and our job was to purify water for drinking and cooking. To do this we needed a source of water which generally was a lake. Back then, in ND, lakes were almost as hard to find as trees. We would set up rubber tanks on the edge of the water source and pump water into the tanks. We had generator trucks to supply electrical power for the pumping as well as other needs. Chemicals would be added to purify it and of course it would need to be tested periodically. Other companies in the battalion would pull up to the tanks with their water tankers and we would fill them with purified water. We had to guard the water supply 24 x 7 to insure the enemy, whomever that might be, didn't contaminate our water supply. They generally used dye to show that the enemy had successfully contaminated the supply. In our war games, the supply was contaminated at least on one occasion but not on my watch even though I may have been watching under the influence.

As a private, I had the privilege of doing many different jobs beside guard duty and setting up and taking down the water purification tanks. Digging latrines comes to mind and setting up and taking down the mess tent and officers command tent. My job was supposed to be a truck driver but I did very little of that. I didn't mind the manual labor and even preferred it over KP (kitchen police) which involved peeling potatoes and washing dishes and pots and pans and cleaning up after a meal. I'm still not fond of those tasks, even at home. I don't mind cooking but I'm a slacker when it comes to clean up.

The weekly meetings were tedious but sometimes enjoyable and on occasion we would have week-end meetings which I hated because I thought I was being robbed of my week-end of pursuing young ladies. In reality, they were just boring with little to do or accomplish, except for the constant hurry up and wait. I would rather be out drinking with my buddies and chasing skirts. For those of you not familiar with the term "skirt", it was apparel that girls wore back in the 50's and 60's and even later.

To my way of thinking we were just a bunch of guys playing soldier. In reality we were being trained to defend our freedoms and way of life. Sometimes, after the meeting was over, a bunch of us, including the teacher I was riding with, would go to one of the local bars in Harvey for a beer or two. Here I am, 17 years old, drinking beer in a bar and smoking cigarettes with one of my teachers. The bar tender never hesitated to serve me or never checked my ID. Sometimes we were in uniform and sometimes in civilian clothes but the bartender knew we had just come from a guard meeting. They probably thought if I was old enough to die for my country, I was old enough to drink.

Just before graduation from high school, the seniors would put on a evening of entertainment for the general public, called class night. Part of the entertainment was predicting what all the seniors were doing 20 years after graduation. Each senior in turn would come on stage and a narrator would tell the audience who it was and what they were doing in 20 years. I was the last one they introduced and came on stage in Army full dress uniform. The narrator said something to the effect that " you can all sleep well tonight because General Dwight Knuth of the Army National Guard is on duty". I saluted the crowd, did an about face and exited stage left.

After graduation, I worked construction work for my Brother-in-law Clifford Kummer out of Williston, ND for Jacobson Construction. We erected steel Butler buildings, grain bins and bomb shelters. I was just passing time until I had to leave for my six months active duty at Fort Leonardwood, MO. I think it was early summer when I left by train for MO. Another fellow from Harvey, Duane Martian and I left together. We were already good friends from spending time together in the guards and we were both privates and about the same age with the same interests, girls. We boarded the train and were off on our next adventure. It was an overnight train trip and the government had gotten us sleepers. Neither of us had experience riding the train in style. Most of my experience with trains was riding in a box car but that's another chapter. We didn't know the protocol or proper procedure but there were double bunks on each side of the aisle with curtains to pull for privacy. We placed our shoes on the floor, crawled into our beds, undressed and crawled under the covers. I slept quite well and in the morning got dressed, crawled out of bed and retrieved my shoes. Unbeknownst to me, the porter came around at night and polished all the shoes setting on the floor. I wasn't aware you were supposed to tip him for this service. I thought it was his job and came with the price of a ticket.

When we finally arrived in MO, the Army had someone there to meet us at the train station along with a whole slew of arriving recruits. They herded us on a bus and took us to Fort Leonardwood. When we arrived at the fort, the hollering and name calling began and the freedom that we were being trained to defend, ended. In the next few days they herded us from one place to another with a theme of hurry up and wait. We were shaved bald, issued army clothes, blankets, towels, shaving/toilet kits, rifles, bayonets, steel helmets or as the army called them steel pots which could be used for anything from shaving to whatever you can imagine. They also issued us any equipment and anything we needed to survive the next eight weeks. We received multiple shots weather we needed them or not and were given physical exams. Bend over and smile. We had to send all our civilian clothes and personal belongings home. Against regulations, I managed to squirrel away my transistor radio with my ear plugs for my personal listening pleasure. I still have that transistor radio and it still works even though it has some olive drab paint on it. We were fed well three times a day. The food wasn't all that bad and was plentiful. What I liked most was you could have all the milk you wanted to drink.

We were tested for days at a time to insure we were close to being sane and that we had partially functioning brains which we were instructed never to use. The Army does your thinking for you, private. Eventually we were assigned to a company and the real fun began.

The eight weeks of Basic Training were pure unadulterated hell. We had a drill Sargent that was very good at making you feel lower than dirt and making programmed robotic zombies out of us. We had several guys go AWOL, several try to commit suicide and the rest of us were just plain scared to death. I think most of us would have committed suicide but we were too scared. I guess we thought if we were successful, they would make us do it over because nothing could be done right the first time.

Dwight E. Knuth

    I don't know why or how it came about but I was appointed Chaplin of our platoon. I know, right? I had to lead the rest of the platoon in the Lord's prayer before bed which was about the extent of my duties except for Sundays when I would have to march the men that wanted to attend church services to the chapel. I didn't mind playing Chaplin and my experience as president of our BYF (Baptist Youth Fellowship) served me well in leading a group in prayer. Once in a while, someone at their wits end would come to confide in me. It was mostly just listening to their concerns and generally they would talk themselves out of their depression, anxiety, frustration or whatever was ailing them. If they needed counseling, I would send them to see the real Chaplin. Most guys wanted to go to church because it meant an hour of peace and quiet and rest. I know I didn't volunteer for the position because I learned never to volunteer for anything. I generally tried to keep a low profile and not draw attention to myself.

    I was assigned to Delta company. Our Drill Sargent was a lifer that was in perfect physical condition and looked and acted more like a marine than a soldier. He named our company the Delta Devils and wanted us to be the toughest, best disciplined, loudest and greatest company the Army ever produced. He wore a T-shirt with a devils' head on it and the words "Delta Devils". I know it wasn't army issue. He must not have been married and not had a family because he was around night and day. It wasn't unusual for him to get us up in the middle of the night to clean the barracks or do physical exercises or practice marching on the grinder. Of course nothing was ever right or good enough and we had to do everything over and over. We sometimes had the feeling that we had joined the Marines or the Navy Seals. We would watch Charlie company across the street and wonder why we got stuck in Delta company. According to our DI (Drill Instructor), Charlie company was a bunch of panty waists and other female names I will only let you imagine.

    The barracks we lived in were world war two vintage. All wooden, built much like a deck on posts about two feet above the ground with air circulating under them. MO is very humid in

This Dummy Pulls His Own Strings

the summer so I imagine it was to try to keep them somewhat dry and from rotting. There was no insulation in them, either in the walls or ceiling and of course not in the floor. MO doesn't suffer from the cold winters as we do on the Canadian border. When we were cleaning the barracks, we used bleach in the water to bleach the floors and make them white. The Army gives new meaning to cleaning from top to bottom. We would get up on the top bunks and from there clean the open rafters so there was no trace of grime or dust anywhere. I don't think I ever saw a spider or any other type of insect, even a fly while in basic training. I imagine it was all the bleach we used for cleaning or the constant cleaning. If anything was overlooked, the inspector would find it and yes they did use white gloves while inspecting. If anything was found to be unclean or out of order, we would first have to be disciplined for our gross negligence and then do it all over again.

One of the forms of discipline was what the DI's referred to as "Elbows and Toes" where you would get down on the floor in a prone position, lock your hands together behind your neck with your elbows on the floor and your toes on the floor. The only thing touching the floor would be your elbows and toes. They would keep you in this position for as long as they wanted. Usually, until the weakest of us would start to sag in the middle and they could then holler at them and berate them for being weak and of the female gender. Another form of discipline they liked to use for the failures in our midst was to have them dig a hole under the barracks 4 X 4 X 4, have it inspected and then fill it all back in with no left over dirt. The advantage to this was that you were in the shade while doing it but you had to do it on your own time, in other words when you were supposed to be having rest and relaxation or as close to relaxation as you ever came to in basic training. Sometimes that required doing it at night and you better do it quiet and not wake up the soldiers sleeping above you. Another form of discipline for those of us that smoked, was taking away our smoking privileges, sometimes for days at a time. As it was, we could only smoke when they told us we could. A familiar phrase on the parade ground when we would take a break from marching, doing physical training (PT), or classes was, "smoke em if you got em" and about the time you got one out and lit, you'd hear "put em out". We would then have to field strip the cigarette so you could not see a strand of tobacco or filter or paper on the ground. Many of us started smoking non filtered cigarettes because they were easier to field strip than the filtered ones. Almost made you want to quit smoking and we did for short periods, not by choice.

Our rest and relaxation time was spent cleaning our rifles over and over. As is said, we could disassemble and assemble them in the dark in very little time. It was stressed that they needed to be clean to be able to be of use and fire when you needed it most, to save your life. I didn't mind the constant cleaning of my rifle, in fact it was rather relaxing to me. What I didn't like was that it was never clean enough until you had done it at least three times. They would always find a piece of lint or some manufactured reason why you didn't pass inspection. They either had much better eyes than mine or better imaginations. The one consolation was that they did this to everyone so you didn't feel picked on.

The part of basic training I enjoyed were the days we went to the rifle range and fired our rifles, even though it meant endless cleaning that night. When we went to qualify at the rifle range, a requirement for graduation, I didn't do as well as I had hoped. If my memory is correct there were about four classifications of your ability to hit the targets. I think I got second from the bottom or as I recall, sharpshooter. It was great fun at government expense. We were using the M1 rifle which was a great semi-automatic rifle but a little on the heavy side, nine pounds, I believe. We had to qualify from the standing, sitting, and prone positions. They had targets of men from the waist up that were electronically controlled to pop up out in a field of brush, grass and trees. Supposedly, a natural setting for fighting a war. The problem was that the targets were always in the same place because they had electrical wires that were buried leading to them to activate them and cause them to pop up. This was before God created wireless. Because of this, they could not be easily moved around the landscape. From all the companies firing on those targets and bullets hitting all around them, there was a discernable path to the target. So you could just locate where all these paths were and keep an eye on them to catch the targets popping up. The target would pop up, stay there for a predetermined time and if you had not hit it in that time frame, go back down. It was supposed to be a test of your observation as well as your proficiency at firing the rifle. Another problem with this type of range was that in front of some of the targets was gravel. So if you hit the gravel in front, it would cause the gravel to bounce forward, hit the target and the target would go down as if you hit it. You could tell when this happened because you could see your bullet hit in front of the target and then the target go down. Some of the guys, once they witnessed this would always aim in front because they thought they had a better chance of causing the target to go down. In reality, some of the targets had soft ground in front of them and when you hit that, your bullet just went into the ground and it was counted as a miss.

There was one set of twins in our company from the hills of TN. They had done a lot of squirrel and opossum hunting back home, out of necessity for food. They were really good at both observation and hitting the target. One of them got a perfect score at the firing range and his twin brother wasn't far behind. I thought they were treated rather badly and made fun of because of the way they talked and acted. Their lifestyle was the typical hillbilly stereotype. They were genuine, honest and probably under educated, but not stupid. In my opinion, they were good, friendly and interesting people and I liked them. They got a little more respect after their performance on the firing range and were treated somewhat better by both the cadre and their fellow soldiers. Labels are hard to overcome, once put in place, and many questioned their intelligence. They were probably smarter than most of us but just didn't have the opportunity for the education. So it goes, life isn't fair but we do the best we can.

Also enjoyable was the grenade range, bazookas, flame throwers, 30 and 50 millimeter machine guns and even the PT

(Physical training). They put old tanks out in the firing range and we would get to fire at them with the bazookas. I was barely over a hundred pounds and most of it was muscle from digging trenches on construction, installing a sewer system in Hunter, ND, working on the farm, training for Boxing, Track, and Basketball in high school. I was in much better shape than most of my fellow soldiers. In fact, at the end of the training, when we took the PT test which you needed to pass to graduate, I scored the highest score in my company. I remember saying to the Lieutenant giving the test when I was doing pull ups, after I had done about 25 of them, "How many of these do you want me to do, Sir". He said with a smirk, as many as you can. I don't remember how many I actually did but probably close to 50 and could have done more but got to thinking that this was too easy and it was probably a trick to tire me out so I couldn't do whatever the next step was. As it was, I did the most of anyone and helped our company take first in the competition. It was easy for me because I weighed so little and had strong arms from all the shoveling, pitching hay and training.

We had to go on bivouac for several days, living in pup tents and playing war games. This was kind of like going camping and it was somewhat of an adventurer. By this time I was used to all the yelling and berating of everything you did, right or wrong. I was pretty good at letting the degrading comments, fault finding and hollering roll off my back like water off a duck's back. Probably because of this and my ability to stay calm under pressure, they had made me a squad leader.

We learned to read maps, use a compass and survive in the wild as if you were behind enemy lines, trying to escape. So I got to take my squad into an area of woods with no man made landmarks, given a map, compass, canteen full of water and our full army packs which included dry socks, half a tent, a mess kit, our steel pot (helmet), first aid supplies and whatever we needed to survive. They also warned us that there were rattle snakes in the area so we should watch out for them. We must have been paying attention in map & compass class because we found our way back in almost record time with no snake bites or even having to pitch our tents. I guess the main part of the exercise besides map & compass was to avoid the enemy and avoid being captured by the enemy, which we did, either by luck or design. We never even saw the enemy, if they existed. Some squads were captured by the enemy so I guess they were there, just concentrating on other squads. Once we successfully completed this exercise we had to repeat it at night. This was a little more difficult but I had a good squad of men and together we made good decisions and completed the exercise, again, without capture, rattle snake bites or spending the night lost.

Another part of the training was crawling through a mine field at night with machine gun fire about two feet over your head. In this mine field, there were mines of course but they were surrounded by sand bags. It being dark except for the tracer bullets flying over your head, you couldn't see where these mines were placed. It was a simple matter of never crawling over a sandbag. If you avoided this, you would never enter a mine or take a bullet in the butt. Just to impress upon us that there were actual mines out there, they would blow one up electronically every now and then. They weren't very powerful and about all that would happen was a loud noise and some dirt, sand or rock spray and if you happened to be right next to the sand bag bunker, you might be lifted off the ground a fraction of an inch or at least feel the explosion. They again warned us that there were rattle snakes in this area and if you came across one, you should take the rattle snake bite rather than jumping up and being cut in half by machine gun fire. Seemed like a no brainer to me. They would tell stories of someone doing that but I doubt it ever happened. It was more than likely just a scare tactic, I can't imagine anyone dumb enough to jump up into machine gun fire, even if you were staring down a rattle snake. In addition, how crazy or suicidal would a snake have to be to crawl into an active mine field. It would have to be dedicated to suicide to attempt it. If in fact there were suicidal snakes, I think a white hanky tied to the end of your rifle might get some attention and if not, if you stood the rifle on its butt, I would think they might see it. We all made it through, with no injuries or snake bites.

In this mine field there were barbed wire fences strung across the course so you had to cross under these fences by putting your rifle under the bottom strand and lifting it up so you could slither under it, without shooting yourself in the foot or face. The bottom strand was placed just a few inches off the ground so it was probably the most difficult part of the course and there were many of these. None the less, it was fun and exciting. It was also good training, especially in saving your ass.

Most of the time, we were doing double time between classes or wherever we were headed. Our DI would have us singing while we did the double time. The songs were generally risqué and about females such as, " I got a girl in south St. Paul, honey, honey". You can imagine what would follow. It was more of a cadence than a song. It was a distraction from the double time and the DI wanted us to be as loud as possible. I'm sure the female population didn't appreciate it as it was degrading and discriminatory. I wouldn't guess that is allowed anymore but the Army does what it wants.

Other training that was loved by all was the forced marches where we would march or jog with a full pack on our back. I think the packs were about 40 pounds and of course we carried our rifles and wore our steel pot helmets. Some of us also had to carry the anti-tank weaponry and of course ammunition. Even this was somewhat enjoyable except for the Missouri humidity. It was so humid there that you could take a shower, dry off and only be dry for a few minutes before you were soaked from the humidity again.

On one of these marches, it was the time of year for the baseball world series. I had my transistor radio along with me, against Army regulations, and I packed it in my pack before we took off. I thought I could listen to it with ear phones on occasion for relaxation. Periodically we would have to stop and hydrate for five minutes and take salt tablets to retain some hydration in our bodies. On one such break, I pulled out my radio and started listening to the world series baseball game. I was so engrossed in the game, I failed to notice the DI walking up. He was uncharacteristically friendly and asked me what I was listening to. I was busted, so I told him I was listening to the world series game. He was a big fan of one of the teams playing, I believe it was St. Louis. I thought he was going to take my radio away but he asked if he could listen too, so I took out the ear plug and turned up the volume and soon the whole company was gathered around and we had an extended break. Not a word was uttered about me having my radio along, ever.

There were other areas of basic training that I found interesting and educational. Hand to hand combat was almost enjoyable. The instructor would sometimes pick me for demonstrations because I was small and probably looked defenseless and with my glasses looked like a geek. They were demonstrating the proper way to gain the advantage and leverage you needed even if your opponent was larger or heavier than you. I found it interesting that I could out maneuver someone larger. In boxing, we fought someone in our own weight class.

Another part of hand to hand combat was fixing your bayonet to the end of your rifle and learning the art of thrusting the bayonet into someone and the proper way to remove it rapidly so you were ready for the next attacker and not caught with your bayonet in the attacker you just stabbed. It could be detrimental to your health and future. Of course we used dummies for this exercise. Bayonet training was something you hoped you never found yourself in the circumstance that you had to use but it was useful training in the reality of war and hand to hand combat. As the Boy Scouts teach, be prepared.

As I mentioned earlier, we spent a lot of time cleaning the barracks. We never had enough mops so we could use the manpower efficiently. We would complain but for some reason the army was very stingy with their mops. Perhaps, the Navy got them all because we never had a shortage in the Navy. Perhaps the Army was requisitioning the wrong thing because in the Navy they were called swabs as in swabbing the deck. At any rate, at one point, most of the mops disappeared. The DI's said that more than likely, they were stolen by another company. I found this hard to believe that we had mop thieves lurking about in the middle of the night. Once I carefully considered the possibility, I came to the conclusion that if other companies were having as hard a time as we were getting mops, perhaps there were mop thieves lurking about. It kind of gave you pause. If the Army couldn't provide a simple thing like a mop, how were they at providing ammunition or rifles or tanks in a war.

I was discussing this with our platoon leader, especially the fact that we had a hard time keeping the barracks spotless as required in the time allotted without the proper equipment. He suggested we should be more creative in acquiring the equipment we needed. As most of you know, I am not very fast on the uptake and sometimes need things spelled out to me. You know, rebel without a clue. Draw me a picture. I asked the platoon leader what he meant and how could we be more creative. He said we should probably resort to stealing mops from the other companies around us. He also said that if we got caught, he would deny telling us to do this. If we got caught and were found guilty, we probably would get sent to the stockade for a while and then have to repeat basic training. A dishonorable discharge could probably be in our future, especially if caught and labeled a troublemaker. I guess the solution is don't do it or if you do, don't get caught.

I guess I must have been bored and looking for some adventure because I recruited a couple of guys I trusted and thought could do the job without getting caught and we made plans to acquire some mops. What's more fun and exciting than a covert operation like mop thievery? We got up around midnight when everyone else was sleeping, went to the latrine with our clothes in tow and got dressed. We had previously scouted out some of the other companies and agreed to steal the mops from Charlie company because they were candy asses and probably didn't guard their mops. They were close enough but not too close and they stored their mops outside the barracks in a rack just like we did. There was some cover we could hide in if there was traffic on the streets

This Dummy Pulls His Own Strings

and some low ground we could lie prone in to be unobserved while the traffic cleared.

We took our time and approached Charlie company barracks. When headlights appeared on the street, we would lie down in a low area until it passed. When we were just across the street from Charlie company we lay down in a ditch and watched the barracks for quite some time to see if the guy on guard duty in the barracks came outside at all. We didn't see a guard in the time we had allotted so we approached the barracks as if we belonged there. We walked right up to the mop racks and were just going to grab the mops and flee the scene but we couldn't get the mops out of the rack. Upon closer inspection, we discovered they had devised a way to lock the rack with a padlock so the mops couldn't be removed. Obviously, they had previously been mop robbed. We didn't have any pry tools with us and it would probably have been too noisy to accomplish the theft. On the other side of the mop rack wall were soldiers in their bunks sleeping. We decided to just give it up and go back to our barracks and bed. This we did, without incident. We learned to work with the mops we had and forget about the covert operation.

Towards the end of basic training, they issued week-end passes to those of us who had passed inspection, both locker and dress. A couple of my friends and I had passes and decided to go into the little town closest to base, Waynesville. We just roamed around the town and enjoyed our freedom and flirted with girls on the street. One of the guys was a little Mexican fellow by the name of Serafin Maldonado. He was a really nice guy, funny, intelligent and a bit shy. The other guy was a little colored guy with the last name of Williams. After roaming the streets enjoying the scenery (ladies), we were going to get a cup of coffee. This was 1960 and as usual, I am clueless. We started to go into a café that had a sign on the door that read, "We reserve the right to refuse service to anyone". When my buddies saw the sign they didn't want to go in. I didn't have a clue why they wouldn't. There weren't that many cafes in this small town so I talked them into going in for a cup of coffee.

When the waitress came, she said I could stay but the other two guys would have to leave. I was of course enraged and didn't know why they were picking on my friends and why I was not included. I, of course, as is my custom, wanted an explanation and am afraid probably displayed some indignation and outrage. They were behaving in a perfect reasonable manner and there was no reason they should be kicked out of the café. Serafin, kept telling me to forget it and we should just leave. Finally the owner appeared and upon my demand of an explanation said it was because they were not white. I had never had occasion to see this type of thing, coming from ND, and was unaware it still was happening. Of course we were in MO below the Mason Dixon line but I thought that war was over. We just got up and left and it was obvious that my two friends had experienced this previously. Being in the military, and in uniform, we didn't dare create a scene and my friends would not have participated in one anyway. I was incensed by it and was really not done protesting when my friends escorted me out. Again, life is not fair.

Part of Basic Training I wasn't fond of was the gas mask training. We were all herded into a building and all the doors and windows closed. They would throw canisters of tear gas in and close and lock the door. We were supposed to get our gas mask out, put it on and make it functional before being overcome with tear gas. Once you had your gas mask operational, you were supposed to help your fellow soldiers that might be having some trouble because they either weren't paying attention during the instruction or were in panic mode because of the tear gas. It wasn't a difficult task but there were those that panicked which made it worse than it should have been.

Upon completion of basic training, one of the officers thought I had leadership ability and should become an officer. This would require a commitment to the active duty army and going to college. I was pretty sure I didn't want to do either. They convinced me that I should at the very least, take the test to see if I was officer material. I passed the test in all areas with most areas in the higher brackets. I'm pretty good or lucky at taking tests. I find that a lot of the questions are very logical and simple logic can give you the answer even when you don't have a clue. Usually your first inclination is the correct one unless you go back and find you misunderstood the question. At any rate, they wanted me to apply for Officer Candidate School (OCS) but I declined and went home on leave.

My orders after leave were to return to Fort Leonardwood for Combat Engineer training. This was another eight weeks of extensive training. It was much easier and more interesting than basic training and they didn't holler at you or berate you unless you were putting yourself or someone else in danger. We learned how to use all the tools of construction, which I enjoyed and found useful. We built floating bridges across rivers so that we could drive trucks and tanks over. We did this in assimilated war circumstances where we had to both defend the builders and build the bridge. We also learned about building roads and did a little of that while defending the builders. We learned how to properly use and care for hand tools of the building trade. After this training, they gave me a temporary assignment at Fort Leonardwood.

At this point they made me a truck driver which made me happy. It was a non-demanding job which involved a lot of sitting in the truck waiting, or at the motor pool waiting, for an assignment. Either way, it gave me lots of time to read which I have enjoyed my whole life. I especially liked it when I got to drive the officers around base in a jeep. Jeeps, like convertibles were fun to drive, I thought.

It wasn't long before they gave me a permanent assignment to the 12th Field Hospital on base. It was a lot like a Mash unit for those of you that remember the TV show "Mash" with Alan Alda. It was an interesting and enjoyable assignment but had nothing to do with truck driving or combat engineers. This is the Army way, give you extensive training in a job and assign you to a job totally unrelated. They just needed some painting done so they put us to work painting barracks during the day. At night we were free to do as we pleased. I was under 21, the age you could legally drink alcohol, so most of our entertainment was movies, sightseeing or playing chess at the barracks. The guys assigned to this unit, like mash, were guys that were nurses or orderlies or as they were referred to in the army, medics. Most of them were very capable at chess or cards, mainly poker. I wasn't that good at chess so I didn't often win but it was a way to pass the time and learn the finer points of the game. I stayed away from the poker games because I didn't want to lose all my hard earned money. I found that if I hung onto my cash, I could double it around payday when everyone else was broke, probably from playing poker. I could lend out ten dollars and get twenty back on payday, sometimes the next day. That was the extent of my gambling. If I didn't know the borrower, I would take something for security until they paid the loan. That was how I ended up with a beautiful set of bongo drums. The guy was reassigned and left base without paying his loan. I came out ahead, as the bongos were worth about twenty-five dollars and he only borrowed ten.

When I had liberty, I went to area tourist attractions. I went to St. Louis once and Kansas City once. As the song goes, "They've got crazy little women there", but I didn't get me one. I also visited the Merimac caverns in MO where it was said Jesse James holed up.

I had bought a car after I had graduated from high school before I left for Missouri, for my six months of active duty. When I went home on leave after basic training I drove the car to Missouri. It was a white 1953 ford hardtop. It was a really sharp looking car with no problems other than a vapor lock from time to time. There were three or four other guys from ND that needed a ride to MO the same time I was going. They were also in the Army and had been home on leave and had to return the same time I did. I agreed to take them along if they paid the expenses. I think there were five us in the car and our Army duffel bags in the trunk. The weight made the springs nearly flat but ignorance is bliss. We stayed overnight in Chicago at one of the guys sisters' home and took off the next morning. We were probably driving faster than we should have and with all the weight the engine overheated. We stopped at a farm to get some water for the radiator. We let it cool down enough to get the cap off the radiator but evidently not enough. We didn't know it at the time but we must have cracked the block. We made it back to base and I used the car around base to go sightseeing. I had to add water quite frequently but I was quite ignorant when it came to mechanical things. I wasn't aware that you should add anti-freeze to the water in the radiator so maybe the block cracked from it freezing or cracked it more.

When I was discharged from active duty and was heading home, I got as far as Rolla, MO before it overheated and I stopped at a service station. The mechanic/owner told me I had a cracked block and probably wouldn't make it to ND with it like it was. My options were to replace the engine or buy another car. He had a 1952 Oldsmobile 98 he said he would sell me. I think it was one hundred dollars or less. It was cheaper than replacing the motor in my car. I arranged to leave my car with him and pay rent for him to store it and would return for it at a later date. That Oldsmobile was a fine riding and driving car. It was big enough for me to sleep comfortably in the back seat. It wasn't great looking as it was black and maroon but it sure was comfortable riding. It got me home and I used it for about a year and then it started using a lot of transmission fluid. I sold my 53 Ford to the guy in MO just as it was. When I joined the Navy, I traded my 52 Olds to the local garage as a down payment on a new car when I got out of the Navy. I never collected on that as I already had a new car when I got out of the Navy.

After returning home from the Army, I again went to work for my brother-in-law, Clifford Kummer, in the construction business, in Williston. I also transferred from the Harvey unit of the National Guard to the Williston unit on temporary duty so I could attend meetings in Williston. While working in Williston and attending meetings there, a military crisis developed in Germany, specifically Berlin. They referred to it as the Berlin crisis and they activated a lot of National Guard units. Williston was one of the units they were sending to Berlin. The commanding officer of Williston said I should pack my bags because I was part of their unit and I would be going with them. I checked with the commanding officer at Harvey and he informed me that I was still permanently attached to Harvey and only temporarily attached to Williston. I told them both, I would do whatever I was told to do and it didn't matter to me but let me know what to do. Actually, I thought it might be interesting to go to Berlin, Germany where my grandparents immigrated from. They came to the agreement that I would not have to be activated and my temporary duty in Williston would be over. That meant that I had to drive all the way to Harvey once a week on Tuesday evenings for meetings. This was a distance of 150 to 200 miles one way. The people at Harvey told me that they could understand if I couldn't make it to all the meetings. I went to very few and still got paid for most of them.

I was always looking for a better job but wasn't having any luck finding one. After the government started activating National Guard units, a lot of employers were hesitant to hire anyone in the guards. They wouldn't come right out and say it but it was a strange coincidence that once they found out you were in the guards, there was some reason they couldn't hire you. My sister Verla, was helping keep an eye out for something for me. She found an ad in the paper for interviews for careers in computer operations and programming. She made an appointment for me and they tested me to insure I had the right aptitude for it. It was actually a recruitment for the College of Automation in Des Moines, IA. I signed up for 3 months of extensive training of computer operations and off to school I went. This was a relatively new field and was training on IBM machines that used the cards that were punched with holes to accumulate and analyze information or as they referred to it, data. Thus the name data processing. After completing those courses, I was ready to go into the data processing field as my new career. I graduated somewhere in the middle of the class, so I was no genius but also was not a complete idiot. While I was going to school in Iowa I transferred to the Iowa National Guard. This involved a honorable discharge from the ND National Guard and then signing up with the Iowa National Guard. When I went back to ND I had to reverse the process. Here I was with two honorable discharges and just a few years in the Army.

Upon my return to ND, I was having the same problem with getting hired as I had prior to going to school. Now I was looking for specific work in data processing and those employers were even more reluctant to hire a member of the Guards even if I did have the proper training. Finally, four of my high school buddies were going to join the Navy and were trying to talk me into joining also. I thought it over and said, why not, it makes sense. When I get out of the Navy, I won't have the National Guard keeping me from getting hired, I'll be finished with my military obligation and I'll have some practical experience in my field and getting a job should be much easier.

I went with my buddies to see the recruiter and he said they could guarantee me the field of data processing as long as I passed the aptitude test for it. The bad news was that I couldn't go in with my friends on the buddy plan as I had prior service and would go to prior service boot camp. If that was bad news, I already loved the Navy. I was not looking forward to another basic training or as they referred to it in the Navy, boot camp. Where do I sign? I was going to go to the Great Lakes Naval Training Center with all my friends and we would just go our separate ways when we arrived there. However, there was a holdup on Mike Toy's enlistment. Finally the other three guys, Charles Toy, Emery Suckert and Bruce Brunner decided to go and I would wait for Mike and he and I would leave together. After a while they finally let Mike know that he was turned down because of a punctured ear drum so I left on my own.

Again, I took the train at government expense and landed in Chicago. We were bused to the Great Lakes Naval Training Center. It seemed to me the Navy was more proficient at processing recruits into the system than the Army. It wasn't very long before I was assigned to a prior service company for boot camp. This was a piece of cake compared to the Army. It was basically just learning the language of the Navy. Port, Starboard, bulkhead, deck, overhead, ladder, line and other terms that are unique to the Navy. Learning the enlisted ranks, officer ranks, ships, knots and the rules and regulations. We also had to learn how to wash our clothes using a scrub brush and scrub table which was the only way they could be washed in boot camp. I guess in case you are lost at sea without a washer and dryer, you should have these skills. A test of your swimming proficiency was mandatory and you could not graduate until you passed it. The hardest part of the swimming test, for me, was staying under water and swimming the required distance under water. Somehow, I always swim on the surface instead of frogman style. I always kept coming to the surface but I managed to pass. I loved the Navy, even boot camp. All things are relative and after the Army this was heaven. The food was much better and they served a lot of things I really liked such as oyster stew every Friday. This was back when Catholics were not supposed to eat meat on Fridays so the Govt. served fish or seafood for them. How times have changed.

 I had a week-end pass almost every week-end. I went to Kenosha, Racine and other towns around base chasing skirts. I still was not very proficient at it and didn't enjoy any success in that endeavor.

 The Navy had a company they called Mickey Mouse. It was comprised of recruits that got into trouble. Some of them had gone AWOL and been caught, some had unsuccessfully tried suicide, some were just plain screw ups and some should have never been accepted in the Navy because they were not able to function in the Navy environment. All these lost souls were waiting to be evaluated and either discharged or assigned another boot camp company for another try or possibly court martialed. Our company, being a prior service company, was assigned guard duty at Mickey Mouse at night. Our primary function was to make sure they all survived until morning and no one escaped. They were housed in regular barracks with no fences or other methods to restrict them from leaving other than us watching them. We would make rounds every hour and do a body count of them sleeping in their bunks. We would have to see skin when doing our body counts because if they tried to escape, they would put pillows and clothes in the bed to make it appear someone was sleeping there. It was a sad state of affairs for these guys, most of whom just wanted out.

After boot camp I went home on leave and spent time with my family, friends and Kathy. My orders, when my leave was over, were to Bainbridge, Maryland for Machine Accountant class A school. This was the field I had gone to technical college in Des Moines, IA for and the career I hoped to have. It was also what the Navy had promised me when I enlisted. I must have learned something in Iowa because I graduated top of my class from the Navy's school with the highest grades ever achieved to that point. What would you expect, the second time around. I had orders to my first choice duty station at Pearl Harbor, Hawaii for the remainder of my enlistment in the Navy. Wow, talk about paradise and dreams come true. The Captain of PAMI CONUS (Personal Accounting Machine Installation Continental United States) called me into his office after my orders arrived. I thought I must be in real trouble because you generally only went to see the Captain for a "Captains Mast" which was kind of like a trial without the jury. He explained that he liked to keep the top two graduates of each class at PAMI CONUS if he could convince them to give up the orders they were issued. He made no specific promises but said he would try to see that I would get a much more rounded experience working for him then at other computer installations in the Navy. He must have been very convincing because I accepted his offer and gave up my orders to Hawaii. I have never regretted that decision.

I started out keypunching and I became so fast and accurate that they quit verifying my work. There was only one other sailor on my shift that shared that level of accuracy and speed with me. There was a section called coding that would code the documents to be key punched. It was a desk job that had nothing to do with programming the IBM machines or operating them. Generally, that was the next assignment after keypunch. They transferred me from keypunch directly to what was referred to as "Transceiver" bypassing the coding assignment. This was a choice assignment, coveted by many. I worked alone in a private locked room. I was my own supervisor. I would take the keypunched cards and place them in a machine that would read them. I would dial one of the other Navy installations PAMI Pacific, PAMI Atlantic, Washington D.C. or other installations and transmit the data in the cards to them. They in turn would transmit data to me. This required a Secret Government Clearance as did working in data processing in the Navy anywhere.

The FBI, unbeknownst to me, had done an investigation of me prior to me beginning school in the Navy. I believe they refer to them now as background checks. My Mom wrote to me to tell me the FBI was in Drake asking teachers, preachers, business people, bankers and others about me. I guess she thought I was in real trouble this time. It was actually for my secret security clearance.

My job as transceiver operator was one level of security up. Generally I would have one outgoing transmission and one or two incoming. We had touch tone dial telephones in 1963 before touch tone was available anywhere else. The rest of the world was still using rotary dial. I would dial the number, talk to the operator on the other end and discuss the weather or whatever we wanted to talk about at the time, exchange information about the data we were transmitting, place the phone receiver in a cradle in the transceiver and sit back and let the machine do the work. Unless there was a card jam, that was all I had to do until it was finished, at which point I would pick up the phone and confirm that it was complete on the other end and we were done. Each eight hour shift only involved about two hours of actual work and the work was relatively easy. The rest of the time I could write letters, read books or sleep on the table top. Once my transmissions for the evening were completed, I could leave. Many evenings I only had to be there a few hours. There was a beautiful dogwood tree right outside my second story window that bloomed profusely in the spring. It didn't get much better than that, I thought. But wait, there's more.

This Dummy Pulls His Own Strings

Dwight, Navy, PAMI CONUS computer room

After working this job for about six months, I was transferred to the computer room operations. Generally, the next step was in the unit record equipment room but again, I skipped this assignment and went straight to another coveted assignment. We had four IBM 1401 computers manned by 3 operators and a shift supervisor and during the day shift, a computer operations manager, usually a chief. By this time, I had achieved the rank of petty officer third class (E4) or as they said in the Navy, had gotten my crow. The enlisted ranks in the Navy started at Seaman Recruit (E1), Seaman Apprentice (E2), Seaman (E3), Petty Officer Third Class (E4), Petty Officer Second Class (E5), Petty Officer First Class (E6), Chief (E7) and I have forgotten the names for E8 and E9 but it was something like Master Chief or King Chief. I believe you had to be at least a petty officer to receive a computer room assignment. I was one of the three computer operators on day shift until I was fully trained in the operations. On occasion, we would help the sailors in the unit record room wire (program) their machines to do various operations such as sorting, collating, printing or calculating data in the punched cards. It was all interesting work and at the time, rewarding, in the accomplishment arena. When I was trained, I was transferred to second shift and eventually to third shift. It was easy work with hours of free time just watching the blinking lights and the turning tapes. The following saying was posted in the computer room.

"ACHTUNG! Alles Lookenspeepers. Das computenmachine is nicht fer gefingerpoken und mittengraben. Ist easy schanppender springenwerk, blowenfusen und poppencorken mit spittzensparken. Ist nicht fur gewerken by das dummkopfen. Das rubbernecken sightseeren keepen hands in das pockets - - relaxen und watch das blinkenlights."

Sometimes a computer program would "blow up" which meant it stopped working. At that point, we would have to determine if it was because of an operations error or problem, computer malfunction or a program glitch. If it was a program glitch we would call the programmer responsible in and he/she would fix it. We played a lot of cards, dominoes, read books/magazines and visited. Eventually, because of people being transferred to other positions or bases, I became shift supervisor. By this time, I had achieved the rank of Petty Officer Second Class (E5). You could be promoted in rank by being in a specific rank for a specified amount of time. Then you were eligible to take a test which tested your knowledge of the job you were working in. Our field at that time, was called "Machine Accounting". So I was not only a Petty Officer Second Class, I was a Machine Accountant Petty Officer Second Class. Big Deal, right?

While working in the computer room as a shift supervisor, another World crises developed. It was referred to as the Cuban Missile crises. It seems Russia was going to give or sell some missiles to Cuba and was bringing them to Cuba via ship. Our intelligence knew about it and our president, John F. Kennedy was not comfortable with Cuba having missiles just off the coast of Florida. These missiles could easily reach US land and some of our major cities. He ordered a naval blockade to prevent Russia from delivering the missiles to Cuba. Our Naval ships stopped the Russian ships and for a time, it appeared we may be going

This Dummy Pulls His Own Strings

to war with Russia. At Pami Conus where all the reserves records were kept, we were ordered to print out orders for thousands of reservists to active duty, in the event of war. We printed hundreds of boxes of active duty orders and had them setting in the computer room ready to be trucked out. This was all done with top secret security and even people with secret clearances were not allowed in the computer room if you didn't work there while we were doing this. The Russians backed down, turned their ships around and the crises was over. All the active duty orders for the reserves were hauled out to the dumpster and taken to the landfill. Had president Kennedy allowed those missiles to be delivered to Cuba we may be living in a different World today.

After getting comfortable as a shift supervisor which comprised scheduling the work on the night shift and assigning the operator to each job as well as making sure the work was done properly, orderly and on time and training my people to do whatever I did, I found I had done such a good job, I was no longer necessary. Any one of my people could run the operation as efficiently as I could, without me. If I wanted to insert some honesty here, they probably could do a better job than I was doing. It was obvious by the amount of card playing, book reading etc. that it only required two people of the four, to man a shift.

I approached the chief and explained the situation to him and asked if we could go to a port and starboard operation where only two of us worked a night and we worked every other night. As I remember, he thought it was a good idea but only for the midnight shift and only for my people who were adequately trained to do my job. He told me I was ultimately responsible for the work getting done on time and correctly and if I had enough confidence in my people to let them take responsibility, it was my decision. However, whenever there were problems, I would be called in and the responsibility was still mine. I didn't have a problem with this because at the very least, my people were as good as I was and most of the time, were better. We went to port and starboard work schedule and I never had the occasion to regret it. From time to time I would get called in on day shift to answer for some "error" but after further investigation it was generally found the "error" was from a previous shift or from erroneous instructions or program error. That is not to say we never made a mistake but usually they were minor or ones we caught ourselves and corrected. By working the port and starboard schedule we could trade shifts if we wanted and get a whole week off. One week we would work Monday, Wednesday, Friday and the next week Tuesday and Thursday so we always had a long weekend. This was especially good for moral and most of us got part time jobs so it helped in the financial department as well.

Because we worked the midnight shift (12 to 8) those of us who lived in the barracks, as I did, could go to the chow hall at 11pm. There were only a limited number of midnight workers so there probably were only 10 to 20 people at midnight chow. The cooks would cook just about whatever we wanted as long as it wasn't too complicated. They would throw a steak on the grill or eggs or whatever was left over from the evening meal. It was almost like being a civilian and sometimes better because we didn't have to pay for it.

Because of all the time off I had, I took several part time jobs. One was pumping gas at the base gas station. Another was pumping gas on the JFK expressway between Baltimore and Philadelphia at an ESSO station. This was also the main thoroughfare between Washington DC and New York city.

One day while working at the base gas station, I was standing by the front window of the station, eating my lunch and watching for cars to pull up to the gas pumps. A Chevrolet Corvair with the engine in the rear where the trunk normally is, pulled up to the pumps. I was about to go wait on it but one of the other guys told me to finish eating my lunch and he would take care of it. From where I was standing, looking out the window, I could see under the car part ways. I could see what appeared to be fire dripping from the engine to the ground. The other attendant was already out by the car and was just reaching for the gas hose to fill the car. I dropped my lunch and ran out to tell him to stop because fire was dripping from the car. The car was still running so I asked the driver to turn it off and have everyone get out of the vehicle. There were four people in the car, two in front and two in back. As I remember it, his two kids were in back and his wife was in front with him. It was only a two door so the front passengers had to exit first so the rear passengers could get out. As soon as everyone was out of the car, the other attendant and I pushed the car away from the gas pumps. Fire was still dripping from it so I grabbed the fire extinguisher setting by the gas pumps. While the other attendant opened the hood, I stood posed at the ready with the fire extinguisher. When the hood was raised, there was a loud whoosh and the entire engine was engulfed in fire. I pulled the trigger on the extinguisher and within seconds the fire was out. No injuries or harm done other than to the car. We assumed there was a gas leak which was confined until it had enough oxygen to fully ignite. I'm sure it took some effort to clean up all the chemicals from the extinguisher as well as replacing hoses and wiring that had damage from the fire, not to mention the leak. I don't know if they ever got it running again or even tried.

Yet another part time job was keypunching for Beta Shoe company in MD and still another was keypunching for Manpower in Willimington, DE. I was employed at all of these at the same time. They were all part time and still didn't take all my spare time. I had a 1956 Ford convertible for a short time and some of my buddies and I would go to Atlantic City, NJ on weekends. We would lie on the beach and view the scenery (bikinis), go swimming and body surfing. On one such occasion, I was body surfing and one of my buddies was taking 8mm movies of me coming in to the beach. I got caught up in a wave that was tossing me all over and turning me in summersaults. One moment I was on the bottom scraping the sand, the next looking at the sky. The wave took me all the way up on the beach and left me laying there on the sand face down. The wave receded back into the ocean. I was going to get up but something was keeping my feet together. Upon further investigation my swimming trunks had slid down to my ankles. My buddy just kept filming. At least I still had my trunks.

Another time we were on the beach, the same thing happened to a young lady only she lost her bathing suit bottoms completely. She didn't get left on the beach and she realized what had happened before she was out of the water. She stayed in the water and there was a mad rush by the guys on shore to try to help her find her swim suit bottoms. We never did find them and one of her friends brought her a towel so she could exit the water.

Another sport was walking the boardwalk, trying to impress the young ladies with our manly physiques and flirt with any that would speak to us. When those things failed we would buy a ticket to the Steel Pier and be entertained there. For one cover charge you could get on the Steel Pier which had a ballroom and a big band playing for your dancing pleasure. They had two theaters with movies playing and an auditorium where they featured popular recording stars with an appearance several times a day and a concert of their recorded songs. I saw Brenda Lee, Trini Lopez, Herman's Hermits, The Jackson Five, Michael was just a little guy and cute then, and others that do not come to mind right now. They had a circus featuring a high diving horse and every Saturday had The Tom Mack amateur hour, a talent show that was televised. There were magic shows and many vendors selling everything you could imagine from kitchen knives to freshly made fudge. All this for the price of an entry fee. You could spend the whole day there and often times we did if the day was overcast and not many scantily clad young ladies on the beach. We followed the crowd.

One weekend, my buddy and cubemate, Jim Gulbranson, asked me to come along with him to New York city to spend the week-end with his girlfriend at her parents. Jim had a VW, four on the floor that was fun to drive and not bad to ride in. We left Friday evening after work and arrived in NYC before dark. I forgot which borough she lived in but it was a row house with one step from the sidewalk to the front door. The sidewalk was three or four feet wide and we parked right in front of her door.

This Dummy Pulls His Own Strings

Inside the door was the living room and after introductions we sat down to watch some TV. Later when it was time for bed, we went out to the car to get our bags with our clean clothes and toiletries. While we were watching TV, just four to five feet from the car and with the door standing open with just a screen door between us and the sidewalk because it was hot out and they didn't have air conditioning, someone broke into the car and stole our bags.

The next day, we went swimming at Jones beach and Jim's girlfriend's father told us we should report the theft to the police. He told us where to go to report it at the local station. We proceeded to the precinct and the officer had us sit at his desk while we gave him the little information we had. After establishing that we were from ND and MN and in the Navy and visiting in NY, he proceeded to inquire about what exactly had been stolen. We informed him it was just our overnight bags with clean underwear, clothes and toiletries. He was very sympathetic and nice. He said, I'm sure being sailors, on shore leave and visiting NYC, you probably had things you purchased overseas that were quite valuable such as expensive cameras, etc. We said, no nothing like that, just a few dollars worth of clothes and toiletries. He proceeded along that line of questioning, suggesting all manner of expensive things we had stolen which of course we denied. Finally he gave up on us and threw his hands up in frustration and told us we would probably not get anything from the insurance co. because the deductible was more than what we were claiming. As it turned out, we didn't claim anything we didn't have and we didn't get anything for what we had. Either Jim didn't have insurance for theft or he didn't want to turn it in and have his premiums go up. The point being, the officer was trying to get us an insurance payment by claiming items we didn't have but being honest mid-western lads, we were clueless and didn't catch on until it was spelled out for us. That was my last overnight trip to that New York neighborhood. I spent quite a few nights in New York City, mostly in Brooklyn and never had my car broken into or anything else stolen. Of course, we had our bags in the back seat in plain view which is inviting a break in. Being from the Midwest, I'm surprised we bothered locking the car doors.

Later that year, Jim and I planned our 14 day leaves to be at the same time. He was driving to Duluth, MN which is just a few hundred miles from Drake, ND. He was taking his girl from New York city home to meet his Mom, Dad and sister and I was riding along to help with the driving. We started our leave by driving to New York City, picking up his girl and heading to Duluth. The VW took very little gas and was relatively comfortable with three people in it. His girl was quite young and didn't have a drivers license so it was just Jim and I driving. The front passenger seat reclined so one of us drove while the other slept in the reclining front seat and his girl sat in the back seat behind the driver. We drove non-stop all the way to Duluth, stopping only at truck stops for gas and a sandwich to go. We made record time and Jim dropped me at the bus stop in Cloquet to catch the Greyhound to Drake. When our leave was over, we reversed the process and returned to New York city and then base. Another year I shared a ride home on leave with another friend from Minot, ND, Rick Alm. He had a new Mercury Comet we drove non-stop home and then back again.

In 1965 I bought a new Mercury Comet, much like my buddy's, Rick Alm, so I had reliable transportation and did more traveling. My cousin, Dennis Kriedeman was going to school at Bainbridge so one weekend we went to Washington, DC to see the cherry blossoms, tourist sights and the Speakeasy. It was a club that featured dancing girls in cages, beer and peanuts. I think the cages were for the girls protection. We went to Philadelphia one weekend, also. I don't remember where we went there but recall we had been drinking, as usual and were heading back to base on a Sunday morning after being out all night. I think we were on highway 40 which was a four lane road with stop lights and we were on the edge of the city near a shopping center. We were stopped at a red light when a car pulled up beside me and started revving the engine and looking over at me. This was an invitation to a drag race when the light turned green. Dennis and his buddies were egging me on. I had a 289 engine in the comet and it was a straight stick and had good tires so I revved my engine also. When the light turned green the race was on. I believe I beat him to the next light but maybe it is just wishful thinking.

There were about three cop cars hidden behind the shopping center and when we squealed our tires taking off, the cops were in hot pursuit. The one that pulled me over chewed me out but when he found out we were in the Navy and on the way back to base, he told me he was a Marine who had recently been discharged and understood what it was like being in the service so he let me go with a warning.

I acquired a boat from one of the guys in the barracks that owed me money. I think he had won the boat in a poker game and had no use for it. He didn't owe me very much, under one hundred dollars but he wanted to get rid of the boat as it was stored on base in a Navy warehouse on blocks with no trailer. It was one of those old wooden Thompson boats that were really heavy and it had a huge engine to power it. The woodwork was all solid and looked pretty good with just a little repair work needed. I was planning to buy a trailer for it so I could launch it at the Navy boatyard at the head of the Chesapeake Bay where the Susquehanna river emptied into it. The Navy had a boatyard where sailors could keep their private boats and either beach them or tie them up to a buoy out in the bay. I never got around to getting it seaworthy or getting a trailer for it.

One day my commanding officer approached me and asked me if I owned the boat that was in the warehouse. I thought I might be in trouble now and at the very least he would want me to get it out of there. I told him I did own it. He asked what I was planning to do with it. I told him my plans but thought it was too heavy for my liking, especially for trailering so would probably just launch it and leave it in the water. He agreed with me and said what a nice boat it was but that because it was wood, required a lot of upkeep and was best left in the water rather than trailering it. He said he had been looking for a boat like that because he liked to refinish them and preserve them.

He said he had built a small run about, around fourteen feet that he had in the water down at the boat yard. He said I should take a look at it and see if I would like it and we could work out a trade. I went to look it over and liked it. It would be easy for one man to trailer and looked to be speedy. I went back and told him I liked the looks of it but would like to try it out and see how it handled. He gave me the keys and told me to go take it out. He said don't worry about capsizing it, I've tried every which way to capsize it and couldn't so just take it out on the bay and have some fun with it. He was right, you couldn't capsize it and it was fun to run around in. It had a big enough motor to pull someone on skis if you only had one other person in the boat.

I went back and we worked out a deal where we traded boats and I believe I got a little cash. I ordered a boat trailer from Sears and I was in business. Some of my buddies and I used to take the boat down the Chesapeake to a deserted beach where there was a deserted shack that was built out of drift wood. We referred to it as our "sugar shack" after the song by that name. We would lie on the beach, swim and drink beer. On occasion we would take some waves (female sailors) with us and have a party. There was an area of the Chesapeake that had a sandy bottom and was only about three feet deep. It was a good place to swim or play games like water volleyball or beach ball. I got a lot of use and enjoyment from that boat. When I got out of the Navy, I took it home to ND with me and used it in the little lakes around home. When I needed some cash to buy a diamond ring for Kathy, I sold it along with the trailer to my brother-in-law Clifford Kummer.

One day while working at the base gas station on a slow day and listening to the radio, we heard that president Kennedy had been shot and killed in Dallas, TX. A few days later his coffin was at the rotunda of the capitol and the public was allowed to pass by the flag draped casket to pay their respect. A lot of the sailors didn't have cars on base so had no transportation. A couple of my buddies talked me into going to Washington D.C. to pass by the casket in the rotunda and again for the funeral procession. I had a movie camera so I thought this would be a good opportunity

This Dummy Pulls His Own Strings

for me to record history. We drove to Washington, a trip of about 70 miles. We went in uniform rather than civilian clothes. I was the senior sailor in rank as a Petty Officer Second Class. We got in the line to pass by the casket and pay our respect. The line was about two to three blocks long.

We had only been in line about a half hour when some uniformed secret service police approached us in line. They told us that military personal did not have to be in line with the general public but could go in front of everyone. They pulled us out of line, took us in the capitol in a separate entrance from the general public and took us to the front of the line and stopped the line that was passing by the casket. While the general public was going by the casket, they had the line moving steadily. Now they stopped it and cleared it out of the rotunda so the casket was the only thing there other than the guards around it which were representatives of all the military services in dress uniform.

Because I was the highest ranking enlisted man of our group, they put me in front of the rest and told me to walk out in front of the casket, alone, execute a smart left face, salute the casket and hold it, do a sharp right face and exit. I didn't know it at the time but they were setting up the major network TV cameras for a TV shot of me saluting. One of the girls I had dated from Turtle Lake, ND later told me that they showed me saluting on the channel she was watching and the announcer said "A sailor saying his final goodbye to his commander in chief and paying his respect to a fellow sailor". I guess they even did a close up of my face while I held the salute because she said she recognized me and called her mother to come look.

After I exited, they let my buddies do the same thing I had done, one at a time and I'm sure they were also on TV. After a few days, when it was time for the funeral, we again traveled to Washington and I took movies of the procession. We were across the street from St. Patrick's Cathedral which was a good location to film the procession entering the church. It was an impressive procession with the horse drawn caisson, the rider less horse, the foreign dignitaries, the politicians and Kennedy clan and then

Jackie, Carolyn and John. The entire route both from the capital to the church and from the church to Arlington Cemetery was aligned with spectators and citizens paying their respect to our fallen leader. They laid him to rest beside his infant child with an eternal flame. It was indeed a sad day in history. I have it all recorded on 8mm film.

As history has written it, Lyndon Johnson was vice president and became president when President Kennedy was killed in office. He served out the remainder of that term and then ran for president and won the election for the next term.

As is the custom, they often have parties for the election workers. My navy buddy, Alan Leavy, was dating a girl from Havre de Grace, MD who was a friend of one of the presidents daughters, I believe it was Lucy, she also had been an election worker. She was invited to the white house for the party and dance of the election workers. She asked Alan to escort her to the party at the white house. Al and I were good friends. He was from Brooklyn and I went home with him on several occasions and stayed at his parents' home. Al told me he had to work the night of the party at the White House and couldn't get out of it. I didn't really believe him because he was the type of guy that could talk the hangman's noose off his neck, so I'm sure had he wanted to, he could have arranged it. He asked me to escort his girl to the party at the White House. Al was a Lady's man and I figured if he didn't want to go, there probably was a good reason and I probably should decline. I gave it some serious consideration but I would have had to wear my dress uniform because I didn't have any other proper attire for a White House party and dance. A dress uniform would have been acceptable attire but then I may be the only enlisted man in uniform. There no doubt would be lots of officers in uniform. I liked parties but thought this may not be my type of party. I hardly knew Al's girl and certainly was not familiar with White House protocol so I declined. In retrospect, I should have said dam the torpedoes, full speed ahead. It would have given me a chance to meet a sitting president in the White House and his family and trip the light fantastic in Washington,

This Dummy Pulls His Own Strings

DC. It may even have opened doors to a political career. Now I'm glad I declined.

One of president and Lady Bird Johnsons' daughter's was married while they were in the White House. It was a newsworthy event on the east coast and some of my buddies talked me into going to Washington, DC to see what all the hubbub was about. We found a spot outside the church where the wedding was taking place and watched the guests and wedding party prior to the wedding. The most notable, other than the president and his family, was George Hamilton IV. After the wedding was over we went inside the church to look at the architecture. It was still decorated from the wedding. They had flown in potted trees from Texas that appeared to be rose trees. They were about 5 to 6 feet tall and they had one tree setting by every other pew on each side of the aisle the bride walked down. There must have been at least 100 of them and they all were in bloom with yellow roses which I assumed were the yellow rose of Texas. I always thought they came from rose bushes not trees but those Texans are a strange lot. ☺ This was for the benefit of my three Texas nieces, Melody, Cindy and Tammy Rau.

Being stationed in Maryland on the Chesapeake bay and having a boat and free use of the Navy marina I considered this an ideal set up. The naval base at Bainbridge was home to the boot camp for Waves and although they were not accessible until close to the end of boot camp, I did date a few, one from Minnesota. The base had a NCO club that I frequented, when working day shift, for a liquid lunch. This same NCO club had famous entertainers such as Louis Armstrong playing for our dancing pleasure as well as others. When Satchmo was playing, I took the girl I was dating at the time and danced within a foot or two of him playing the horn until the song was over. While he was wiping the perspiration with his hanky, I spoke with him and requested a song. He was a very happy, humble and nice gentlemen as well as a talented artist.

The base had a golf course, riding stable with horses of course, movie theatre, fully equipped gym with boxing gloves and anything you could imagine, a wood working shop, a fully equipped mechanics garage for working on your car, with about a dozen bays for cars, some with lifts, ball fields, grocery store, navy exchange, café, a chapel and most anything you could want. At Christmas, the officer's wives would wrap your Christmas presents for you to send to your family or girlfriend. Baltimore was 30 miles away with a USO for entertainment like Johhny Cash and hootenannies or baseball and football games. Washington DC was 70 miles one way with the cherry blossoms in the spring and all the monuments and museums. Philadelphia was 60 miles in the other direction and New York city just a little over 100 miles and Atlantic City, NJ about the same, as well as Ocean City, MD, Wildwood, NJ and many other seaside cities, all ideal, shore leave destinations. The Aberdeen Proving Ground was just a few miles away with a great NCO club that we frequented for taking a date dining. I had a good job, I loved, good liberty, three part time jobs with decent pay, many friends and lots of girls and dates. It was the best time of my life.

On many weekends, there was drag racing just a few miles from base at the Cecil County Drag-O-Way. There were cars, trucks, super-stock, nitro burning racers as well as stock, road worthy automobiles and funny cars. They also had what they referred to as the powder puff derby for the ladies. Plymouth/Dodge/Chrysler seemed to be the favorite at this time at least at this track. It was good entertainment and relatively inexpensive but hard on the ears.

It goes without saying we lived up to the reputation of sailors and drank plenty of alcohol. Bainbridge, our naval base, was situated in a rural setting just above the village of Port Deposit on the Susquehanna River as it flowed into the Chesapeake Bay. There were other streams that also flowed into the Bay. It was a serene setting of rock, waterfalls, streams, wooded areas along the streams, curvy two lane roads and farms. There was a small shallow river that had a swimming hole with a tree that had a branch extended over the water with a rope hanging from it we would use to swing over the water and drop into the swimming hole. We often would go there in the evening to swim, listen to the radio, sing and drink beer. In other words party. Sometimes we had our swimming trunks and sometimes we didn't. One time we were having a party and consuming some beer with some waves (female sailors) and we decided we wanted to go swimming but no one had their swimming suits. We hadn't consumed enough alcohol to convince the waves to go skinny dipping but they agreed to swim in their underwear (panties/bras). The guys also swam in their shorts. We all went to our vehicles to strip down and deposit our clothes there. None of us had towels. We were walking back to the swimming hole. A couple fellow sailors and I were in the lead followed by another sailor with a couple waves, one of which was his girlfriend. As we were walking, one of the waves ran up behind me, grabbed the bottoms of my boxer shorts and pulls them down. Of course, I stopped walking. It's difficult to walk with your shorts around your ankles. I reached down and pulled them back up and was about to turn around and do the same to the guilty looking wave.

    I thought better of it because the guilty looking wave was the sailors' girlfriend and I wasn't quite sure how he would react to it. I think I said something to the effect, if you want a better view, just ask, honey. I had been told by several females I had a cute butt. However, I wasn't aware it was irresistible. We continued with the party, swimming and drinking. When we ran out of beer the party broke up and the guy I rode with and I convinced a wave to ride back to base with us. I tried to convince her to get out of her wet underwear before she caught a chill but she put her dry clothes on before she removed her wet ones.

    With the port and starboard work schedule and the way I had been treated in the Navy thus far, I was seriously considering making the navy my career. By the time my enlistment was up I already had eight plus years in the service towards my twenty year retirement, leaving me less than twelve to go. I was eligible to take the E6 Petty Officer First class test and there was no reason I shouldn't pass it. Then there was the re-enlistment bonus which was roughly a brand new car depending on your taste. In

1965 I bought a new Mercury Comet for $1,800.00. In weighing this decision I looked around and observed that a lot of career sailors were alcoholics. Besides, I had just bought a new car. By this time I was assigned to day shift so I could do all the things necessary to "muster out" of the navy. I was going to the NCO (Non-Commissioned Officers) club every day for lunch and having a beer or two, sometimes with a sandwich and sometimes just beer. I was concerned if I continued along this path I would become an alcoholic if I already wasn't. When I had duty, which meant you couldn't drink alcohol and were the NCO on duty and had to handle any crisis that might come up, I would get a six pack of beer and hide it in a toilet tank in the head (bathroom). If someone found it, they couldn't prove who put it there. The water kept it cool enough to drink, especially if you flushed the toilet frequently which filled the tank with fresh cold water. I had my own room with a lock on the door so the risk was relatively low. To me this also pointed at alcoholism.

About this time, the Vietnam war was heating up and when I had less than a month left on my enlistment, all enlistments were extended by six months. What a bummer when your short timers calendar has six months added to it and it is now seven months. Not so short anymore. My next duty station would more than likely be on a ship and chances were it would be a large ship like an aircraft carrier that had data processing (computer) equipment on it. Up to this point, I was a dry land sailor and wasn't sure how much fun sea duty would be. Chances were that an aircraft carrier, during a time of war would be off the coast of wherever we were fighting and probably at one time or another under attack from air, sea or by submarine. This was not the travel I had in mind. Being the coward I am and a logical thinker, logically, if I wanted to stay alive and breathing and not become an alcoholic, I should probably go back to the safety of the missile silo sights in ND.

I decided not to take the E6 test because if I was promoted to E6 it would be harder to reject reenlistment. After all, this would be my fourth honorable discharge. How honorable can a guy like me be. It might be best to quit while I'm ahead. The four honorable discharges are. 1. From the North Dakota Army National Guard to join the Iowa National Guard. 2. From the Iowa National Guard to rejoin the North Dakota National Guard. 3. From the North Dakota National Guard to join the Navy. 4. From the Navy at the end of my enlistment. Thus when my enlistment was up I headed for the plains of ND and a shapely beautiful young lass by the name of Kathleen that I was becoming more smitten with as I got to know her better. So ended my Army and Navy careers. I don't regret either of them nor do I regret ending them and going home to pursue, court and brainwash Kathy. There he goes, it's Kathy's clown.

While I was complaining because my enlistment had been extended six months, worried about my health because I was drinking too much, swimming with the female sailors (waves), bikini watching in Atlantic City, NJ and living the good life, some of my friends and classmates were more worried about their life and if it would continue or if they would be another casualty of war. Following is a story my friend and classmate and fellow veteran, Arlo Blumhagen related to me about his duty in Viet Nam, in his words.

On Memorial day, 1967, I and 6 other soldiers and civilian contractors were on our way home from Viet Nam, by First Available Flight out of Saigon. I don't remember for sure, but I for one, was heading home on an Emergency Leave, due to my Fathers having had a stroke. (I don't remember if the other 6 were going on Emergency Leave Status, as well) As we waited beside the cargo plane, on the tarmac, in the glaring floodlights, one of the other fellows remarked, "We won't be traveling alone", as he noticed aluminum "boxes", which were obviously caskets, being loaded as well. It was the most somber, thoughtful Memorial day of my entire life, making that journey with 49 fallen comrades. (You may note the "7" of the live people and 7 times 7 who were not, as 7 being a Biblical number.) We rode "jump seats" in the cargo hold, with the cargo. The cargo hold wasn't pressurized very much for several reasons. Normally it wouldn't have been anyway but being not pressurized it stayed much colder. Part of the reason was by keeping it colder, the odor of the formaldehyde wasn't as strong. For us it was on the cold side, so we were given extra jackets and took turns riding in the cockpit with the pilots to keep warm.

Arlos' story puts everything in perspective. While we are enjoying the comforts of freedom, there are men dying, giving the life God gave them so the world can enjoy freedom. These are men with Mom's, Dad's, Brothers, Sisters, Wives and Children whose lives are changed forever. God Bless the brave men and women of our armed forces and their families that also sacrifice.

I was serving in a much lessor capacity but I considered it honorable as did the Navy. The following are things my commanding officer, Lieutenant Commander T. E. Craig, said about me in my performance evaluations:

Knuth has, through his positive attitude and desire to increase his knowledge, turned in a continually efficient and effective performance of his duties. He is doing very well in getting good results from his men and at the same time works well with them. He is the type of petty officer that the Navy needs. Knuth's behavior is above reproach. His appearance leaves nothing to be desired. Knuth continually strives for perfection in the minute details necessarily involved in a complex data processing operation. His initiative and willingness to take on additional work has added immeasurably to the efficient operation of the computer center. Knuth's command of the English language, both written and orally, is good. Highly recommended for advancement and for reenlistment. Knuth's behavior has continued to be exemplary. He demands much from his men but has maintained complete control without creating animosity and he has assumed the position of shift supervisor in a most proficient manner. He sets a very fine example in appearance. He will be a loss to this Command and to the Navy.

This was at the ripe old age of 23 and I was quite proud of my service in the Navy. Much of the credit for the praise by my Commander goes to the sailors that worked for me and with me, especially my good friend John Dempsey. Some of these sailors out ranked me in pay grade but that was not a problem, either for them or me. We worked as a team and had a good working relationship. It was a great time of my life, I don't regret at all. It resulted in many fond memories, a great experience and many wonderful friends, some are part of my life yet. Some of these friends made a career of the Navy, others gave their life in the service of their country. Thanks for your service and the memories.

6

Crushes, Love, Romance & Foolishness

Let me tell you about the birds and the bees and the flowers and the trees and the moon up above and a thing called Love. Birds do it, Bees do it, even itsy bitsy fleas do it, let's do it, let's fall in Love. (song lyrics)

Love, not time, heals all wounds.
No one's perfect until you fall in Love with them.
From the book, Live & Learn and Pass It On, volume II;

This Dummy Pulls His Own Strings

Dwight, 1960, my Buddy Holly look alike impersonation

From the time I began going to school, which was first grade, I was very much interested in girls. There was something about girls that made my tingle want to mingle. I couldn't put a finger on it then and still can't but the excitement of mingling tingles was there. Charlie Toy and I were in the same class and we were interested in a couple of first grade girls, Ladonna Zeigler and Jeannie Jans . Ladonna had Charles interest and Jeannie had my interest. They showed some interest in us also and told us about a big mean sixth grade girl that followed them home from school and harassed them. Back then we didn't have school buses. The farm kids went to country, one room schools through the eighth grade. High school kids were driven to school by someone in the family or stayed with a family in town. All the town kids walked to and from school, uphill and against the wind both ways.

These girls asked us to walk them home for protection. They lived next door to each other. We were honored to be asked and gladly accepted this manly and honorable task. We had several encounters with this would be bully and she soon discovered that the fun was gone so she stopped. Maybe it was that we were more accurate at throwing rocks than she was. Of course, we continued to walk the girls home, just in case of trouble. You never know when trouble chooses to appear. We had crushes on these same two girls all through school, off and on. When Valentines day was close, we would pass the little heart shaped candies that had romantic sayings on them, between us. Later, when we were older, perhaps eighth grade, when my parents had gone out of town for the weekend, we tried to entice the girls to my house on the pretense of a Birthday party for Charles. I believe his birthday is May 11, springtime, when a boy's fancy turns to love. We went to the store and bought a do it yourself Jenos pizza, a cake mix, frosting and sodas. This was before God invented frozen pizza or home delivery. You got all the pizza ingredients in a box, mixed up the dough, spread it on a pizza pan, poured on the sauce, sprinkled on the cheese and sliced the pepperoni and put it on the pizza, then baked it in the oven. We also had to mix up the cake mix, bake the cake and then frost it with canned frosting. It all went very well and was surprisingly edible and even tasty, at least we thought so. The girls came but of course when they found out my parents were out of town and that we had made the pizza and cake, they didn't linger. I believe they had a piece of cake and a coke but maybe it was just a coke. Latter on in high school, we still pursued them from time to time but they had other interests and higher standards.

I remember after one church function when I was in the eighth grade, asking the girl crush from the first grade if I could walk her home after it was over. She agreed and I kissed her at her door. It was my first kiss. I guess there was no chemistry because nothing developed from it. I believe I half heartedly pursued her from time to time but the pursued was faster and fled.

I believe I was a junior in High School when Charles Toy convinced me to accept the role of president of BYF (Baptist Youth Fellowship). His ulterior motive was that with me as president we could control how many parties and what kind of parties we had and who we invited. That way, we could invite other churches where there were other girls, who didn't know us so well, one of which he was dating and later married. Of course, being president would mean that I would have to stand in front of my friends and lead the meeting. This being a Baptist church fellowship group, it often involved praying and leading in singing. As most people are, I was terrified of public speaking and to me this was public speaking. However, I knew that with it came the popularity of being a leader and popularity might add up to more opportunities with the girls. I weighed the options and the sex hormones won over the fear factor. See how teenage boys think or should I amend that to males? I accepted the challenge, ran for president, I believe unopposed and won. It turned out Charles scheming was successful. We went to Minot for roller skating & swimming parties, had hayrides and parties in the church basement.

The only opportunity that being president led to, was a date with a girl from a church in Minot, I think it was the Methodist church. Our youth organizations got together for some reason, probably to scout out dates. A friend, Ralph Cushing, introduced us and I asked her out. She was pretty and God had endowed her with a shapely body. In fact she had won the miss Minot competition and come in third for miss North Dakota, or so I was told. I only dated her once and we had a good time if unmemorable. I believe she was more interested in herself than me but I couldn't blame her for that. I was more interested in her than me, also. As president of BYF I became more comfortable with being in a leadership role and speaking in public which helped me all my life.

My Mother was head cook at the North Dakota state Baptist camp on Lake Bently just west of Drake. My Father was the caretaker there and had helped in establishing and building it.

I would attend the summer camp for my age group for a week each summer. I think I did this from first grade through about eighth grade. These were kids from Baptist Churches all over North Dakota. Of course there were girls there and I generally left camp, In Love. One year it was a girl from Berthold, Carol Mann, another year, one from Minot, Darlene (Dee Dee) Janke and yet another year a girl from Stanley, Jane Eidem who had a twin sister, Joyce. David Jans and I were often competing for the same girl but the year of the twins, we didn't have to compete. They were identical twins and they would sometimes switch to see if we could tell the difference or perhaps out of boredom. We had Bible classes, swimming, games, crafts, meals, church and a lot of singing around the campfire before bedtime. Most of the day was spent flirting and avoiding one another until it was campfire time when we would sit next to each other and hold hands. After the campfire we would walk the girls back to their cabins. There were not many good night kisses as we were closely supervised. After camp ended for the summer, we usually wrote letters for a short period of time until one or the other lost interest. It was not unusual to receive a letter that was sealed with a lipstick kiss and bathed in perfume. It makes my heart skip a beat just thinking of it. ☺

Later on when we were too old for summer camp or thought we were (probably 15) Charles Toy, Gary Richards from Tacoma, WA and I went to see my Mother who was head cook at camp, to look over the crop of counselors who were generally teen age girls. We struck up a conversation with three of them. We told them we were camping just across the road from the camp in a grove of trees and that they should come visit us that night. Of course, at night the camp was gated and locked down so no one could get in or out. The girls were adventurous and thought they could wait until everyone was in bed and under the pretense of using the outhouse, get dressed and leave by climbing over the fence. For those of you that don't know what an outhouse is, it is an outdoor toilet, used where there is no running water or plumbing facilities.

Anyway, the girls agreed on a place and time to meet and they scaled the locked fence and came to visit us. Those Baptist girls are adventurous and looking for excitement. I guess we were a little more excitement than they wanted because they didn't stick around long. There was some arguing between them about whether they should stay or go but I guess the necking scared them off.

I would say the next phase of my romantic life was after I got a drivers license and could use my parents 1952 Chevy. Dad bought it new but it wasn't really a chic magnet. It was a four door, straight stick, six cylinder, gray in color with no accessories like ash trays, cigarette lighters or a radio. I bought a really good transistor radio that cost me in excess of fifty dollars back in 1956 which we used in the car. The Chevy did have some get up and go and I could beat some of my friends' fathers' cars in a short drag race. Most of them had automatic transmissions and were much heavier cars so were slow off the line. I got my driver's license earlier than my friends so for a while I was the only one who could get the family car. These were the times when there was one car in most families.

I was 14 when I got my license, I still have it in my memorabilia. My Dad had been in a farm accident which kept him from driving so they gave me permission to take the driver's test and get a license. My Mom didn't drive. Generally, you couldn't get a license until you were sixteen. Dad had a big circular saw, the blade of which was about three feet across. He would hook this saw up to the tractor with a big belt that would turn the saw blade. He then could cut up firewood. He was all alone at the farm cutting firewood and somehow got his hand by the saw blade and cut it really bad at the wrist. He had to drive himself about 10 miles to town and the Dr. They bandaged and stitched everything up and he was OK but couldn't safely drive one handed, especially a straight stick that had to be shifted. Somehow, they thought a teenager was a safer driver. I would drive Dad to the Dr. in Harvey and of course, Mom to the grocery, to church three times a week and anywhere we needed to go. I remember the first time I drove Dad to Harvey to the Dr. I had never driven on the highway and probably never over 20 mph. There was no power steering in 1952. I kept moving the steering wheel from side to side and of course going all over the road until Dad did a little coaching and got me settled down. It took me a while to get my speed up to 50 mph. Once I caught on, you couldn't keep me from behind the wheel. I would even go to church, willingly, just so I could drive there and home.

It wasn't long until I was a good enough driver that the folks would let me have the car for cruising on Sunday afternoon. I would pick up some of my friends and we would cruise the streets of Drake picking up girls and riding around, dragging main. Gas was only about 25 cents a gallon at that time but Dad insisted that I pay for my own gas. He would fill the car up before I took it and after I brought it home, fill it again. Whatever it took to fill it up the last time is what I owed him for gas. If I didn't have the money to pay him, he would deduct it from my allowance. We had set up an allowance where he paid me a sizeable allowance weekly and I would take care of all my expenses including school supplies, gas, clothes, and spending money. I think it was somewhere between three and five dollars a week. Of course, I had to buy my cigarettes and beer out of that also. So when we cruised around I had everyone chip in for gas even the girls we picked up. There wasn't a lot of romance on those Sunday afternoons but there was some heavy flirting. As my driving skills improved and I became more trustworthy, I got to use the car in the evenings, supposedly for dates. In reality it was for riding with my buddies in search of beer. I found I was more likely to get the car if I said I needed it for a date. I just never said the date was with my drinking buddies. I was shaving by the time I was fifteen so by the time I was 16 and 17 I could get served in a few bars. Generally we would pick up some girls and ride around drinking beer, smoking cigarettes, singing songs with a little necking once in a while. We went to a lot of dances but generally there was more fighting than dancing going on. One of the bars I could buy beer at was a bar on highway 14 that was called midway because it was about half way between Towner and Drake. It was out in the country with nothing else

This Dummy Pulls His Own Strings

around which is probably why I could get served there. It was right on the way to Karlsruhe where a lot of the dances were held.

In this phase of my life, my idea of romance was a six pack of beer for my date and I, a deserted farm for parking in the trees and spending the evening drinking beer, smoking cigarettes and watching submarine races while listening to music on the transistor radio. It wasn't until I was in the Navy and had a couple buddies who were ladies men, that I learned the finer points of dating. They educated me in how to impress the ladies and I learned there was more to romance than a six pack of beer.

My Navy buddy, Alan Leavy was from Brooklyn, NY and was a real ladies man. He always asked every girl he met for her phone number and recorded them in his address book with notations about the girl. Shortly after meeting her, he would call her and try to make a date and most of the time he was successful. He also thought you should make several dates, at least two for the same night in case one cancelled on you or as he put it, in case one was boring. I guess in Brooklyn, that happens often, at least the canceling part. If a better offer came along they would accept and cancel the first one. Often times he would take one girl out and if the date wasn't going that well would make an excuse to take her home, the classic headache excuse and then pick up the other girl he had made a date with. He would apologize for being late and make excuses, in other words, lie through his teeth and most of the time they would still go out with him.

Another Navy buddy, Sam, was from Cleveland and was more sophisticated about his dating. He would wine and dine the ladies and bring them flowers and candy and try to make them feel special. I sometimes went home with Alan on weekends to Brooklyn and we always had dates and parties to attend. If one party was boring, we would leave and head to the next one we were invited to or just find one to crash. We defined boring as everyone there being too drunk or high to have a conversation. Alan generally was invited to several parties and we usually hit most of them. They were parties that you could get just about anything you could afford to smoke or drink. There was never any pressure to use drugs or smoke pot. Most people were glad if you didn't want their drugs or pot. I never tried any drugs or pot other than what the medical Drs. prescribed for me. I was comfortable with alcohol and it generally flowed freely. I was afraid to lose complete control of my thought processes so I stayed away from other substances. That can happen with alcohol also but I learned early, if I stuck with beer, I got full before I lost the ability to think or lost control. I didn't say I could think clearly or was in full control but the thought processes still functioned although much slower. My judgment sometimes left a lot to be desired but I could generally stay out of trouble and keep breathing.

    An example of alcohol induced bad judgment was one New Year's Eve in Brooklyn when I parked in a snow removal area while it was snowing and I got an expensive parking ticket. We had been drinking and we had a lot of partying to do. I couldn't find a parking spot so just parked where no one else was. I ignored the parking ticket and still haven't paid it. That was back before they had data bases of violators and they arrested you when you went through a toll booth at a bridge or toll road.

    I dated several girls in NY City but none of them more than once. I actually preferred Sam's method to wine and dine the ladies.

    My first steady girlfriend was probably when I was a freshman. I still had a paper route and would walk by her house every night. Her little sister, Jodie, who was about 10 or 12, would tease me that her big sister was in Love with me. Her big sister, Diane, was a year younger than I. Before long Diane would be outside when I went by on my paper route and I would stop to talk to her. Soon we were dating and going steady. I don't remember how long we dated. I remember walking on most dates or riding bicycles. I know that all of a sudden she avoided me and the rumor going around was that she had broken up with me. I didn't know anything about it other than the rumors but we never really broke up, just faded away. I had heard that she was dating others and I guess I was interested in another girl so just let her fade into my past. She eventually became a cheerleader but never really went steady with anyone else that I was aware of. I guess she couldn't find anyone that could match my qualifications. ☺ Maybe she still thought we were going together since we never broke up. ☺ It's still a mystery to me what went down but then I've always been clueless. I think her Dad worked for the railroad and they moved out of town before either of us graduated from high school.

My next girlfriend was when I was a sophomore and she was the sister of one of my good friends, David Traiser. Her name was Faye and she was a freshman. I started to notice her when I would go to David's to study when I was a freshman. At that time she was attending country school which was a one room school where eight grades were taught by one teacher. Both of my sisters taught school in these one room schools. When Faye started high school at Drake she would ride along with her brother David who drove to school in his Dad's car. David would pick me up before school and we would ride around and smoke cigarettes. Sometimes Faye would be with him and sometimes Dave would drop her off at school before he picked me up. It wasn't long before I was going to David's at night, allegedly to study but mostly to see Faye. David had a pair of skis and we would attach a long rope to the car and pull each other on the skis behind the car in the ditch. We drove very slowly on country roads that had no traffic. Kids, don't try this at home. Some of them were snow covered and then we could ski on the road instead of in the ditch. It was winter and of course dark so we could hardly see whoever was on the skis from inside the car. Sometimes when we were going down a hill the skier would pass the car. It was great fun and generally there were three or four guys and of course we would take Faye along.

I soon tired of the skiing and was more interested in keeping Faye company and learning the art of necking. This romance lasted several months and then one morning when David picked me up he parked the car and went into my friend's house and left Faye and I alone in the car. She informed me she was breaking up with me. I was heartbroken for several days. She was soon dating some of my class mates. I was the typical male, unaware of the ways of the opposite sex and what they wanted from the male in their life without ever telling us. They just assumed we were born with that knowledge. Actually, typical male may be over stating it. Perhaps I was under typical and knew less than the average male about the opposite sex and how they do or don't think. I still don't have that ability but I'm still trying. As my wife describes me, I'm very trying.

After that I didn't, "go steady" with any Drake girls. They were on to my ignorance and rejected my proposals and advances. I dated one or two several times but we were not committed to each other. Perhaps, I thought they were fickle and didn't know a good thing, me, when they saw one or in reality they knew me too well.

One that I dated was Janice Gross. She was a very sweet, nice and pretty girl. She had siblings that had died of some disease that escapes my memory. I believe it was some form of cancer. It was rumored that she also had it and was dying. I remember dating her several times. Others had the idea we were going together but in reality we were just dating. I guess back then in Drake, if you dated a girl more than once, you were going with her. I did meet her parents but back then it was common practice when you dated a girl for the first time, you went to the door for her and generally were invited in to meet the parents. After the first date, you still went to the door to get her but sometimes she would answer the door and you would leave without going in. The parents would usually tell you what time they expected their daughter to be home.

I especially remember one New Year's Eve that my friend, Gary Richards from Tacoma, WA and I double dated. He took out Kathy Flatlie and I Janice. We had a great time that night. We took the girls to a New Year's Eve dance in Anamoose and danced the night away until midnight when according to tradition everyone counted down to midnight and then kissed, hollered Happy New Year and activated their noise makers. I especially liked the kissing part.

I dated Janice a few more times after that. Gary had been at Drake for Christmas vacation to visit his grandparents and he went back to Tacoma for the rest of the school year. Kathy and

Janice were close friends and double dated most of the time. Now Gary was gone and I didn't know anyone that was dating Kathy so Janice and I stopped dating. I believe it was the following year Janice died. She was only 16 or 17. I talked Charlie Toy into going to her funeral with me. I remember sitting right behind Kathy Flatlie and her parents. I always admired Kathy for being such a good friend to Janice. I believe Janice was the last girl I dated from Drake. Not that I didn't try to date them, they just were smart enough to say no. When you are young, you don't think much about death and certainly don't think you or your friends are going to die. When one does, it kind of reminds you that none of us are permanent residents here and there are no guarantees. It kind of makes you re-evaluate your priorities.

As a teenage boy, your priorities kind of revolve around girls and pursuing them. With the Drake girls onto me and not wanting to date me, it was time to expand my territory of pursuit. Mike Toy had a girl he was pursuing in Underwood, about fifty or sixty miles from Drake. I guess saying he had a girl isn't quite correct. He and another fellow were pursuing her. He always wanted me to go along with him in that pursuit because he said there were a lot of good looking party girls there and he may have noticed I wasn't dating the local girls. It's nice when your friends are looking out for your interests. He also needed someone with a car because he didn't have access to one. I thought it was a good trade, a ride to Underwood for introductions to the fine ladies there.

I could make the bars in Kief and Butte and some around Underwood so we would pick up a few six packs of beer or a case if there were enough of us and head for party time in Underwood. The first of several steady girlfriends in Underwood was a girl named Maryann. We dated, wrote Love letters, exchanged Christmas presents and then she informed me she had other interests and I was no longer one of them. Again, I was broken hearted for several days. I was not very perceptive and was completely clueless. As my wife says, I'm a rebel without a clue. I wasn't aware when a girl had lost interest in me or why. I just assumed they would love me forever, what's not to love?

In retrospect, I can understand why these girls would dump me. I was a guy who was really into music. One of my classmates told me she remembers me walking by her house with my transistor radio blaring. When in the car, we would listen to my transistor and most always, sing along with whatever the disc jockey was playing. I knew the words to all the Elvis songs as well as Buddy Holly, The Everly Brothers and most rock and roll songs. I sang in the church choir and was told on several occasions, by girls I was dating and their friends that I had a good voice.

As a five year old, I was asked to sing on the radio on one of my Father's friend's gospel programs. They had it all set up but at the last minute, I chickened out. So I've been singing all my life as both my parents did. I imagine the young girls I dated were not impressed with me when a good song came on the radio, in the middle of necking and I would interrupt the kiss to sing along with the tune. It might have been a mood breaker. Rebel, without a clue. However in my defense, I had several of these young ladies, tell me I was quite good, so if you're going to feed my ego, don't complain.

When we would be driving around, drinking beer, smoking cigarettes, singing along to the radio, eventually you needed to empty your bladder. Generally we would be out in the country where there were no rest rooms except for the wide open spaces. North Dakota girls were not shy about using the wide open spaces to empty their bladders and make room for more beer. They would have you stop the car on a lonely country road and go out behind the car. Usually there would be about three of them and they would all go together. Of course, they would converse with one another during this bladder emptying. On more than one of these occasions, my girlfriend would come back in and say that so and so thinks you're a really good singer. Sometimes, they would even impart this information directly to me and really swell my ego. So, of course, I wasn't aware, that some of these ladies would rather be necking, than singing. Again, rebel without a clue. Once in a while, someone would tell me to quit singing so they could hear whoever was singing the song on the radio. That didn't usually keep me quiet for long.

Mike went on a crusade to find a replacement for Maryann. I dated several different girls but didn't "go steady" with any of them until I was a senior. For my junior prom, I took an acquaintance of Mike & Charlie Toy. My friends looking out for me and setting me up. She lived in Max and was a beautiful girl. Her Dad and Mom were either separated or divorced. Her Dad lived in the hotel in Drake and she lived with her Mom in Max. I remember she wore a beautiful white formal and I wore a white sport coat, black slacks and a pink carnation with white buck shoes. This was the year that the song, "A white sport coat and a pink carnation" was on the hit parade. I thought we made quite a striking couple.

Before the prom we went to see her Dad at the hotel where pictures were taken and then to see my parents. My parents thought it sinful to go dancing, yet they let me use the car and never said a word about me going to the prom. I think the young lady's name was Judy Stevens. We got along fine but there was no spark. I was a nervous wreck and in awe of her beauty. I was on my best behavior and she was a wonderful date but I never felt any chemistry and am sure she didn't either. We were out most of the night and got back to Max about sunrise. Her Mother insisted that I come in and sleep for a few hours before driving back to Drake, which I did. We never saw each other or communicated after that.

In my senior year, Mike Toy fixed me up with a girl he knew from Underwood, Sharon Schell. Another very pretty girl that was very shapely. Built like a brick one, as the saying used to go. She also was a very nice, intelligent girl who I really liked and enjoyed her company. She was easy to be with, interesting to talk to and we had fun. She appeared to have other interests beside herself and one of those interests seemed to be me. She was a very wise lady. Before long we were going steady and she was wearing my graduation ring, " up around her neck, to tell the world she's mine, by heck ". We went together for quite a while and I thought we had a good relationship.

One night, Mike and I came to town with a case of beer in the trunk and a pint of vodka under the seat. There was another kid from Drake along, I think it may have been my friend, Dennis

Hinsz. Anyway, there was a car full of kids. I assume Mike had a date and probably Dennis also. There were at least six of us in the car. While driving around trying to figure out how we would spend the evening, it was suggested that we go to the dance in Garrison. Garrison is just a hop, skip and a drive from Underwood, so off we go. I'm driving and Sharon is snuggled up to me probably because someone is sitting next to her. Remember, no seat belts to confine us. I had my Dad's 52 Chevy, bare bones, no radio, ashtrays or cigarette lighter. I did have my trusty battery operated portable transistor radio we listened to and sang along with. We arrived in Garrison and being unfamiliar with the town, the girls had to tell us how to get to the dance. After driving around and looking for a place to park, someone suggested I park in the parking lot next to the building. It had snowed and there were a couple inches of snow covering most everything except the sidewalk. I drove into what appeared to be an empty parking lot and one of the girls said that this was no parking lot but the persons' yard that lived next door. She mentioned I might want to get out of there before they called the cops. Having had a few drinks and a being a bit of a showoff, I did a couple donuts on his lawn, went back to the street and parked in front of the dance in probably a no parking area. We all got out of the car and went into the dance.

    The Drake boys or at least the ones that kept dating the girls from Underwood had a bit of a reputation for being a bit on the wild side. We were kids who never really got into trouble but were skating around the edge of it. Mike, quite often got in fights over girls with the locals who thought they had first rights to them. Of course we all smoked, drank alcohol, drove a bit reckless and probably were loud and obnoxious, so you can see where that rumor started. It was reported by some of the girls we dated that when we drove into town, the whole town knew we were there in less than one half hour. Some even said their Dad's told them they couldn't go out with us. So of course that would make them want to go out with us and they would conspire to meet us at a friends' or down town so their parents wouldn't find out. We used to joke about it, that the locals were locking up their daughters because we had arrived in town. This "bad boy" image didn't really hinder us when chasing skirts. It often times worked the opposite. To the daughters, it spelled excitement in an otherwise boring town.

We played the part of teenage boys of that time. Ducktail haircuts in the fashion of Elvis, shirt collars turned up, leather jackets, cigarettes rolled up in the sleeve of your shirt, tough guys trying to impress the ladies and intimidate the guys. At any rate, weather it was my imagination or wishful thinking, when we walked into the dance, it felt like a scene out of a James Dean movie. Everyone's attention shifted to us and to Mike Toy specifically. He had that Toy Charisma that just demanded and got attention. He kind of had the "Fonzie" persona, for those of you that remember that generation. We hung around for a while but soon got thirsty and knowing we had beer in the trunk, we went back to the car parked out front.

We all got in the car, I got the pint of vodka from under the seat and took a swig before taking off to find a location where we could get the beer out of the trunk and have one. While sitting there swigging on the vodka, I hear a knock on my window. Looking out, I see a police officer standing there. I hand the pint of vodka to Sharon and she makes it disappear. It seems she had places I wasn't familiar with where a pint of vodka could be stored in her blouse.

I got out and Mike got out also. The officer told Mike to get back in the car which he did after protesting. The officer walks around back of the car and starts writing down my license plate number on a ticket pad. He says It was reported that I had been driving in someone's yard in a reckless manner. Of course, I denied it and said it must be someone else. He asked for my driver's license and we were talking as he was writing. As was my custom when trying to get out of a jam with the law, I was being very polite with a lot of yes sir, no sirs. Mike again got out of the car to try to help but the officer told him to get back in the car. The officer had just asked me to open the trunk and I was stalling, pretending to look for my keys, hoping for a miracle. At this time in history police didn't need a search warrant to search a vehicle.

They just did it routinely. The officer finally suggested that I may have left the keys in the ignition, which I knew I had, so the stalling was over. I walked around the car to retrieve the keys when this big fellow ran up huffing and puffing. I knew him; he was Dennis Anderson from Underwood, the son of the cop at Underwood. He was a friend of ours and sometimes hitchhiked to Drake and stayed at Toys.

I was just about to say hi Dennis when he stopped in front of the officer and said, do you know where I can find a guy named Dwight Knuth. He was supposedly in Underwood and left for the dance here. My Dad got a call that his Mother had a heart attack and is in the VA hospital in Minot. The officer said well matter of fact this is he. Dennis told me I was supposed to get to Minot to the VA hospital as soon as possible. The officer said, you better leave now, son, but drive carefully and don't speed. I suspect you may have been drinking but you seem OK to drive. There were no breathalyzers, at least not in ND. The sober test back then was walking a straight line and touching your nose with your finger. It was not an accurate test and I passed it another time when I was definitely inebriated. The officer probably thought this test would take too much time and he already expressed that he thought I wasn't that impaired. I thanked Dennis and the officer and asked for directions out of town to get to Minot. Just as if I actually was going to go to Minot. We headed out of town towards Minot, went down the highway a few miles, enough to know we weren't being followed, stopped and got some beer out of the trunk and then proceeded back to Underwood.

I believe I saw Dennis once after that and he said the Garrison police never followed up with his Dad to see if the story was true and he never got in trouble for it. They obviously never checked with the VA hospital either because he had my license plate number on the ticket he was writing out so he must have thrown the ticket away. It was a good act and fast thinking and my Mother was never a veteran so I knew it was a made up story. I don't think we ever went back to a dance in Garrison. It's good to have friends that have your back.

This Dummy Pulls His Own Strings

In the spring I took Sharon to the senior prom and again we stayed out all night and got back to Underwood in the early dawn or perhaps it was full daylight. I believe we double dated with another couple but I can't remember who it was. One of my friends told me it was Janet and Mike and I have no reason to doubt that it was, so I'll go with that. Evidently I was too enamored with Sharon to pay attention to my surroundings or alcohol might have entered the equation. Again, I believed I had the most beautiful girl at the prom. Everyone knows the prom is just a beauty competition and about the girls dresses and hair. My date again would have won that competition had there been one. It's not really about dancing and it certainly wasn't about the hokey-pokey which I don't believe God had invented yet. Well, it may also be about having a party and drinking alcohol but mostly about who is with who and all the gossip that goes with that.

That should teach the Drake girls that I was a good catch and a desirable date, despite what they may have heard or observed. Just look at the beautiful out of town girls I brought to the proms. I can imagine the gossip in the ladies room now, that poor girl, wait till she really gets to know him.

Some weeks after the prom, Mike and I went to Underwood unexpected. We went looking for our girls and found them out with other guys. I asked Sharon for my ring back and she surrendered it quite willingly which prompted me to think this was her way of telling me we were finished. She returns my ring without defending her actions or without protesting our breaking up or an apology. If she is dating someone else and doesn't seem to care she was caught doing it, she must be done with me. I may be naïve, clueless and slow but I'm not stupid. Oh wait a minute, in retrospect what did I think she would use for a defense. I sort of caught her going out with someone else when she was going steady with me. I suppose I was broken hearted that she would cheat on me and was going to teach her a lesson, not to ever do that again. Guess what, she never did but how did I benefit from it?

We didn't discuss the circumstances of it and years later I heard that she was really heartbroken over our break up. I didn't get that feeling at the time. When I heard that, I felt bad that I had handled it badly and perhaps I had over reacted to what had appeared to be a betrayal. The lesson here would be, open honest communication is important. I still feel bad that the communication never happened and again I proved to be a rebel without a clue. I could have been more understanding and forgiving but I guess we learn from our mistakes.

This was the first girl I had broken up with. Usually it was I who was getting dumped but this time it was I doing the dumping. Probably because of my inexperience, I handled it badly. That's my story and I'm sticking to it.

I'm not exactly sure of the time line but I know I spent six months in MO for Army National Guard training, some time in Williston working construction for my brother-in-law Clifford Kummer and three months in Iowa going to the College of Automation for Data Processing. This whole period of time seemed to be quite a dry spell where romance was concerned. I didn't have Mike Toy finding girls and dates for me. I wrote to a few girls that I knew and one that my sister Verla was trying to set me up with but nothing developed from the correspondence. I did try to date a girl in my class in Iowa by the name of Virginia Thomas from Epping, ND. She only seemed moderately interested and then only because of the urging of her friends. She seemed to be timid and shy and may have been as clueless as I was but not a rebel. Or perhaps she was not clueless and knew the score and had me pegged as a loser.

I gave up on her and pursued a nurse that was going to nursing school in Des Moines by the name of Evelyn Beckett. She lived in an apartment with two other girls going to nursing school. There were two guys from ND that were attending the same school as I. Together we rented an apartment. The three of us started dating the three nursing students. We would get together at their apt. mostly because we couldn't even afford Henry Hamburgers at nineteen cents each much less a date. When we weren't seeing the girls or studying we went to the bowling alley to watch bowling because we couldn't afford to bowl, eat or drink. How bored are you when your entertainment is watching bowling? When one of my fellow apartment dwellers broke up with the girl he was going with, the other guy and I just kind of faded into history. It was more of a companionship relationship and an excuse not to study than a romance. In retrospect, I think Evelyn wanted it to be more than companionship but I still remained clueless. Back then the girls did not pursue the guys. The guys were the pursuers while the girls were the pursue'es.

Towards the end of the school, one of our classmates who lived in Des Moines, had a party to celebrate our graduation. She had moved all the furniture out of the living room and set up a record player for dancing. Her younger sister who was about 17 took an interest in me probably because I was one of the few guys dancing and could do the twist which was the new "in dance". Her name was Rosie and she was a pretty Spanish teenager that was very well built with many curves where they are pleasant to view. We danced the night away but I never saw her again because I was soon leaving Iowa to go back to ND.

That brings me to a young lady by the name of Janet I met from Underwood, ND. I had been acquainted with Janet for quite some time but had never dated her. She was one of the girls from Underwood that came with us on our escapades. I even double dated with her on occasion when dating her friend Sharon Schell. Again, Mike Toy was fixing me up with a girl he thought would be right for me. She was pretty, with long blond hair, shapely, intelligent, fun loving yet reserved and refined. I guess pretty is not the correct adjective to describe her. Beautiful is a better word to describe her. I liked her from the time we met but always thought I wouldn't stand a chance with someone as beautiful and classy as she. I guess you could say I placed her high above me, too good for the likes of me. Me being a rebel without a clue. When Mike set me up for a date with her, I was ecstatic. On our first date, she seemed to tolerate me better than most. We seemed to hit it off quite well but that might have been because she thought she would never see me again.

I had just joined the Navy and she was going to Philadelphia to stay with her sister and family and help take care of her sister's kids. In my mind, we had a great first date. There was some spark, maybe even fireworks, at least for me. Mike and I stayed overnight at a friend's house and the next morning, Janet with a friend came by to see me. I got her address in Philadelphia so we could communicate but of course assumed under the circumstances, it would be awhile before we saw each other again.

As it turned out, I was stationed just 60 miles from Philadelphia where Janet was.

Two of the five guys I enlisted with, Emery Suckert and Bruce Bruner, were stationed at Bainbridge, Maryland for Radioman school and came to see me. These fellows were on the Golden Gloves Boxing team with me and good friends. They wanted to go to Philadelphia for the weekend on liberty. I mentioned I knew a girl there from Underwood, ND and that perhaps she had some friends and we could have a party. So off to Philadelphia we go by bus. All I had was her address, no phone number but if three of the Navy's finest can't find an address in Philadelphia; our Country might be in trouble. We all were in uniform which usually generated cooperation and friendliness from the civilians or natives, as we referred to them. This was before the Viet Nam war had escalated and become controversial.

We stopped in a department store and asked directions to the address I had for Janet. After we told the lady we were all from ND, the lady at the counter took considerable time to explain how the subway/elevated trains worked, where to catch them, what parts of the city might not be safe, how to make transfers and how to get to the address we had. She enlisted the help of her co-workers in this endeavor. I think because we played the ND card, she felt sorry for us and thought we probably wouldn't survive in the city.

With three of us all getting the same instructions, it was not surprising we each interpreted them differently. After a few drinks at a bar to build our courage and confidence, the instructions became much clearer and we succeeded in finding the address and Janet was in fact there. Both Janet and her sister, Elaine

This Dummy Pulls His Own Strings

welcomed us and seemed glad to see us. I think Janet even called some of her friends to try to set something up but on such short notice was unsuccessful. That's my mode of operation, surprise them so they don't have a chance to run. I believe we may have gone somewhere but I can't remember where. Probably a neighborhood bar. I believe I set up a date for the next week end with Janet. My buddies were just out of luck and had other fish to fry.

When I went to see Janet the next time, her sister and brother-in-law offered me their couch to sleep on. From then on I became a permanent week-end house guest unless I had week-end duty. Janet's sister, Elaine and her husband Francis were wonderful people and became friends and an added bonus to our relationship. They were always kind to me and treated me with open arms and kindness. They would go out of their way to make me feel at home and welcome and would include me in their weekend and family plans. They bought a house and invited me to come and help get it ready so they could move in, which I did. The Army had given me extensive training with a paintbrush so I was well qualified in this area. These were good times of making new friends and for Janet and I to get to know each other, our personalities, interests, sense of humor, faults, hopes and dreams.

Janet and I took the bus to New York City one week end to see the sights. I called one of my buddies from Brooklyn or the Bronx and he took us around the city. We also took a paid tour of the city. Several weeks later we decided to go to Washington DC to see the sights. We took the bus again and took a tour in DC. We had been having fun together and seeing each other every weekend and I thought our relationship was possibly getting serious. I even chased off a possible suitor one week-end I was there. I guess he took one look at me and knew he didn't stand a chance. ☺ Either that or he thought if she dated the likes of me, she wasn't worth pursuing. It was a fellow she worked with and after that he didn't show any interest, at least that I was aware of. I digress.

Janet and I took a break in one of the many parks in DC and were sitting on a bench in the park by the Jefferson memorial, taking in the beauty of the park, having a conversation, enjoying the moment, getting to know each other and I had to go and spoil it all by telling her I Loved her. It was not pre-meditated just spontaneous. We hadn't even been drinking but were holding hands on a park bench in DC and possibly exchanging saliva. I guess I was feeling romantic or maybe it was cursing hormones or perhaps it was the necking that got the lust going because I not only told her I loved her but asked her to marry me. I was brought up by Baptist parents that had a lot of old fashioned views and morals, more like Quakers or Pennsylvania Dutch, which my mother was. One of these values was you didn't participate in sex unless you were married. I suppose, being a healthy male with raging hormones and a tank full of lust, I thought it necessary to marry her before trying to get her to sleep with me. She was taken completely by surprise at my proposal, as was I, and at first was leaning towards a no answer but as my sainted mother often said to me, you should be a lawyer because you will argue over anything and won't quit until the other person gives up just to end it. So eventually, I wore her down and she agreed to my proposal. I think part of the proposal was, just give it a try and if it doesn't work out, no harm done. Wouldn't it be fun? We spent the rest of the day, intoxicated on Love and/or Lust. We took a late bus back to Philadelphia and at one of the bus stops in a little town by the name of Elkton in MD there was a sign that said you could get married there with no waiting.

    This is the same town you see in movies that advertise instant marriage on the east coast. They also had slot machines at the bus stop. A typical gambling paradise, marriage and gambling or perhaps, marriage is a gamble. I guess they are similar, one is taking a chance on love, the other with your money. Janet saw the sign and suggested to me we should get married right now, right here. Wow, I really am convincing. By this time, my hormones had settled down and it was my turn to be surprised and to lean towards a no answer. I kind of thought we should get to know each other better first. Isn't that the whole purpose

This Dummy Pulls His Own Strings

of an engagement? In my Baptist upbringing, marriage went on forever or until one of you killed the other, as it says in the vows, till death us do part. I hadn't even gotten her an engagement ring yet since I had not planned any of this. I expressed to her that I thought we should wait, get engaged with a ring and plan a wedding that our families could attend. She half-heartedly agreed but to me she seemed disappointed. Maybe it was just my over active imagination.

Obviously, we were not on the same page with our emotions. Earlier, I was thinking with my heart and not so much logic and now we had switched places and she was thinking with her heart and not so much logic or perhaps my lust had abated and hers had been kick started. So, this proves my persuasive powers as my mom always said, I could talk anyone into or out of anything. On the same day, I talked Janet into marrying me and then talked her out of marrying me. Do you think she might have been confused by any of this? I had the poor girl going in circles. No wonder she dumped me later. As intelligent as she is, I'm surprised it took her as long as it did. Also, keep in mind, my memory of these events and my description of them may be different from her memory of these events, so if she tells a different story than mine, I would go with her version.

It may have been divine intervention. Anyway, we stayed on the bus and proceeded to her sisters where, of course, we broke the good news. Sometime in the near future, whether it was the next day or next week, we went to a local neighborhood jewelry store to acquire a ring for her finger. She picked out the one that I could afford and that she wanted in that price range and was very pleased with it. Remember, I was a sailor so my price range left a lot to be desired but I think she did a fine job of selection. Perhaps the jeweler was as taken with her beauty as I was so he gave us a deal. I think she fell in love with the ring as was witnessed when she ended the engagement but wanted to keep the ring. I told her the ring and I were a team, she couldn't have one without the other. I mentioned previously, Janet is an intelligent person so she took less than a second to think about it and did the smart thing and removed the ring and the ring and I went down the heart break trail to the heartbreak hotel.

You can't really blame her for wanting to keep the ring. After all, diamonds are a girls' best friend. I probably should have given the ring to her because putting up with me for as long as she did, she should have benefited in some way other than experience. I believe I gave her my 8mm Bell & Howell movie camera for either her or her sister so they could take movies of the children, Jackie and Michael, who I also had come to love.

We had much happiness, in our short engagement. I don't recall a lot of disagreements and no fights. She was easy on the eyes and it was not a difficult task to Love her. She was very loveable as well as adorable. She had two lips that insisted on being kissed and it was my pleasure to accommodate them.

We, of course, spent holidays together, Including Thanksgiving with her sister, sisters' husband and kids. At Christmas her parents and younger brother came from ND and I met them and thought they were wonderful people. Her mother was a very classy lady which made me quite happy because I had heard that many times the children eventually turn into their parents. This is an important thing to keep in mind when selecting a mate. Get to know the parents and see what kind of people they are because chances are your life mate will have many of their qualities, good or bad, as you mature. Ask yourself if you can live with those qualities because the only person you can change is yourself. So I was pleased with her parents and the qualities I witnessed in the short visit we had. I was also pleased with her siblings and their qualities. All her siblings had good values and were good and kind people with good moral fiber. At this point, for me, all was good and I was becoming more in love as time went on. Here again it could have been more in lust but I like to think that I have a logical mind and though I suffer from lust as all males and perhaps all humans do, I can separate the lust and logic. Looking back, I had no indication that Janet felt any different than I did. Here again, I'm a rebel without a clue and a slow learner. Everything seemed to be going well except

This Dummy Pulls His Own Strings

we had not set a wedding date but there didn't seem to be any reason to rush it.

Sometime in the spring, I bought a 56 ford convertible. It had a Mercury engine in it and was leaded in on the frame to keep it from rolling over. As was often the case back then, cars were not very reliable so it was not always in top running shape but it looked really good. It was yellow with a black top. The motor for the top was burned out so it was a manual process to raise and lower the top which was a small inconvenience. Sometimes I would pick up Janet at work to impress her co-workers and because she needed a ride home. Just imagine, this handsome sailor driving up in a convertible, top down, to pick up this beautiful, shapely blond and they drive off into the sunset. What, no imagination? Let me tell you, the beautiful, shapely blond part was true and requires no imagination. Besides, imagination is crazy, you start asking a daisy what to do.

One summer evening I was going to Philadelphia to spend the weekend with Janet, driving along route 40 with the top down, listening to music, wind blowing in my hair, I still had some. I guess I was a little distracted because I took a wrong turn and ended up in the ghetto or hood. There were no signs that said ghetto or hood but I knew I shouldn't be there. Not a good place to be in a convertible with the top down, being a white boy and not in uniform. Remember, the motor to raise and lower the top was burned out so it was a manual procedure to put the top up which required pulling off the road, getting out of the car and manually raising it. This was a procedure that required about 15 to 20 min. I decided I was probably better off to keep going and find a safer neighborhood to put the top up. I was getting lots of stares and there were a lot of young black men standing around in groups of three or four. I was very nervous or you might say downright scared. It wouldn't be difficult for anyone to walk up to the stopped car and jump over the side into the car. I tried to time the stop lights so I wouldn't get caught at any but in heavy city traffic that is almost impossible to pull off. The law of averages caught up to me and there I was stopped at a red light with a car in front of me. A group of punks standing on the sidewalk started sauntering over to my car from the driver's side sidewalk. This meant they had to cross a lane of road before getting to me and they had to wait for a car that was turning the corner to pass before they reached me. Luckily for me, the light changed and the car in front of me took off in a hurry and I followed suit. After that, when driving in unfamiliar territory in the city, I kept my top up and tried to stick to known routes.

Back to romance. While engaged to Janet we did things that a sailor and working girl could afford such as movies, the mummers parade on St. Patrick's day, wedding dances, shopping and staying home talking and listening to music, drinking beer and necking on the couch and holding hands. Janet spent a lot of time washing her hair, sitting under a dryer and fixing her hair which always looked great. We didn't go out very often so the hair care seemed like an exercise in futility to me. She had beautiful long blond hair but it seemed to me it was in curlers most of the time which didn't really bother me. I thought she was cuter than a bugs ear, even in curlers or especially in curlers. When in curlers, the long blond hair didn't take your attention away from her perfect face. That is still one of my favorite memories of her, sitting under the hair dryer in curlers. Her cute smile and often a somewhat embarrassed expression on her face, probably from something I said. Good memories.

On one rare occasion we went to a movie. I'm not sure of the location of the theater but I know we took the elevated train to get there and I don't believe it was city center but a neighborhood theater. I wore civilian clothes rather than my uniform because by this time the Viet Nam war was somewhat controversial and some people would call you names such as baby killers and cuss you out and spit at you. Most places I went off base, unless I was hitchhiking, I would wear civilian clothes to avoid this.

We hadn't been seated very long waiting for the movie to start when some rowdy teenagers came down the aisle. They may have said something to us as they passed but I'm not sure. If they did, I ignored them. When they got to the front of the theater, they started fooling around, putting on a show for the people in the theater, swearing loudly, throwing things at the screen and being obnoxious. My first instinct was to go down there and give them a piece of my mind but I knew I couldn't spare any. Besides, I didn't want to leave Janet alone and unprotected and the deciding factor was they outnumbered me by three or four.

So we sat there and tried not to attract their attention. After some time had passed one of them got up where the screen was and pulled out a switchblade knife and started slashing the screen. No one attempted to stop them. Eventually someone came and escorted them all out. After the movie, when we were leaving to catch the elevated train home, there was a guy standing in front of the theater urinating. Perhaps this was not the best part of town or a good place to take a lady for a date. In my defense, it was Janet and her sister that had chosen this theater because I was unfamiliar with Philadelphia but in their defense they picked it for the movie that was playing not the neighborhood it was in. For once I wasn't the only clueless one. All the way to the elevated train stop, I was looking over my shoulder for any sign of being followed or possible trouble coming our way. We escaped with only a bruised dignity. That may have been the last movie we attended.

I thought our relationship was good. We seldom disagreed, fought or were unhappy. We laughed a lot and generally were happy. Maybe that is only how I felt and she didn't express her discontent and I didn't pick up on it, if there was any. I've heard that guys are clueless. I guess my first clue, there may be a long "row to hoe" ahead was when I was moved from the couch in the living room for sleeping to a roll-a-way in the basement. I justified it with I was kind of in the way in the living room and disrupted everyone's morning when they had to pass through my bedroom. I thought of it as a more permanent arrangement, my own room, with privacy. Maybe it was the first sign that paradise had left the building. I was happy with the arrangement and grateful to Fran and Elaine for their hospitality and accommodations. I would have slept on the floor, just to share time with Janet. Fran would often make us all bacon and eggs for breakfast.

It wasn't too far down the road when Janet told me she was breaking off the engagement and going back to ND. Of course, I was clueless and had not seen this coming.

There must have been signs and looking back perhaps I had my head in the sand. In retrospect, I believe she was still in love with her previous boyfriend and wanted to give that relationship another try. I mean really, how could she not love me. I'm just that loveable. I choose to believe that, rather than accept responsibility for screwing up the relationship. She adamantly proclaimed it was not me but that she was having doubts about her love for me. I also believe she was more mature than I was and was looking for a man instead of the boy I was. She said I would thank her someday for doing this. After some probing, she admitted there was a former boyfriend that she wanted to reconnect with. As I said before, she asked if she could keep the engagement ring and I denied that request. She returned the ring, we broke up friends and broke out a bottle of booze, the strong stuff and I proceeded to get drunk and retire to my basement roll-a-way.

I continued to come to see Janet on weekends until she left by plane for ND. She encouraged this and we parted friends and I still consider her a friend. We even had a going away party for her where I brought a car load of guys from the base. She requested that I not go to the airport with her when she left. Her sister and brother-in-law took her and I stayed at her sisters with her sisters two kids. I thought I was devastated by the breakup but it wasn't that long before I was going to Atlantic City to the beach with my buddies and getting on with life. There's nothing like looking at bikinis for healing a broken heart. I apparently wasn't as broken hearted as I thought at the time because It didn't take that many bikinis before I was dating again and she was a distant memory.

What I learned from this experience was that any relationship that is one-sided will not be a happy and fulfilling one unless you can keep your head in the sand. It would also help if the sand you have your head in, is a beach filled with bikinis. If you are in a relationship with someone and they want to end it, don't fight it, walk away and move on. Don't prolong the agony.

This Dummy Pulls His Own Strings

Part friends, if possible. If you can, talk about it and see if there is something specific about yourself that you can improve on, for future relationships. Keep in mind, you are opening yourself up to a world of hurt and you need to be able to take constructive and/or destructive criticism, without lashing out. Remember this is a learning process and a self-improvement process. We all think we are perfect but reality disputes that.

Don't offer any suggestions to the other party unless they request it and then only if you can do it in a spirit of love and helping them, not trying to hurt them or point the fickle finger of fault. Remember that sometimes it is not all about you. It may be that their heart is somewhere else and with someone else. That is just the way life is. They can't help how they feel about someone else, no more than you can control how you feel about them. Emotions (feelings) are not something you can turn on and off. You each have your emotions and theirs are as important to them as yours are to you.

If you talk them into staying with you when their heart is not in it, you may live to regret it and your love may turn to hate. If you take the wedding vows with them, until death us do part may come sooner than necessary. I would prefer to lose someone but retain my love for them and the memory of that love, the rest of my life than turn my love into hate. That is just me and we are all different but I'm just saying, put some thought into your breakup before you allow your emotions to cause your mouth to say things that can never be unsaid. Put distance between you so that time can heal the broken heart. Find someone else to share your time with and build a relationship with and "fall in love with".

In actuality, time doesn't heal a broken heart. Love heals a broken heart. Sharing love is the meaning of life. Even if your heart is broken over and over, love is worth it and sharing your time, space, thoughts and experiences brings much joy and happiness. Anytime you spend time, getting to know someone and learning to love them, if it doesn't work out there will be a broken heart. Getting to know someone is the key phrase here. Do they make you happy, make you laugh? Do you want to be with them and share thoughts, feelings and life? Do you miss them when you're apart and wish you could share the moment? Do they feel the same about you? Don't settle for any reason, walk away if it is not right.

Don't be afraid of a broken heart, it will mend. For guys a generous amount of skimpy bikinis speeds up the healing and for the girls, well I'm clueless. I can't imagine not having someone to share my life with or not loving someone and being loved. My simple mind, just can't grasp that concept. I guess when it comes to love, you would call me needy. I am thankful that Janet had the intelligence to know her heart and follow it. I only hope that her heart brought her the love and happiness she was hoping and searching for. She deserved to share love with someone that felt the same way about her.

Here is a little side story of one excursion to Atlantic City. Two of my buddies and I were driving down Atlantic Avenue in Atlantic City with the top down on the convertible, all three of us in the front seat. I stopped at a stop light and three pretty young girls walked up to the car, jumped over the side into the back seat and asked where we were going. They literally flew into the back seat, without an invitation. I guess the convertible was a chic magnet. I had been trying to pick up girls all my life, with very little success and now they are literally jumping into my vehicle.

After I recovered from the shock, we struck up a conversation. They wanted to know where we were from and all about us. We saw no reason to deceive them or lie to them so we told them we were sailors and stationed in MD. At the next stop light they exited the car the same way they entered it. After getting the lay of the land in Atlantic City, we discovered that most of the girls there were rich girls going to college and that was what they were looking for, college guys, preferably rich which excludes sailors. From then on we were college guys even if we weren't rich. At least there was a possibility perhaps someday we would be rich.

I did go to see Janet in Underwood the next time I was home on leave or perhaps it was after I was discharged. She was working at the Dairy Queen with her mother who was the owner/

This Dummy Pulls His Own Strings

operator. I went to the order window and asked her mom if Janet was around. Her Mom recognized me and was very gracious, as always and gave me the impression she was glad to see me. She went to get Janet and we talked. Her Mom told her she could leave for the day so we went to the bar for a drink and to catch up. I got the feeling that Janet wanted to be seen in public with me and was using me to make someone jealous. Now remember, I'm a rebel without a clue. It may have been my imagination but she didn't send me any signals that she was really overjoyed to see me but yet she wanted to spend some time with me. Maybe I was just being clueless and immature again. Then again, Janet is a compassionate and caring person so she probably would take it slow so that she would not lead me on only to break my heart again. I found her to not be a deceptive person but very private and cautious.

I may have been sending signals of my own that discouraged her, having had my heart broken by her previously. Too bad we can't just lay our cards on the table and say this is how it is, fold or stay. That evening she suggested we go fishing at the lake with her other sister, Diane and brother-in-law, Jim. Again, to me it was mixed signals. Why did she want me to meet her other sister and brother-in-law who to this point were only names. Was it, perhaps, that she wanted witnesses so she had proof positive that nothing happened between us or perhaps she didn't want another proposal from me and with her sister there, it would be more unlikely? I didn't know if she was still in a relationship and I didn't ask. That would be my bad. I guess my thinking probably was if I didn't ask, I wouldn't be disappointed. My track record, to her, was probably that I was unpredictable so she should cover the bases. With my limited ability to read peoples' intentions, it indicated to me that there might not be a future for us and she was using me to make the other guy get serious, if in fact there was another guy.

On the other hand, if she was trying to rebuild our relationship, wouldn't she want to spend the evening alone with me and discuss our future? I came to the conclusion that, A. we didn't have a future and 2. She might be using me to make someone else jealous and further another relationship. You see how my convoluted mind doesn't work? Just my perceptions and as my wife says, I'm a rebel without a clue. That was my last encounter with Janet. I still have loving feelings for her and good memories of our time together. Loving feelings in that I wish her well in life but am not in Love with her. She was a beautiful, classy, lady, like her mom and sisters with many admirable attributes. Many of those attributes were pleasant to look at. I am grateful she had the sense to turn down my marriage proposal, especially since she wasn't as committed to it as I was. I can't imagine that anyone else could have made me as happy or loved me more than my wife has. Speaking of my wife, my greatest Love, Romance and Crush; she has her own chapter in this book titled "Love of my life, my Happiness". For the rest of the story, go to that chapter.

For you young guys, looking for a life mate, partner, wife, significant other or whatever the culture is now labeling them. Early in the relationship, meet her mom. This is the woman she very likely will turn into in the future. Get to know her and find out if this is the kind of woman you want to spend your life with. I didn't say that the daughter will be a clone of her mother but there will be many similarities. In my life, I've seen it happen over and over. Even girls who don't especially like their mothers and some of their characteristics acquire some of the same ones and if you were to point this out to them, they would not be able to recognize it. I spent a lot of time with my wife's parents before we were married. I got to know both of them pretty well and fell in love with them and the whole family as I was falling in love with Kathy. It cements the marriage and insures that there is a better chance of it succeeding. Kathy acquired many of both her mothers and fathers characteristics for which I am grateful. She is the best of both. Just saying.

One weekend, one of my buddies from Maine asked me to accompany him home for the weekend. I had nothing better to do and thought perhaps I would get some home cooking. He also promised to fix me up with one of his girlfriends, girlfriends so how could I refuse. He lived on a farm outside one of the quaint villages in Maine. You know, church bells chiming on a Sunday morn, remind you of the town where you were born. There are lots of ski resorts and covered bridges in Maine. A serene setting. I actually visited a general store much like the one in Kief, ND owned and operated by Sam Karpanko. The one in Maine had a wooden barrel of pickles where you could get one pickle or as many as you desired. I believe in Sam's general store he had wooden barrels of black olives and barrels of pickled herring. Sam also had ice cream in the two and one half gallon containers and would scoop you out a generous ice cream cone for a nickel. In Maine, the general store had a pot belly stove where the locals would gather to get warm and chat and possibly play a game of checkers or chess. A Norman Rockwell scene. My buddy lived on a farm where they raised racing horses. They had a large barn with separate stalls for the horses and the double doors where you could open the top half so the horse could stand with their head outside.

They had a small house by today's standards. I imagine it was designed that way so it was easier to heat in the winter. All the bedrooms were upstairs and there was absolutely no heat in any of the bedrooms. The beds all had feather beds on top of the mattress which was like a huge bed sized pillow for those of you not familiar with a feather bed. There were flannel sheets and huge thick wool quilts. You were only cold getting into or out of bed even when the temperature was below zero. Most people wore a head cover to bed which held the heat in and kept you warm. I didn't have a night cap so I would have to pull the quilt up over my head to keep from freezing. My buddy was true to his word and set me up with a date. We double dated. My date was an Italian girl by the name of Andrea Bellando. Again, as was my custom, I went to the door to get her, even though we had never met and this was a blind date. She invited me in to meet her parents. I remember the whole house smelled of Italian cooking and I was almost as interested in that as their daughter. The Maine girls are like the ND girls. They enjoy watching submarine races, so that was the extent of the date. Like ND, there are not many options in a small village unless you are old enough for the local pub. We had an interesting date and enjoyed each other's company. We even wrote to each other for a while but she thought I was a bit conceited and I agreed with her. If you don't love yourself, you might be unlovable and no one else will love you either. Again, what's not to love. ☺

After I became disengaged, I started working several jobs to fill the spare hours. In the Navy I worked night shift in the computer room as shift supervisor. As supervisor, I could designate who worked and when. With the knowledge and blessing of my Chief, I went to a port and starboard work schedule, work one night, take the next night off. With all the time off, we had a lot of hours to fill and the more time you had to spend money the more money you spent. I decided that if I was working, I wouldn't be spending money but in fact earning money so I went out looking for part time work. Back then, no one pumped their own gas at a gas station. That was what service station attendants did.

There was a gas station on base that I got a part time job at, pumping gas. I enjoyed doing it, sort of a mindless job with physical exercise and social interaction with the customers. The biggest challenge of the job back in the 60's was trying to guess where they hid the gas cap in the car design. Some had it behind the license plate, others behind the tail light and some in the oversized fins. In fact, I liked pumping gas so well I got another part time job at a gas station on the JFK expressway a few miles from base. It was the main road between Washington DC and New York City. Many politicians and celebrities passed through on their way to NY or DC. I waited on more than one celebrity and politician. Some were friendly and sociable, others not so much.

We not only pumped gas but washed your windshield, checked fluid levels, belt wear, tires and opened your car door for you to stretch your pretty legs, unless you were a male. In which case, you could open your own door and we would ignore your legs. We often received tips for this level of service and admiring legs.

I also had a part time job working for Bata Shoe Company, doing data entry or as it was called then, keypunching. We converted shoe orders from retailers to punch cards that could be read by the computers. It was interesting that many retailers ordered their shoes from the same company. We had orders from J. C. Penny, Macy's, K-Mart, Montgomery Ward and many other retailers.

I also worked for Manpower out of Wilmington, Delaware doing data entry or keypunching. With all these part time jobs, I was working more than full time which didn't leave a lot of time for romance. Also, I was seldom on base at chow time so I had to eat at Cafes or fast food places. When you eat at the same place a lot, the food servers (waitresses) and cooks get to know you and you them. There was a young teenage girl by the name of Elizabeth Fox working at one of the places I frequented who was very friendly to me and would flirt with me. She often would come sit with me to talk to me while I was eating, if it wasn't busy. I thought she was a little young for me but finally asked her out. Even as clueless as I am, it was obvious that she wanted to go out with me. Soon we were dating quite frequently and she invited me out to her birthday dinner with her entire family. I guess we dated for close to a year but she was still in high school and there was another high school girl in ND that had my full attention or maybe it was that Elizabeth lived on "Love Run Road" out of Rising Sun, MD that scared me off but whatever it was, I ended it. Truth be told, I was interested in a sweet farm girl from Kief, ND. Elizabeth was the last local girl I dated in the Navy.

When I would go home on leave I would date Kathy almost exclusively except for one of Mike Toy's former girlfriends from Turtle Lake, Bernadine. She was older than Kathy and could stay out later then Kathy so on occasion I would take Kathy home and drive to Turtle Lake and take Bernadine out. Berna wrote to me while I was in the Navy and our relationship was more friendly than romantic. We knew each other and enjoyed the others company. In fact she would tell me about the guys she was dating and even asked me if I thought she should marry the guy she eventually married. She may have been testing me to see if my interest was beyond a friendship. Again, clueless me, say what you mean and mean what you say, don't expect guys to have a clue. I advised her to follow her heart.

Berna and Kathy were acquaintances and I asked Berna for advice on how to proceed with Kathy. Berna advised me to go slow with Kathy and not pressure her too much. Here again perhaps she wanted more than just a friendly relationship with me and I was too clueless to realize it. I was also too smitten with Kathy to recognize any budding signs of romance with anyone else. It turns out her advice was "spot on" and I followed it. Obviously Kathy was and is my last and greatest romance.

I would recommend, based on my experiences, to seek out romance whenever the opportunity is available. As Sidney Poitier says in his auto-biography, "Love is a many splintered thing". I found that assessment to be quite correct, in that you expose yourself to very serious heartbreak and at the same time, when everything is going smoothly, the greatest high you can experience in life. The trick is to nurture Love and guide it to a successful relationship. As the "Love Chapter" in the bible says, it requires patience, self-less-ness, hope, endurance, kindness and truth. In my alleged mind, when you find it and nurture it, it is worth all the pain and heartbreak suffered in the prior experiences to get to the part that causes you to be higher than a kite can fly, floating on a cloud, dancing on a rainbow and all the other euphoniums used to describe the indescribable emotion of Love.

As I bring this chapter to a close, I'm sure many of you were expecting to read about my sex life. You just did. In my youth it was pretty much non-existent. As I explained previously, I was raised by Quaker like values and mores. My maternal Grandmother being Pennsylvania Dutch and my parents being Baptist of the northern variety. My Father had gone to school to be a minister and in fact had his preachers license, although that was not his occupation. I was taught that sex was only for married couples. I didn't necessarily accept this but it must have played a part in my sub-conscious because sex avoided me until I was in my 20 something's. As most teenagers, I pursued it but when it became available wasn't sure how to approach it. There were times I even turned it down because I thought I shouldn't take advantage of a situation or perhaps it was a trap. In retrospect, I suspect some of the girls I dated, quit dating me because they were looking for more excitement than I was giving them.

I even rejected encounters with ladies of ill repute. Once, in the Army, when my friends and I went to St. Louis we asked the taxi driver to take us to a whore house. This he did. We entered the house and were asked to wait in the parlor. Soon a parade of scantily clothed ladies (perhaps ladies is the wrong pronoun) paraded through the room and we were asked to choose one. Two of the guys I was with did but one other fellow and I declined. We of course came up with the excuse that they were too old but in reality we were scared, confused and had not drank enough courage. I also think the price may have entered into our decision.

Another time was, again in the Army, when someone knew where girls worked in the oldest trade, outside of base, in a café/coffee shop. We stopped for a cup of coffee and sure enough a couple girls came and sat at a table with us. They offered their services for $3.00. These were young girls about our age. I didn't feel right about it and I wasn't the only one as two of my friends declined the offer also. Only one soldier accepted. She escorted him out back of the café to a trailer house. He said there were several others there making use of the bedrooms and he was back before we finished our coffee.

An opportunity presented itself to me one time when a young lady wanted me to get a hotel room. I was raring to go and rented the room. I guess, inexperienced as I was at this, I made the mistake of going to a nice, respectable hotel. I liked this lady and wanted her to have clean sheets at the very least. She couldn't help that I was so un-resistible. This was back in the day when some hotels had door men and elevator operators. These people expected tips. Not being a customer of this class of hotel, I was unaware of this tipping practice and did not tip them. The result of that was when the lady and I went to my room, the phone rang almost immediately. It was the front desk telling me that if we didn't leave at once, they would be there to throw us out. We of course did as they requested. So ended that encounter and we were both too embarrassed to pursue it any further.

In the Navy, it seemed like there was always a sailor sleeping with another sailors' wife. I guess the wives get just as horny as their husbands. What do you expect when they are out to sea for six months. One of my buddies had a buddy who had to go away for the weekend so he asked my buddy to stay with his wife in off base housing over the weekend while he was gone, to provide protection for his wife, I imagine from other sailors. I think it was his wife's idea. My buddy took his tooth brush and PJ's and moved in for the weekend with the husbands blessing. In the middle of the night, the wife ventured out to the couch in her lingerie where my buddy was sleeping. She told him she was scared and would he please come sleep with her. What could he do, he promised her husband he would protect her. So he did.

Of course, it wasn't only the wives that were sleeping around and it wasn't only when the husbands were out to sea that the wives were doing the hanky panky. I had a friend whose wife was rumored to be unfaithful to him whenever he had duty and couldn't come home for the night. They were a young married couple, teenagers and she had just joined him in base housing. Prior to that he had been living in the barracks where I was also living. We sometimes had conversations and thus got to know each other and became casual friends. One night when he had duty, his wife called me and asked me to come see her and bring a pizza. She said, by the way my husband has duty so won't be home all night. I told her that was not happening for many reasons. She was not that disappointed, probably because she knew she could find a sailor that would accept her offer and all night it would be offer, honor. Neither did she give up on me. I think she considered me a challenge. She talked her husband into asking me to take her to a job interview because they didn't have a car and he worked day shift while I was off during the day because I was working evening or night shift. This was not a dumb girl. She knew if she asked me, I would refuse but if her husband asked me, I couldn't refuse without an excuse or explanation. She probably had all the lies ready in the event I made accusations about her to her husband. I viewed him as quite naïve when it came to his wife. He trusted her completely which is how it should work in a marriage.

When I picked her up to take her to the interview, she told me the interview had been canceled but wanted me to take her around doing errands while she flashed her legs and other body parts getting in and out of the car in her mini skirt. This I did and must admit enjoyed it until she suggested we go out to a parking area in the woods. The realization hit me that I was being played and was on the verge of giving in to her wiles. I am not that strong and she was clearly an expert at these games while I was a novice. I just turned around and took her home. This time she was very angry.

Just to be clear, I like the female gender very much. God also bestowed an abundance of horny on me but he also gave me uncommon sense. At that time in my life, I would consider a tryst with a single woman, if the conditions were right, however a married woman was off limits to me. This was not because I was standing on high moral ground but for self-preservation. There are many people of both genders that are emotionally unstable. When the jealous emotion kicks in, anything can happen, up to and including death to any of the parties involved. I say live another day and perhaps other opportunities will surface. Try to think with the brain God gave you and use the other parts of your body for what God intended them to be used for. For everything there is a season.

I was staying overnight at a friend's house out of town and had gone to my bedroom to retire for the night. He had a sister whom I knew but had no romantic or sexual inclinations toward. My bedroom for the night was actually her bedroom normally. I viewed her as the little sister but unnoticed by me, over the years she had matured into a good looking and bodily mature girl. As I was undressing for bed, she entered the room and began removing her clothes. She was standing there in her panties and bra and I must admit was quite tempting. I was pursuing another young lady I was fond of and didn't want to ruin my chances with her if she found out. I was also very suspicious of this behavior and imagined perhaps she was pregnant and would try later to convince me I was the father. These were the days before DNA testing. On the other hand, how many opportunities should one turn down? She threw back the covers of the bed and was about to climb in when her Mother called to her through the closed door and wanted to know why she was in my bedroom. Awkward and busted. She made up some excuse like she was looking for clothes to wear for the next day, got dressed and left. I never stayed at that friends' house again.

One time after I was married I went on a business trip to New York City for a week. I usually took my wife, Kathy along when I went out of town on business. Kathy liked to travel and see places she had never been to, do some shopping and read books by the hotel pool. For some reason, Kathy didn't come along on this trip. I stayed at Lowe's hotel just a block from the Waldorf Astoria and a few blocks from the theater district. In the evenings I would eat at one of the nicer places with the Company picking up the tab and then go to a play. It was summer and the weather was pleasant so I walked to Sardi's restaurant right across the street from the theater I was going to and then the play. When the play was over I walked back to my hotel. A block from my hotel as I was walking by the Waldorf Astoria, a very nice looking, well dressed lady approached me and made me an offer she thought I couldn't refuse. The offer was sex for money. I first told her she didn't have enough money. She laughed at my attempt at humor so I then told her she didn't measure up to the standards my wife had set for me and she couldn't compete with my wife, so thanks for the offer but no thanks. I wanted to let her down easy. A girl has to make a living. You can lead a horse to water but you can't lead a horticulture.

So you see, my sex life before marriage was pretty much non-existent and I don't regret it. As a man thinketh, so shall he

This Dummy Pulls His Own Strings

also be. Neither do I regret the tests of my will power. I believe it helped me in my marriage in that I never had the desire to stray or cheat on the one I love. I do enjoy the scenery when the opportunity presents itself. Especially the bikini covered beaches in Hawaii. The one lesson I would like the reader to take away from these experiences is, pull your own strings. You don't have to jump off the proverbial cliff. If you are comfortable with jumping, go for it but on the other hand if you are doing it because everyone else is doing it and you don't want to stand out by being a non-conformist, don't do it. Don't be afraid to take chances but don't let others make bad decisions for you. In making your own bad decisions, ask yourself if you are the only one that is going to get hurt or if you will hurt someone you love.

7
Boxing, Bar fights & other sports

My first introduction to boxing was prior to starting school. My Mother was a member of the Baptist ladies aid. This was a time before Mothers worked outside the home, generally speaking. Two of my lifetime friends, Charles and Mike Toy's Mother was also a member of the same ladies aid. The ladies aid would meet monthly at one of the ladies home. In those days, they didn't hire babysitters. They just took the kids along and the kids would play together while the Mom's did what Mom's do at ladies aid. In this era and at our church, ladies aid was referred to as "Mission Circle". I'm guessing that was because these ladies raised money to support missionaries around the globe.

    The Toy boys had boxing gloves and we would put them on and box with one another. As a preschooler I was a timid child. I didn't have any boys my age I played with regularly, other than my cousin Bill who lived in another town, and I only played with girls, so being aggressive in play and wrestling or fighting was foreign to me. Most of the other boys were used to the aggressive play of boys their age and welcomed it. I didn't want to be a momma's baby so I participated, albeit reluctantly and with great fear. We were quite little so I'm sure there was some crying, probably from me. I think Charlie and Mike were the only ones who knew what they were doing. Their Father had been a boxer and had taught them a little about boxing.

This Dummy Pulls His Own Strings

When I was a Junior in High School, Mike and Charlie Toy talked me into going out for Boxing on the golden gloves boxing team. I reasoned that if I was out for boxing the school bullies would not be as likely to bully me and if they did, I could defend myself. The Toy boys convinced me that it would be fun and I certainly could use the skills I would learn. Up to this point my fighting experience was a sucker punch to a classmate who I kept tackling in physical educational football. He thought they were illegal blocks, which they were, but the guys officiating weren't calling them. Because of our somewhat questionable playing, our side was winning. He told me if I didn't knock it off he was going to pound the crap out of me after school. He was the same size as I was but I had a higher opinion of me than he did, so it didn't intimidate me. I imagined I was more coordinated than he was or at least I assumed I was, because he was a farm boy and it was generally thought that farm boys are uncoordinated when it comes to organized sports. They were good at throwing the bull over the fence, some hay but sports, not so much. Anyway, I continued to pull his chain and when school was over asked him if he was still inclined to clean my clock. Of course, since he made the threat, he couldn't save face and back out. Now who's the bully? He told me he wouldn't fight me around my friends, meaning Charlie and Mike who were known fighters and opined the best and toughest in town, so I suggested we drive out in the country, just the two of us, and may the best man win. He agreed to this and we got in his car and drove out of town about a mile on a graveled road. He parked the car at an approach and we both headed down the ditch and stood facing each other, waiting for the dance to start. I offered to let him throw the first punch but he must have thought it was some kind of a trick because he insisted I start the fight. I obliged him, without ever putting up my guard, gave him a sucker punch to the stomach and the fight was over. It took quite a while for him to breath properly again and when he could talk said he was done fighting. We both got back in his car and he gave me a ride back to town. I digress. Anyway, the point I was making is I could use more boxing skills than a sucker punch.

Boxing provides you with more skills than self defense. You learn motivation, dedication, coping, thinking on your feet, pacing yourself, planning, coordination, ambition, patience as well as pride, to name a few. You enhance your imagination because you even imagine your peers respect you for your courage and skills. Sometimes, just stating that you were a golden gloves boxer kept someone from pounding the crap out of you. I had a Navy buddy that liked to inform anyone that threatened us with bodily harm that I was a golden glove boxer. It didn't always deter them.

I liked that boxing was one of the few sports that you relied on your own skills for your success. You either succeeded or failed mostly on your own. I say mostly on your own, because other boxers taught you skills they already had learned, and of course there was the coach, Mr. Drake. I attribute most of what I learned to Charlie Toy. His brother, Mike was a good fighter also and taught me a lot but Charlie communicated with me better. He explained how it should be done and why this was the best way to do it. I might not have been such a good listener because, according to Charlie, he showed me one time what he was trying to teach me. I have a vague memory of it but Charlie described it for me. This was one time Charlie wasn't pulling his punches. We were sparring and Charlie gave me a solid punch to the solar plexus. We may have taken a short break for me to recover and for me to express my displeasure which didn't hinder Charlie from getting his message across to me. He again hit a solid left to the gut. I assume there was some break and swearing following the second punch but Charlie came back with a third solid punch to the gut. At this point I must have realized I am a slow learner and the cussing wasn't helping because I threw my gloves on the floor and walked away, probably mumbling or cussing under my breath because I was without breath. Mike was also good at showing me. Both of them seemed to pull their punches when teaching me the fundamentals of boxing. Other boxers didn't do that, probably to impress the coach and instill fear in you. Back in the late 50's our high school sports were an after school activity, usually from 4pm to 6pm. The training was much the same for boxing as it was for other sports. Running laps around the gym, running up and down the bleachers, working out on the bags, shadow boxing and sparring with others.

There were some of the boxers that were difficult to spar with because of the different style they had and some that were easy. One that was easy for me was a little guy in my weight class that was determined and had lots of spunk but not many skills. Because of his lack of skills he often became frustrated and angry because he thought of himself as a fighter. One time when I was sparing with him he came charging at me arms and fists just a flying, I stood my ground with my guard up and when he came within arms length, threw my left jab straight and hard. I think his forward charging momentum caused him to run into my jab, perfectly timed, and he landed flat on his butt. Of course, this did not, happy, make him. He got up and repeated the same course of action, as did I. Again he ran into my jab and again he landed flat on his butt. He was really angry at this point and obviously a slow learner, not unlike me, because he repeated it for the third time with the same result. I think the coach came over at this point and paired us up with different sparring partners. I don't know if he learned anything from it but I certainly learned that getting angry doesn't help you and generally hurts you. I also learned, if something isn't working, you should probably try something else. The first thing you should do when you find yourself in a hole is to stop digging.

We only had a few matches a year probably because we were the only high school around with a boxing team. There was a team in Parshall, ND, The Minot Air Force Base and The Mandan Training school which was a school for Juvenile Delinquents (tough guys), Fargo, Washburn, Velva, Whapeton and a few other schools. I don't know how the coach chose the boxers for matches in a boxing card. I know that most of the cards had the best boxers in their weight class. There were 20 to 30 boxers at Drake and each boxing card only had 10 matches. I was chosen to fight in boxing cards two to three times. Why I was chosen is still a mystery to me, I didn't think I was the best boxer in my weight class. I suspect it was because I bled a lot and often and the crowd liked blood. Perhaps I was the sacrificial lamb.

I also fought in a boxing card in Sidney, MT after I had graduated from high school. The coach at Parshall often needed boxers for cards he was organizing. When this happened he would call Charlie to see if any of us from Drake wanted to fight. The coach at Parshall also owned a bar there and he had a picture of all the boxers that had fought for him on the wall in his bar. I stopped in to see him once in the latter years but he was in ill health so I didn't get to see him but my picture was on the wall in the bar. I lost the fight at Sidney but true to my usual form, I bled all over my opponent. I did make it all three rounds. I never lost by a KO or TKO. All my losses and there were many, were by the judges decision. I admit, it wasn't a difficult decision. Obviously, my guard wasn't all that good and invariably I would get hit in the nose and it would always bleed. I should have been protecting my nose instead of my solar plexus.

At the fight in Drake, I was fighting a guy from Fargo by the name of Leslie Large. I thought he lived up to his name of Large but I actually had him in weight. He was 128 lbs and I was 133. However, he was a former District champion. I smoked all through high school and drank alcohol whenever it was available. My opponent, and most everyone, was in much better shape than I was and by the time I got to the third round, I was just hoping I could keep from getting knocked out. Here is where staying power, determination and thinking on your feet come into play. I think it was in the second round when he broke my nose. That started the blood and I could no longer breathe through my nose. I really guarded my nose from that point on, in fact, my focus for the rest of the fight was protecting my nose. I was very careful when jabbing or throwing punches not to leave any openings that allowed him to hit my nose. There was a lot of clinching by me. I figured if I was hugging him, it would be difficult for him to hit me in the nose again. Also, while hugging him, I bled all over him. This made it look like he was in as bad a shape as I was because he was covered in blood. He won on a unanimous decision.

This Dummy Pulls His Own Strings

After the fight I went to the locker room and cleaned up. My nose was really hurting and crooked. I tried moving it around to straighten it and all of a sudden it went back into place and didn't hurt anymore except if I would press on it too hard. I could even wear my glasses. Later in life, Drs asked me if I had ever broken my nose because I had a deviated septum.

My Mother wouldn't come to the boxing matches but my Dad was there to see me get pummeled. At least he learned I wasn't a quitter but he probably also learned, I was not too bright but stubborn.

Boxing was the only sport in high school I lettered in. I played other varsity sports but wasn't good enough to letter. I played basketball and even made the A squad for a couple games but you had to score points to letter. I blew my chance at that. I think the coach had to put me in at the end of one game because everyone else had fouled out. It was a close game and as I remember it there was just a few seconds left, we were one point behind and I had the ball coming down the court. I was fouled so the game rested on my shoulders. If I make one free throw, we're tied, if I make them both, we win. No pressure. I missed them both and we lost. I was not a popular person in school for a few days. That may have been when I decided to go out for boxing for self-preservation. I actually liked playing on the B basketball team better than the varsity team because I was on the first string on the B team and got to play a lot more which was the whole point of going out for basketball. I even scored points on occasion.

I also went out for track all four years of high school. My track coach called me Marlboro butt. Marlboro was a brand of cigarettes and the coach knew I smoked, thus the nickname. I had a lot of fun but didn't excel at anything and thus never earned a letter. I really liked football but was told I wasn't big enough to play football. I should not have listened and played anyway, just for the fun but at least I don't have any old football injuries.

When I was a Junior in High School I joined the ND Army National Guard. We had meetings once a week in Harvey, ND for a couple hours. Every summer we would go to summer camp for two weeks near Devils Lake where we would play soldiers and drink beer. We also got paid for this. A pretty good deal for a 17 year old. We were a Combat Engineer Co. It was our job to make potable water from lake water for the rest of the ND National Guard companies. Towards the end of the two weeks, all the companies in the ND Guards would compete in Boxing and Wrestling. My company commander had seen me fight in a Golden Gloves match in Drake so he was aware I boxed and bled. He asked me to compete in this Guard sporting competition. I agreed and one of my buddies by the name of "Tiny" Hirschcorn was asked to compete in Wrestling. Tiny was a big boy and strong and he had been wrestling in high school so was very competent. Several years after this I ran into Tiny at a bar in Minot. He was the bouncer there. By agreeing to compete for our company, we got special treatment so we could train. We got out of many of the less than desirable tasks they liked to assign to the lower ranking enlisted men, like KP (Kitchen Police). I still haven't figured out why they call it kitchen police. There is no policing of anything other than brooms, mops and potato peelers.

We did a lot of running, shadow boxing, working on the heavy and speed bags, jumping rope etc. A couple days before the matches, we weighed in. I discovered I was a couple lbs. over the weight limit for my usual weight class, probably because of all the beer I was drinking. The next couple days I did a lot of running, sweating and spitting to lose a couple lbs. It worked and I was able to qualify for my usual weight class. The night of the fight, as usual, I didn't eat an evening meal. There are two reasons for this. One is to be sure I wasn't too heavy for my weight class and the other was so I wouldn't get physically sick during the fight. Generally, I would get butterflies prior to a fight but once I got in the ring, everything was fine. After the weigh in, prior to the fight, I warmed up by working out a little on the heavy bag and speed bag and did some shadow boxing. This was mostly to show off and try to intimidate the competition. Part of any sport is mind games, trying to intimidate your opponent. I had to wait for my fight because there were a few fights prior to mine and all the wrestling matches. I think my fight was the next to last fight. The warm up to the main event.

Tiny won his weight class wrestling match which wasn't a surprise. He was fast, well built and in good shape. Me, I had been to a bon fire the night before, drinking beer and smoking cigarettes and singing songs. I recognized some of the officers in the ring side seats from the night before. One Major who had been on the opposite side of the bon fire, had heard me singing quite loud and had come over and put his arm around me, told me he liked my voice and asked if we could harmonize together on "the old mill stream". If I had any thought process at that point, I probably thought, it couldn't hurt to have friends in high places. I certainly wasn't going to say no, go back to your side of the bon fire. So we started harmonizing to the old mill stream, Capella, barber shop or just drunks singing. We did this for one song after another until our voices played out. I was having a good time and I thought I would never see the guy again but here he was, ring side. I believe he recognized me and probably was taking bets from his fellow officers. He was probably betting against me because he knew I had been partying the previous night.

The guy I was to fight for the championship was a skinny guy, slightly taller than me which meant he had longer arms, therefore a longer reach. That meant I probably should do a lot of counter punching. When he throws a punch, block it or duck it and quickly throw a punch. It sounds easy enough but in the heat of battle, it doesn't always work the way you planned it.

The first round started with each of us kind of feeling out our opponent. A few jabs, a lot of clinches and the referee breaking us apart. I got a couple lucky punches in, one of which really seemed to hurt him. The ring side cheering section of officers was hollering for me to go get him and finish him off. This was a bit unusual for me. Usually I was the one that was bleeding all over everyone and my opponent was trying to finish me off. I was thinking this is kind of fun. If I finish him off, the fun ends. At this point I was pretty much having my way with him but wasn't really trying to knock him out, just showing off and scoring points because most fights were won or lost by a decision of the judges and referee.

When the round ended my coach was after me to go get him and end it before he recovered. The officer cheering section was going crazy when the second round began. I began to actively pursue him. It was more difficult than I had imagined because he was trying to stay away from me. His coach probably told him to stay away and hope for a decision. He was backing up faster than I could go after him. I managed to get him on the ropes a time or two but he either clinched or the referee broke it up. About half way through the round, I got lucky. I landed a solid left jab that caused him to drop his guard. As soon as his guard dropped, I followed it with a right cross to the side of the head and I could see in his eyes it had hurt him. This time I didn't hesitate but followed it with a hard left uppercut to the jaw. His knees buckled and he went down, prone, flat on his back, hello canvas. I went to a neutral corner while the referee did the 10 count. He was down longer than the 10 count and I was beginning to worry that I had really hurt him but he came to and was trying to get up to continue the fight. He didn't know it was over. The first fight I had won by a knock out. Probably the first fight I didn't bleed all over my opponent. The crowd was going wild, most of them from my company plus the ringside officer section. I guess I did my job and got the crowd warmed up for the main event.

The main event was between a fellow from our battalion and another battalion and it was a heavyweight fight. I don't think either of them had ever been in the ring before or had on a pair of boxing gloves. It was a slug fest of trading punches. Neither one was too careful about their guard, just bring it on, is that all you got. I thought the guy from our battalion was better at taking punches than the other guy and I believe he took more. He did land some good hard punches that would have had me kissing the canvas. It was a good fight that went the distance and I believe our guy lost by a split decision. I thought it could have gone either way.

The next day they had a presentation of trophies. There were two of us in our company that had won fights. With both Tiny and I winning our fights, it gave our company the most points and our company won the overall competition trophy. It was a huge trophy about 3 feet tall. Your tax dollars at work. Each of us who won our matches were presented smaller trophies, six inches high. Mine was engraved with "Boxing Champ, North Dakota Army National Guard, 145 lb., 1962". For the presentation, we were called up to the stage individually, saluted, received the trophy, shook hands, saluted again, did an about face and exited, stage left. What a production. After the ceremony, there was picture taking and that week, Tiny and I had our picture on the front page of the Harvey Herald with the story of our individual conquests. The Army sent us copies of the picture and the Harvey Herald newspaper.

Dwight & Tiny Hirschcorn with boxing and wrestling trophy's

I don't know if it was imagined or real, probably just wishful thinking, but some of the guys in our company treated us with a little more respect after that. One guy, Paul Miller, who owned a clothing store in Harvey and was in the guards, came up to me and said, "I didn't know you were a boxer. You pal around with the Toy boys in Drake, don't you? That's a pretty tough crowd, isn't it?" My answer was that, yes the "Toy Boys" were two of my closest friends and most of my friends are in boxing, if that is what you mean by a tough crowd. And yes, if you cross them or give them reason to, they will punch out your lights but they will then pick you up, give you their last cigarette or beer and will be your friend. I guess the rumor mill was in full gear prolonging my moment of fame.

While I was in the Navy, my good buddy and cube mate Jim Gulbranson, would inform anyone that made threats to us that I was a former Golden Glove boxer. I threatened to use my boxing skills on him if he continued to do that. I guess it was helpful because I never had to prove it. Perhaps that knowledge made them think twice about taking on two skinny guys.

There was one fellow who was also a friend and cube mate of mine at one time, who was a self proclaimed martial arts fighter. He was from the Bronx of New York and usually a very nice fellow. He would tie a bean bag from the ceiling about head height and practice kicking it. He would also dance around the cube shadow boxing and doing martial arts moves. He would thrust his hands into a container that had dried beans in it to build calluses on his fingers. He claimed he was the holder of a black belt. He was about 5' 10" well built and in good physical shape. He was also black but that never was an issue in our relationship. In fact, we both arrived at base about the same time for the class A computer school and while we were waiting for the next class to start, they had us painting anything that didn't move. We painted side by side for weeks so got to know a little about each other. One Friday after a day of painting, he was planning to catch a bus to New York for the week end. The Chief told us when we got our brushes cleaned we would be done for the week. I told him to take off and I would clean everything up and put it all away so he wouldn't miss his bus because I wasn't going anywhere for the weekend anyway. He thanked me profusely over and over. I, not thinking or even remembering that he was colored, said, " don't worry about

This Dummy Pulls His Own Strings

it buddy, I'd do the same for a white man." He thought that was hilarious and was still laughing as he left to catch his bus.

That was a saying we used to say to each other in ND as kids where we never saw black or people of color. When you said it to one of your white friends, it was meant as an insult, inferring he was black. Kids can be cruel. Discrimination was still present, even in the north and perpetuated by those of us who thought of ourselves as unbigoted. I realized what I had done when he started laughing but it was too late then and we made jokes about it the whole time we were stationed together. He'd come up to several of us and say where are you guys headed. We'd tell him, to chow or the movie or whatever we were doing. He'd say, do you mind if I come along and of course we'd say no, we don't mind. You're welcome to join us and he'd say, you're not going to make me walk a few paces behind, are you? So we had a good relationship and were friends.

One time, I don't remember what precipitated it but for some reason he wanted to fight with me and was really serious about it and appeared angry. I told him he would regret it because he would get all bloody (probably my blood) and broken and parts of his face would probably be moved from one side to the other. He, in turn, told me he would plunge his hand in my chest cavity and remove my heart and hand it to me. I didn't think that was actually possible but wasn't quite ready to find out, because I was pretty sure I needed my heart, beating inside me, so I told him I wasn't going to fight with him and apologized for whatever misunderstanding we had. He took that as a victory and backed off. I still don't know what set him off but we were friends again after that. Perhaps, someone suggested that a boxer could take a black belt. Who knows, someone was probably trying to stir the pot.

With Jim advertising that I was a Golden Glove boxer, It was common knowledge in the barracks. We had a nice gym on base complete with weights, mats and all the equipment you could want including boxing gloves. One fellow wanted me to teach him how to box. I think he may have been an Iowa farmer. He was a very large boy about 6 feet tall and weighing about 250 or at least I thought so. He reminded me of Hoss Cartwright on Bonanza. I was 5'8" and weighed about 140. I explained that in boxing there were weight classes so you fought someone that was in your own weight class. He maintained he didn't want to box with me he just wanted me to teach him what I knew. I figured that should take less than a minute so I finally agreed to it.

After teaching him what I knew about boxing, he wanted to spar a little to try out his new found skills and knowledge. He was a lot like some of the street fighters I've seen. He wanted to kill you with one punch. Me, being lighter and smaller, I could move in and quickly land a few jabs and move back outside his reach. He wasn't a dumb kid and he quickly figured out what he had to do. I knew if he ever connected with even a jab with his weight behind it, I would be hurting or not feeling anything at all. He wasn't in as good as shape as me and because of his size, quickly tired out. Eventually the law of averages caught up and he connected with a good solid punch. I told him I thought he had learned enough for one day and we quit for the day. We went back several more times but I taught him how to pull his punches so he wouldn't kill me. I believe I had several more students but none as big as he was.

While in the Navy, stationed at Bainbridge, MD, my buddy Jim Gulbranson and I would go to Lancaster, PA about an hours' drive from base. We went there for several reasons, mostly because it was a relatively small town as opposed to New York, Philadelphia, Baltimore or Washington, D.C. It was located in Amish country and it was interesting to see how the Amish people lived. It was also fun to talk to the young Amish girls, flirt with them and watch the reaction of their parents, especially their fathers. I think many of them talked to us just to get a reaction from their parents or as an act of rebellion. Jim and I also frequented the shopping district of Lancaster, especially a department store by the name of Watt & Shand, where we both had credit accounts. It was a clothing store and it allowed us to stay fashionable in civilian clothes and learn what the "in" thing was from the clerks at the store, many who were young females and up to date on fashion. We wore civilian clothes most of the time when we went off base because of the Viet Nam war and the opposition to it. It was better most of the time if no one knew you were a sailor, unless you were looking for a fight. After we purchased our civilian clothes, we would take it to the tailor shop on base and have it tailored so it fit perfectly. We would do this with our uniforms also. Aside from that, we liked Lancaster because it had a USO and we liked to go there to dance with the USO girls and on occasion get a date with one. There was a bar right across the street from the USO and we were both 21 so before, during and after the dances we would wonder over for a glass of courage. Usually I drank only beer because hard liquor was not a friend to me.

For whatever reason on this particular evening I was mixing the beer with an occasional Old Fashioned. I guess because I like them. They had a band playing at the bar and I think we spent more time at the bar than the USO club. I know I was feeling no pain but was in great spirits and having a great time. I remember standing towards the back of the bar talking to a guy I didn't know or had ever seen before. The guy reminded me of my wrestling buddy, Tiny. Maybe in my drunken state, I thought it was Tiny. I believe Jim was dancing because he wasn't around. The next thing I was aware of I was standing facing the guy I had been talking to with my guard up in a boxing stance. I don't know if he said something that offended me or if I said something to anger him. I didn't even see the punch coming but there I was sitting on the bar room floor.

Two bar tenders jumped the bar and before I could get to my feet, each took hold of an arm, lifted me up and literally carried/dragged me out of the bar and deposited me on the sidewalk. The sidewalk went from the bar to the street and there were some no parking signs next to the street. As I drunkenly assessed the situation, I saw three colored guys standing there looking at me. Again, I don't know if they started something with me or if I initiated it but the next thing I know I'm duking it out with one of them. I had him backing up and was backing him toward the no parking zone sign when this new mustang pulls up to the curb and the passenger door opens and I hear the driver holler for me to get in. I sort of hated to leave the fight that I thought I might have a chance of winning but then I thought of his two buddies, I quickly took my buddy Jim up on his offer and got in his car. Jim squealed out of there and headed back for base. I had a really sore jaw the next day but because of Jim's quick action, nothing more. I guess he witnessed the bar tenders literally throw me out and he went out the back door, retrieved the car and picked me up. It's good to have buddies that have your back.

After the Navy, while dating Kathy, I felt it was my duty or should I say right, to threaten any of her former boyfriends or guys that showed an interest in her. Generally they were more civilized and sober than I was and didn't want to fight. One guy took me to his car for a private conversation and told me what a wonderful person Kathy was and how I should value our relationship and realize what I had. I, being not so articulate, probably told him I was aware of what I had which is why I was going to punch his lights out if he didn't stay away from her. At any rate we drank a few beer and parted friendly.

One weekend while working at the Bank in Grand Forks, one of my good friends, Danny Schaefer, was coming to Grand Forks from Drake to see his Dad who had a stroke and was in the hospital. I arranged for him to bring Kathy along and for her to stay with my boss and his wife and kids. Danny had just returned from fighting a war in Vietnam. A war that was unpopular for many reasons. The military fighting it were not the ones that should have been persecuted. These soldiers were made to do things and witnessed things that no one should ever see or experience. In a war, you follow orders or you may end up a casualty yourself. If they can't blame your death on the enemy they chalk it up to friendly fire. Both Danny and I were Vietnam veterans, the difference being Danny was actually in Vietnam. My contribution to the war was having my enlistment extended six months but serving it on US soil. Anyway, I thought it would be good if Danny could forget the war and take his mind off his Dad's stroke.

So, Kathy, Danny and I went to the American Legion, of which Danny and I were members, for some party time. They had a black jack table there as well as a band and a dance floor. Kathy and I did a lot of dancing and occasionally Danny would come to dance with Kathy and tell me to take over for him at the Black Jack table using his money. We were celebrating pretty good and long and closed up the Legion. When we came out of the Legion we went to my car which was a 1965 Mercury Comet that I had bought new for $1,800.00. This was 1966 so it was still a new car to me. We got in my car, I started it up and the next thing I knew the car in front, backed into me. It then pulled forward and backed into me again and kept repeating the process. I opened my car door and flew out of the car and went up to the driver and started cussing him out. He got out of his car and I was ready to tear him apart but as he exited his vehicle, it was more like he unfolded. He must have been 7 feet tall. He was apologizing profusely and as I looked up to him, literally, my anger dissipated. I accepted his apology and went back to my car where Kathy and Danny were laughing hysterically. I don't think they ever did stop laughing until I dropped them off at their respective abodes. Another lesson in keeping your anger under control.

After I married Kathy, my bar hopping & drinking days diminished. I had seen what happens to a marriage when one or the other of the partners go out drinking without their partner. It generally doesn't make a happy or long lasting marriage. Other than a few beer at the bowling alley when bowling with my bowling team or a few drinks at supervisors club, I generally took Kathy with me if we were going drinking at a club or bar. This I found to be a good practice. Many of my friends who didn't do this, had relatively short marriages.

After I was married, I joined a bowling team with some of the guys I worked with. One night a week we would bowl league bowling. I maintained about a 152 average, nothing to brag about but it provided my team with some handicap. Our team did win the league championship a couple years which provided some trophy's to occupy space next to my boxing trophy. I also picked up a 7/10 split which provided me with a patch for my bowling shirt. I was a consistent bowler but with that much room for improvement, it kind of left me frustrated when I couldn't accomplish that goal. Rather than put the effort into a sport that was supposed to be relaxing and enjoyable, I relaxed, enjoyed and maintained. When it became too frustrating, I gave it up.

For several summers I played slow pitch softball. I played mostly fielder positions but on occasion would play infield, first base or shortstop and catcher once or twice. I enjoyed it but many of the players were die-hard players and thought the game was all about competition and winning. I, on the other hand, thought it was about camaraderie and exercise and perhaps the beer after the game. When it got to be an obligation to play rather than looking forward to it, I gave it up to spend more time with my wife and kids.

8
My Hometown

The things that count most in life are the things that can't be counted.
                                                    Zig Ziglar

My hometown or home village, Drake, ND is also my place of birth. That isn't true anymore for most of the people that claim Drake as their hometown because there no longer is a hospital there, so therefore very few births. I say very few, because I imagine there are those who choose to have home birthing and then there are North Dakota blizzards which would necessitate a home birth.

When I was born, it was a farming community in central North Dakota located on U.S. Highway 52 about 50 miles east of Minot, 100 miles north of Bismarck, 100 miles west of Jamestown and 100 miles south of the Canadian border. It was named after the founder of the village, Herman Drake. Several of his descendants lived there at the time I occupied space there. I have a straight edge razor with his name engraved on it, probably acquired at an auction sale.

It is a village of mostly German ancestry but several miles away is the village of Kief which is Ukrainian ancestry. There are also others who came from European countries but the population in the area was predominately German. Some families even spoke German in their homes and most of us could say a few German words, most of them profanity. My grandparents emigrated from Berlin, Germany but I believe they were of Danish ancestry prior to that. (see chapter, Family-Heritage)

Drake has had no famous/infamous characters although just 25 miles west of Drake is the village of Velva where the newsman Eric Sevareid, a WWII war correspondent for CBS news, was born. One hundred miles in the other direction is Jamestown where the singer Patti Page and author Louis L'amour hailed from.

Probably Drake's most famous citizen was the medical Dr. at the local clinic. He was the most intelligent and educated citizen as well as a compassionate and caring individual. I ran across this article by Jen Rosel Juenger, a former resident of Drake and with her permission have included it here.

A Simple Country Doctor-An International Hero

In 1981, I met the smartest man I've ever known.

His name was Dr. Bohdan Hordinsky, and for most of the time I knew him, I only knew him as a small-town, country doc, who had a thick accent, and a brain full of knowledge. I didn't really learn about *him* until 1991, when they had Doc's 80th birthday. By then he was "semi-retired", which means he worked most mornings, and took afternoons off, except when someone called and needed to see him, or he was bored, or because he simply wanted to go back to work.

Because to Doc Hordinsky, working *was* life. And serving others was his mission and joy. He was a true hero, around the world. And most people have never heard of him.

But those that met him once, never *ever* forgot him.

Doc was born in 1911 in the Western Ukraine to an aristocratic, intellectual family of scientists and artists. The Hordinsky family has always held scholarly pursuits in high esteem, something that was passed on from his parents, and that he, in turn, passed on to his children. This was to be true throughout his life, and he passed this on to everyone he met.

Doc survived many things with his family, including being in occupied countries during World War II. He graduated from Medical School in Lviv, Ukraine in 1935, even having as one of his teachers – the father of psychiatry – Sigmund Freud, who Doc claims taught him how to listen. He recalled "Freud told us, 'Take as much time as you need with each patient. Don't look at your watch, but if you have to, take his pulse – and then look.'"

Dr. Hordinsky was, at various times, the physician to some very prominent people in the Ukraine. Including during World War II. I personally was told by Doc that he was Josef Stalin's personal physician for a while. He also told me that he used to watch another famous man walk to work every day, before he became famous. This man was Adolf Hitler. I asked him once about that, and whether he was ever tempted to "not" take care of those men, especially after learning what those men were doing in his country. But he was a dedicated man, and his Hippocratic Oath was his life's motto. *First do no harm.*

As WWII raged around him, Doc provided what aid he could to Jews that were being shunned, then persecuted. He treated their medical needs when others were being executed for simply providing them with food. When the Jews were in hiding, and someone would die, Doc would quietly sneak the bodies out, piece by piece, in his doctor's bag, so that they would not be found by the Germans.

He was also pursued by the Germans, who wanted him to serve in the SS as their doctor, because he was considered the "Perfect Aryan". Doc, however was "always too sick". He would fake high blood pressure with caffeine shots, and sugar injections to emulate the onset of diabetes.

When Doc finally escaped the war with his family, including his wife, Irene and children, Jerry and Walter, he came to the United States, searching for the chance for his children to learn and grow in an environment of freedom. His daughter Maria was born some years later, in the same year he opened his office in my hometown.

Once, I was given a chance to ask him some questions for a research paper, and he told me about coming to the United States, and his welcome, and his reason for moving his family to North Dakota. He told me "When we came to the States, I applied to many hospitals, and they all told me that they didn't want a *German* doctor, because people were bitter about the war. When we were offered a home, and practically *begged* by the community to come to North Dakota, which was so much like our beloved Ukraine, we jumped at the chance. We have never regretted our decision. And when those large-city hospitals came back to me, years later, and begged me to come to them, because of my reputation, I told them 'You didn't want me when I first got here because of my heritage, and now I don't want you because of the same reason.' Even though we were Ukrainian, not German, it didn't matter. I was welcomed with my family into this community with open and grateful arms, and I could not turn my back on those people."

Doc did many things that gained him world-wide renown, including helping to develop medication to dissolve gallstones, which was later discovered to also lower cholesterol. He specialized in skin diseases and allergies. He had remarkable success with a medicine to control asthma. But he was always certain that the real key was the patients.

In 1987 a newspaper in Fargo quoted him as saying "You can trust machines too much; of course, machines are good, but they make mistakes... some physicians rely so much on sophisticated equipment that they forget to *listen* to the patient."

In 1991, my hometown held something called "Doctor Hordinsky Days". It was a celebration of their most-famous and most-humble physician. A map of the globe was placed on a stand, and everyone that came put a pin in the map for where they came from. There were pins in that map from all over the world, including Japan.

Doc and his wife, Irene, also traveled back to their beloved Ukraine on a regular basis, taking supplies like shoes and other things that we take for granted back with them. They would even buy a car, have it stripped of the valuable things, like the stereo (because they would be stolen and sold on the black market), and they would give these things away when they got there.

For the whole time I knew the Doc, he always prized education above all.

Doc never charged the teachers that came to see him, or their families. He wanted them to spend their money on other things, not on him. He knew that small-town teachers don't get paid much, and he wanted to give back to his community as much as he could.

I always swore that Doc had a photographic memory. He had a wall in his office that was full of nothing but medical books and magazines. If you had a question, he would go to exactly the magazine or book he wanted, flip to the page, and point out exactly the answer.

He was an amazing man, a true hero to all the people that met him, and is greatly missed by the community. He diagnosed Eldest Daughter's allergy to milk, when we couldn't figure out what was making her sick all the time. His advice? "One serving of milk a day, and no more. She will grow out of it, given time." He was right.

Doc Hordinsky was a simple country doctor.

Doctor Bohdan Z. Hordinsky was an International Hero.

He was a man who loved his family, his community, and his work. In that order.

P.S. I forgot to add earlier, that much of the information for this post, other than personal quotes he told me himself, came from the Doctor Hordinsky Cookbook that was created and published by my hometown, in honor of the Doc, for the celebration in 1991.

End of article by Jen Rosel Juenger

I recall as a lad, being bitten by a dog on my paper route. It was after hours, probably about 7:30 pm when I called the Dr. at his home and told him what had happened to me. He asked me to come to his home so that he could look at it. I only lived a block and ½ from him so went over to his home and knocked on the door. It was obvious that the family was in the middle of their evening meal but he immediately examined my dog bit leg, gave me a tetanus shot, called the local police to have them capture the dog and keep it to insure it didn't have rabies, for the specified amount of time. I'm sure his dinner was cold by the time he finished with me. I asked him how much I owed him and he said, "there is no charge".

On another occasion after I was an adult and married and lived elsewhere, I was home to visit my parents and my wife's parents. My Dad took me aside and told me he was having some health problems and one of them was blood in his urine. There was lots of blood and I panicked and called Dr. Hordinsky at home. I would guess it was about 8:00 pm. I described the problem and doc told me over the phone that it more than likely was prostate cancer. He no doubt could tell I was panicky and he tried to reassure me that it was a slow growing cancer and it wasn't an emergency. He could tell from my questions that I was not well informed and he told me to come to his home so we could sit down and talk, face to face. This I did and he proceeded to explain what was happening and what we should do. He recommended that I take Dad to see his Dr. in Williston where my sisters lived and his Dr. there could determine what was going on. This way he would have my sisters for support because I would be going back home and to work soon. I called my sisters, packed up my parents and off to Williston we went, immediately. His diagnosis was correct without ever even seeing my Dad.

On another occasion, I went to see the Dr. during office hours. I was about 15 or 16 and had a wart growing on my lip. I was very much interested in girls but thought I might not have a lot of success with the fairer sex with a wart on my lip. I couldn't imagine any of the girls wanting to kiss a wart, even if it would turn into a prince. I showed the Doc my wart and asked if there was something that could be done about it. He seemed to be quite excited about it and went to his wall of shelves of books, retrieved one and opened it and showed me the explanation of what it was and how to treat it. What was amazing to me was how fast he found the right book, on the first try and then turned right to the page in the book he was looking for, without consulting an index or anything. I was so impressed by this that I hardly noticed the article.

He told me he could freeze my lip, burn the wart off and give it a couple stitches. He said in no time there would be no trace of it ever being there but there was a slight chance it could come back. I told him to go ahead and do it. There was no signing of papers or calling my parents for their OK, he just went ahead with the procedure. As I recall, it was painless and you could barely notice the stitches. Anyone that noticed, I probably told I bit my lip or someone punched me. You should see the other guy. It healed just fine like the Doc said it would and left no visible scar. Because I was at his office and his employees frowned on him not charging his patients, there was a small charge but it was so small I'm sure it raised some eyebrows of his employees.

I had the privilege of being friends with Jerry, Dr. & Mrs. Hordinsky's youngest son, for about a year. During that year I was able to witness the family life of these fine people. Jerry had the same ability as his father of instant recall of facts and where to find the printed verification of the facts. He could tell you what page, paragraph and sentence an answer to a test in school could be found and because of this ability, could win all arguments with the teachers. It was rare for him not to have a perfect score on tests and only happened when it was a trick question or if the question could be interpreted several ways. I soon learned that it was a losing battle to argue with Jerry about anything. The difference between us was, I thought I was always right but Jerry always was right and could prove it. Because of his intelligence and ability, his parents sent him away to military school after the 8th grade because they felt the local school wasn't a challenge to his learning abilities. We lost touch and went our separate ways.

Drake was/is a farming community. A farming community is one that is supported by the farms around it and its existence depends on those farms. When I was growing up the small farms consisted of from 40 acres to probably about 300 acres. Each farm was lived on by a family with several children and most had houses, barns, machine sheds, granaries and perhaps a chicken coop. The farms generally raised grain to sell as well as hay and feed for the livestock. Some farms would raise cattle for the production of milk and cream, called dairy farms and some would raise cattle for the beef and/or pigs for the pork. Many would also raise chickens, ducks, geese and turkeys. The farmers would sell the eggs where they did their grocery shopping and the milk or cream at the creameries in the local towns. The poultry generally was for their own use. My mother would can chicken in the canning jars. It was a simple matter to open a jar of chicken, heat it up on the stove and have your meat for a meal. This was often the solution when unexpected guests were there for a meal. The canned chicken was also good eaten cold right out of the jar.

When I was a child it was customary and polite when someone was at your home around meal time to ask them to join you for the meal. Often times they would politely decline but in my parents case, they were quite good at convincing them to stay and break bread together. My mother was an excellent cook and could whip up something in no time. We always had fresh bread and baked goods as well as winters supply of home canned goods, including fruits, vegetables and meats.

The farmers would buy whatever supplies they needed in the town that generally was closest to them or where the best sales were. Such a town was Drake. The village of Drake was where the farmers came to buy the groceries that were not grown and preserved on the farm as well as farm machinery they needed and the things they needed in the operation of the farm.

In addition to the farmers that supported the businesses of Drake, there were railroad people who lived, worked and shopped in Drake. The Soo Line railroad was on the edge of town with a depot at the south end of main street and a roundhouse was located just west of town. The purpose of a round house, as I understand it, is to turn the train engines around. Trains don't do U turns.

The business community of Drake had two hotels and cafes. The railroad people were the main ones utilizing those services but the towns people frequented the cafes, especially for coffee and catching up on gossip. There were two grain elevators the farmers could sell their grain at or buy coal or feed. There was a

Farmers Union gas station/garage and store that sold fertilizer and things farmers frequently purchased. In addition there was anywhere from two to four more gas stations and garages. There were three to four farm implement dealers and three car/truck dealers. We had a Laundromat, bakery, a bank, a drugstore, two hardware stores, a post office, a general store, a J.C. Penny store, two grocery stores in addition to the general store that also sold clothes and groceries.

Drake had a funeral home, two Lutheran churches, one was a German speaking church, one Catholic Church, one Baptist church and one Evangelical United Brethren (EUB) church that later merged with the Methodists. There were also some country churches that still had services. Two were Lutheran, one south of Drake and one north of Drake and there was a Baptist country church with its own pastor south of Drake. This was one ND village that the churches outnumbered the bars. We did have three bars and at one time a bowling alley. There was a Creamery that bought and sold milk and cream and had a butcher shop and freezer plant that rented freezer lockers. There was a wholesale house that sold items such as tobacco, candy, snacks and various items to all the stores/bars in Drake and the surrounding villages. There was also one to two more creameries that bought cream from the farmers and shipped it by rail.

We had the Soo Line depot and passenger trains several times a day as well as many freight trains. There was a Movie Theater that had movies on week-ends. We had a weekly newspaper that printed all the gossip about who was at whose house for coffee and everyone's ailments, vacations, trips and guests. It was a busy and prosperous community. Probably the most notable business was the medical clinic and our Dr. Hordinsky. This brought people from far and wide to seek his wisdom and cure their ailments.

All the farmers would come to town on Saturday nights to do their shopping, visiting with friends and neighbors, take in a movie and perhaps have a cold beverage at one of the bars. The two blocks of Main Street would be packed with parked cars, Kids would be running up and down the sidewalks playing with their friends. The businesses would pool their resources and have drawings giving away prizes or money. This was a community where everyone knew everyone else and they knew more about you than you would have liked them to know.

This was a community that attended church and had a strong moral fiber. Wednesday night was considered a church night so school activities were not scheduled on Wednesday evenings. The Baptists believed that dancing was a sin and fought having dances in the school or city. I think the city fathers just tired of fighting the Baptists and didn't allow dances in the city until after I was out of school. We never had any school dances, street dances or city hall dances while I was in school except for the prom. We all went to dances in the surrounding villages, even the Baptists. There were dances at Anamoose, Karlshrue, Butte, Balfour and Orrin. Most of them were wedding dances and were free but there would be an occasional pay for dance like New Years' Eve. Surprising that when the Baptist church closed its doors permanently, the city of Drake started renting out the city hall for dances and having street dances. At least that's how it appeared to me. I wasn't living there anymore so don't know the history and/or gossip leading up to allowing dances.

I'm not faulting the Baptists' for their beliefs' or for fighting for what they believe in, they provided me with a good Christian upbringing that has served me well. However, I do disagree with them on the dancing issue. I found dancing good entertainment as well as good exercise and before I was married, a good way to make a pretty ladies acquaintance. A good social venue for the single people. After I was married, I never was comfortable dancing with anyone but my wife. To me it just didn't feel right. Also, I was not that great of a dancer when I danced with anyone else but when dancing with my wife we just clicked. Just proves how talented Kathy was. That's just me and I believe dancing to be good for anyone, single or married.

I am no longer a Baptist, partly because my wife is Lutheran and I liked the Lutheran religion. It seemed to me, the Lutheran religion promoted Love and forgiveness above judgment of others and how they live their life. Kind of a "Live and let Live" philosophy. The Lutheran philosophy seemed to be, we will explain salvation as we believe it and let you decide. Some religions try to force feed their beliefs, rather than letting God do his work after you've made the information available. This philosophy I learned from my parents who would try to lead you to Christ and salvation but after giving you the information would allow you to come to your own decision without the added pressure. The only person you can change is yourself. They relied on prayer and God to do his work in His own time. They never gave up and prayed for you, endlessly, and had faith that their prayers would be answered. I remember them praying for certain individuals all the time I lived in their home and those individuals eventually became a Christian years later.

I also noticed that many Baptists preached one thing and did the opposite such as condemning dancing, drinking and playing cards but doing it anyway. This is not unique to Baptists but to me, probably because they have more "thou shalt nots", it seemed more prevalent in the Baptist religion. At an early age, 17, I was able to "make" or be served at many of the local bars, usually for takeout but occasionally would be allowed to stay and have a few drinks. I would notice that the Baptists that like to bend the elbow, on occasion, would either go to a village close to Drake for their elbow bending or would come in the back door of the local bars and leave by the same way. To my way of thinking and here comes my Baptist upbringing of judgment, on them, you should be true to yourself as my daddy was. If you are going to preach against something, you shouldn't do it. On the other hand if you think it is OK, then don't preach against it. To be fair, it was mostly the women of the church that were against these things. The men just went along with it to keep the peace in the family. I would guess that some of these men were of different faiths than Baptists prior to their marriage so didn't totally go along with all of the Baptist "do not's". I believe we should be tolerant of the lifestyle our friends and neighbors choose and just because we choose a different lifestyle doesn't make ours right for everyone or theirs wrong for everyone. Just saying. Anyway the point I was trying to make before I side tracked myself on a minnie sermon was that the people of Drake had good moral character and high standards but were also human beings that fail, even themselves, like we all do.

The German people of the Drake community were stoic, hardworking, get it done, take responsibility for your actions, brusque people. To others they could appear to be a selfish, not caring about others feelings, people. I found this to be just the opposite but sometimes it could give you pause. An example was my Fathers' funeral. I was the executor of his estate and of course there are no secrets in a small town. When the funeral was over and we were filing out of the church sanctuary to go to the graveyard to bury him, a friend of my father, who had been parking his boat in my Dad's yard with Dad's permission, stopped me on the way out behind the coffin and asked if it would be OK to continue to park his boat there. I was of course, grieving and there were tears but that just seemed like the right time, to him, to approach me about parking his boat. Not a "sorry for your loss", just kind of a suck it up and get over it and by the way, I need a place to park my boat. I think to most people, that would appear to be insensitive to say the least. After the initial shock, knowing him, I told him he could continue to park his boat where he was.

He meant no harm and was not a man of low intelligence. He probably did not have a college education and perhaps not even a high school education as many of that generation were only educated through the eighth grade, if that. They were needed on the farm to work and provide food for the rest of the family so didn't get the chance to further their education. A lack of education, doesn't make you stupid. I've known many very intelligent people without an education. This individual probably did not have much social contact outside the community and had not been exposed to society as a whole. Whatever the reason, that is how he was and I found many people of German heritage, including some of my relatives, to be somewhat like that. They speak their mind, tell it like it is and are not always sensitive to the feelings of the person they are speaking to. Sometimes their mouth speaks before their brain has thought it and you say to yourself, did they just say that out loud.

So perhaps you have an image of the community and the people of the village that raised me. They were good people even though their social manners may have not always been perfect. They were not perfect people but were very logical thinking and intelligent. Not that different from people the world over. They didn't overthink a problem but analyzed it, came to a decision, and executed it. They didn't need approval of the masses or care if it was politically correct or even necessarily care what others thought about it. If it was right for them and the majority it affected, do it.

An example of this is the book burning by the Drake school board in Nov. of 1973. It seems it came about because a young 26 year old English teacher by the name of Bruce Severy had decided to assign his sophomore class a book by Kurt Vonnegut. It was Kurt's 1969 novel "Slaughter-House Five". The teacher claimed that some of the students that were "C" and "D" students were writing "A" papers after he assigned that book. However, one student was opposed to the profanity in the book and the use of four letter words. She told her mother about the book and assignment and her mother in turn, complained to the school board. The school board ordered the 32 "Slaughter-House Five" books confiscated and burned as well as about 60 copies of "Deliverance" by James Dickey and an anthology entitled "Short Story Masterpieces" with works by Ernest Hemingway and John Steinbeck, among other famous writers.

In a Minot Daily News article, the board president, Charles McCarthy, was quoted as saying, "We didn't approve of its obscene language. It might pass in a college, but not in this school." Another board member said he read the book after the meeting and didn't think it should be read by anyone. Two clergymen from Drake attended the school board meeting and blasted the book. One was a Catholic Priest and one was a Methodist pastor. Most of the sophomore class signed a letter of protest to the board and many of them refused to turn in their copy of the book and said their copy had been lost. The board ordered their lockers searched and had the administration call the students' parents.

This "book burning" got national attention and Playboy magazine printed an article about it as well as newspapers and TV news across the country. I was working full time at my career, married, raising a family, going to college on the G.I. bill and living in International Falls, MN at the time this occurred. I was either in a college Literature class or a Creative Writing class when it hit the national news. My teacher, somehow found out I was from Drake. During one of our classes, she questioned me about the village of Drake and the people who lived there who would take such drastic measures. As much of the country was, she was surprised, scandalized and outraged that there was a book burning in Drake, ND, a neighboring state, no less. Who are these people?

I explained to her and the class, as best I could, that the people of Drake were ordinary people who were moral with high standards when it came to religion and family, not that different from the people in this town we live in now and people all over. They want what they believe is best for their children and believe it is their right and responsibility, even if it means censoring what they read or watch on TV. They not only want this but believe it is their duty as parents to do this. Their thought process may have been that, we censor movies children watch under a certain age, so how is censoring what children under a certain age read, different?

As always, the news reports blow things out of proportion and sensationalize stories to sell their papers or news programs. The school board, in my opinion, went overboard when they ordered the books burned but in their defense, it was probably a knee-jerk reaction and not thought out. They possibly thought that if the books physically existed in the school, other kids would get access to them and read them. Probably a little like the book "Peyton Place" when I was growing up. I think every kid who could read, read that book. Many parents forbid their children to read it but that only insured they would read it. It's quite easy to be

This Dummy Pulls His Own Strings

a Monday morning quarterback and say what should have been done but being in the heat of battle is quite different.

In hindsight, the school board may have been better served to donate the books they thought offensive to a public library somewhere. As I explained previously, they don't over analyze, just get er done. The Catholic priest did say that he didn't approve of certain parts of the book but didn't think they should be burned. He didn't say if he told the board this but he told a reporter it, after the fact. At any rate, Drake had a brief moment of infamy in 1973, only 13 years after I graduated from the same high school.

As long as I am on the subject of high school, let me tell you about my high school experience in my hometown. These were the years of Rock and Roll and American Bandstand, 1956-1960. Elvis had just appeared on the scene along with Buddy Holly, The Everly Brothers, Rickey Nelson, Dion, Bobbie Vee, Bobbie Darin, Brenda Lee, Connie Francis, Roy Orbison, Duane Eddie, Fats Domino, Jerry Lee Lewis, Bill Haley and the Comets and many more. The Beatles hadn't appeared yet. We, as impressionable teenagers were caught up in the rock and roll fever and the Elvis era.

We were rebels without a clue. The school administration was trying to keep order and discipline and in that endeavor were very controlling. We wore our hair long for that time, pre Beattles, with it combed into a ducktail like Elvis or else Buddy Holly style with a curl or point in the middle of the forehead. We went beltless and lowered our jeans to our hips. When the school administration ordered us to wear belts in our jeans, we cut the belt loops off our jeans and wore the belts at our waists and the jeans on our hips until a few students were sent home. We grew our sideburns long and turned up our shirt collars. Most of us smoked cigarettes back then and when not in school would carry our cigarette packs rolled up in our t-shirt sleeve. Most of us wore leather jackets and some wore motorcycle jackets.

The girls had to wear skirts in school and in ND in the winter that is not comfortable or practical. They could wear jeans under their skirts on the school bus until they got to school and then had to remove the jeans. Skirts had to be a prescribed length. It was common practice by some of the girls to wear the prescribed length of skirt when leaving home and then roll the skirt at the waist when they got to school to make it shorter.

Of course, students were not permitted to smoke in school or for that matter anywhere. If a teacher saw you smoking anywhere, you could and would be expelled for three days. Never mind that the smoke in the teachers' lounge was so thick, you couldn't see to the other side of the room. One of my friends was smoking at home in his living room with his parents' knowledge and permission. They had a big picture window that he was sitting in front of. A teacher went by his house and saw him smoking and expelled him.

I was on the golden gloves boxing team. Most of us on the team smoked and since smoking was not allowed in the school except for faculty, who had a smoking lounge, the guys would go to the parking lot and sit in one of their cars and smoke over lunch hour. The boxing coach saw them one day and gave them a choice of punishment. They could either be expelled from school and kicked off the boxing team or they could give him permission to beat them with a rubber hose. I believe they all chose the rubber hose. I wasn't one of those unfortunate kids who got caught. I only lived two blocks from school so I would go home for lunch and smoke in my room. Many of the farm kids would walk downtown to the Laundromat to smoke and the kids that drove cars to school, instead of taking the bus, would drive around in their cars and smoke. There were a few occasions when we were desperate and we would smoke in the locker/shower room in school because the coach was in the faculty lounge smoking and we thought he was occupied. We would post a person by the door outside to warn us when an adult was coming.

When I was growing up in Drake and I specify Drake because I'm still growing up, we had one policeman. He also served as the water meter reader. His name was Ferdinand and everyone referred to him as Ferdinand the bull. He was the step dad of one of my friends. On Halloween, it was customary for the little kids to "trick & treat" but when you were too old for trick and treating, it was all tricking.

Generally about the time the little kids went home after filling their candy sacks, the older kids would begin setting up road blocks by pushing farm implements from dealerships into the streets and anything that wasn't tied down was also piled in the streets. Sometimes, once we got the implements in the street, if they were implements with tires, we would let the air out of the tires so it was harder to undo what we had done. It was great fun trying to stay one step ahead of Ferdinand. We were always careful not to damage or break anything, just make life difficult for the cop and his helpers. In the latter years he would deputize a bunch of the town councilmen or business leaders so he would have some help. Of course many of these deputies would be fathers of my friends.

We sometimes were not very quiet when doing our mischief and someone would call Ferdinand to tell him where we were and what we were up to. Of course this was the time before cell phones so all that was available was land lines to his home or jail. He was out busy patrolling the streets so he wouldn't get the message until he stopped at home or someone from home went out to find him and deliver the message. He would come in his car and of course couldn't get by the roadblock we had set up so would get out of his car. We would all hide on the opposite side of the roadblock until he got out of the car and started shining his spotlight around. Then we would all take off running in different directions and obviously he could only chase one of us. We would usually have a designated area to meet up again so we could continue with our mischief. You might call this organized mischief.

One time he got out of his car and hollered for us to stop or he would shoot. He then fired a warning shot into the air. One of his step sons hollered something like, "you got me, Dad". I'm sure the next day Ferdinand confronted his step-son and his step-son claimed it was somebody else trying to get him in trouble. You got no proof.

If Ferdinand or one of his deputies caught any of the mischief makers or tricksters, they were taken to city hall, booked and put in jail. The parents would get a phone call and would have to come get you out of jail or leave you there as punishment. I never was caught so I don't know if they had to pay a fine or bail or what the process was. I think one of my friends had to spend quite some time in jail, maybe even over night because his parents couldn't be reached or chose to let him sit it out.

I had one close call. There was a group of us, probably about 20, pushing farm implements out onto the street from a dealership and setting up a roadblock. One of the deputies, probably the owner of the dealership, walked up behind us while we were moving a piece of equipment. We thought he was one of us until he started talking. Everyone took off running but I was the unlucky one he started chasing. I ran around a combine in the lot, dropped to the ground and rolled under it. He was a few steps behind me and didn't see me roll under it but knew I couldn't disappear into thin air so he stood there for a while. I could have reached out and grabbed his foot he was so close. Of course, I had to try not to breath too loud, cough or sneeze. He stood very still listening and assessing the situation, then walked around the combine and among the other implements. I just lay still and tried to wait him out until he left. I had the advantage because I was laying on the ground and could see his feet and watch his movement. I think he hung around for about a half hour before he finally walked away and I quietly and carefully snuck away. I found the rest of the gang who were back together and continuing the mischief. The benefit of these actions was it was good exercise for all concerned, the chasers and those being chased.

Back in the early days it was common on Halloween to tip over out houses. An outhouse is an outdoor toilet that sets over a hole in the ground. Everyone had them before indoor plumbing was installed and even after the city had water and sewer available, some people couldn't afford to hook up or for other reasons didn't want those modern conveniences. Some people resist change and those modern inventions. There were not many outhouses left

This Dummy Pulls His Own Strings

when I started tricking on Halloween. There were a few and some of the owners got tired of getting their outhouse tipped over every Halloween. They would load their shotgun with rock salt or something other than the regular shells. These would sting but not do serious damage. They would lay in wait for the outhouse tippers. A shotgun makes a lot of noise and can give you quite a scare especially when you don't know what kind of shells they are using. Of course when we were doing our mischief, it was dark so we had the cover of dark to hide. We would generally stake out an outhouse for a period of time to make sure no one was lying in wait and three or four of us would run up behind it and give it a shove and it would tip right over. Of course we had to be careful not to step or fall into the hole that it previously covered. Talk about being up to your neck in it, quite literally. I never heard of that happening but I'm sure there were close calls and maybe even a few tricks like moving the outhouse off its hole but upright in front of it so when someone ran up behind to tip it, they would fall in the hole. I don't recall that happening either but I would not be surprised if it did.

One Halloween we were going to get a fellow who supposedly shot his shotgun at tippers. We thought we would watch his outhouse until he came out to use it, generally right before you went to bed, and after he had his pants lowered and sitting down, would rush up and push it down on the closed door making it impossible for him to get out. We waited and were about to give up when he came out. It was too dark to tell if he had his shotgun with him or not. He went in the outhouse and we waited a reasonable time until we thought he would have his pants down and be seated. I think there were four of us or maybe even five. As quietly as we could but as fast as we could we ran up behind the outhouse and pushed as hard as we could. Nothing happened. He apparently anticipated this and had somehow staked the outhouse down so it was not just setting over the hole but was anchored. Of course he came roaring out the door. We didn't linger to see if he had his pants up or down. Luckily we were on the opposite side of the outhouse so we all took off in different directions and we found out he had his shotgun with him. He fired a shot or two or three but didn't hit anyone. By the time he got a shot off we were in the next county or at least far enough away so we could barely hear the blast. I think that may have been the last outhouse tipping for us, at least for that Halloween. What an adrenaline rush.

I've heard other Halloween stories, some before I was old enough to participate. One was about barrels of coal ashes. Everyone burned coal for heat in the winter time before God invented fuel oil and natural gas. Coal produces ashes and everyone had an ash pile come spring, from the winter heating season. Even by Halloween it was cool enough for people to be heating, burning coal and have ash piles. There was a bowling alley at the time and it was located underground on Main Street, I believe below a bar. The entrance was down steps on the outside from the sidewalk and through a door. Some kids called the police officer and told of a disturbance at the bowling alley. Of course the policeman responded and as soon as he went in they started dumping barrels of ashes in the stairway, in front of the door. They dumped enough ashes so when the policeman came out he had to wade through the ashes and was covered in ash. They may have even saved some ashes to dump on him when he exited, in which case you could say they got him in the ash hole.

Believe it or not, I was a Boy Scout for a short period of time. I even went to summer camp one summer. However, the scout master caught me smoking, probably at the ripe age of 13, and kicked me out of the scouting program. Another example of the moral judgment of the community and the strict adhering to rules and not over analyzing the situation. Today, some organization and a truck load of lawyers would probably come to my defense and make a big deal out of it. I deserved the outcome but in modern society, they would probably have ascertained that even if I was smoking, I would be better off in the Boy Scouts and would probably learn to be a better person and give up smoking eventually. (over thinking or analyzing) Back then you followed the rules or suffered the consequences. Their reasoning was that I was

This Dummy Pulls His Own Strings

a bad example to the other scouts, especially the younger ones. I couldn't argue with that. On top of that, I didn't dare appeal to my parents to fight on my behalf. They always told me, If you get a licking in school or any other punishment, if we hear about it, you'll get one from us also. Double the punishment. My parents didn't approve of my smoking either and my Mother always told me, "if God wanted you to smoke, he would have put a chimney on you". I smoked in front of them but without their approval.

Ferdinand, the cop, also had the pleasure of insuring all the children of the community were off the streets by curfew time which was shortly after ten PM. The city whistle would go off at 10:00PM and shortly thereafter all kids were supposed to be off the streets unless accompanied by your parents or another adult. There was an exception to this rule for nights that there were sports being played at the high school. My friends, Charlie and Mike Toy lived way across town on the east edge of town and I lived on the west edge of town. A distance of about 6 to 8 blocks. Many nights we would gather at the Toy residence and play cards, battleship or just hang out together. When the 10:00PM whistle sounded, we would finish whatever we were doing and then head to our respective homes. By this time it was probably 10:30PM and we should have been home. If Ferdinand saw you walking home he would stop and generally holler at you and tell you to go home and sometimes follow you in the car. On one occasion, I think I hollered back at him and asked him where he thought I was going. This did not make him happy and he ordered me into his car. I thought I was in trouble but he was just trying to scare me and without any more conversation, drove me home and dropped me at my front door. The lesson here was, if you want a ride home, just sass the cop and you can get a ride home, rather than walk.

Perhaps I should have been more respectful of the local constable, Ferdinand. He seemed to not like me very much and appeared to be out to get me. I, on the other hand, could sense this and was usually within the law. That is not to say, I didn't misbehave, tempt fate or ever break the law. I quite often drove my fathers' car in a reckless manner. It was more of exhibition driving. Most of the roads in Drake were gravel which made it easy to slide around a corner or spin doughnuts in the middle of the road. Before doing any of this I would generally figure out where Ferdinand was and usually leave town shortly after.

My father was hard of hearing and always drove a straight stick. He would rev the engine until he could hear it to make sure the car was running and then pop the clutch and take off spinning his wheels, throwing gravel. Because of this, it was difficult to know if it was my father driving or me. Perhaps the local citizens were hesitant to report my father. I had one of the citizens tell me once when my father was older and still driving and I no longer lived there that everyone knew when George was coming down the street because they could hear the engine roaring and everyone just got out of his way. When I was a teenager, my friends called me George, after my Dad because they said I drove like him. Why wouldn't I, he taught me to drive.

Ferdinand and I nearly came to blows one night. There was a basketball game and of course we all went to the game. I had my Dad's car and after the game gave a whole bunch of kids a ride to Toy's house. There were four or five cheerleaders plus a couple of my buddies. There were no seat belts or seat belt laws so you could pile in as many people as would fit and allow you to drive.

I believe there were rumors of a party at Toy's after the game. I'm sure Mike and/or Charlie were along. Some of the cheerleaders had not changed out of their cheerleader outfits but brought their clothes along in a paper bag. When we went in Toy's house they left the paper bags of clothes in the car. Shortly after we went in the house, Ferdinand drove up and parked across the street and just sat there. The cheerleaders decided they wanted to retrieve their clothes from the car and change clothes at Toy's.

None of the girls wanted to go out and get the clothes with Ferdinand setting there. I, being one to never pass up a chance to be a hero or rescue a damsel in distress, said I would go get their paper bags of clothes for them. At this point we didn't have any beer or alcohol but we were making plans to get some. With everyone looking out the windows, I now had an audience; I boldly stepped out the door and walked to my car. I waved to Ferdinand who was parked directly across from my car. I then opened the back door and searched for the bags of clothes. I found them and put them under my arm and turned to go back in the house and there Ferdinand was standing, blocking my way.

He told me to give the bags to him. I told him no, I wouldn't do that. He didn't appear to be kidding or even in a good mood when he told me the second time to hand over the bags. I again refused. He had his one hand down by his gun and I saw it move rather quickly and thought he was drawing his gun on me. It turned out he pulled his Billy club out and gave me a quick bop on top of the head. He was not in a good mood and was using a lot of expletives to describe me and what he was going to do to me if I didn't turn over the bags. We were practically nose to nose and I looked him in the eye and refused again. I guess I was grateful it was his Billy club and not his gun so thought I wasn't in real danger. Besides, that first smack had kind of dulled my senses and pissed me off just a little. He smacked me a little harder with the club and since I was still standing upright, did it one more time for good measure.

My knees started to buckle so I handed him the paper bags without uttering a word. I think I was incapable of speech at this point and lucky to still be standing. I was probably out on my feet but too stubborn to fall down. He reached in and started pulling out the girls clothes. I'm sure he thought there was alcohol of some shape or form in the bags. He probably had overheard some kids talking about a party at Toy's so he parked there. He was a bit embarrassed and not very happy. He inquired as to why I had bags of girls clothing and wanted to know what I was going to do with them. I told him they belonged to the cheerleaders in the house that wanted to change out of their cheerleader outfits and I was taking them in to them so they could. He muttered some threat to me, stuffed the clothes back in the bag and handed it back to me. He probably thought I had set him up. I believe he got in his car and drove away and never bothered us the rest of the night. I, on the other hand had a knot on my head and a bit of a headache for a day or two.

If that had happened today, there would be lawyers and protestors all over with lawsuits and protests. That was a different time. It was my own fault for refusing, even though he had no right to look in the bags. You can't fight city hall. I was just being a dumb teenager, showing off to my friends. See, I'm so thick skulled you can't knock me out with a Billy club. One more wop and they would have been carrying me in the house. After that, Ferdinand treated me differently and didn't appear to be out to get me. We were never friends but got along just fine.

In the summertime, before we had drivers licenses, the kids of the town would get together and play softball, baseball, kick the can, moonlight-starlight, anti-I-over, Red Rover, football, hide & seek, and many other games. In the wintertime we would play in the snow, slide on the streets, ice skate, have snowball fights, build snow forts, play king on the hill and invent games to play. These were the days before television. When television came to town it was all black and white, no color, with only a couple channels and only a few people had it. You knew who had a TV by the antenna on the roof. It was a status symbol. One hardware store had a TV set and the Farmers Union had a TV set. My Dad and I would walk the two blocks to the Farmers Union to watch wrestling on Saturday night. It was black and white with a lot of snow. The Farmers Union employees would set up folding chairs and we would all sit glued to the snowy picture. Generally there were ten to twenty people watching. Everyone was on a first name basis and everyone tolerated everyone and usually most of them were friends or friendly.

It was a village of friendly people raising their families and trying to make decent, law abiding, authority respecting, individuals of their children. If they couldn't succeed at the task before them, there was a state reform school to help and the military could always lend a hand in doing the job. Sometimes a judge would sentence the offender to join the military service of your choice or go to jail, your choice. Generally, the choice was military service.

Drake had many social organizations such as a sportsman's club, commercial club, volunteer fire department, American Legion, Senior Citizens club in addition to the church organizations like the Knights' of Columbus and ladies aids. My parents didn't participate in any of them, except the church organizations, probably because they didn't imbibe in alcoholic beverages and most of these activities included alcohol. Just going to get the mail at the post office or going to the grocery store or Dr. was a social activity. You knew everyone and would visit with them when you encountered them. It's one of the reasons I maintain a post office box today. I get to see people I otherwise wouldn't see and exchange greetings, small talk, news and gossip.

Dad grew raspberries and strawberries and sold them to the people in town and farmers in the area. They would call on the telephone to inquire when he would have some or when they saw him around town, ask about them. He always had more customers than he had berries. The Dr. especially liked his berries because Dad didn't use any pesticides or fertilizers. They were all organic and natural before it was poplar and labeled. Sometimes when we went to see the Dr., he wouldn't charge us for the visit but say just remember me when you have berries. Dad and Mom also grew a big garden and shared the produce with neighbors and towns people and sold some to the local grocers.

In the days of my youth, there was a gentleman, John Backmier, who lived on the northeast edge of town and had a team of horses. He would plow peoples' garden plots with a horse drawn plow for a small fee. This was before God invented roto-tillers. He would go from house to house and anyone who had a garden would have him plow it. Back then most people grew gardens. The kids would follow him around to watch as he drove the horses and plowed. It was somewhat of an art to drive horses, walk behind the plow and hold onto it and keep it in the ground and plow a straight furrow. When you reached the end you would have to turn the horses and plow around and go the other direction. No small feat requiring strength and coordination.

He also was the garbage collector. He had an open wagon he hitched the horses to and drove down the alley emptying peoples' garbage cans into his wagon. He would give voice commands to the horses to have them move forward or stop. When the wagon was full of garbage, he would get onto the seat and make a trip to the dump ground to unload the wagon and return to town to continue picking up garbage. He also hauled ash piles out to the dump ground in the spring. They were called dump grounds because there was nothing sanitary about these land-fills. He was a hard working man making an honest living, providing a necessary service at a reasonable price.

Football and Basketball game nights were a big night in Drake. Especially Friday nights. Most of the town would go to the games to cheer the teams on. This was also a social event. The kids would go to the cafes after the games for a hamburger and coke to socialize and flirt. The adults would go to the bars for the same reasons.

It was a nice, safe environment. You didn't have any worries about safety as a child unless you were being bullied by an older kid for some reason. That happened very seldom and usually, the bully just wanted to scare you, not do you physical harm. There were no gangs or drugs to worry about and the streets were safe, night and day for anyone, young or old, male or female. Everyone knew their neighbors and spoke often with them, either around town, on the telephone, in church or on the front porch. It was a comfortable feeling to know everyone in town and who was related to whom or who was having relations with whom. If a stranger came to town, it didn't take long for the whole town to know about it and who the stranger was and why they were there. Without television, computers, or smart phones, face to face socializing or the land line telephone was the only way to network and socialize. For entertainment, we listened to the radio, played card or board games in our homes or went to church or school events such as concerts, plays and sporting events. It was a simple, relaxed life with plenty of work to keep boredom at bay and give you a good night's sleep.

I fear the day that technology will surpass our human interaction. The World will have a generation of idiots. Albert Einstein

We had a full time policeman whose biggest worry was catching teenagers speeding or drinking. Once in a while he might have to break up a street fight between a couple of teenagers or a bar fight. These were fights involving fists only. There never were knives or guns involved. Usually there was alcohol involved and nine times out of ten, it was over a female. Nature taking its' course.

For the most part, my hometown had good, friendly people. They had good intentions most of the time but were like anyone else and could get emotional and sometimes let the emotions take over their common sense. We all do that from time to time. I am grateful for my hometown and the people in it that helped shape the person I am. I may not be perfect but I pull my own strings. I may not be an outstanding World citizen but I have managed to stay out of jail, most of the time. That doesn't mean I have never broken the law or that I followed all the laws of society, it just means, I have not been caught, often.

Drake has residents that don't like change and actually fear and fight change. Change means uncertainty. Such was the case, I believe, not so many years ago. The farm that I lived on for the first few years of my life is just about 10 miles north of Drake. My siblings and I were given this farm by my parents while Dad was still living. We formed a partnership to keep the land in the family and it automatically passes to our children and their children. None of us are farmers so we rent the land to a local farmer. Many of the local farmers farm many small farms now. We rented our land to a farmer just across the road from our farm. He farmed it for many years until he retired and sold his farm to an Amish family. In his opinion, they were a nice family but of course they live differently than most of us. They farm with horses and have no motor machines including vehicles. They don't even use modern conveniences such as plumbing and electricity. In fact, they tore out the plumbing and the septic system at this farm and went back to using an outhouse.

I have seen worse lifestyles than the Amish and in fact kind of admired them and their way of life. I had some exposure to the Amish people when I was stationed in MD when I was in the Navy. Our base was a few miles from Lancaster, PA where there was an Amish settlement. My buddies and I used to go to Lancaster to the USO there for female companionship. We would see some of the Amish girls on the street and stop to talk to them which didn't set well with their parents. My mother originally came from this area and was raised as a Pennsylvania Dutch, a close relative to the Amish so I was interested in their way of life. I was always interested in females so it wasn't much of a stretch to talk to any that would talk to me. Some of them were just trying to get a reaction from their parents, typical teenagers.

The Amish that moved in across the road from our farm needed firewood for their cook stove and our farm had a shelterbelt with old and dying trees. They asked if they could clean out the shelterbelt of the deadwood and use it for fuel. I told them to go ahead and thanked them for doing it. We also had an old cupboard that my Dad had built in the farmhouse they liked and wanted to buy from me. I told them they could have it because if anyone else liked it they would take it without asking. We had an old cook stove in the kitchen that was made of cast iron and very heavy. I would use it for heat and cooking when I went to the farm to duck and goose hunt. Someone stole it, prior to the Amish people moving there. These honest people wanted to pay for the cupboard and I thought their honesty should be rewarded, so I gave it to them. Our former renter, the farmer that sold them his farm, befriended them and would do hauling of cattle, horses, horse pulled farm machinery and other things with his pick up and trailer. They would pay him for his time, gas and trouble when he would let them.

There were some residents that were not too neighborly towards the Amish farm family. I heard that they were afraid this family was only the first of many that intended to buy up farms in the area and start an Amish settlement. What a disaster that would be. Honest, hardworking, peace loving people driving slow moving, horse drawn vehicles on the roads and literally spreading horse crap. More than likely, all home schooled kids and their own churches. Just wouldn't fit into the community. However, the community should feel privileged that these people wanted to move there and live there and raise their families there. I would think it speaks to what they thought of this community and the people that live there. I guess they misjudged the character of some of the residents.

These people stand out because of the way they dress and live and in fact are somewhat of separatists. I would classify the Amish as friendly separatists that will not bother you and hope you will not bother them, especially their children. They don't like their daughters talking to drunken sailors especially if the drunken sailors are trying to pick up their daughters. You can't blame them for that. Many of the residents of Drake didn't approve of their daughters speaking to me even before I became a drunken sailor.

It seems some residents of the Drake area wanted to keep the Amish from buying up farms and moving into the area. This particular family was harassed by some area residents when they would go to town with their horse and buggy to get groceries, mail or whatever the reason. Nothing too serious, just un-neighborly and in my opinion, un-Christian. I'm sure, they are probably used to this, wherever they go because of their dress and lifestyle. There are bullies everywhere. However, the people of Lancaster, PA seemed to be friendly with the Amish people there. The Amish family at Drake seemed to tolerate it quite well until people started driving by their farm and firing guns. I choose to believe that they were not firing at the people or buildings but that is not known. I do believe, one of their dogs was killed. I'm not sure if that was with a bullet or if it was run over by a vehicle. The Amish farm family believed that this was a pretty good indication they were not wanted in the area and perhaps their lives could be in danger. They packed up and left, I'm sure with some financial loss not to mention the trauma.

Anytime you and your property are threatened, especially in your home, you are traumatized. I have experience in this. You lose your sense of security and wake to every noise. In my case, sleeping with a shotgun by the bed hoping you don't have to kill an intruder and if you do, it is not a child, drunk or on drugs. I have some experience in the trauma of a home invasion. The setting of these stories is in my current home town of International Falls, MN as opposed to my birth home town of Drake, ND.

Memorial Day of 2014, Kathy, my wife, went shopping which removed the car from the garage. While she was gone and the garage was empty, I thought it would be a good time to clean the garage. She wasn't gone long or I'm just slow because I hadn't finished with the garage when she returned. I told her to leave the car in the driveway and I would put it away when I finished cleaning. Somehow, I never got the car put away. The next day I noticed my solar yard lights were pulled out of the ground and the tops thrown about the yard and broken. My first inclination was to blame it on some drunken teenagers that had been walking by, saw them and decided to have some fun. They were quite unusual and noticeable as they would change color to all the colors of the rainbow. Kathy discovered that one of the metal stakes that the light rested on above the ground had been used to scratch a symbol into the hood of the Cadillac I had not put away the night before. It covered the entire hood and was a circle with a diamond inside the circle. The diamond points all touched the inside of the circle. It appeared to be a gang symbol but research on the internet turned up nothing and the police didn't know to who or what it was associated. I still have no idea as to the meaning of it.

After talking with the neighbors, we found out that we were not the only ones vandalized. One of our neighbors across the street was sound asleep when they heard a noise. He got up to investigate and found the window air conditioner pushed inside the house. Evidently, by whoever was trying to gain entry to the house. Other neighbors in the area had the same symbol scratched into their cars. People reported that their cars were unlocked with laptops in them but nothing stolen, yet the symbol

This Dummy Pulls His Own Strings

scratched into the car. Now it appeared that this was either gang related, with the symbol or drug related or both. It appeared this person or persons were not afraid, indicated by trying home invasion while people are home, which often means they are using drugs and are looking for more prescription drugs so they target older people or the infirm that are more likely to have prescription drugs. People on meth, especially, are often fearless and unstoppable until there is no life left in them.

It was obvious we were home, our car was in our driveway which was vandalized, so obviously they noticed it. I also noticed when I got up in the morning and went outside, our back storm door was propped open using the door closer slide and bells that we had stuck to the entry door were lying on the deck. I thought this unusual but dismissed it as my grandson playing around. When we discovered the vandalism, I looked more closely at the door and noticed scratch marks on the door locks as if someone had been trying to pick the locks. They had propped the storm door open so it was not in the way while trying to pick the locks. I of course reported all of this to the police.

My theory, I shared with the police, was that it was someone who used to live in International Falls and was home for the Memorial Day holiday and was either on drugs or was vandalizing before they left town. The police disagreed with my theory and thought it was a young kid that had been breaking car windows and stealing things out of cars. They said he didn't have parental supervision and was running wild but they hadn't caught him at it yet and didn't have any proof. I mentioned that there were unlocked cars with laptops in them that were vandalized but nothing was taken and no car windows had been broken. They didn't have an explanation for that. Once you get an idea in your head, it's hard to displace it. I'm just as guilty of that with my theories. I admire the police and the work they do and the sacrifices they make to help and protect us.

I was feeling threatened and uncertain what was going on and vulnerable. I am an Army and Navy veteran and was trained in hand to hand combat in both services. I was also a golden glove boxer in high school and won the Army North Dakota National Guard championship in my weight class one year. I taught boxing for a short period in the Navy, albeit to a class of one. I was confident I could handle myself in a one on one situation even with a much younger opponent. I was 72 but in fairly decent shape. However, if you bring drugs into the equation or several opponents, I may not be the super hero I imagine myself to be. I retrieved my twelve gauge pump shotgun from the gun rack. Took the trigger lock off and placed it in my bedroom closet. I also put some shells in my night stand. I didn't want to load the shotgun because of my 5 year old grandson spending a lot of time at our home.

I was planning a trip to North Dakota to do some research for this book. Kathy was not feeling well and we just found out her cancer had returned. She was not planning to go to ND with me. Kathy saw me put the shotgun in the closet and asked me to review with her it's use so when I was gone she could use it. I told her first of all that I didn't believe she could shoot anyone, nor would I want her to be put in that position where she would have to make that decision. Secondly, if you don't shoot the perpetrator, they may take the gun away and shoot you. Thirdly, if you do shoot them, you may go on trial for manslaughter or worse. Lastly, I had decided not to go to ND without her, partly because of her diagnoses of cancer and partly because of this vandalism, I wouldn't leave her alone unprotected and I wanted to spend as much time with her as she would allow me. She was not up to the trip so I canceled it.

The fourth of July was on a Friday and was the next holiday. If my theory of a former resident returning on holidays was correct, our vandal might strike again on or around the fourth. Friday and Saturday passed with no vandalism. Sunday night, the last night of the holiday weekend, we were sound asleep in bed sometime after midnight. I was awoken by a noise and the sound of glass breaking. I have always had the ability to come wide awake in an instant and have my thought processes in full gear. It probably stems from when I was a computer programmer at a bank and

This Dummy Pulls His Own Strings

would get calls at three AM because a program quit working. I wear my underwear to bed, shorts and t-shirt but no pajamas. I jumped out of bed in my underwear, barefooted, grabbed the 12 gauge shotgun and shells and started walking to the dining room where I heard the glass breaking and still dropping to the floor. These dining room windows open onto the deck. We have central air conditioning so all the windows are closed and locked all the time. As I am walking toward the dining room, barefooted, I hear glass dropping out of the window onto the floor, some of it breaking, one piece at a time. As I'm nearing the dining room, I have inserted several shells into the gun and I work the pump action to fully load it, ready to fire. As I do this and as I come around the corner to the dining room, I hear footsteps running across the deck. This person heard me work the pump action of the shotgun, which is distinct and quite recognizable and presuming it was a he, took off running. He had been calmly standing there, picking pieces of glass out of the window frame so he could step from the deck into the dining room. Had I had the shot gun fully loaded and not had to work the pump action, I would have been able to catch him or if he ran, got a shot off, at that close range, probably killing him. I would probably have been writing this from prison. As I told the policemen when they came, I don't want to kill a kid over a break-in but if I believe we are in danger, that could very well happen.

When I jumped out of bed, Kathy asked me what was happening, I simply whispered, stay in bed. When I heard this person running across the deck, I ran to the window, in my bare feet over all the broken glass to try to get a shot off at him. There was nothing to shoot at and no noise in the woods that are on three sides of our home. When I turned around after looking out the broken window for the culprit, Kathy was standing there. She never has listened to me so I wasn't surprised she didn't stay in bed. The surprising thing was that I didn't cut my feet even though I was stepping on broken glass.

I dialed 911 and described what had just happened. The lady said the police were on the way and she was staying on the line until they arrived. She verified my address with me and we talked as we waited. She told me the police were pulling up to my house and I argued with her that there were no police cars around or in the vicinity of my home. I asked her if she had given them the correct address and she verified my address with me, again. I told her they probably went to 7th Ave. west instead of 7th Ave. east. She asked them where they were and found out that is what they had done. She re-directed them and in a few minutes said again, they are pulling up in front of your house. This time I could see their vehicle pull up in front of our neighbors with the lights out. One officer came to the door and the other walked around the house, looking for evidence or the perpetrator. I met the officer at the door. I was holding the shot gun wearing only my underwear. At this point, I noticed the storm door, propped open as before, with the slide on the door closer. Obviously, he had been trying to pick the locks again to gain entry and when he was unsuccessful decided to break a window.

    I put on some clothes and joined the officers in their investigation, still holding my loaded shotgun. I have several lights outside that can light up my yard like daylight. I turned them all on. One officer picked up a piece of glass from the dining room floor that had circular marks on it, each circle smaller than the one next to it. I was told this was made by a glass breaker that ambulance EMT's use to break automobile windows in rescue attempts. I again, verbalized my theory that this was someone from out of town that came back to town for holidays and on the last night of the holiday, before they left town again, they did the vandalism and break-ins. The officers had no comment on my theories and in fact had very little to say. They looked around, aimed their flashlights into the woods and even walked into the woods at several points where the access was not difficult. I set about finding something to cover the window to keep the mosquitos, spiders and vandals out. To do this I had to go to some sheds that were next to the woods to get some boards and plastic to nail over the broken window. I carried my loaded shotgun with me which made carrying the other things awkward. The officers completed their investigation and told me they were leaving. I asked what I could and should do in the event the perpetrators returned. They said do whatever you need to do to protect your family and home. That was what I wanted to hear in case I had to shoot someone. I put plastic over the broken window to keep out bugs and rain and then nailed boards over the plastic to keep out intruders. My loaded shotgun always by my side and at the ready.

That same night, I later learned, they broke into a rental house a few blocks from me that was unoccupied. They painted their calling card, the circle symbol with diamond and foul language and talk is cheap on the walls and floor, then dumped the left over paint in the window air conditioner. They again did some vandalism of other homes in the vicinity. At one home about a block and one half from me, a woman woke up to see a man standing by her open bedroom window, cutting the screen. She said something to him and he took off running. That fearlessness, suggests drug use to me. This was a tall man and not a child or kid that was lacking supervision.

Only one person has ever been seen but the police now believe there is more than one person. They base it on the break in at the unoccupied home where the window that was broken was too high for one person to reach without a ladder and there was no ladder around. They believe there had to be two of them. One to boost the other up to the window. I suggested that perhaps that wasn't the entry point and perhaps he had successfully picked the door lock and entered through the door and had either broken that window as vandalism or it was his escape route if there was activity out front. After all they had on two occasions tried to pick my locks. They didn't buy into any of my theories. They perhaps thought I watched too many police shows on TV like Castle and Chicago PD.

Later I was talking with one of my neighbors and telling him what had happened. He was asking questions about the time it took place and when the police left. He told me that he heard a noise outside his home about the time I was talking about. He got up and looked out the windows but couldn't see anything except that his motion lights were on. He assumed there was an animal, probably a raccoon, roaming around getting into mischief, so he went back to bed. The next day he was talking to his neighbor on the other side and learned that the neighbors' teenage girls had been sitting outside in the back yard with a fire in the fire pit until about midnight. When they went in, they neglected to put out the fire in the fire pit and left the canvas chairs they were using setting around the fire pit. The following morning they found all the chairs in the fire pit, burned up.

From this information we surmised that whoever broke into my place probably hid in the woods until the police left, probably watching what we were doing and listening to our conversations. He may have been thinking if I didn't cover the broken window, he could come back and gain entry noiselessly by just stepping through the opening. Luckily, Kathy is more afraid of spiders in her home than vandals so I sealed it up securely both against spiders and vandals. When the police left and he saw I was sealing up the window, the perpetrator proceeded down the block, setting off motion lights, stirring up the fire in the fire pit and burning the canvas chairs. This information I gave to the police for which they had no comment.

It wasn't too long after our break-in that there was an incident at Ray, MN, a little village south of International Falls. It seems that an individual was at the door of a family in the middle of the night. When they woke up and went to the door, he forced his way in and started attacking them and beating on them. The husband ran to get his gun but the intruder then quit beating on the wife and ran after the husband who had a long barreled gun by this time, but had not had time to load it. The intruder was coming at him so he swung the gun and hit the intruder in the head, breaking the stock of the gun. The intruder at this point left the residence, got in his car and drove away. 911 was called and the Sheriff was sent to investigate. There were two small children in the home that slept through the whole thing.

The intruder drove down the road and stopped at a home a few residences away. The lady living there was either up or got

This Dummy Pulls His Own Strings

up when he drove in and was looking out the window. She was an EMT and noticed a man wondering around her yard with a bloody head. She thought he needed help so called to him from the door asking if he was in need of help. He came to the door and forced his way in. Again, he started beating on the woman and had her on the floor, beating her head against the floor. The man living there had retrieved his gun and told him to stop beating the woman. The intruder lunged at the man and the man shot him. Again 911 was called and the Sheriff was just up the road a few houses investigating the first incident and the ambulance came to transport the intruder to the hospital. He died a short time later.

My information came from the newspaper and the grapevine so may be inaccurate but the general outline is correct. It was learned that the intruder was camped at a lake a short distance from Ray. His girlfriend was a friend with a girl from International Falls who was getting married. The intruder and his girlfriend were here to celebrate the upcoming wedding, the girlfriend going to International Falls to be with her friends and the intruder staying at the campsite. When the girlfriend returned to the campsite, her boyfriend was missing so she called to report him missing. No one knows why he did what he did. His father said he was a recovering alcoholic but it was never reported if there was alcohol or drugs in his blood. It sounds to me like there were drugs and his actions somewhat mirror the actions of the intruder we experienced.

He was fearless and didn't appear to care if he was caught or not. Kind of like drug users act. He only did these things when it was a holiday or weekend. He was from out of town but had connections to people living here. I went to the Sheriff and expressed these concerns, that perhaps this was the same person that had previously broken into our home and vandalized others including the man who cut the ladies bedroom screen while she lay in bed watching him with no fear of being caught. She described him as a big man and this individual was a big man. The Sheriff said he didn't think it was the same person because his girlfriend said he had never been in International Falls. Well, if he was out prowling around in the middle of the night while she partied with her girlfriends, she would never know and if she did know, probably wouldn't tell to protect his reputation. After he was killed, the vandalism, at least in our neighborhood, stopped. Another indication it could have been him.

    I went to see both the Police Chief and the High Sheriff to verbalize my theories and concerns and confided in them that my wife was dying of cancer and just wanted to die in peace in her home. I also confided that we had considered and were talking about having a family reunion, renting a hall for it and having some meals catered. After our second vandal attack and home invasion, we were kind of leaning toward not doing that, partially because some would be staying with us and we didn't want their cars vandalized as ours had been and partially because we were somewhat traumatized by the home invasion. We were not sleeping soundly and waking up at every little noise.

    The police encouraged us to go ahead with our plans. There could have been in excess of one hundred out of town family from as far away as Montana and North Dakota. I wasn't so much afraid for my wife's family's safety as I was for the intruder, had he decided to strike while they were here. Many of her family are gun toting cowboys who know how to use a gun and are capable of using a gun and can protect their families. I was more afraid that an intruder would be shot and killed and one of my relatives would end up in prison for it. My wife had the same fear and did not want to take that chance. We may have been a bit paranoid but I know that if I had had the opportunity, I probably would have shot a fleeing intruder, especially one that was trying to break into my home while I was in bed sleeping. One that had done this repeatedly and would do it again, I would want to put an end to it. This individual had already robbed my wife of the right to die in peace and I was angry enough to shoot him. The police promised more patrols by our home and the motels where our relatives would be staying but Kathy and I decided to give up our plans for a family reunion. The police kept insisting that it was some local kid which was more reason not to kill him. I disagreed with their reasoning

This Dummy Pulls His Own Strings

but they probably had information I didn't and that they were unwilling to share with me.

Because I was insecure, not sleeping well and not wanting to spend my final days in a prison cell, I started looking into security cameras. The police suggested game cameras that are battery operated and can be disguised easily. I wanted a camera that was clear enough to identify the vandals and this is not an undercover operation where I need to disguise the cameras. If vandals and thief's see a home is protected with cameras, wouldn't that be a deterrent? In my research I learned that the wireless cameras often get interference from other wireless devices such as police radios, garage door openers and others. As we move into the wireless age, I could see this interference increasing so I started looking for the hard wired type. It turned out that the wireless were the new technology so the hard wired ones were selling for little or nothing. The downside to the hard wired ones is it is hard to string the wires in a 200 degree attic in the middle of summer.

I found a set that had a DVR (Digital Video Recorder) with one terabyte of memory which would allow 8 cameras to record 24 hours a day for about 3 months before re-recording over. So I could take a trip to Denmark for 3 months and still catch the vandals when I came home. Actually it has the ability to view all the cameras recording from your laptop, Ipad, tablet or smartphone. It came with 8 night vision cameras and 8 channels and the wire to hook them up. It was capable of capturing sound but the cameras did not have sound on them. Do the vandals talk to each other and call each other by name? Unless they are on meth, probably not. They were so reasonably priced, I bought two sets. One for my home and one for my daughters.

I started installing the cameras and stringing the wire. I think I only had one of the eight installed when my son showed up on the scene and took pity on me and helped install the remaining 7. He did all the attic work while I enjoyed the outdoors. It was relatively easy, once Eric took over the attic job. That is, easy for me.

So back to the Amish farm family, I can understand how they felt, being harassed and bullied. You feel violated, afraid for your safety and life and that of your family. It's a form of terrorism because you feel terror. I don't blame them for packing up and leaving. Why would you want to live among bullies and terrorists? You have no idea how far these people will go in their crusade and if they are on drugs at the time of these incidents, there is no predicting what may happen. These are not the people of the friendly village of Drake I grew up to know and love.

I still enjoy going back to my hometown for a visit. I don't know everyone in town anymore and every time I return there are fewer that I know. However, those I do know, especially my old friends, I feel as if I have never been gone. We just pick up as if we see each other every day. We have familiarity and history and know each other's character and are comfortable with one another. It's a good feeling with emotions of friendship, honesty, caring, compassion and love. I get this feeling with my Army/Navy buddies, classmates and most people I have really gotten to know and shared life's meaningful moments with. So it goes.

9
Family - Heritage

Knuth

Preferred pronunciation is 'Ka-nooth' or 'Ka-noot'.
German dictionaries describe the name's true meaning as a 'noble family'.
In Swedish, the name means "clan" or "family".
English translation: old German word for "Noble", "Titled", "Aristocratic".

In the summer of 1885, my grandparents, William and Amelia Knuth, emigrated from Berlin Germany to New York City via boat with their baby Paul. At this point I am trying to trace where their origins were prior to Germany. There are Knuth's presently in Denmark. One of these, Christoffer the Count Knuth, who is in charge of Knuthenborg and the castle there, is in the process of refurbishing it. He thinks my ancestors were the branch of the family that immigrated to Germany. They were from the barony of Knuth-Conradsborg. If that is true, it indicates they were part of the nobility of Denmark. I can only speculate why they left and went to Germany. Perhaps it was for a better life, perhaps it was for freedom as opposed to the absolute monarchy and rule of the King. Did they leave before the fall of absolutism and the start of a democracy in 1848 or was it after that political change? Perhaps they were a lot like me and couldn't hold their tongue and got in political trouble and were forced out, which would be preferable to be-heading. The stories

I've heard are of a flight in the middle of the night to Germany by whatever means available, leaving their castle, wealth, nobility and most of their possessions behind. My imagination has a field day with the possibilities that would cause this.

There may have been jealous husbands or scheming wives involved or irate fathers or competition of relatives or just plain wanderlust. Christoffer doesn't know why they left either but has hundreds of pages of documents that he is willing to share with me. The problem is he is refurbishing the castle and it is a mess and he doesn't know where those documents are located at this time. I would speculate that we are related but just how, we don't know yet. Perhaps, when the castle is finished, he will locate the documents and share them and I can include any discoveries I make. Just in case that doesn't happen, I have his permission to share what he has shared publicly on the internet. This is about his family in Denmark and some history of it. I copied the article which was written by Christoffer or his family. If there are comments or further explanations in a different font (*Lucida Calligraphy*) they would be written by me not by Christoffer or his family. That information follows;

The History of Knuthenborg

Knuthenborg was first mentioned under the name of "Arsmarke" in 1328. Until 1662, the old stately home was favoured by some of the members of the ancient aristocracy who, through the imperial Diet, were the real wielders of power in Denmark, Norway, and the Faroe islands. The king was elected by the Diet.

In politics, a diet is a formal deliberative assembly. The Imperial Diet is an assembly and means the highest representative assembly in the empire. The term is mainly used historically for the Imperial Diet, the general assembly of the Imperial Estates of the Holy Roman Empire and for legislative bodies of certain countries.

The Urne family was one of the most powerful families at that time. Three generations of the family owned Arsmarke from 1527 – 1667.

When King Frederick III (1609 – 1670) introduced Absolutism, and with it the absolute monarchy in 1660, he brought new men into the nobility that he collected around him. One of these men was Cornelius Pederson Lerche, a career diplomat, and, in 1667 he became the owner of Arsmarke amongst other properties. In 1667, his daughter, Sister Lerche, married the Mecklenberg nobleman, Christoffer von Knuth, who was in the service of the Danish King Christian V (1646 – 1699). The Knuth/Lerche married couple proved to be excellent for Arsmarke, enlarging it through building, acquisition and exchange.

Their son, Adam Christoffer Knuth, became the first count in the family in the year 1714 under King Frederick IV. The old Arsmarke became the new county of Knuthenborg.

Counties, baronies and manor houses were constructed as a consequence of Absolutism. The large manor house estates underpinned the system and could not therefore be mortgaged, loaned or broken up. These estates were to be handed down intact to the oldest son, just like the kingdom itself. It was the duty of the liege/feudal lord to reflect and maintain the King's glory and be his representative in the estates. This was a tax-free position, but with the same responsibilities as those of a mayor in a local authority.

After the fall of Absolutism in 1848 and the introduction of the new charters in June 1849, the Diet concluded a declaration of intent on the dissolution of the counties, baronies and great houses. These were the fiefdoms of Absolutism, so they were no longer in keeping with the new spirit of democracy. In 1919 the declaration passed into law and in the following years the manor house estates passed into private hands. As a countermeasure, the majority of the land and the art treasuries went to the state. The land was distributed to smallholders and many of the art treasures are today in private collections or in museums all around the world. In many cases, the manor house estates survived with new owners, but Knuthenborg today is still the property of the thirteenth generation of the same family.

Dwight E. Knuth

The Danish Knuth Family

For twelve generations the Knuth family has been responsible for the growth and development of the great estate of Lolland. Chance, in the form of, for example early death, has had an influence on many of these generations.

There can only be one Count in a family, and this is also true in the Knuth family. First, when the current Count dies, will the oldest son become the bearer of his title. It was agreed in the law of 1919, mentioned above, that the holder of the title of feudal Count would keep it for three generations. After that, the head of the family will be a normal count, and his wife a normal countess. The same rules apply for to the previous feudal barons. That the current countess of Knuthenborg is also called Bille Brahe lies in the line of descent of her own family, one of the ancient Danish nobility with strong Scanic (Swedish) ties.

This concludes Christoffer the Count Knuth's documentation.

The German/American Knuth Family

My uncle Rev. Herman & my aunt Nettie Knuth (top) and my paternal grandparents William and Amelia Knuth (bottom).

This Dummy Pulls His Own Strings

Back to my grandparents whose parents or grandparents, we believe, fled from Denmark to Germany. My grandfather had served in the German Army for the required amount of time all young men of Germany had to serve. It appeared to him that he might have to go back in the Army and serve some more time so he decided to go to the United States where he already had a brother living. My grandparents immigrated by boat to the United States.

There is the story of them arriving in New York City with a baby that needed to be fed a bottle. The year was 1885 and they were both 26 years old and had been married about one year. Grandpa was busy getting their belongings off the boat, trunks of personal belongings and clothes, all their possessions they brought with them from Germany. They couldn't speak any English and grandma needed to heat a bottle for the baby. They had a little portable kerosene stove with them they used to heat the milk on so they could feed the baby. This stove was with the possessions grandpa was retrieving from the boat. The baby, Paul, was hungry and crying. Grandma managed to communicate with signs and speaking German to let the clerk at the store know she needed milk and cereal for the baby. When she got the milk, she had no means to heat it but somehow managed to get materials together that would burn. I would guess probably old newspaper, scraps of wood from packing crates or whatever was available. On the streets of New York, she started a bon fire and heated the baby's milk. Once grandpa retrieved their possessions, they had the little kerosene stove they could use to heat the baby's' milk and whatever else needed heating, perhaps their hands.

I have a stove that is identical to the one they used. I bought it at my sisters' auction. She had gotten it from my cousin Tyler Kriedemen who had bought it at an auction and given it to my sister. When my sister showed it to my Dad, he got all excited and said it was identical to the stove his parents brought from Germany and used to heat the baby's milk.

I can relate to being in a strange country and not speaking their language and trying to communicate. My wife, Kathy, daughter, Kimberly and my wife's sister Vivian Larson and I took a trip to Italy and rented a Villa outside the village of Lucca. None of us could read or speak Italian. We also rented a car for our transportation. Some of our language barriers were using an ATM (Automatic Teller Machine), using a telephone, reading the road signs, asking for directions, shopping in a grocery market, shopping in general, ordering at a café or bar, using toll booths, filing a lost luggage report, communicating with Italian police officers after they had our vehicle towed and the list goes on. I'm sure Grandpa and Grandma had different communication needs than we did but I can empathize with what they went through.

Like my Grandmother, I didn't give up until I accomplished my goal and the Italians seemed to appreciate the challenge of communicating with someone with little brain. Bonjour.

My grandparents and baby Paul took a train from New York City to Vinton, Iowa where grandpa got a job on a farm and grandma did housework for others. They saved their wages until they had paid back all they owed for their fare to America, which had been financed by grandpas' brother Charley. I've been told that Grandma's wages went to repaying the debt for coming to the U.S. while Grandpas's earnings went for living expenses and savings for their future. When they had enough saved to begin farming they went to Plymouth County near LaMars, Iowa. They cash rented land and farmed there for 5 years. Their second child, Elizabeth, was born there on Dec. 16, 1886. All the rest of their children were born here except for Elsie.

One of my Grandfather's brothers, Rev. Fred Knuth was sent to North Dakota as the first missionary from the Evangelical United Brethren Church. He saw the land that was available and wrote to his brothers, telling them about it.

Grandpa and two of his brothers heard of the governments homestead act which gave 160 acres to farmers for settling the prairies and they went to North Dakota to find an area to homestead. My grandfather, two of his brothers, August and Louis Sr. chose homesteads north and east of Balfour, ND. They then returned to Iowa to move their families and possessions to

This Dummy Pulls His Own Strings

ND. The family took an immigrant train from Iowa to ND. The immigrant train had a car for the cattle and horses and any other animals they were bringing along with space for feed for the animals and any farm implements they were bringing. It also had space for them to sleep and eat on the trip. The three brothers and grandpas' two oldest boys, Paul and Louis rode in this car while the ladies rode in a passenger car on the same train from Iowa to North Dakota.

I can imagine that after arriving in Balfour, the car with the farm implements and animals was unloaded. The wagons would have been loaded with their possessions and the horses hooked up and off they would go to their homesteads which were probably about 10 to 15 miles from the train station with one small river to cross. They may have had to make several trips as I'm sure they brought some farm implements with them such as a plow and probably a stove for cooking and heat. I would guess they had to construct temporary living quarters and shelter for the animals until something more permanent was erected.

There were no trees, just barren prairie with grass for miles. The only shade would be from buildings, wagons etc. I would think they would have thrown up a barn of sorts for the animals. They would have had to haul all the farm implements from Balfour where they got off the train and of course bring all the farm animals with them. I was told they built a granary next to the barn, sharing one wall of the barn with the granary to save money. All the lumber would have to be purchased and hauled presumably from Balfour where the train station was. This granary is what they lived in until they had the house built which I'm sure was done immediately so they could free up the granary to store grain after the first harvest.

I was also told they had to haul all the water for their use so I'm sure digging a well was a high priority. They didn't drill wells back then but physically dug a hole that was about three feet square, give or take a foot. As they proceeded to dig deeper in search of water, they would shore up the sides with timbers and lumber to prevent the sides from collapsing. They would also create a ladder on one side so there was a way to go down the well to the bottom to clean out the sand that would flow into the bottom along with the water. I helped my father clean out our well on our farm located about a mile from grandpas. I would guess our well was about 40 feet deep with about two feet of water at the bottom. It was deep enough to be completely dark at the bottom. I would go down to the bottom with a pail and shovel and fill the pail with the sand that had accumulated. Dad would pull the pail of sand to the top using a rope and pulley, dump it and send the pail back down. We would do this until we had a couple feet of water at the bottom. As you would pump the water out of the well, water would flow into it underground from wherever the source was. In a few years it would again fill up with fine sand and we would have to clean it out again.

They also had to break up the prairie so they could plant a crop. For this they used horse pulled farm implements, called gang plows. They probably didn't worry too much about fences because they had some young lads to herd the cattle and there was plenty of prairie grass for the cows and horses to eat. They did have to make hay and store it to feed the cattle and horses in the winter. At least they didn't have to cut down trees and pull out the stumps before breaking up the sod and planting a crop. They did have to clear the land of rocks and dig out the large ones and drag them into piles so they wouldn't break the farm equipment. It was a hard life of work from sun up to sun down.

One option that some homesteaders used for a house and other buildings was a sod house. I have seen at least one sod house that was built south of Drake on a homestead. This was a house built of prairie sod which is the roots of the grass and the earth held together with the roots. Much like the modern day sod used for making an instant lawn, only much thicker, probably six inches to a foot thick and was cut in rectangles or squares that were manageable to be lifted and stacked much like block construction. The roofs were of poles with sod laid on top of the poles. Grandpa did not build one of these sod houses but built a wooden frame house which indicates he had enough money saved to allow him to do this. As my Dad and many of his siblings said, he was a good provider and manager of resources.

They hired a carpenter to build a house on the farmstead and "old uncle", great grandpas' brother Carl Theodore Knuth, told them if they would allow he and his wife to live with them, he would pay to add an extra room for their bedroom onto grandpa's house. This they did. My grandma was very grateful to "old uncle" because when they had a crop failure in Iowa while they were cash renting the land, "old uncle" mortgaged his home and lent the money to grandpa and grandma so they wouldn't be evicted and could farm it. He also helped Grandma any way he could and did a lot of work in the garden. My dad gave me the hoe he used in the garden which appeared homemade and was quite short which is the way he wanted it. I also have the table he kept beside his bed where his Bible rested. My cousin, Rev. Tyler Kriedeman, son of my Aunt Lillie, gave me the table. Tyler was also a man of the cloth and served as a minister for the Congregational denomination in many locations. Tyler was probably the first of his generation of Knuths' to complete college.

There was plenty to do on the homestead to keep everyone busy and out of trouble from daylight to dark. Once they were settled with a house, barn, out buildings and fences there was time for socializing with neighbors who were mostly relatives. The neighbors got together and built a church on the main road to Balfour, now known as highway 14. Of course where there is a country church, there is a country cemetery. The church was later sold to the Lutherans and moved into Butte but the cemetery is still there and was being cared for, at least mowed several times a year. There are some of my relatives buried there including old uncle and his wife. Once the church was moved, the cemetery no longer received occupants. Most former church members were buried in the Balfour cemetery which is where my grandparents, parents, some aunts and uncles and cousins are buried. The church is still standing in Butte and was functional but I am not sure if it still is. I attended the wedding of my brother-in-law there at which time it was still a Lutheran church and was situated next to the home of the bride, Pamela Federanko. She married my wife's brother, Michael Hoffman.

Things went well for the homesteaders and my grandfather started buying more land. More land meant they needed more horses for planting and harvesting. At one time grandpa had eighteen horses and I'm not sure how many acres. Of the 10 children, he provided 8 of them with wedding gifts of 80 acres which adds up to 640 acres of land plus his homestead of 160 acres making 800 acres. That was a lot of land back in the early 1900s when they were farming with horses. One of Grandpas' boys, Frederich, died young and one of his daughters never married. He had seven sons and three daughters so there were plenty of men to do the work. All of the land was adjacent or close to the homestead. Perhaps he was repaying them for all the hard work they had done to make a go of the homestead and expanding it. Also, as the kids got married and left home, there wasn't enough manpower to farm that much land.

The only daughter that never married, did not have a farm. The story I was told is that she had a suitor but grandpa did not like him for some reason and chased him off and promised her she would always have a home with him and grandma. The suitor must not have been worth his salt if he let that discourage him or he was not in love but was looking for a cook and housekeeper. That was probably a test by grandpa to see if he was worthy of his daughter. She was probably better off without him.

There were not many roads established and maintained when the homesteaders arrived. There was however what was referred to as section lines. A section of land is one square mile and a section line would be around that section of land. This was used to determine land boundaries and these section lines usually had a track where the farmers drove from field to field with the wagons. If the land was prairie, you could drive anywhere on it but if it was cultivated land you wouldn't want to drive on the crops. Therefore the farmers used the section lines for roads. They consisted of two wheel tracks, just enough room for one way traffic.

By the time the homesteaders arrived on the scene, 1901, the Indians had been assigned to reservations so these homesteaders did not experience the Indian battles or wars in this area. Their biggest challenge was the weather which could be brutal, both in the summer and winter. They needed rain for the crops, gardens and feed for the animals. They were pretty much self-sufficient if they got enough rain. The winters were especially brutal partially because there weren't any trees for windbreaks around the farms. It didn't take long for the farmers to plant trees to break the wind, especially in the harsh North Dakota winters. Just north of the homestead was an area known as the sandhills and north of them was the Souris (Mouse) river. There were trees and bushes growing in the sandhills and along the river. The sandhills had chokecherry and juneberry bushes whose fruit was used for pies, jellies and jams. The river had cottonwood trees among others. Many of the farmers transplanted young trees from the sandhills and river for wind breaks and the berry bushes for the fruit. Another danger was prairie fires. If a fire was ignited on the prairie from lightening or railroad trains or other sources, it would race across the prairie burning everything in it's path. Once the land was plowed around the farm it provided a fire break.

Someone commented on Ghost's of North Dakota web site that a young teacher and six of her students were caught in school with a prairie fire approaching with a fierce wind driving it. She and the children ran across the prairie toward a plowed field but the fire caught up to them and they all perished. The wind was blowing so hard that it pushed the fire right past the school without burning it. If they had stayed in the school they would have survived. Before the teacher died she said she had made a mistake.

Some of the difficulties of tracing the roots of my family is the fact that many people changed their names or spelling of them, either by chance, error and sometimes on purpose. Remember, many immigrants were running from the law in their native land and it is no stretch to imagine they would change their name out of fear of being discovered. Some were in trouble in their native land, politically and did not want to be found.

Such may be the case with my great grandparents if they indeed did flee Denmark under the cover of darkness. My Father said that his ancestors fled for their lives in the middle of the night because they were part of the ruling family that was overthrown. They only took with them what they could carry. My grandparents also have inconsistencies in their names. We always thought their names were William Knuth and Amelia Nehls. William was born June 13, 1858 in Klein Luke, Germany. Amelia Nehls was born Dec. 13, 1858, I assume also in Germany but don't know. I have not seen either birth certificate and the names on them if they exist. According to a family Bible, it records that they were married April 14, 1884 and it lists their names as Julius Christian Wilhelm Knuth and Augusta Emilie Johana Nehls. If these were their birth names, they adopted variations of their third and second names, for whatever reason is not known. William appears to be a derivative of Wilhelm, possibly an Americanized version. Amelia appears to be a derivative of Emilie, again, possibly an Americanized version. They came by boat to New York City in 1885 but the Ellis Island computerized records only go back to the late 1890s. In a 1900 census of household members, it lists "old uncle" Carl Theodore Knuth as Charles Knuth age 69. I myself have experienced a name change by an error of the government. When I applied for my social security card as a lad, the government added an extra L in my middle name so it is spelled Elldon instead of Eldon as it should be.

This Dummy Pulls His Own Strings

Grandpa & Grandma William & Amelia Knuth
Homestead as it appeared in the 1940's

Family picture – missing is Herman Knuth
(assuming he is taking the picture)
Top row L to R, George Knuth, Charley Knuth, Grandpa's oldest brother Great Uncle Charlie Knuth, William Knuth Jr., Grandpa William Knuth Sr, Grandma Amelia Knuth, Minnie August Bartles Notbohm holding Carl Jr. Notbohm, Anna Knuth (Paul's wife). Bottom row L to R, Elsie Knuth, Elizabeth Knuth, Louis Knuth, Lillie Knuth holding Erma Notbohm, Carl Sr. (Charley) Notbohm holding Fred Notbohm, Paul Knuth holding his son Henry Knuth. Louis died in 1918 from the influenza outbreak so this photo would be prior to that.

Dwight Knuth

Dwight age 3 1/2

I was born Dwight Eldon Knuth on March 24, 1942 during a North Dakota blizzard at the hospital in Drake, ND. My Father, George Harvey Hugo Knuth had taken my Mom, Margaret Alma (Valentine) Knuth to the hospital in Drake, ND. They lived on a farm about 10 miles northwest of Drake or about 3 miles northwest of Guthrie, ND. Guthrie is now a ghost town of ND. The last time I drove by, it had returned to prairie with no visible buildings.

They had cows to milk, horses, pigs and chickens to feed and probably other farm animals as well as kids, so staying with my mom after I was born, even though it was snowing and blowing, was not an option for my dad. The cows needed milking twice a day, morning and night. My twelve year old sister, Verla had

This Dummy Pulls His Own Strings

gone to the country school that morning so when school was over she would be alone at the farm house. The school was only about one and a half miles from the farm so she could walk but she had cousins that also went to that school and lived across the road from the farm so they would either walk together or our uncle Paul Kriedeman would pick them all up from school. These were the days before telephone land lines in the rural areas and God hadn't invented cell phones yet, so there was no telephone communications. There wasn't any electricity to the farm or running water either. Kerosene lanterns were used for night lighting along with candles and with their use came the danger of fire. To heat the house, coal and wood were used in a cook stove or parlor stove. That day, night and for several days there was a blizzard. When the blizzard stopped, all the roads were blocked.

According to my sister Fern's story, who was four at the time, it was already snowing when my parents and my sister Fern, headed for Drake in the sleigh pulled by horses. Everyone, especially the children would be bundled up in blankets or quilts because in a sleigh you are exposed to the elements. The adults often draped a blanket over their lap and legs. It was about a 10 mile trip from the farm to Drake but they were planning to stop at Guthrie, just about 3 miles from the farm to drop off Fern with my Dad's sister, Aunt Elsie. This was my Mother's fourth pregnancy but they were still apprehensive and in a hurry because of the snow. Fern, being only 4, had no clue as to what was taking place. She loved to stay with Aunt Elsie and Uncle John but for some reason, unknown even to her, she didn't want to stay that day but wanted to go along to town.

I can imagine there were some hushed conversations between my parents and quite possibly some anxiety and Fern probably picked up on it and was either frightened or thought they were on some sort of a secret adventure. She says she was quite insistent and perhaps there were tears. Dad promised he would bring something back from town that she always wanted. She did want a baby in the family but in those days, pregnancies were not discussed, especially with young children who had no clue about babies, how they came about or their birth. Neither was it proper to try to explain babies to young children. Instead, they would tell the children when a baby was born that "the Stork" brought the baby and dropped it down the chimney. Sounds like a derivative of Santa Claus. I'm surprised that the pre-school age siblings never tried to play stork and deliver a baby by dropping it down the stairs, possibly their newborn sibling they were supposed to be watching.

Fern said that while mom was pregnant with me, if mom was not feeling well or suffered any of the symptoms of pregnancy, they simply explained them to her as mom was having heart problems. My mother often said I caused her much heart burn and other heart aches, even after my birth. Even more than a baby in the family, Fern had been wishing for a doll baby buggy, so when Dad promised to bring her something she always wanted, a baby buggy is what she thought she was getting.

Fern stayed in Guthrie with Aunt Elsie and Uncle John who owned and operated a Garage/Implement dealership/general store. My parents continued their journey to Drake to the hospital there, with the horses and sleigh and the snow coming down and the wind blowing, commonly referred to as a blizzard. As the storm intensified and the hour grew late, Uncle John and Aunt Elsie discussed weather George, my dad, would be able to make it back or would have to stay in town. They knew if it was at all humanely possible, he would try to make it home because he had chores awaiting him at home. Cows to milk, animals that needed feed and water and an older daughter, Verla who was 12, home alone keeping the home fires burning. There was always the worry that someone would get caught in a blizzard, get lost and freeze to death. I can imagine that this was the case at this time. In fact, my maternal great grandfather Switzer had frozen to death in ND but that is a story for later.

After the dinner hour or supper hour as it was referred to back then, came and went and dad was not back yet, the anxiety grew. Somewhere around 7:30, dad showed up and Aunt Elsie insisted he eat as she had saved him some supper. Dad said they had to get going right away or they wouldn't make it back to the farm. If he quickly ate or didn't is not clear in my sisters memory. Fern was too excited to see what her daddy had brought her and happy to see her daddy to remember all the details. When Fern inquired as to what he had brought her, Dad told her it was something she always wanted and that her mother was in town with him and it was a baby brother. As Fern described it; "I was so sure I was getting a baby buggy plus my mother didn't come home but stayed in town with that baby brother, so I was crushed". She reminds me to this day what a disappointment I was. I've been pretty good at upholding that reputation.

Dad bundled up Fern and they proceeded to the sleigh and horses and into the storm and on to the farm. They were a lot braver and tougher back in those days but it was a necessity to survive. Horses were quite good at finding their way back to the barn and it's warmth and feed and water. I can remember dad telling of just letting the horse find the way home sometimes when it would storm. I don't know if I could have that much faith but I suppose with experience your faith would grow. Without communication such as telephones, there was a lot of anxiety and worry for your loved ones. I'm sure mom was concerned about dad and Fern out in the blizzard and wondered if they made it safely home and dad was concerned as to the welfare of mom and his new child.

Fern said it stormed for several days and when it finally ended the snow was blown into snow banks that were five to ten feet tall. I would guess from my own childhood, that there were snow banks higher than that in places. I can recall snow banks as high as some houses and other buildings. They had to shovel a path to the barn from the house and the snow banks in the yard were nearly as tall as dad. It was like a tunnel to her, walking to the barn through the path with snow walls 5 feet tall. In years to come they referred to this blizzard as the blizzard of 42.

Fern proclaims she was a daddies' girl but she wanted her mommy, desperately. She was already disappointed because she didn't get a baby buggy. Now she was not the baby of the family anymore but had a baby brother that would compete for and demand her parents and siblings attention. Already, the sibling rivalry begins and I'm not even home yet. Since she was miserable, she was going to make everyone else miserable. It is common for children to act up when a new sibling comes along especially if you were the baby of the family to this point. Verla was on her hands and knees scrubbing the kitchen floor. Fern laid down on the floor right in front of where Verla was going to scrub and would not move. Every time Verla would come to move her she would scream and kick. Dad happened to come in from the barn and witnessed this behavior. Fern got her first and only spanking from him.

I guess you could say, I was responsible for it and she hasn't let me forget it either. Dad was a very patient and compassionate man but Fern believes that her orneriness had finally gotten to him. It was probably the last straw after all he had been through the last few days and with the additional worry for his wife and newborn son. Fern said she shaped up after that and was on her best behavior.

All the roads were blocked and even the horses and sleigh was not an option to get to town so dad used the only available method to get there, his feet. Dad walked the Great Northern railroad tracks which were about a mile SE of the farm to Guthrie and then walked the road to Drake. I'm sure he had to reverse that to get back home to do chores. When the roads were cleared of snow enough for the horses and sleigh to travel on, dad went to town and brought Mom and I home. I remember it well or perhaps not at all.

Dad was still farming with horses when I arrived on the scene but owned a case tractor with lug wheels. Fern said she hated those lug wheels because they made big holes in the farm yard. I'm sure that made it difficult to push her baby buggy which she finally acquired or to pull a wagon filled with cans of water from the well to the house, one of her tasks as a child. Dad used the case tractor to power the threshing machine at threshing time.

This Dummy Pulls His Own Strings

Prior to the case tractor Dad owned a threshing machine that was powered by steam and Dad would have to get up early enough to get the steam built up to power it. Dad owned a threshing machine and it was shared/rented with all the relatives and neighbors at threshing time. Generally, threshing the grain was not only a work event but a social event. They found by working together, they could accomplish much more and get the grain harvested and in storage quicker.

The process to do this was to first cut the grain with a binder which was so called because it would cut the grain and make sheaves or bundles of grain tied together with binder twine. These bundles would be dropped behind the binder in the field on the ground. The farmers would then have to stand these bundles up in the field in bunches with bundles leaning against one another to keep them upright. This was referred to as shocking the grain, as in standing it up. The groups of bundles standing together in the field were called shocks. This would keep the grain heads off the ground so the dew or rain didn't cause the grain to sprout. When the threshing machine was available on the farm, these bundles would be gathered by the farmers into hay racks and hauled to the threshing machine. Using pitch forks, they would be pitched into the threshing machine from the hay racks and the threshing machine would do the job it was designed to do, separating the grain from the straw and chaff.

The threshing machine was a unique machine that was quite large and looked somewhat like an elephant with it's long flexible snout. This snout was where the straw came out and was blown into a straw pile. These piles of straw had many uses. The main purpose was to use the straw for bedding for cows, horses, pigs, sheep or whatever animals that you raised. Cats would make nests in the straw in the barn and have baby kittens, dogs would make beds in it to stay warm when the temperatures dipped below zero and it made clean beds for the cows or other animals. Out in the field, these huge piles of straw were used by the wild animals to burrow into to keep warm in the winter and many of them such as fox, badgers, skunk, raccoons would use them for dens to have their babies. Mice also loved them as there were always some seeds of grain among the straw. Travelers that were caught out away from home, often used these straw piles to make a bed for the night and if it was cold could burrow into the pile of straw and stay warm. Railroad Hobos or bums would use them for sleeping and then go to the nearest farm to raid gardens, chickens, eggs etc. Sometimes, depending on the person, they would ask for a meal or some would work for a meal.

The threshing crew was usually the farmers themselves but sometimes there were for hire crews that would go from farm to farm with the threshing machine to harvest the grain. These crews would consist of sometimes 10 or more men. There were hay racks that brought the grain to the threshing machine, wagons that hauled the grain to the granary for storage, men to drive these and load and unload them as well as the men that were required to keep the threshing machine running and the steam pressure at the right level for an efficient operation. All these men needed to be fed and they often times had a cook wagon that traveled with the threshing machine and crew with several young ladies cooking most of the day to feed the crew.

My mother and many of my aunts worked on such a cook wagon when they were young ladies, wives and mothers. With my Dad's threshing machine, the farmer whose grain was being thrashed provided the food and his wife did the cooking for the threshing crew. My sister recalls threshing time as a lot of work but lots of fun. Some of her tasks, before she was 5 years old were to bring in corn cobs to burn in the cook stove for the food preparation. She also had to pick the garden vegetables and weed the garden. After she turned 5 her tasks increased to include milking some of the cows, pump water for the cows if the wind was not blowing and the windmill not turning to pump the water, haul water to the house from the pump in her wagon and after my arrival, watch me and keep me happy and entertained. She informed me she got over her disappointment in me being her surprise rather than a baby buggy and was quite proud of me and thought I was a cute little bugger.

This Dummy Pulls His Own Strings

My parents grew a large garden and would pick bushels of cucumbers, tomatoes and beans. They always tried to pick all the strawberries, watermelons and muskmelons (cantaloupe) before the threshers came because at the end of the day of threshing, the threshers would raid those patches and clean them out if there was anything left.

My uncle, the Rev. Herman Knuth and his wife, Nettie, did not have any children. They would get foster children from the children's home in Fargo to give them a home to grow up in. Of course, being part of the family, they would have to do their share of work on my uncles' farm. He was the minister at the Guthrie Baptist church and later moved to Stanley, ND to be the minister there. While he was still on his farm just about a mile from my Dad's farm, in addition to being the minister of the Baptist church, he also farmed. He had two foster sons.

One was William Benbow who was my brother Dorel's best friend. When World War II started and after the attack at pearl harbor and the US entered the war, both Dorel and William joined the Navy. William was serving aboard the U.S.S. Farragut as an electrician. He was in the process of adjusting the position of an electric fan in the after deck of the Engineers living compartment. He was being assisted by one of his shipmates of whom there were several in the compartment at the time. He had finished positioning the fan as desired and then stood on a deck locker to insert the electric plug into the receptacle nearby. After doing this he reached for the switch to turn the fan on. After touching the switch, he was observed to be unable to let it go for several seconds. Finally, he did succeed in letting it go, whereupon he stepped down from the deck locker onto the deck and started to shake his hand. At this time he slowly fell to the deck. One of the sailors in the compartment immediately ran for the medical officer who arrived on the scene shortly thereafter. William had already begun cheyne-stokes breathing when the doctor arrived. The doctor was unable to perceive any heart action and sent for some adrenalin to use as a heart stimulant which he applied as soon as it was brought to him. Neither the stimulant nor the artificial respiration, which was continued for about 40 minutes, was effective and he was pronounced dead by the doctor at 1515, 7 December, 1943. In the opinion of the doctor his heart had stopped almost immediately after receiving the shock.

A loose wire in the switch connections was believed to have shorted the body of the switch causing it to be "hot". The weather was very warm at the time and Benbow was sweating profusely. This plus the fact that he was standing on a metal locker top probably combined to thoroughly ground him thus greatly increasing his susceptibility to the effect of the shock.

The other foster child of Uncle Herman and Aunt Nettie was James Muldoon. He was the intellectual type and probably not cut out for the farm life. He went on to college and became an English high school teacher and pursued his education, attaining a Masters degree in English. As the story goes, Jim was very apprehensive around horses and was not very adept at controlling them. Horses are smart animals and can sense this. Horses normally move around a bit stamping their feet, swishing their tails, shaking their heads and this activity would make Jim nervous and cause him to nervously talk to the horses saying, "whoa daisy, easy daisy" when in fact the horses were only doing what they normally do. It was well known by the area farmers and the threshing crew that Jim was nervous around horses and sometimes, for excitement, someone would spook Jim's team so they would take off and they could watch Jim panic and have a good laugh.

My Dad, being the compassionate man he was, would always give Jim a gentle team of horses that was not spooked easily and was laid back and easy to control and drive. Often times it would be my brother Dorel that was the one that would spook Jim's horses at the end of the day, when the threshing was finished for the day and everyone needed a good laugh. I'm sure there were others encouraging Dorel to do it. The horses would take off with Jim in a panic, holding on for dear life and trying to get the horses stopped. It provided some entertainment and a few laughs after a hard day's work. Jim was a good sport and although he was not happy about being the object of their entertainment,

This Dummy Pulls His Own Strings

he wasn't one to lose his temper easily or to fight. Had it been me, I probably would have returned to punch the perpetrator in the nose, brother or not. That would have provided more entertainment for the threshing crew.

I guess it was lucky that there was close to a 20 year age difference between my brother and I. He enjoyed teasing but was not fond of being on the receiving end of it. His temper was quicker to show itself than Jim's. I can remember Mom saying to him when someone would get the best of him by teasing him, "you can dish it out but you can't take it". I think she may have said the same to me a time or two. I guess we were alike in more than one trait. Dorel was a boxer in the Navy so I am sure he could defend himself and probably do some damage to his opponent. I was also a boxer but we never got into a fist fight or used our boxing skills against one another, probably because of the age difference. I believe it would have been a close contest that could have gone either way. He was tough, strong, sinewy, determined and quick so even though he was older could have given me a good contest and probably cleaned my clock.

It was interesting to me that my Father, who was a gentle soul, had two sons that liked to box. I think my Father just had better control over his temper and emotions and suppressed the urge to fight. I know Dad enjoyed watching wrestling and boxing on television and could get quite excited while watching it. Even when he had good reason to, I don't believe my Dad ever threw a punch. It wasn't that he lacked the courage, he just had his emotions under better control than the rest of us.

Back to the Threshing crew. When they were threshing my Dad's crops, it was my mother's duty to feed the crew, some of them breakfast and all of them lunch, around noon, and supper at the end of the day. These were long days because they started as soon as it was dry enough in the morning and went until dark some days, if there was a threat of rain and they wanted to finish up. Another of my sister Fern's tasks was to take the lunch out to the threshers. Lunch would probably consist of cold left over fried chicken, hard boiled eggs, fresh tomatoes, pickles, fresh buns or bread. I imagine they did not stop threshing but as farmers often do, ate lunch on the run. I would guess that when a thresher came in with a load of bundles, someone who had already eaten would unload the bundles while the driver of the horses, found a patch of shade and sat down to eat a quick lunch. At supper time, everyone would come to the farmhouse where Mom would serve as many as she could at the table, either in shifts or the rest would find somewhere outside to sit and eat, probably sharing the bones with the dogs. They would have several basins of water set up on the porch so everyone could wash up prior to the meal. These were men that would be black from the toil of threshing.

My Mom would get up at three AM to do her baking before the heat of the day set in. She would have fresh baked buns, fresh out of the oven, for their breakfast. She also baked many, many pies for the evening meal every day they were there. My mom was a great cook and the threshers knew they would be well fed at my mom's table. Later in life, she was the head cook at Camp Bently, a Baptist camp at Drake, where she fed a hundred or more campers, three meals a day. She had help in preparing the meals but was responsible for the menu and planning as well as preparing the meals.

Even though she was feeding a multitude, it always tasted like home cooking, not like institution food, such as you get at a hospital or even some restaurants. For the threshing crew, she had to prepare most of the meal the same day because there was no electricity and no refrigeration. Fried chicken was a staple in the fall because the baby chicks that were purchased in the spring would be all grown up and ready for eating. They would need to be killed the same day, dunked in boiling water to make picking the feathers easier, gutted and cut up for frying. All this would need to be done just prior to frying them.

There was usually fresh from the garden, corn on the cob, boiled or mashed potatoes, lots of them, wonderful gravy for the potatoes, fresh baked bread, fresh tomatoes from the garden and possibly fresh peas or beans from the garden and they probably were cooked in fresh cream from the cows. Of course there was always some sort of fruit pie, apple, strawberry/rhubarb, peach, juneberry (saskatoon), and on occasion, mincemeat. This could continue until the crop was all harvested and in the grain bins which could take a week or more depending on the crop that year, the number of workers and the weather. When they moved on to the next farm, because the threshing machine and tractor was owned by my Dad, our family would be invited to join the threshing crew for the evening meal. Back then, it was standard practice that even the women guests would help with the preparation of the meal and the serving of it to the men. You pitched in to help. You didn't sit around waiting for the hostess to serve you.

When I reflect on the hard work of my parents and their parents from sun up to sun down, I can understand why God set aside a day of worship and rest for them. My parents always observed the Sabbath and did as little as possible on that day. It was a day of socializing with friends, neighbors and relatives and of attending church and honoring and worshipping God. When I reflect on what our society has evolved into, complaining if the coffee isn't ready when we arise, much later than the sun, it seems like we have turned into a society of whiners and complainers. If we have to park our car more than a few paces from wherever we are going, we complain and many park in the handicap spaces. Then they probably go to their exercise club to maintain their health and again want to park in front of the door.

When you compare what our ancestors went through every time they went anywhere of any distance, they had to first catch the horse or horses, harness or saddle it/them, hook them to the wagon/carriage/sleigh and then ride or drive them to their destination, usually unprotected from the elements. When they got home they would have to unhook them from the vehicle they used, unharness or unsaddle them, rub them down, feed and water them and let them out in the pasture. Our common sense of yesteryear has turned into un-common sense of today. Our parents worked very hard so their children could have a better life than they did. I think they did a very good job, perhaps too good of a job so we have turned into whiney brats. See, just like our society, we don't accept responsibility or blame ourselves for our laziness but say it is our parent's fault for making our life too easy for us. So it goes.

To help with the perspective of the time of my birth, 1942 compared to our current time as I write this in 2015, my mother kept a sugar bowl on the top shelf of a cupboard my father had built in the kitchen. She kept 50 cents in the sugar bowl to buy medicine for the children, if any of them got sick. This was their health plan or health insurance and it was adequate. In comparison, when I retired in 2000 at the age of 58, I was no longer covered by work place insurance but had to purchase it myself. I spent in excess of $12,000 a year for each my wife and I for our health insurance. We still had co-pays to pay in addition to the insurance premiums and anything the insurance co. did not cover. When my wife, Kathy got cancer and had to have a mastectomy, chemotherapy, and radiation, I had to take out a mortgage on our home for $50,000 to pay our share of the medical bills. I must say, it was well worth it or any price because it gave her eight more years of life and you can't put a price on that. I would give all I have just to see her smile again and hold her hand.

Upon my birth, I joined my brother Dorel Harvey Knuth who was 18 years old and in the Navy fighting a war against Japan and Germany, my sister Verla Jean Knuth who was 12 years old and my youngest sister Fern Beverly Knuth who was 4 years old. My parents chose to name me Dwight Eldon Knuth after a cousin of mine who died when he was several months old and was named Eldon Dwight Chole. His Mom was my Dad's sister, Elsie Chole. Her husband, Walter Chole died the same year as their baby. Just imagine the grief of losing your husband and child in less than a year. This was before they had anti-depressants and other drugs to help you cope. The method of coping was work until you were so exhausted you could sleep and then get up and do it over again. Aunt Elsie later married John Kofstad and of course became Elsie Kofstad. Aunt Elsie and I shared the same day of birth as did my Mother's only sister Rebecca Brieher.

My Birthday partners, Aunt Elsie Knuth Chole Kofstad and Aunt Rebecca Valentine Brieher. Elsie is Dad's sister, Rebecca is Mom's sister.

At the time of my birth, my paternal grandfather lived on his homestead just about a mile away. One of his daughters, Aunt Lillie and her husband, Paul Kriedeman and their youngest son Delos lived with grandpa for a brief period. For whatever reason, they had lost their farm in foreclosure, possibly because of a failed crop, which was not uncommon. Not too many years later, grandpa sold the homestead and moved to Guthrie next to Aunt Elsie and Uncle John. Aunt Lizzy moved in with him there and did the cooking, cleaning and house work. Uncle Paul, Aunt Lillie and Delos moved to Minot.

My Father came from a large family, (9 siblings) most of whom were living when I entered the scene except for my paternal grandmother, Augusta Emilie Johana (Nehls) Knuth (she went by the name of Amelia) and one son, Frederich. My grandma had died of complications of diabetes. My Grandpa, Julius Christian Wilhelm Knuth, (he went by the name William) became my buddy and let me sit on his lap and play with his pocket watch. Back then they wore three piece suits that consisted of a pair of pants, a vest and a suit coat. Most vests had a little watch pocket to hold your pocket watch that was on the end of a chain which was attached to a button hole on one end and the watch on the other. You simply took hold of the gold chain and pulled the watch out of the watch pocket to see what time it was. These watches were usually fine crafted pieces of jewelry that were very fascinating to a little boy.

Grandpa had a full white beard and in my view was better than Santa Claus who I had never seen, much less sat on his lap. Grandpa lived in Guthrie right next to Aunt Elsie by the time I was old enough to remember. His unmarried daughter, Aunt Lizzy, as we called her, was a quiet lady that treated me as though I was special and I think she had it right. I would go from Aunt Elsie's to Grandpa's and Aunt Lizzy's and she would give me raw vegetables of whatever she was making. The heart of a cabbage, a peeled carrot or potato, celery or cucumber. Uncle John, Aunt Elsie's husband, had the only general store, gas station, garage and farm implement sales in Guthrie about a block from their home. Uncle John's gas station/general store was a gathering place for the local men to visit and pass the time. When I would go to see him at the store, he would give me a bottle of soda or as we called it, pop and sometimes a candy bar. Aunt Elsie always kept Hershey's chocolate bars and would give my sister Fern and I each one when we would come if we hadn't already received one from Uncle John. I'm sure they did this for my cousins as well as most children that came.

I also had a cousin who was the same age as I that lived in Guthrie. Her name was Glory Ann and she was the daughter of my Dad's brother Bill and his wife Francis. We played together on many occasions and were in the same graduating class in high school. My Dad's other sister was Lily Kriedeman, married to Paul. Dad's other brothers were Paul (Anna), Louie, Herman (Nettie) and Charlie (Lizzy).

My Mother only had one sibling and that was Aunt Rebbeca, married to Rev. William Brieher who was a minister for The Evangelical United Brethren Church which later merged to the Methodist Church. Dad's brother Herman was also a minister in the same denomination, different location.

Dad's brother Louie died in the 1918 influenza epidemic, Nov. 6, 1918. He was in the army at the time but was home on furlough. His furlough was up and he was supposed to report back but he asked for another week to help with the harvest. He was 30 years old at the time of his death. My Dad told me Louie was so sick and suffering so much and thought he was dying, either from the influenza or when he returned to the army, that he begged my Dad to take the gun and shoot him. Of course, my Dad didn't even consider it but his thoughts of the request was that Louie was not rational from the fever and pain. I'm sure there was some trauma of war that also was causing some depression but back then, it wasn't talked about.

My father later learned about pain prior to the birth of my sister Fern and of course prior to my birth. He was having a lot of leg pain and the Drs. told him it was rheumatism. Today they don't use that diagnoses anymore because it doesn't tell you much because it includes over 200 conditions. It is described as a regional pain syndrome or soft tissue rheumatism which can cause significant discomfort and difficulty. It is a painful condition of the joints or muscles in which neither infection nor injury is a contributing cause. Dad was farming but could not do the farm work so he hired one of the Strege boys, full time, to do the work. At one point, the Dr. in Balfour gave him a shot in the thigh, I would imagine for the pain. The sight developed a sore or boil and Dad went to the Dr. in Drake where there was a hospital. The Dr. in Drake put Dad in the hospital and proceeded to lance the boil. For years after, people would tell my sister Fern, they could remember the day they heard my Father scream when they lanced that boil. They said they could hear him three blocks from the hospital. They kept him in the hospital for quite a while because he was not healing. This was fall when farmers harvest their crops and he of course wanted to get home and help with or at least oversee the harvest. He asked the Dr. when he could go home. The Dr. told him he would be home for Thanksgiving. Time passed and it was getting close to Thanksgiving and it didn't appear that Dad was a whole lot better and Dad again asked the Dr. when he would be going home and reminded the Dr. that he told him he would be home for Thanksgiving. The Dr. replied, you can go home for Thanksgiving but when I told you that before, I didn't expect you to be alive at Thanksgiving.

They sent Dad home, even though he wasn't ambulatory. Dad would crawl on hands and knees to get around until he could stand upright at which time he graduated to crutches and then eventually to a cane. I'm sure from not getting any exercise and lying in bed for months his leg muscles had atrophied to the point they were useless. God hadn't made physical therapists yet. I experienced some of this when I was hospitalized for just three weeks. My leg muscles would not work normally. If the Drs. prognosis for my Dad had come true, neither my sister or I would have been born. Thank goodness, Drs. are not always correct in their diagnosis or predictions. Dad lived to the age of 89 and always had trouble with and pain in his legs.

Maternal Grandparents, the Valentine and Switzer Families
The Murder of David Switzer

My great great grandparents were David Switzer and Anna Mary (Varnes) Switzer. This story was told to me by my Mother, Margaret (Valentine) Knuth. I had her write it down to preserve the story as she told it. The following is her story as she wrote it.

Grandpa Switzers parents moved to Missouri from Pennsylvania, I don't know what year, with their family of four girls and Grandpa. His mother, Anna Mary (Varnes) Switzer, died in Mo. in 1857. One night the Jesse James outfit came to rob them. In trying to protect his family there was trouble and shooting commenced. Jesse James shot Mothers' Grandfather, David Switzer and killed him. There was another family that had moved with them when they moved from Pa. to Mo. This family packed up and took the orphaned children, four girls and one boy back to relatives in Pa. The children were Arabella, Susan, Mary Ann, Hulda and Winfield Scott, my Grandfather. When Grandpa was old enough he married Rebecca Ernest and they made a home for his four sisters. He and his wife had six girls and one boy.

Winfield and Rebecca Switzer, my Grandparents, had six girls and one boy. Next to the oldest of these girls was my Mother, Alma Margaret Switzer. We lived in Pa. until I was about eleven years old. Grandpa and Grandma Switzer came to Des Lacs, ND four years before my parents, Alma and Harvey Valentine. We came to Des Lacs, ND in 1910. We came on an immigrant train. It had a box car for machinery and animals and a separate passenger car for the people. There were twenty four people that came to ND at that time. I have lived in ND since that time. I lived at Des Lacs with my parents until I was married in 1920. I lived at Drake ever since.

This is the end of my Mother's written auto-biography.

The previous two paragraphs came from her hand written auto-biography I requested, before she started having Alzheimer's like symptoms and when her memory was intact along with her ability to think and communicate her thoughts. Her version of what happened to my great great grandparents, David and Anna Mary Switzer differs from one published in a history book titled, History of Johnson County Missouri. There are two of these books by two different authors but tell close to the same story that comes from newspaper articles or minuets of meetings of the vigilance committee. The authors of the two books are Ewing Cockrell and F.A. North.

I also found some inconsistencies in the history book version. For example, the history books say at the time of the robbery/

murder Anna Mary, his wife, was still alive and present. Death records give her death as 1857, 10 years prior to the robbery/murder. In the history books they spelled Switzer with an additional e, as in Sweitzer. In one chapter of the book they say there were three men that robbed them and in another chapter they say it was two men. The media is still the same with inconsistencies and inaccurate reporting.

I believe that the survivors that were present at the time of the actual murder probably thought it was members of the Jesse James gang and the murderer even had similarities to Jesse James and in fact could possibly have been him. There was never any real trial of the murderer and proof that he did it, so the wrong man may have been hung for it. It was a vigilante trial and execution. As for the history book inaccuracies in the wife's' death and spelling of the name, it is possible the records were inaccurate or the reporter got it wrong. I have to believe the children, one of which was my Mothers Grandfather who was 16 at the time of his father's murder, would know if their mother was alive at the time of the murder and the death records support that she was not.

I will attempt to glean details of the story from the history version and correct what I believe to be errors and merge what was told to me by my Mother. Understand that this is my version and assumptions and my logic enters in to my version of the story. It is probably just as accurate or more accurate as the media at that time.

First some background of the time of these events. The setting of the story is Missouri, in Johnson County, just southeast of Kansas City. The time is February 1867. The Civil War is barely over and Missouri was a border state between the North and South. Some of the citizens were Confederate supporters while others were Union supporters. They more than likely had men fighting on both sides in the war. The state sent representatives to both governments during the war. Added to this were soldiers that had returned from the war from both sides. Some of these soldiers had been taught the ways of war which was taking what you need or want, robbing, pillaging and yes, murder of innocent citizens,

This Dummy Pulls His Own Strings

not to mention rape. War is a lawless endeavor with much hatred and vengeance and can make honest law abiding individuals into gangs with a mob intelligence.

This was the case with the Jesse James brothers of Missouri. They were sons of a Baptist minister/hemp farmer. At the age of 16 Frank joined ranks with the confederate side in the civil war. He ended up with Quantrill's Raiders and when his younger brother Jesse turned sixteen, he joined Frank and the confederates. They had some issues of laws and treatment after the civil war and decided to take the law into their own hands. For a time they were considered the modern day Robin Hood and were thought to be robbing the rich to give to the poor. This proved not to be true. They were keeping the loot for themselves and were avenging deaths and alleged mistreatment of gang members and friends. This was the case with many of the citizens and former soldiers of both the Union and Confederate armies after the war. It was a violent and lawless environment especially in Missouri.

These gangs or mobs would terrorize the citizens by riding their horses into stores and shooting merchandise off the shelves and walls, striking defenseless men with their guns, riding into public gatherings, political or religious, shooting their guns and breaking up the gathering. Most of the time they wore some form of disguise to avoid detection but even when detected they were not punished for their deeds. These were the worst passions of the worst men, much of it learned and practiced in the civil war. Civil Authorities were afraid to interfere or powerless to do so. Courts, Juries and Judges were terrorized or bought off, returning the outlaws to the streets. One of these outlaws was Dick Sanders, a gang leader. Two of his men were Brackett Sanders and Bill Stevens. They were residents of Johnson County around Fayetteville, Hazel Hill and Warrensburg.

Some of the citizens were trying to bolster the resolve to rid the community of these outlaws. One such individual was General Frank P. Blair who was advertised to speak at Warrensburg. He was a champion of the peoples' rights. He was to speak of the lawlessness of the time and area. Bill Stevens, one of the areas lawless gang members, had threatened to kill Blair if he spoke. Gen. Blair was advised against speaking. He would not back down and ascended the platform to speak. He was interrupted and insulted by the lawless scoundrels in attendance many times. Around 2:00pm Bill Stephens came to the front of the platform insulting Gen. Blair and declaring his speech a damned lie. He was ejected but didn't give up and tried again and was again ejected. According to the history book, around 100 pistols were drawn and cocked and aimed at Gen. Blair. During all this commotion, someone knifed and killed Jim Stevens, Bills son. Bill Stevens took his dead son and left and was followed by his followers. Gen. Blair continued to speak and finished about 6:00pm.

Feb. 27th 1867 was cold and stormy. The wind was driving rain and sleet out of the north. David Switzer, a respected farmer in the area, was at home in his apartment with his five children, about eight miles north of Warrensburg. One room of the Switzer apartment was occupied and lived in by Mr. Younger and his wife. It is assumed this is the couple that came from Pennsylvania with the Switzer's but it is not known. Perhaps they were living with the Switzer's to help with the five children whose Mother had died ten years previous in 1857.

The history book states in two different chapters that two men or three men entered the room the Youngers were occupying. Weather it was two or three men they appeared to be under the influence of alcohol and were disguised. Disguised is probably another way of saying they had bandannas or handkerchiefs over their faces as outlaws of that era often did. They asked to stay the night because it was a cold nasty night and wanted shelter from the storm. Mr. Younger told them there was no room for them and they would have to leave. Mrs. Younger was frightened by their appearance and behavior and went to fetch David Switzer from another room. David came and engaged them in conversation, asking where they were from. With David in the room, it either evened the odds of males or made it two to three. One of them was dressed as a soldier, which I would assume to mean in uniform. The history book doesn't say if it was a Union uniform

This Dummy Pulls His Own Strings

or a confederate uniform. They told David they were from Ray County which was a short distance away and asked David where he was from. David told them he was from Pennsylvania. They instantly drew their pistols and fired two shots, both of which missed their mark, which was David. The mention of Pennsylvania by David Switzer, indicates to me that they were ex-confederate soldiers and assumed David was a Union sympathizer because he was from Pennsylvania, a union state. Therefore the guns appeared and shots were fired. I assume they missed the shots at close range on purpose because they wanted David alive to tell them where his money was. They told David, we want your money. This indicates they were there because they had heard that David, a fellow from Pennsylvania, had purchased a farm and had the money to pay for it in his possession.

Shots had already been fired, David's children were in the Apartment, the men had asked to stay the night and they appeared to be under the influence of alcohol. With these facts going through his mind, David may have thought he was going to be killed before this was all over. Whatever his reasoning and thinking, he attacked them and tried to disarm them. This was obviously the bedroom of the Youngers because there was a bed in the room that they fell across in the struggle that ensued. David literally threw them off of him and the bed and it was noted that he was very strong for an older man. They still had their guns and fired two more shots. One bullet struck David in the forehead and the other in the back. David immediately dropped to the floor. The men went through David's pockets and found $130.00. They didn't bother the Youngers or the children but probably had what they came for and were not afraid of repercussions, so just left. It is quite possible they were drunk because the next day $120.00 was found in the road near Hazel Hill, the route they would have taken, after leaving.

They knew this was the route they took because after leaving the scene of the crime, they met Jack Redford on the road and fired several shots at him, killing his horse which they found on the road the following day. Jack escaped. It's a mystery why they tried to kill Jack Redford, yet didn't kill the Youngers or David's children. They probably intended to rob Jack also.

The next morning the storm had abated but the rain had frozen and everything was covered in ice, roads, trees, homes, fields and even the grass which looked like fields of icicles. The news of the robbery/murder spread to Warrensburg by the next morning and the citizens were outraged. Of course there was much speculation as to who it was that had done it. One possibility was a neighbor of David's. By the description of the outlaws, it was thought that it was Dick and Brackett Sanders. With the outrage came the mob mentality of, we are fed up and not putting up with this anymore. As with most mobs, bravery and lack of rational thought increases. The bravest and most outraged become instant leaders. They swore to avenge the death of their fellow citizen, David Switzer.

A meeting was held at the court house at one o'clock to discuss the method of disbanding the outlaws. They appointed Colonel Isaminger chairman and N.B. Kline as secretary. Professor Biggar said at the meeting, "It is our duty to ferret out the murderers of our peaceable citizen, who has so lately been killed, and bring them to justice. Murderers may any day walk our streets with safety, and it is necessary that we engage detectives. We have not the same advantages that larger cities enjoy, and whatever action is taken now, is for our safety. I am opposed to summary vengeance, but when law cannot be enforced, and violators brought to justice, it is necessary for the people to take care of themselves if the law does not, is an indisputable right. We must unite and put down lawlessness."

At this meeting they drew up a document of whereas's an wherefore's and be it resolved's that pretty much said we are fed up and the authorities and courts aren't doing anything so we are taking matters into our own hands. It was reported that about 400 men attended this meeting. One minister, Rev. J.W.Newcomb addressed the crowd and said the meeting has his hearty approval. He also said that "He that draweth the sword shall perish by the sword". There were many respected citizens

This Dummy Pulls His Own Strings

who spoke and many former officers of the Union Army, Generals, Colonels and Majors. All agreed if they were to be rid of these lawless gangs they would have to do it themselves and quickly and quietly. A committee was appointed and the Whereas's and be it resolved's were accepted unanimously. The final Resolved was, that we will support a vigilance committee in executing summarily, all murderers, robbers, horse-thieves wherever they can be identified with certainty.

The vigilance committee first dealt with the desperado, the notorious Dick Sanders, the recognized leader of the band that allegedly murdered David Switzer. A posse of about 100 men went to Fayetville where they were joined by some townspeople. They proceeded to the Sanders home. They woke the occupants after surrounding the house and demanded their surrender. Dick refused to surrender until he learned a man he knew and trusted was along and then said he would surrender to him only. Dick and Brackett Sanders and another man came out and surrendered.

They were taken immediately to a place in the woods about a mile north of the Sanders home where the rest of the vigilance committee was waiting. It was about midnight.

The committee elected a Judge and they proceeded in a systematic manner of accusing the prisoner. Dick Sanders was brought before the Judge who addressed him as follows: "Richard Sanders, you are charged with one of the most infamous crimes known to law, not one but many. You are charged with murder and to make it still more infamous on your part and more horrible to a fine community I will add assassination."

Sanders interrupted the judge, saying "It's a damned lie". The Judge, without acknowledging the interruption continued; "You are charged with horse stealing; you are charged with murder and robbery, in the broadest sense of the word; you are charged with being at the head of a band of murderers and marauders who have for years made Johnson County the scene of death and destruction. And to crown your long reign of infamy I charge you with being the murderer of David Switzer. You have again spilled blood without any just provocation. The man whom you assassinated came to you in confidence not suspecting your murderous intentions. He asked you what you wanted. You said 'your money and your life' and you shot him dead."

"This was the story of Mrs. Groninger," said a man in the crowd. Sanders said, "It's false, she lied." Sanders was livid as well as nervous and had lost his audacity. He looked around the crowd and realized the determination and feeling of the mob. Had this been a civil arrest it would not be as serious but this was a mob mentality and it was obvious, his fate was sealed.

"Mrs. Groninger didn't lie," said the judge coldly, "for the crimes you have committed you must die. If we turn you over to the civil authorities you will escape or by some of your comrades in infamy, prove an alibi and be turned loose again upon society. If perchance you were tried, found guilty and sentenced to death by a civil court, there would be a chance for you to escape justice or you would stand on the scaffold if found guilty and jest with the hangman, or I fear profane the name of God with your dying breath. This must not be. You must die in secret, tonight, now. It will save your mother the shame of a son dying on the scaffold and she can say, he was murdered, killed by a mob. Listen, you are not the only one. Many of your companions will follow and that soon. This last outrage is more than we can bear. Your crimes demand an extraordinary reparation. You have broken in the houses with arms in your hands; you have committed another murder. You must die here. I now sentence you to hang by the neck until dead."

Sanders appeared to be dumb founded and did not reply. He was placed upon a horse and a hangman's noose placed around his neck with the other end tied to a tree limb above. The judge again asked Sanders who killed Switzer and he replied, "I don't know, I think Morg Andrews". A voice in the crowd said, "Oh hell, Dick! Drive up the mule". The horse was driven from the prisoner and Dick Sanders met his maker while his body swung from the rope.

His brother, Brackett Sanders and the other captive were released and the committee quietly dispersed. This author does not understand why his brother was released when it was thought he accompanied Dick and was present during the murder of David Switzer. Two shots were fired twice. The last two were from the front and back so it would indicate two individuals fired them. There were witnesses to the murder, the Youngers. Why hang one brother for the murder and not the other?

This is my speculation of what was taking place. Dick Sanders was the leader of the gang. They wanted to rid the county of him and put fear into the other gang members. They did not have proof positive that Dick and Brackett Sanders were the murderers. The Youngers, who lived with David Switzer, were never mentioned as to telling what happened or for the identification of the murderers. A Mrs. Groninger was the one who told the story and identified the murderers. She was not an eye witness to the crime. The murderers were supposedly disguised but it is never said how they were disguised, except one was dressed like a soldier. Did they have covers over their faces to hide their features? Were they dressed differently than they were known to normally dress?

My theory is that, they appeared to be Jesse and Frank James. My mother's story says that is who murdered her great grandfather. That information would have come either from her grandfather, Winfield, who was there or the Youngers who were also there. I believe the vigilance committee heard it was Jesse James but thought it was useless and dangerous to apprehend Jesse James. They took advantage of the opportunity to rid the county of a terrorist outlaw and claimed it was the Sanders brothers who murdered David Switzer. The committee said they were wearing a disguise, thus probably appeared to be someone else. I believe the Youngers were the family that my great great grandfather David Switzer went to Missouri with and because his wife died, they lived with David to help with the children. It was in their bedroom David was murdered. I also believe they were traumatized after the murder and possibly thought the Jesse James brothers, whom they believed were the robbers/murders, would come after them and kill them because they could identify them. Either Mr. Younger was an elderly man or had more feelings for self-preservation than David. There is no mention of him trying to come to the aid of David when he attacked the robbers and had them lying across the bed. I believe the Youngers packed up and fled Missouri, taking the children back to relatives in Pennsylvania as soon as physically possible, probably the following morning. My mother said the family that immigrated to Missouri with David returned the children to relatives in Pennsylvania. I would guess they did that as soon as they could, trying to avoid Jesse James and his gang.

    The vigilance committee may have knowingly hung the wrong man but took advantage of the circumstances to rid the county of some of their outlaws. How could so many people be wrong? If you have ever witnessed mob mentality, first hand, you can understand that the truth is what they want it to be and has nothing to do with facts. Dick Sanders never admitted to the murder of David Switzer and I wouldn't expect him to even if he was guilty. He did offer another name of a possible suspect while trying to literally save his own neck. Jesse James lived in Clay county, a short distance from Johnson county. When David asked the soon to be murderers where they were from, they replied Ray county which is adjacent to Clay county. Jesse fought for the Confederate army and when he learned that David was from Pennsylvania may have shot him because he was from a Union state. He had a reputation for doing things like that. Jesse James felt he was being persecuted by the Union soldiers and often murdered them when the opportunity was presented. For Jesse James, the war was not over. This is all speculation and just my conspiracy theory. I know my mother believed, whoever she got the information from, that they believed Jesse James was the murderer and I had her put it in writing so I would know it was not my imagination.

    What difference does it make? It doesn't make a difference except that it sheds doubt on truth as history tells it. Not everything is as it appears which we have discovered over and over in the telling of historical events. Just as in this book, the author has a

This Dummy Pulls His Own Strings

biased view and wants to portray events so he/she looks good to the reader. We are all guilty of this to some degree.

The story of the vigilance committee and the pursuit of the local outlaws continues. It was assumed that Bill Stevens would take over leadership of the gang after the demise of Dick Sanders. He was perceived to be a "bad man" and was heavily armed. The committee resolved to find him and kill him outright, not taking any chances. One night about twenty men armed with double-barreled shot guns loaded with buckshot, and carrying revolvers, surrounded the home of Bill Stevens. They hid and waited for dawn and for Stevens to appear. At daylight, Stevens appeared at the door in his shirtsleeves to assess the day and perhaps use the outhouse. The committee fired immediately without warning. He fell riddled with buck shot in the doorway. He was taken into the house by his family and died about noon.

It appears the tactics of the vigilance committee worked because the other gang members were now the ones being terrorized and they all left the country with the exception of a few that were more stubborn or fearless or both. The committee continued to pursue those that stayed.

Their next victim was Jeff Collins. They heard he was about to leave the country so they surrounded his house with about twenty men with double-barreled shot guns. The same method used with Stevens. They again waited for his exit of his home but this time warned him. Collins home was in Warrensburg, so I suppose there could be witnesses to the proceedings, which is why they probably warned him and didn't shoot immediately on his exit. He saw the shotguns leveled at his chest and heard the commander of the party say, "Jeff Collins, we want your surrender!" Reportedly, Jeff was not a coward but neither was he stupid. He put up his hands and said, "I surrender". The commander said, "drop your pistols". Collins reached for his guns like he was going to draw and the commander hollered, "Stop, unbuckle your belt and drop them". Collins followed the command and the committee took him prisoner.

That evening the committee gathered in the livery stable and put together a court for the conviction and sentence of Jeff Collins. The Judge sat on a stool in a stall of the livery barn and the jury stood in a line across from him. Jeff Collins was brought before the court with his hands bound behind him. His mood was defiant but relaxed. There was no positive proof that he had ever committed murder but there was circumstantial evidence and his reputation did not help him. The judge made the accusations in the same manner as those against Sanders except for the murder of Switzer. Collins response was a simple, "Well". The judge continued with, "You are charged with being a member of a band of robbers that have for so long infested this country". Collins again replied, "Well". The judge then asked, "What have you to say in defense of these charges?". Collins reply was, "nothing". "Are you guilty as charged?" "You are the judge, not I". "Then you have no defense to make". "No, it would be of no use. Your court sits to convict, not try". "Confess your crimes and it may not go hard with you". "I confess nothing". The judge then addressed the jury, "Gentlemen, what shall be done with the prisoner?" The jury replied, unanimously, "Hang him". The judge then said: "Jeff Collins, I sentence you to be hanged by the neck until dead". They led him out along a railroad bridge to a black jack tree where he was hanged. Before the hanging took place the judge asked him if he had any last words. He said, "Yes, tell my mother that I died a brave but innocent boy."

The outlaws the vigilance committee next pursued were Thomas Stevens, son of Bill Stevens and Morg Andrews. Morg was the outlaw that Dick Sanders said may be the murderer of David Switzer when he was asked who he thought it was. Why he may have thought that and why he would offer that information, we will never know except he was trying to save his own neck. The civil authorities of Johnson county were informed that these two men were presently in jail at Lawrence, Kansas. They pursued the legal channels to have them sent to Johnson County which included the governor of Missouri filing requisition papers and the governor of Kansas honoring the request of those papers. The two prisoners were young men, about 18 years of age.

This Dummy Pulls His Own Strings

When the train transporting the prisoners to Warrensburg arrived, it was met, at the depot, by around 400 men, most of who were from the Fayetteville area. When the guards removed the prisoners from the train, they proceeded to the county jail by a circuitous route, anticipating possible trouble. They had not gone very far when they were stopped by about 50 armed men. These men overpowered the guards and took the prisoners.

The committee was assembled on the north and east sides of the public square. They put the prisoners in a carriage or hack and the committee formed a line behind them much like a parade. They proceeded in this fashion in the direction of the Post Oak Bridge out Gay Street. Close to the bridge was a huge elm tree with a limb that extended over the road about thirty feet above it. Two ropes were suspended from this limb over the road that hung down about six feet above the road.

The carriage or hack with the prisoners was positioned under these ropes. Andrews was begging for mercy and his life. Stevens was silent and relaxed, looking at his surroundings.

A man from the crowd stepped forward and read the charges against the prisoners. The charges as he read them were, "You were with the party that killed and robbed Switzer; your comrades are disappearing one by one. You go tonight: Your last hour has come. Prepare for death. If you have a prayer to offer to your God, pray."

Stevens stood tall and straight and said in an unwavering and firm voice, "I have never in all my life spilled a drop of human blood. The charge of my killing Switzer is false. I know that you are going to kill me and there is no use in my wasting your time in talking." He then pulled a small purse from his pocket and emptied it into his hand. There were a few coins and some trinkets. He then asked, "Is there one man in this crowd who will do me the kindness to deliver this to my young sister. It is small but all I have." Someone stepped forward, took it and promised to carry out his wishes. Stevens then said, "Tell her to accept this from her brother who dies an innocent boy. You will find her in the city."

The rope was tightened around his neck and the driver told to drive forward. It was obvious to Stevens that the end was near so he jumped off the carriage and the force of the jump and his weight on the end of the rope, broke his neck. He died instantly.

Andrews' was quite different and showed no bravery or acceptance of death. He begged for mercy and his life but it was not to be. His noose was tightened and the driver told to drive forward, which he did. Andrews body hung by the neck until dead over the road.

The vigilance committee was not finished with its' reign of terror regarding outlaws. It had resolved to rid the county of the lawless and they believed their work wasn't finished. The next victim was a man named Hall, by the Fayetteville committee. Details are not clear but it was reported that he was captured, confessed to the killing of several men, and he was hanged.

The next target of the committee was Thomas W. Little in Warrensburg. It was reported that someone was robbed near Post Oak Bridge. He was accused of this and tried by the committee. This time it didn't follow the pattern as he was acquitted for lack of evidence. They did put him in jail, even though he was declared innocent of the charges. Evidently some of the committee was not satisfied with the outcome because several nights later the committee tried him again, weather it was for the same charges or for new charges, it was not reported. There were some prominent citizens from Dover present at this trial who provided the prisoner with an alibi. The vote to hang the accused by the committee was three hundred forty four for acquittal and twenty eight for hanging. He was still taken back to jail, even after his second acquittal. That night, about twenty men battered down the door of the jail, retrieved Little and hung him from an Elm tree on Main Street. This act was publicly denounced by the vigilance committee and was made known that this was not the action or did it have the approval of the committee. Justice gone bad.

This didn't put an end to accusations as another lad James M. Sims, a reported irresponsible youth, was accused of stealing a horse from a boy near Post Oak bridge. He was taken captive southeast of Clinton on the Grand river. The authorities who apprehended him were thinking there would be trouble in transporting the prisoner to Warrensburg. Their thinking was correct. They were stopped on the way at Smith's Mill by about fifty armed men. The prisoner was taken and hung from a tree there. This was the ninth man executed and the last one. Nine alleged outlaws, paid with their lives for the murder of my great great grandfather, David Switzer. It's possible, none of them had anything to do with his murder.

Great Grandparents Winfield & Rebecca Switzer

My Maternal Great Grandparents, Winfield Scott Switzer, born Dec. 7, 1851 in Mifflentown, PA, the son of David Switzer, and Rebecca Ernest, born Jan. 20, 1856 In Mifflentown, PA, were united in marriage in 1878 in Juniata County, PA. They moved to a farm one mile south of Des Lacs, ND in 1906 with 6 of their 7 children and spouses of the married children and at least one sibling of Winfield, possibly more. The one child that remained in PA, my grandparents, Alma and Harvey Valentine, followed them to ND, four years later, in 1910.

In research of Rebecca Ernest, I found several spellings of her surname Ernest, Earnest and Ernst in different census records. When census takers were recording names, they often misspelled them or wrote them so they were hard to interpret. I have seen this many times where names are recorded differently from census to census. Also, many people were named several names and sometimes chose to use their second or third name rather than their first name. For example, my maternal grandmother was named Margaret Alma. She chose to go by the name of Alma. On the other hand, my mother was named Alma Margaret and she chose to go by Margaret. I would guess to avoid confusion, my mother chose to go by Margaret or else, for the same reason, her parents referred to her that way.

Great Grandma Rebecca (Ernest) Switzer died at the age of 87, June 1943. Great Grandpa Winfield Switzer died at the age of 93, Nov. 3, 1944. His death was somewhat unusual and recorded in The Minot Daily News newspaper. He had accepted a ride with a neighbor farmer and asked to be let out of the car about a mile from Des Lacs because he was going to walk north from the highway, he told the farmer. No one knows the reason. I would speculate for exercise or to look at something from his past or perhaps he had Alzheimer's or like my mother, hardening of the arteries and was unaware of where he was or what he was doing. Whatever the reason, when he didn't come home, the Ward County Sheriffs' department started searching for him. They found him the next day, frozen in a field. The newspaper article said the cause of death was exposure. He was found one and one quarter mile east and one mile north of Des Lacs in a corn field. The Sheriff said it appeared he had crawled inside a corn shock to try to stay warm but was found outside the corn shock. He had been a farmer most of his adult life, until he retired and moved into Des Lacs. His father, David Switzer, had been murdered when Winfield was 16, reportedly by Jesse James. He had been orphaned by this act as had his 4 sisters.

Top row, left to right: Anna, Millie (Camillia), David, Grace, Esther Victoria. Bottom row, left to right: Alma, Winfield Scott, Rebecca, Orpha.

This Dummy Pulls His Own Strings

The Winfield Scott and Rebecca Ernest Switzer family. Winfield's father David Switzer was murdered in MO. Winfield also named his son David.

Their seven children are my Grandma, Mrs. Harvey (Alma) Valentine, Mrs. Albert (Camillia, (Millie)) Spicher, Mrs. Wilbur (Orpha) Tracy, Mrs. Elmer (Anna) Dokken, Mrs. Jay (Grace) Hornberger, Mrs. Rev. Marion C.(Esther Victoria) Roser, and David B. Switzer.

While I was growing up or more accurately, in my youth (I'm still growing up), Alma, Orpha, and Millie all lived in Des Lacs. All three were married and had children but were either widowed or had chased their husband off. We were never allowed to speak of this so I wasn't aware what had happened to whom. The truth would have been probably better than my wild imagination.

Aunt Orpha was a telephone operator in Des Lacs. She often stayed overnight at the little central office that housed the equipment for the telephones. I would say she stayed overnight most of the time except when she could arrange for a high school girl to watch the office overnight. There was a desk type piece of equipment, she sat at. It had a set of wires with a metal plug on the desk surface and a set of holes in a vertical back that the metal plugs were plugged into. She wore a headset and when someone called "central" by turning the crank on their telephone, she would somehow turn that incoming call on so she could speak to them through her headset. She would know who was "ringing her up" by the connection that was blinking. She would identify herself as "Central" and inquire as to who they would like to be connected to. Often times, because she knew everyone with a phone, there would be an exchange of pleasantries, and perhaps some local gossip or passing of information. She would plug their line from the horizontal incoming call to the vertical outgoing call and the two parties could converse. Aunt Orpha would periodically listen in to see when they were finished talking so she could disconnect them. She had a cot in the little office and a coal parlor stove to keep warm in the winter. As I remember it, the central office was located next to Aunt Millie's home or perhaps their Evangelical United Brethren Church was between them. I would often go to Aunt Orpha's office and sit on her cot and watch and listen while she did her job. I found it fascinating and so high tech for the times.

Aunt Millie had a huge, at least it was huge to a little boy, two story house and lived alone most of the time except when her son Winfield was home. He generally worked out of town and lived wherever he worked. This house was the home of my Grandpa and Grandma Valentine before Grandpa either left Grandma or Grandma kicked him out. Grandma rented out rooms, much like a hotel but after her and Grandpa separated, she sold the house to Aunt Millie and moved in with Aunt Orpha whose husband had died as a result of a car crash. I believe Aunt Millie rented out rooms to anyone that was in need of one, by the night or longer, for a while. She probably provided meals for them also.

My Maternal Grandmother was Alma Mary (Switzer) Valentine. My maternal Grandfather, Harvey Banks Valentine was no longer with my grandmother, when I was a little boy, because of some womanizing he allegedly got caught at, or so the gossip goes. The version I heard was he infected my grandmother with a STD (sexually transmitted disease). My grandma Valentine was from PA before moving to ND and was raised as a Pennsylvania Dutch, a cousin to the Quakers, Amish and Mennonites. She was from around Harrisburg or Lancaster which is mostly Amish and Pennsylvania Dutch country. I know that my Grandmother Alma and Grandpa Harvey were married when Grandma was 16 years old. I also know my Mother was born six months after they were married. I'm not sure if a shotgun was involved in the wedding or not. Grandpa Valentine was 21 at the time of the wedding. Grandpa worked at the Ward County Courthouse in Minot, possibly as a jailor. When he and Grandma split up, he stayed in Minot, possibly at the jail until he moved to Washington.

I can't fault Grandpa Valentine for robbing the cradle because I also robbed the cradle with my bride having the same age difference, 5 years. My bride was 20 years old, I was 25. Harvey and Alma had a second child in 1903. The marriage must have survived for at least eleven years because my Mother says she was eleven when they moved to ND and Grandpa Harvey moved with them and lived with them. It may have lasted that long because before they moved to ND, they were living in PA in a duplex with my Grandpa's parents, who probably kept their son on the straight and narrow and their daughter-in-law's demands reasonable. They never did get a divorce but Grandpa's place of death was in Washington. Grandpa was never mentioned or talked about and we were not allowed to talk or ask about him. I never met him. He once wrote to my Mother after she was an adult and married but she didn't respond. My sister, Fern, wanted to invite Grandpa to her wedding but Mom wouldn't allow it. I imagine my Grandmother planted some hatred and may have had good reason for it. However, I don't think my Grandfather was totally to blame. I'm sure there was enough fault to go around. Grandma had her faults too. As my Mother often said about some individuals, "They are so Heavenly minded, they are no Earthly good." I would not declare my Grandma, no earthly good but she certainly was Heavenly minded. This may have had something to do with my Grandfather straying from the martial bed.

I loved my Grandma and respected her but she was just as human as we all are. I spent several weeks with my Grandmother Valentine one summer. She was a fine Christian woman and was kind to me. Her lifestyle was not conducive to the enjoyment of life as much as it was to serve the Lord in all she did and thought. I'm sure this lifestyle could and did drive some men to stray. I would guess the wedding should never have happened but it was a different time then. Generally if a girl got pregnant out of wedlock, she was sent away to have the baby and often gave it up for adoption or there was a forced marriage. They didn't want to bring disgrace on the family. After Grandpa left, I can't imagine he was celibate, especially since he got my Grandmother pregnant out of wedlock. It's possible I have some half Aunt's and Uncle's somewhere that we are unaware of. Grandpa may even have married again, despite he never was divorced and his new wife and family may be unaware of his previous marriage and children.

Aunt Grace lived in Minot. She was married to Jay Hornberger who was the Jailer at the Ward County Jail in Minot. It's possible he took over Grandpa Valentine's job when he left but I do not know that for certain. We visited Aunt Grace and Uncle Jay often and even stayed overnight with them on occasion. Their daughter, Joyce was a Baptist Missionary to French West Africa. All the Switzer sisters were good cooks and we always dined bountifully.

The rest of my Grandma Valentines' siblings were ones I hardly knew. Anna Dokken was married to Elmer who died at the age of 43 of pneumonia. He was a farmer at Berthold. He died before I was born. He left three young sons, Duane, 15, Earl, 9, and Linden, 7. His parents homesteaded at Berthold. Anna died Dec. 1961 at the age of 64 in a Minot Hospital. Her funeral was at the Evangelical United Brethren church of Des Lacs. She obviously continued to live in or around Des Lacs after her husband, Elmer died. I don't remember visiting her. An old newspaper article in Grandma Valentines' scrapbook honors her for her service as a telephone operator in 1957. I believe she did this in Berthold but the article doesn't say. That would be the same job Aunt Orpha had in Des Lacs. The widowed sister telephone operators.

I believe Grandma Valentines' brother David lived in Oregon but don't know where or what he did or anything about who he married or his family.

Grandma's sister, Esther Victoria, went by the name Victoria and married a minister, the Rev. M.C. Roser. I believe they lived in South Dakota and don't recall meeting them either. My sister Fern says their son had a turkey farm on the MN SD border and every thanksgiving would send a large turkey to Des Lacs and the whole family would gather at Aunt Millie's large home. The kids would have the run of the house and it was lots of fun playing with all the cousins. There were so many people that they couldn't fit at a table so they would dish up and sit wherever they could find a spot. The kids usually sat on the steps. I have no memories of these gatherings.

My Maternal grandmother was a very religious person who lived a very disciplined life much like the Quakers. My grandfather

This Dummy Pulls His Own Strings

may have been less religious and disciplined than my grandmother. Knowing my grandmother, and her disciplined Christian beliefs and practices, I probably would have strayed from the straight and narrow also, and in fact did when subjected to her rules. They observed the Sabbath on Sunday and did only what was necessary to survive on the Sabbath. If you were a farmer you could take care of your animals but the day should be spent at church or at home visiting and gossiping. Gossip was the entertainment of the time and with Aunt Orpha being the telephone operator, she knew all the local happenings and gossip. No games were allowed to be played on Sunday and as little cooking as possible. Most of the Sunday meal was prepared on Saturday night.

To illustrate the strictness of the religious rules Grandma Valentine lived by, one Sunday, while visiting Grandma Valentine, my cousin Bill Brieher, the minister's son who was my age, and I were playing ball in grandmas driveway. Grandma came out and told us we couldn't do that on Sunday. Back then, kids listened to the adults, so we stopped playing ball. We were sitting around with long faces and Bill's dad, Rev. Brieher, came and asked what the problem was. We told him Grandma wouldn't let us play ball because it was Sunday. He said, "well boys, just walk down the road about a block to the school house down there and go behind the school and play ball out of sight of your grandmother". This we did.

Not everyone practiced all the rules Grandma had but most of us respected them and obeyed them when around her, especially at her home. Grandma Valentine had lots of rules, many of which did not pertain to the Sabbath. You couldn't drink soda pop because it was in bottles at that time. Her reasoning was that beer also came in bottles so therefore soda was a gateway to beer which was evil and sinful. Of course, everyone else drank soda but when Grandma Valentine came we weren't allowed to have any except on a few occasions. One time Grandma was visiting Rev. Brieher and Aunt Rebecca. Grandma was thirsty and wanted some cool aid or juice and Aunt Rebecca couldn't find any. She did have some soda hidden away so she got out a bottle of Grape

Ni-Hi and poured it in a couple glasses and gave one to grandma. Grandma thought that was the best grape juice she ever had.

Another time, Grandma, Aunt Rebecca, Uncle William, Mom, Dad, Billy and I were going to Lake Metigoshe on the North Dakota, Canadian border to rent a cabin for a few days of swimming and fishing. We stopped at a Gas Station to get gas and Bill and I wanted to have a pop, forgetting that when Grandma was around, this was forbidden. Aunt Rebecca said we couldn't have one because Grandma was along and would disapprove. Uncle William overheard and said, "oh, let the boys have their pop". So we did. I don't know what Uncle William said to Grandma, if anything, she never chastised us for drinking it. It's possible she didn't see us drinking it because back then there was a deposit on the bottle of a few cents. When you brought the bottle back you got your bottle deposit back. I'm guessing we drank those sodas right down before we left for two reasons, so grandma wouldn't see us and so we got the deposit back.

Grandma didn't like boys or men to go bare chested either and as a boy I hardly ever wore a shirt in the summer time. I would try to remember to wear a shirt when Grandma was around but would sometimes forget, especially if swimming. Grandma would get on her soap box and complain about me not wearing a shirt. One time, when washing the car in my swimming suit and no shirt, she asked me how I would like it if she went bare chested. I must have been fed up or else just my normal self and told her it wouldn't bother me a bit if the whole world was bare chested. She was not happy with me and my disrespectful mouth. She also thought it was sinful for females to wear jeans or outer pants of any kind. Females should only wear dresses and they should be well below the knees, I'm sure she preferred them to the ankles.

Alcohol and the drinking of it was a sin as was smoking and playing cards except for cards such as rook which were the exact same thing as gambling cards except they had four colors instead of suits and they were numbered through fourteen rather than having Jack, Queen, King and Ace. Dancing and movies were strictly forbidden. There were many things that were unacceptable for females to do. My Mother, having been raised by Grandma with her Quaker like beliefs was relatively modern and reasonable in things we could do. I attribute it to Dad's influence on her. His dad liked a strong drink from time to time and they would have the neighbors over and clear the furniture so they could dance. They also played cards. Mom would never allow me to go to Movies, Dances or play cards. However, when I reached my teenage years, I did all of those, sometimes with her knowledge and she never said anything to me. I just knew enough not to ask her if I wanted to do them. Just do them without her blessing or permission. I also smoked in front of my parents as a teenager and most of my life and Mom only said that it wasn't good for my health and if God wanted me to smoke, he would have put a chimney on me. I also imbibed strong drink but only Dad knew, when he would find leftovers or empties in his car that I had borrowed. He would just ask me what I wanted him to do with it. I would reply, give it to me, I'll take care of it. This he did, without a sermon or lecture.

Maternal Ancestors of Note

Grandpa Valentines Grandfather, Samuel Valentine fought in the civil war for the North. He would be my great great grandfather.

If you go back seven generations from Grandpa Valentine you have Samuel Gettys who helped finance the Revolutionary war. He was so broke after the financing of it that he was faced with bankruptcy. He obviously believed that it was more important to be free of British rule than to have any money. He did have quite a bit of land but no money so he sold his land to his son James. James sold off parcels of the land to form the town of Gettysburg. Samuel Gettys would be my great great great great great great great grandfather or great grandfather to the 7th power.

Samuel Gettys was born in 1706 to James Gettys and Mary Margaret Muir. They were born in Ireland and emigrated to the US. Samuel was born in Cumberland, Adams County, Pennsylvania, USA. His history on the internet says he was a tavern owner.

Dwight E. Knuth

About Samuel Getty's;

Samuel Getty's was a settler and tavern owner in the late 1780s. The borough of Gettysburg, Pennsylvania founded in 1786, was named after him.

He gave funds to the Continental Army, but soon after they won, he was rich in land but had no funds. Samuel Getty's decided to sell off his land in order to be financially stable. His son, James, bought his land and sold it off in parcel lots.

His wife was the sister of Reynolds Ramsey, grandfather of historian J. G. M. Ramsey.

from: http://en.wikipedia.org/wiki/Samuel_Gettys

Taverns were not only an integral part of colonial life in America, but were also a necessity. The modes of travel and transportation of the day mandated the location of a tavern every few miles on the main thoroughfares, where tired and hungry travelers could find food and drink and a bed or floor upon which to sleep. Most colonial taverns were the only available public meeting place in early American towns and countryside's.

The first tavern in this area was operated by Samuel Getty's in 1772; Mr. Getty's son, James, helped Reverend Dobbin found, and lent his name to the town of Gettysburg.

Men from all walks of life met inside the Getty's Tavern to transact business, discuss politics, gamble and gossip over hearty food and a bottle of wine, a bowl of punch or a tankard of ale. The Tavern served as the first town hall, news center, general store and military station. The local militia mustered there to join ranks with the Continental Army during the Revolutionary War.

Colonial tavern keepers were men of consequence. Mr. Getty's received his guests graciously, providing a good bill of fare and a choice selection of wines. Throughout the colonies everyone drank liquor, from babes to ministers, due to their rigorous lifestyle, scanty diets, bitter cold winters without home heating and lack of medicines. Adams County families drank homemade wine, brandy, and ale made from the apples of the many trees they planted.

It could very well be that James Getty's good friend and fellow community leader, Alexander Dobbin, sat before a crackling fire in a colonial tavern room similar to the Springhouse Tavern, discussing the possibilities of creating a new town and county seat for a new country...in a new United States.

from: http://www.dobbinhouse.com/taverns.htm

George and Margaret Knuth (Authors' parents)

George Knuth Family, Top - Dorel, Verla;
Bottom – Dwight, Margaret, Fern, George.

This is the world I was born into. My parents were very religious but not terribly strict. They were members of First Baptist Church in Drake. Dad was a deacon and Mom belonged to the ladies aid. Dad had graduated from Northwest Bible College in Minneapolis to become a minister. He obtained his preacher's license, which I have in my possession. Before he served as a minister in a church, his health and hearing failed him and he gave up on his goal of becoming a minister. Because of his schooling and because he was respected by the other members of the church, they often asked him to preach a sermon on Sundays' when the minister was unavailable. He was a good speaker and preached from and about the Bible. I am a bit prejudiced but I thought he was very good and would have made a fine minister. He had that understanding and forgiving quality and was a very patient man, slow to anger. Others must have thought so also because they had him fill the pulpit many times. Perhaps it was because he donated his time and service so there was no cost to the congregation. They were conservative in many ways.

We attended church twice on Sundays, morning and evening and again on Wednesday evenings for "prayer meeting". Daily, we had morning and evening devotions where a member of the family would read a chapter or two from the Bible and then we would all get down on our knees facing our chair seats and each, in turn, would say a prayer. We did this even when we had overnight company and would ask them to join us and participate if they so desired. This was a healthy, wonderful and forgiving environment. My parents were God fearing and God loving people. They were happy people who worked hard and prayed without ceasing. They both sang hymns while they worked. Often times they sang different hymns and within hearing of each other, at the same time. It never seemed to bother either of them that the other was singing or humming a different tune. They were obviously deep in thought and didn't hear the other one. I loved to listen to them, it was a comforting environment. They walked their talk.

We always had plenty to eat, never went to bed hungry or without a goodnight hug and kiss. There was plenty of hollering at us, especially me, but it was generally well deserved for not doing what was expected of me as far as my chores or responsibilities were concerned.

I only had one spanking and that was after repeated warnings that I ignored. I was about six or seven and my friends lived a couple blocks away at the edge of town on a farm. They had a slough that filled up with water every spring. We would build rafts out of dead trees and old boards and we would get poles and pole across the slough on our rafts. It was great fun and exciting. I was

This Dummy Pulls His Own Strings

supposed to come home for dinner or as we called it back then, supper, when the six o'clock town whistle blew. I generally followed that and all was well until spring came and a very young lads' fancy turns to rafting. I would be having so much fun, I would stay an extra few minutes and each day it would get a little longer until I was a half hour late or someone would have to come get me. After many warnings of, "you're going to get a licken if you do it again", it came true. Dad got a stick out of the wood box by the kitchen stove and spanked my behind. Not very hard but of course I started to cry almost immediately before it got too serious. I thought if I cried, Dad would stop. He never did hit me very hard. It was mostly the threat of the unknown and the idea of disappointing my parents that was most traumatic. Mind over matter.

One time while rafting, I had a bit of a mishap. We used long tree limbs for poles to push the rafts across the slough. The rafts were built of dead trees that floated with boards nailed across the top of the horizontal logs to form a platform. These rafts were quite heavy. It took a strong and long pole to push them across the slough. You would put your pole into the water and push it down to the bottom and push the raft across the slough in this manner. Sometimes a breeze would come up and try to push the raft back the way you came from. If you had your pole stuck in the mud and muck of the bottom of the slough, the raft would push up against it making it difficult or impossible for a child to extract it from the bottom. You would then have to use your pole as a lever to move the raft.

On one such occasion, both of us were using our poles as levers to push the raft against the wind. The wind gust stopped and the raft took off. My pole was so imbedded in the bottom that I couldn't get it free but the raft kept moving away from my pole. Not wanting to lose my pole I hung on to the pole now sticking straight perpendicular to the slough as the raft moved away from me and left me clinging to my pole, stuck in the slough bottom. My feet dangling in the water. My raft partner soon realized my predicament, probably from my hollering, and changed directions to retrieve me. You would have thought the pole would have tipped over into the slough and deposited me on the bottom but it was so buried in the mud that it stayed upright with me hanging on for dear life. Eventually, my rafting partner got the raft back to me and I was able to get back on the raft. I don't believe we were able to retrieve my pole but we did reach dry land.

It wasn't unusual to come home with wet feet when rafting so I either lied to my parents about what happened or wasn't asked. I don't think the water was very deep but I was a very short person at this time in my life so it probably would have been over my head. The slough bottom was mud so there were probably several feet of mud to sink into and at this point, I couldn't swim and didn't have a life jacket or floatation device.

Dad was "hard of hearing" and had a hearing aid that he seldom wore because of background noise (wind, etc.). In order for him to hear my Mom and understand what she was saying, Mom would have to holler. To someone that wasn't familiar with the circumstances, it would sound like she was angry with him. In reality, they loved and respected each other and I can't remember them exchanging a cross word or having a fight. They would argue but it would always end amicably. They celebrated 60 years of marriage and beyond.

We lived on the farm until I was about 2 years old at which time we moved into Drake. The year was 1944. The only memory I have of the farm is that my crib was in my parents bedroom. I woke up one night and started crying and shaking my metal (brass) crib, which made a terrible noise, until I woke up my parents. Mom wanted to go get me and take me into bed with them but Dad said she should just let me cry and I would eventually go back to sleep. He being hard of hearing, the noise probably didn't keep him awake. Turns out Dad was right and I did eventually quit crying and went back to sleep. I'm told we had a big St. Bernard dog that I used to ride like a pony but I have no memory of it.

The house we moved into in Drake was the one I grew up in. It had a small bedroom with a closet under the stairs on the first floor which was my parents' bedroom and there were two bedrooms upstairs. Verla had one bedroom upstairs and Fern and

This Dummy Pulls His Own Strings

I shared a bedroom until Verla left home and Fern moved into Verla's. There was a huge kitchen/dining room and a livingroom or as it was referred to, front room. There was an unfinished full basement which was where the coal furnace was and a coal bin large enough to hold enough coal for the winter as well as some wood for the cook stove in the kitchen. There was also a large pantry in the unheated basement where we kept all the home canned meats, fruits and vegetables as well as several hundred pounds of potatoes, onions, squash etc.

There was a bathroom but it was not functional when we moved in. We had an outhouse which we still used. In the winter we used "slop jars" which were enamel pail like potties. They had lids to keep the smell in and of course in the morning someone would have to carry them out to the outhouse and empty them and clean them out. It was either use a slop jar or get fully dressed and put on coats, hats and boots and go out into the cold and snow to use the cold outhouse. At least in the winter, you didn't have to worry about spiders biting you in the butt. We didn't live in town long before Dad had the bathroom finished and the sewer hooked up. Back then it was unheard of to have more than one bathroom in a house. Even the new houses that were being built had only one bathroom. There was no lingering in the bathroom and you planned ahead. If you were taking a bath, you told everyone and everyone else used the facilities first. There were many times when as kids we would wait until the last minute to go to the bathroom and if it was occupied there was a lot of knocking on the door and dancing waiting for your turn.

We had a coal furnace in the basement and a coal/wood stove in the kitchen. We really didn't need the coal cook stove for heat but sometimes it felt pretty good and it was good for drying mittens on the oven door. Most of the winter, Mom would have a copper boiler setting on the cook stove and fill it with snow. She would use the melted snow for washing hair and anything else she needed soft water for, such as watering her plants and the sprinkling bottle for ironing. The cook stove also had a boiler on it that you could fill with water so you had a supply of warm to hot water depending on how hot the stove was. This could be used for washing dishes or other chores you needed hot water for. Of course, with a coal furnace, Dad had to keep it going by shoveling coal into it periodically and taking the ashes out. The ashes would be carried by the pail full out to the alley where everyone had an ash pile. Every spring you would need to haul the ash pile to the dump grounds (now called sanitary landfills) or hire someone to do it for you. Sometimes when it was really cold out and the car wouldn't start, Dad would put a pan of hot ashes under it to warm it up so it would start. Very few people had garages and the cars were outside, subjected to the elements.

Having a coal furnace, restricted the amount of time we could be away from home because you had to come home and put more coal in the stove to keep the fire going and keep the water pipes from freezing. Dad would get up before everyone else in the morning and get the fire going so the rest of us could get up to a warm house. I can remember some cold winter days when we would be invited to a friend or relatives house for Sunday dinner after church. This was how we spent most Sunday afternoons, either at someone else's house or having company at our house.

The women would get the dinner on the table and we would all sit around an expanded table with benches unless there were too many and then sometimes they put up a card table for the kids to eat at. After dinner, the men would go to the living room and visit or in the summer outside to visit or play horseshoe or croquet. The women would clean up the dinner and do dishes. In the winter time when the dishes were done, the adults often played board games such as pachise, kick-off, sorry, flinch or rook. The kids would find their own entertainment, either playing games or with whatever toys were available.

Sometimes the company would be asked to stay for the evening meal which was called Supper. If it was cold out, sometimes you couldn't stay for supper because you had to go home and put coal in the furnace. After supper and dishes it was back to church for another hour or more. When you became a certain age and were considered a youth, you were expected to go an hour before

Sunday evening church services to what was referred to as BYF or Baptist Youth Fellowship. We would read the Bible, pray, sing, conduct any business that needed to be taken care of and play games in the church basement such as shuffle board and ping pong. My maternal grandmother would have been scandalized had she known we were playing games on "The Lord's day" and even in the church, what a sinful disgrace.

On Wednesday nights which was known as a church night, no school functions were scheduled. This was referred to by the Baptists as "prayer meeting" where the minister would read the Bible and preach a short sermon and we would do a lot of hymn singing. The hymn singing was my favorite part and the attendees got to choose the hymns we sung. You could always count on Mr. Toy to request, "What a Friend we have in Jesus". Toward the end of the service, we would all get down on our knees by the church pews and pray out loud, one person at a time in turn, as you felt moved to do so. They were straight forward prayers for God's blessings and protection and they were sincere. Instead of complaining about the politicians, we would pray for them and God's guidance in their leadership and endeavors. There was no talking in tongues. As I remember, there was a lot of praying for the salvation of friends and relatives that had not been "born again". Everyone just prayed as they felt the need.

There were those who would pray, trying to impress the others that were listening as opposed to humbling themselves before God. This, I would guess is an age old problem and I find myself doing it. That is probably why Jesus taught us to go into a closet and pray instead of publicly praying. That advice was for those of us that are trying to impress the public.

For those of us that sang in the choir, there was choir practice an hour prior to Wednesday night prayer meeting. So to sum it all up, Sunday, 10:00AM was Sunday school for everyone, regardless of age, 11:00AM was church. Sunday evening, 7:00PM was BYF and 8:00PM evening services. Wednesday evening 7:00PM choir practice and 8:00PM prayer meeting. So that was 6 hours of church a week. In addition, every morning and evening in our home, we had our devotions. I had a very religious structured childhood. I am not complaining, in fact, am grateful for it. I had a very loving family and secure childhood and the structure of our life helped in what successes I have enjoyed. Also, I am convinced, my Mother's prayers kept me alive and out of serious trouble.

As a child, I had very few haircuts by a barber. Dad always cut my hair and his brothers and my cousins. He had a hand clippers that you squeezed the handles together which made the blades move back and forth to cut the hair. Later, he got an electric clipper and I would cut his hair with it. He had a homemade stool that was higher than an ordinary chair, much like a youth chair. He would put Sears and/or Montgomery Wards catalogs on the stool to raise the seat level and bring our head even with his eyes for easier cutting. Dad often cut anyone's hair that would ask him too, thus saving them the price of a trip to the barber.

Uncle William was the minister in the Martin, ND Evangelical United Brethren church. Martin was only about 10 0r 15 mi. from Drake. The whole family would come over for the evening and Dad would cut everyone's' hair and we would make homemade ice cream.

As a child I was very selfish as most children are. I was a young lad and all my school mates were joining the band which meant their parents were buying them band instruments such as trumpets, trombones clarinets and saxophones. I wanted to learn to play the trumpet and join the band. My friends, Charley Toy, Denise Hinsz and Danny Schafer all had trumpets and were in the band. Band instruments were relatively expensive in the late 40's and early 50's. We were not wealthy and there was very little for extras. I asked my parents and they informed me that at this time we couldn't afford it. As I've said before, I am quite persistent and not easily discouraged. Mom had been working summers at the Baptist camp and saving money for a carpet for our living room. At this point there was no carpet, only linoleum with throw rugs. Mom had been wanting a carpet for a long time and had been diligently putting away a little at a time to get one. She finally had enough to purchase one and realize her dream. When they found out they couldn't buy me a trumpet, Mom offered up her carpet savings and purchased a trumpet for me. I still have that trumpet, I know how to play it but it requires practice to be able to play it well. I'm lacking in the practice arena.

Another time, I wanted to drive the family car to a BYF convention in Williston, ND, about 200 miles away. My Father would need to go along as an adult supervisor. He informed me, the car needed new tires and we didn't have the resources to buy them. Somehow he figured out a way to get new tires so we could make the trip. This is where my siblings would interject that the youngest gets anything he/she wants and is a spoiled brat. I probably wouldn't disagree. My parents worked hard and sacrificed a lot for me and I'm sure my siblings. They always treated all of us the same. If they did something for one child, they found a way to do that for the other children.

Siblings

George and Margaret Knuth Family all grown up.
Top left to right: Verla, Dwight, Fern
Bottom left to right: Dorel, Margaret (Mom), George (Dad)

Dwight E. Knuth

My brother Dorel was off fighting a war when I came into this world. He joined the Navy after Pearl Harbor was bombed. I'm not sure of all of his naval stations but I know he served aboard the USS Richland (YFD - 64). This was an AFDM 3 class medium auxiliary floating drydock. She was towed to the Philippines and Guam where she served until war's end. In 1946 she was placed back into service to support submarine maintenance at Guam for the next forty years. The awards he received that I am aware of are American Campaign medal, Asiatic – Pacific campaign medal, World War II Victory medal, National Defense Service medal. He served from 9/29/42 to 2/21/46. His service number was 7300735. When he was discharged he was a Carpenter's Mate First Class (E6), Knuth, Dorel Harvey. His remains were buried at the Bismarck, ND Veterans cemetery. Upon his death his body was donated for medical science. Before his death, Dorel wrote his life story for his kids who gave me permission to include it in my book. Following is his life story as he wrote it.

Dorel's Life Story (Authors' Brother)

I Dorel Harvey Knuth was born to George and Margaret (Valentine) Knuth on October 21, 1923. Like my Aunt Elsie Chole Kofstad who was born on the homestead, I was born across the road from my Grandfather William Knuth's place, which he homesteaded. One of my recollections of that place was being sort of scared. I woke up and it was dark outside. How old I was at the time was I suppose somewhere under three and there I was alone. I remember knowing they had to milk and I went to the window to see but couldn't see no light so by and by mother came in and of course asked if I was scared. They also tell me I got lost in the corn field with the dog but that I don't remember. Elsie Kofstad owns the place, she sold the house and barn but believe there are granaries still there.

When I was real small I lived with Grandpa and Grandma and aunt Lizzie took care of me. Grandpa had dirt that he banked

This Dummy Pulls His Own Strings

the house with that I would play in. The reason I lived there is because my Dad and Mother both worked out. In the winter we lived in Minneapolis when I was small. My Dad was studying to be a minister at I think my Mother's pushing. But he told me in later life that he gave that up as he had trouble hearing.

Later we moved to the farm we still own, I suppose I was four years at the time. There was lots of work and I was willing to help. The folks bought me a wagon and it was used mostly to haul wood, cobs and water. We also milked cows which I started before I went to school. I could just milk the front teats at first and mother would come along and milk the back ones.

Coming back from Minneapolis, Dad had a Model T and it was sort of windy. I had a little old hat and I was always afraid it was going to blow off and guess it did a few times. My Mother had a uncle and aunt Marian and we would stop there for a visit. They lived in the corner of ND, MN and SD.

My Dad got sick with rheumatism and we had been to the fair and he had got a shot and he got sicker and he got staff infection and was in the hospital at Drake but he pulled thru. We went to church at Drake and when the preaching was going on I would go out to see my Dad. He would give me his ice cream that he got for dinner to eat.

I remember going with my Dad and uncle Walter Chole to bury their baby. Was just the preacher, uncle Walter, Dad, I and the undertaker there and it wasn't very much longer we buried my uncle Walter. What I remember about uncle Walter, he was fun.

I couldn't start to school till I was seven and then we had to go two years to first grade. She called one year primary. We had a mile and one half to school and there is where I got my book learning. Wesley and I was in my class and then the folks got Walter Gandy and he was in our class. He was from the home in Fargo, was Indian and sort of on the lazy side.

At first we went to church at Balfour. One time when Verla was a baby, Dad and I went to church. We got to Balfour and no church. Instead of going home he said he knew there was church at Drake so there we went. Going home there was no curtain on my side and I darn near froze. They put my feet in cold water. In those days boys had to wear cut off pants only to the knees with long stockings. Crazy. Later they went to church at Drake. Uncle William was minister then. Then Uncle Herman came and he preached at Guthrie church and that's where we went.

We farmed 640 acres, part rented from my Grandpa's. Farmed with horses and that kept us going. As soon as I was big enough I worked in the field. When I started plowing I had one time getting it out of the ground. Our recreation was playing games, softball, hunting.

When I was growing up we wasn't supposed to go to shows, go dancing, drink, smoke, play pool or bowl or hunt on Sunday. It would just about kill my mother if she had to sew a button on, on Sunday. When Grandma Valentine came to visit we had to keep our shirts on.

In 1941 my good friend William Benbow that stayed with Uncle Hermans and my best friend joined the Navy. He was in boot camp. I and some young folks had went to church in Balfour. Coming home we were going to Drake and there was a rabbit in the road and I lost control and we rolled over. That wiped me out, money wise. No one got hurt as we wasn't going fast but didn't do the car any good. Then, later William came home on leave and he got a telegram to report back. So he left and that night I did too. I got as far as Minot and they caught me. William was assigned to the USS Farragut. I joined the Navy on Sept. 29, 1942, went to boot camp, had a short one, four weeks and one week was mess cooking, the only time I had to work in the mess hall. I took the coffee pitchers around. Then was sent to Mare Island, a destroyer and submarine base and was fire guard as they redone the ships. Then in Jan. was sent to Hawthorne, Nevada to ammunition depot. That was hard work so I went for carpenter and got it. After a while we was shipped to Clearfield, Utah. From Clearfield to San Francisco and overseas. Caught a dry dock off the island of Samar and Leyte in Philippines. We took ships out of the water, worked our butt off. After the war was over they wanted to send us to China but we refused to go because our skipper was

This Dummy Pulls His Own Strings

to go home but he said he would stay on if we wanted to go. But they sent another one like the one I was on. I was sent home and on Feb. 21, 1946, the old sea dog was discharged.

And you lucky kids, on the 21st of March, 1946, I got married. I laid around awhile then went to work for George Ulman. I worked on that building on the corner of Mandan and First which is a grocery store. Think they had a fire in there this fall but had me doing everything else too and so I quit and got a job with The Core of Engineers as carpenter building Garrison Dam. I worked there seven years. Was a volunteer fireman. Was at fire school when Bill was born. Then farmed and worked in elevator and you know pretty much the rest of the story.

To my dear children: I love each and every one, also my grandchildren. Remember and trust your God. When it comes to the last mile of this life, all that matters is your faith in God. The key is John 3: 16. Confess your sins, we are all sinners saved by Jesus death on the cross, believe.

This is the end of Dorel's life story.

I think I was about four years old when I found out I had a brother. My parents never told me about him, I suppose because they wanted to spare me if he was killed in action and didn't come home. I may have heard them talking about Dorel but had no clue who that was and never asked. My sister, Fern tells of not hearing from Dorel for months at a time and not knowing if he was dead or alive. She remembers my mother pacing the floor with tears running down her face many times when they hadn't heard from Dorel for a long time.

When Dorel finally returned from the Navy and the war, he didn't live at home but had a job at Fort Lincoln close to Bismarck. He had a girlfriend in Bismarck by the name of Laura Peterson. He eventually sold his motor cycle so he could buy Laura a ring and married her. I remember their wedding because Dorel had bought me a navy blue woolen sailor suit and I was forced to wear it to the wedding. Dorel wore his uniform for the wedding also. Brothers in uniform, how cute. I didn't want to wear the sailor suit because it was made of wool and itched and I complained about it the whole night. As I said before, I was four years old.

Eventually they produced a baby girl, named Linda who became my good friend and playmate. They also had a baby boy, named William, after Dorel's best friend who was killed while in the Navy. Then came the baby of the family, Jeannie Marie. Dorel and his family moved to my Father's farm when I was a teen ager and I worked for him one summer on the farm and lived with them. He had crohn's disease and had to give up farming because of it. He first moved to Woodworth, ND to a rented farm where he raised pigs, some cattle and worked at the elevator. Even this was too much for his health. They moved back to Bismarck and his wife Laura went to work at the ND capital in the tax department to support the family.

My oldest sister Verla only lived with us a short time. She was a senior in high school when they needed teachers for the one room country schools. They offered to let the seniors take a test and if they passed it, allow them to finish high school by teaching in one room country schools. She did this and we only saw her on weekends. After the school year she got a job in Minot, I think in a nursing home and lived and worked there. On occasion she would come home for the weekend and always brought me some toy when she came. She continued teaching at one room country schools south of Drake and there met her future husband, Clifford Kummer. They had two boys, Douglas and Dean. They rented my uncles farm for awhile and tried farming but the weather didn't cooperate. Between hail and drought and rust in their years of farming, it was a losing operation.

Clifford got a job on the railroad to subsidize the farm and pay off debts and eventually they gave it up. Verla went back to teaching school and Cliff worked construction and did very well at it, becoming a foreman. Many customers would not do business with the construction company unless Cliffs' crew was the one doing the work. I worked on his crew and knew first hand, why that was. He was conscientious and honest and did not cut corners or take shortcuts. He was proud of his work and did a good job. There wasn't anything he couldn't accomplish. The difficult was done post haste and the impossible took a bit longer.

This Dummy Pulls His Own Strings

A more intelligent, kinder, gentler, forgiving, fair and honest man, would be hard to find. He was also a wonderful husband and father and a good friend.

My sister Fern was only five years older than I. We grew up together or at least she grew up, I still hold on to my childhood. As siblings we fought a lot and looking back can assume I initiated most of it. As I still do to this day, I would stir the pot or yank her chain whenever the chance presented itself. In my defense, she was very good at presenting opportunities for pot stirring and chain yanking. On the main floor of our house, when you entered from the back door, you could go left into the kitchen which was connected to the dining room. To the right of the dining room was the living room and to the right of the living room was my parents' bedroom which had a door leading to the back entrance. So you could go full circle inside the house. When I would irritate Fern, she would reach a point where she would come after me. I, not quite a complete idiot, would run. Around and around we would go. I would have two avenues for escape. If I got far enough ahead, I could go into the bathroom and lock the door or I could exit through the back door to the outside. She was bigger and older than I so I guess I thought if she caught me she would do me bodily harm. I guess I was in it mostly for the thrill of the chase. I don't remember her doing me bodily harm so maybe she never caught me.

Sometimes, by the time I escaped, we forgot what we were fighting about and ended up laughing. In retrospect, there were times I deserved bodily harm. We each had our chores and share of work and responsibility. We started out by sharing the responsibility of doing the supper dishes together. One would wash and one would dry. We would sometimes fight through this chore and I think Mom got fed up with it and had just one of us do the dishes, both washing and drying on alternating evenings. This was before God invented dishwashers. Fern was in high school and dating a fellow from the Air Force by the name of Clarence Rau, whom she later married. When he was home on leave, she would go out with him. When it was her night to do dishes, she would offer to pay me to do them for her. I would refuse until she paid me an exorbitant amount. If I had been her, I would have resorted to blackmail. I'm sure there was much she could have blackmailed me with, threating to tell my parents. Quite the opposite, she was very kind to me and put up with my obnoxious behavior.

One birthday, she enrolled me in a book club and I got a whole stack of books she paid for. I owe my joy of reading to her. After getting those books, I started reading and using the public library and even the state library. One of the books she gave me was "Swamp Boy" and I still remember it as one of the best books I ever read and it made me hungry for more. I advanced to the Little House on the Prairie, The Bobbsey twins and then Nancy Drew.

After high school, Fern attended college in Minot at the State Teachers College there. I believe she also worked in Minot. When Clarence Rau, the Air Force dude, was discharged, they continued to date. It wasn't long before they decided to marry. They were married a day after Christmas. Clarence attended Wahpeton State School of Science to become an auto body repair person. After graduation he worked in Wahpeton and then Fargo as an auto body repair person but discovered he was allergic to the paint so switched to upholstery in the auto body shop. They later moved to Dickinson, ND. From there they moved to Williston where my other sister Verla and husband Cliff lived and he opened his own upholstery business there. He did quite well in his business and my sister Fern was the front office receptionist/ bookkeeper/ office person. Together, they built a successful business that was successful because of the reputation of not only the work done there but the treatment of their customers. They always had more work than could be done by one person so had to hire help. Some customers would be on a waiting list for months to get the work done by them rather than going somewhere else.

Fern and Clarence had three lovely daughters and a not so lovely son. He was a fine son, just not lovely. Their firstborn was Melody Dawn. Next was Cynthia Kay and then Tammy Jean. Wayne Curtis was the baby of the family. His mother often referred to him as Dwight when he was in trouble, probably because he reminded her of me when I was being obtuse and irritating. She sometimes refers to me as Wayne, probably for the same reason. I guess neither of us is lovely. The girls are nothing, if not lovely. They take after their mother and aunt Verla. Their father is an extraordinary person who has many qualities he passed on to his children that I wish I possessed. He is a valued friend and loved by all who know him. He is a person that is easy to be with and hard to offend but interesting to talk with and not afraid to voice his opinion and beliefs. A kind and loving man with good values and high morals. A good man and there are few of us left.

Both my sisters were school teachers and taught school in one room country schools. They taught all eight grades if there were students in each grade. Each of them stayed with one of the students' parents on a farm.

When Verla married, she and her husband Clifford lived in part of the school. One winter Cliff was working construction in Williston and would come home on weekends to their school house home. During the week he would stay in Williston. At this point, they had two boys, Douglas and Dean. The boys were not very old so Verla would have to take care of the boys while she was also teaching school. This arrangement allowed the boys to be by themselves, unsupervised, on occasion. One winter day while Verla was teaching a class, the boys ran outside. As I remember it, Dean had only his under shorts on and was barefoot. He ran through the snow, climbed the slide and slid down the metal slide with nothing on but his under shorts. I believe Doug was dressed in shirt and jeans and followed him out. I don't think they were out very long because their mother saw them and brought them in. Doug was the older of the two and I would guess Dean was probably three or four. Dean was much like his uncle Dwight, a rebel without a clue that pulled his own strings.

My siblings were all hard working, loving and kind people. My brother had a lot of health problems early in life. He had crohns disease and at that time, they didn't know how to treat it so he had a limited social life when his crohns was not controlled. He also suffered from effects of the war, which he wouldn't talk about.

My sisters were like my Paternal Grandmother, Amelia, always taking care of those who needed caring for. When my Mother had hardening of the arteries and would not remember who she was or what or how to do most anything, my sisters would take turns having her live with them until she finally had to go in a nursing home. The last time I saw my Mother alive, she was scared of me and thought I was the devil. I could see I was upsetting her and she was convinced I was the devil so I just left so she could calm down. She called me a "little devil" many times in my rebelled childhood so perhaps some part of her memory was functioning. She could be lucid and know you one minute and the next minute, not know you or be scared of you. She could carry on a perfectly normal conversation with you for five or ten minutes and then all of a sudden not remember any of it and start the same conversation all over. It was sad and hard to live with, yet my sisters and husbands and their families took excellent care of her and my father. My wife and I took care of her for one week so my sisters could have a break and it was almost more than we could handle for one week. My sisters and their husbands did it for an extended period of time, and still kept their sanity. In my book and this is my book, they are candidates for Sainthood.

Fern and Verla also took in Aunt Lizzie to live with them alternating between them. Aunt Lizzie never married so her only relatives were her siblings and nieces and nephews. Aunt Lizzie would cook, clean and do housework while she was able but later when she was unable would visit with you and keep you company. Fern said when Aunt Lizzie lived with them, they never needed to read the newspaper because while Fern was doing the housework, cooking, ironing etc., Aunt Lizzy would read the newspaper out loud to her.

When it was time for Aunt Lillie to go in a nursing home, her kids chose the one in Williston, the city my sisters lived in. I'm sure in part because they knew Fern and Verla would visit often. Not only did Fern and Verla visit often but their husbands, Clarence and Clifford visited often. They would also bring her to their home to celebrate holidays and special occasions.

When my Father couldn't live alone anymore, he lived with one of my sisters and her husband, alternating between the two homes. That was my sisters' nature, care for and share your home with anyone in your family that was in need of a home and care. I've heard from other relatives, my paternal grandmother Amelia Knuth was the same way. You took care of and cared for your family, doing whatever needed doing.

My brother Dorel was the first born in our family and I was the last born so there was nearly twenty years difference in our ages. Because of this, I never got to know my brother very well. I was closer friends with his kids, Linda, Billy and Jeannie than with him because his kids were closer to my age and I grew up with them. That was also true of Verla's children, Doug and Dean but because I lived with Verla and Cliff, I also became friends with them.

I never lived with my sister Fern and her husband Clarence but I broke bread at their table with them often and can tell you Fern is an excellent cook and they are great hosts. I also got to know their children, Melody, Cindy, Tammy and Wayne quite well. There is not a bad apple in the barrel. They come from good stock.

Youth & beyond

A good portion of my miss-spent youth is described in the chapter, Crushes, Love, Romance & Foolishness. Also in the chapters, Work, Friends and Army & Navy.

Once I received my honorable discharge from the Navy, I spent a good amount of time in the pursuit of the Love of my Life and somehow brainwashed her into marrying me. There is another chapter describing that.

We made our first home in Grand Forks, ND where I worked at First National Bank as a computer programmer. The pay was less than poverty level because of all the prestige that went with working at a bank, or so the bank thought. You can't eat prestige. Luckily, Kathy's parents gave us a half of pig for a wedding present and my parents provided us with canned goods, berries, baked goods and fish. We couldn't afford Henry's Hamburgers at nineteen cents each, much less a six pack of beer. I managed 12 apartments so we got a reduced rate on our rent or we would probably be homeless. The bank was long on promises but short on follow through. They kept promising me raises that never materialized. When I gave my notice of termination because I applied for and got a job at the University of ND, they promised me equal pay if I would stay. I liked the people I worked with so agreed to stay. The equal pay never happened. I appealed to the president and the next day was fired. Of course the job at the U of ND was already filled.

My Navy buddy, Jim Gulbranson, got me a job with Boise Cascade in International Falls as a computer programmer. We bought a small house in International Falls, packed up all our worldly goods in a U-Haul and attached the car to the truck and went down the road, without a glance back. The disadvantage of this move was that we were another 200 miles further from both our parents so now we were 400 miles away. It made the trips home a less frequent adventure. The advantage was we now were making a living wage and could afford hamburgers and beer. Even before my first day of work, I received a raise and they kept coming with regularity as did the promotions. When I agreed to go to work for Boise Cascade, they thought they would be able to pay my moving expenses. My boss, Lee Dornhecker, called me and told me they wouldn't be able to pay my moving expenses but would instead give me a raise over what we had agreed to. This was a much better deal. Moving expenses are a one time payment. A raise is more money every pay day. I had not worked one day and already got a raise. A much better work environment as well as great people to work for and with.

We made a trip to International Falls to look for housing. We thought we would rent something until we found a suitable home. After looking at several rental units we changed directions and decided we would look for a house to buy. We looked at several homes that didn't impress us and the real estate agent finally showed us a nice home that had been on the market for quite a while and the owner who had moved to Minneapolis was wanting to sell. Kathy made an offer and the real estate agent said he didn't think the owner would accept but he would relay it and see what happened. He rejected the offer but made a counter offer. Kathy stood firm and said we wanted the house but at the price she offered. She told the agent to show us some more houses because she wasn't willing to pay the counter offer. The agent called the owner and he accepted Kathy's offer. Kathy then told the agent they had to leave all the draperies and curtains and matching bedspreads with the house. They offered to sell them to us but Kathy again would not budge. No deal without the draperies and bedspreads. I guess she thought we would have bare windows if we didn't get them. They were expensive, custom made draperies and she really wanted them. Again the owner caved and we bought the house complete with custom draperies and bedspreads at the price Kathy offered. She missed her calling. She should have been a union representative on a negotiating team.

The early years. 1974, Kathy, Dwight, Kim, Eric (I grew a full beard because all the male members of the George Knuth family grew beards that year)

When I shaved my beard Kim didn't recognize me. After her nap and my shave, I went to get her out of her crib. She started crying when I picked her up. When I would talk to soothe her she would stop crying but when she looked at me she would start in again. Kathy came to see what was wrong with her baby and realized Kim was confused because I didn't have a beard anymore. I went to the wastebasket and retrieved the beard and alternately held it to my face and removed it. You could see in her eyes and her expression that she got it and everything was OK again. Shortly after we went to the Littlefork fair and were in one of the animal barns. I was carrying her but she wanted to get down possibly to pet one of the animals. She wandered around and when more people entered the barn she went over to a bearded fellow and grabbed onto his leg. I saw what was happening and went over to retrieve her and when I went to pick her up she started to cry until I started to talk to her and she recognized my voice. I'm still pretty good at confusing people.

Our home was a modest three bedroom with a bath and one half. Room enough for out of town guests such as our parents. We had a TV room upstairs with a hide a bed couch. We also had a living room on the first floor, without a TV, with a hide a bed couch, so technically we had four beds. Kathy didn't have a drivers license but we were within walking distance of downtown, my work and a grocery store. We didn't have a washer and dryer so we had to go to the laundromat and because Kathy couldn't drive, I had to take her. It wasn't long before we purchased a new washer and dryer. We also didn't have a dishwasher but that seldom affected me and Kathy said she didn't mind doing dishes.

We even could afford to start a family. We decided it was time and Kathy became pregnant overnight. I guess that is how it generally works. After nine months we were thinking a baby should arrive. When it didn't happen, the Dr. thought he could help it along by inducing labor. That didn't work either. At the ten month mark, Kathy finally went into labor and our first born, a son, Eric came into the world. Life was never the same again. Gone were our carefree days but the happiness that he brought with him was worth the loss of sleep and any other freedom that vanished.

We had a fenced yard so Eric could play outside. He was a very smart child, already exploring his world by taking all his toys apart and finding out how they worked. He had a small desk with a seat that was put together with wing nuts. He was three years old when he took it apart and had all the pieces laying on the floor with the screws. He had figured out how to lower the side of his crib so he could get out and after his nap, crawled out and proceeded to dismantle his desk. Kathy heard him in his room and came in and saw the results. She scolded him and told him he better be able to put it back together and he shouldn't come out of his room until he finished.

She never expected him to accomplish that goal but thought it would occupy him for awhile and make him think about demolishing his toys in the future. After a short time he came out to get his mom and show her his accomplishment. He had finished putting the desk back together correctly. It's no wonder he later became an aircraft mechanic in his adult life. He still has the ability to take a look at anything and tell how it should work and if it is broken, how to fix it. In his youth he was a lot like his dad whose teachers always told my parents that I was not working up to my ability. His teachers knew he was capable of more than he was doing. He also had a very logical mind especially when he wanted to express himself but didn't know the words yet. He would call his shoes, his "walks" because that is what he used when he went for a walk. When out walking he would sometimes say walk be front of me. If you walk behind the opposite must be walk befront. He coined many expressions that we still use.

Kathy and I had decided we wanted two children. Eric was two plus years and a delight so we thought perhaps it was time to increase our family. Life was good, my job was as secure as any job ever is and I was doing well, getting raises and enjoying my work. Kathy became pregnant and again was a happy, glowing person. She was happy before she was pregnant but when she was pregnant she just glowed. She did get quite large and had a hard time getting around and was anxious to have the baby. Again, nine months of pregnancy came and went and the Dr. said with past experience, just be patient. The baby will come when it is ready. After ten months, our beautiful daughter was born and we named her Kimberly Kathleen. She was a very good child and was daddies sweetheart. She had an older brother who would try to get her in trouble. Most of the time she would try to keep him out of trouble. Eric and Kim were sharing a bedroom and we had become used to using the other bedroom as a TV room. We liked having the TV in a separate room from the living room because when we had company we could visit with them without having a blaring TV. If one of us wanted to watch a TV show that the other was not interested in, the non-interested party could go to the living room to read a book or do other things. It worked well for us. Even now we have a separate room for watching TV. Although we have a TV in the dining room, it is never on during meals if there is more than one person eating. Just a rule we created to enjoy our meals with conversation. We never have the TV on for background noise. If no one is seated, watching TV, it is turned off.

So we didn't want to give up our TV room for a bedroom for one of the children. We had some unfinished room upstairs that I thought I could convert to a bedroom. My parents visited us and Dad brought his carpenter tools so we could put in a window for light, ventilation and fire escape. I began wiring for electric heat and lights and installing floors and walls. In the meantime we decided that perhaps we were outgrowing our cozy little home and should look for something bigger.

We looked at quite a few homes but nothing we fell in love with. Either they wanted too much or they needed too much fixing up. Kathy talked to one of her girlfriends, Marsha Shuff who told her about a house that she knew was for sale that she thought we might like or perhaps, her and her husband Tim would like. They were also looking for a house. She asked if we would like to make an appointment to look at it and we could all go together at the same time. Kathy mentioned it to me and we decided we might as well go along and look. Someone set up a time and after work we all went to look at the house. It was Dick Walkers house that he had built himself for his late wife. You could see he put a lot of time and love into it. They built the basement and lived in the basement while they were finishing the upstairs. His wife died before the completion. There wasn't a kitchen upstairs but there was a fully functional kitchen in the basement where they had been living. The rest of the upstairs was completed which consisted of three bedrooms, a living room, a dining room, a full bath with shower and the kitchen which needed cupboards and appliances. The downstairs had a huge family room a bedroom under the attached garage, a pantry, a kitchen, a laundry/furnace room and a bedroom attached to the full bathroom with shower. There was the one car attached garage and a basement walk in shop on the down side (back) of the house on the hill that it sat on. This all sitting on a huge lot with plenty of room for the kids to play. Outside it had woods on three sides for privacy.

All the first floor, floors were narrow hard wood. This was when everyone was doing wall to wall carpets but we preferred bare hardwood floors. The front of the house was split native rock and the living room had one wall done of split native rock with a fireplace. I had taken a college course from the gentleman that did the split rock walls on how to build split rock walls and fireplaces so I was aware of the work and talent that went into it. There was a brick fireplace in the family room in the basement. Each fireplace had its own chimney and there was a separate chimney for the furnace. The basement floors had ugly tile. The first floor was all plaster walls and ceilings. The price was reasonable and we liked the house.

The only thing that was holding us back was selling our cozy little house. I did some calculations and came up with a figure that we would have to get for our house so we wouldn't be living in poverty again. I didn't think we had a chance of getting what we needed for our house, which was nearly double what we paid. Kathy thought we could and said, just let me handle it. We advertised it and didn't go with a real estate seller. We had quite a few lookers and all seemed to like it but couldn't afford our asking price and Kathy would not budge on it. Finally, when it looked as though we would not be able to sell our house and therefore not be able to buy the new house, a Native American lady looked at it and wanted to buy it. She was getting help from the government and they agreed to the price and went ahead with inspections. They found some dry rot in the main beam in the basement and required that we replace it, which we did. They gave us the asking price and we received a nice profit, nearly double what we paid. Only the government could afford our outrageous price. This allowed us to purchase our dream house. Kathy again came through with her bargaining skills. From then, henceforth, Kathy did all the bargaining and bickering.

More than once I witnessed her bargaining with salesmen that thought they had made the lowest possible offer and she would refuse it. At least on two different occasions I heard them say, "how much would you like to pay". Once she told them how much money she had on her, which was minimal and way below the asking price, but they took it. When bargaining for some jewelry once, the salesman asked her how much she would like to pay and she said she would like it to be free. He surprised us all by actually giving her the piece of jewelry.

Now we had to get the new house ready for occupancy. Kathy wanted fresh paint on the walls so she went about repainting the whole house. She would take the kids with her and paint from morning until night with the kids getting used to their new digs and yard. Some of Kathy's friends gave her a hand with painting when they could. Meanwhile I was getting things packed up and ready to move.

One day Kathy told me there was a dog laying on the back steps that would not let her in the new house to do some cleaning. I went over and sure enough there was this gray mangy looking mutt laying on the back steps. When I approached him he would snarl and growl and show his teeth like he was going to rip me apart. I would back off and he would be fine. I went around to the front door and the dog just stayed by the back entrance. I went in the front door with no objection from the dog and went to the back door and opened the door, keeping the storm door between me and the dog. The dog just looked at me like we both belonged where we were. He was not upset that I was in the house. I finally got brave enough to open the storm door and the dogs tail started wagging and he got up and was treating me like his long lost owner.

I thought perhaps he was the previous owners dog but that proved wrong and no one in the neighborhood knew where he belonged or where he came from. From then on, even though he was friendly with me, I had to go in the front door and out the back door whenever I came or the dog wouldn't let me in the house. We didn't want a dog but he thought for some reason this was his home. We let him occupy the back porch until we had moved in. Not being familiar with the dog, we were afraid he might bite one of the kids so I had the dog catcher come and get him. The dog catcher lived next door.

The kids wanted to keep the dog but Kathy and I didn't really want a dog even though we had become somewhat attached to him. I checked with the dog catcher daily to see if someone had claimed him or adopted him. He told me that after three days they would put him down. Kathy and I discussed it and said we couldn't let that happen so after three days I went back to the dog catcher and got him. I had to pay for his board for three days and license him. We then took him to the vet to get shots and check him over. We learned from the vet he was a few years old and a mix of a poodle and probably some type of husky.

All went well, the kids loved him and he wasn't much trouble other than when we would leave him outside, he would run through the neighborhood like a crazy animal, scaring the neighborhood children with his exuberance and running through yards and gardens. We decided to name him Tramp. I had to invest in a chain to put him outside so he wasn't a neighborhood nuisance. He was a house dog for a short period of time until he started using our new basement carpet for a bathroom. He quickly became an outside dog. I found a nice dog house for him that was insulated and had a light in it for warmth in the winter. I ran an electrical line to the dog house with the switch in the house so I could control it from inside. I got straw bales and stacked them around the dog house to further insulate it. Most of the time, he ignored the nice cozy dog house and lay on top of the straw bales, outside. If it got very cold we would bring him into the back entrance even though the dog house was heated.

He was a good watch dog and kept the animals out of the yard for the most part. The black bear liked to tease him. They obviously knew he was on a chain and could only go so far. The bear would go to the garbage can, get a bag of garbage, walk down to where tramp was chained, sit down just outside his range and tear the bag of garbage open and sit there and eat or lick out cans. Tramp would tear out of his dog house at full speed toward the bear and hit the end of the chain and flip over backwards. He was a slow learner because he did this repeatedly. One day he finally got the best of a young bear and chased it up the tree that was by his dog house. I came home from work and the whole neighborhood was in my yard looking up the tree at the bear. We called the department of Natural Resources and they told us to take the dog in the house, tell all the neighbors to leave and eventually the bear would come down and go away. They were right. It got to be an annual event where the bear would tease Tramp. They never attacked Tramp, just teased him.

On one occasion we had a pack of dogs come into our yard and Tramp took on the whole pack. There was blood let, both on the pack of dogs and on tramp. Kathy called the police but by the time they got here, the fight was pretty much over. One more reason, if there is a leash law, you should keep your dog leashed. If I keep my dog leashed and you don't, my dog is defenseless and can't even run away.

One time I took Tramp grouse hunting with me. He was not a hunting dog and I knew that. I just took him along so he could have a good run in the woods. He wasn't good at coming when you called him so I just let him run while I hunted. I had my son along and when it was time to go we called and called Tramp to no avail. Finally I told Eric we would just have to go home and leave Tramp. Of course he didn't want to do that but it was obvious

Tramp was not coming. With our heads hanging we got in the pickup, started it up and began to slowly drive away. Here comes Tramp running at full speed out of the woods. Eric opened his door and Tramp jumped in all excited. That was Tramps last hunting trip.

1984 –Eric, Kathy, Dwight, Kimberly

We took many vacations while the kids were growing up and living at home. We thought it was important to build memories. In retrospect, not all the memories were good ones. Our vacations usually consisted of visiting relatives while doing some sightseeing. They usually involved a great deal of travel, many times to Montana where Kathy had siblings. We generally took Kathy's parents along with us. I thought they were great vacations but the rest of the family was not always so appreciative. I enjoyed stopping at relatives or friends to visit and break bread together. The kids especially, didn't care so much for the visiting. It got to be a standard question when planning vacations, does dad know anyone there? The kids, at least Kim would prefer to spend the evening in a motel room watching TV. If the kids were fighting in the back seat of the car, on the trip, we would take away the TV when we got to the motel. It turned out this was only punishment for Kim as Eric didn't care if we had TV or not. I guess I should have threatened to visit someone.

Our two kids. Our greatest contribution to the world.

Eric, 22 years old, an aircraft mechanic.

Our Darling Dimpled Daughter Kimberly, in Italy

This Dummy Pulls His Own Strings

We went to Yellowstone and Glacier national parks. Of course, mountains are involved in those parks. Both Kathy and her Dad were not fond of travel in the mountains. If the down side of the mountain was on their side of the car, they would lean in towards the center of the car. We decided to carry a pint of vodka in the trunk of the car for medicinal purposes. When we would stop at a rest stop or scenic stop we would get the pint out for Kathy's dad, Wester, to build his courage. He chewed tobacco and drank straight out of the pint so no one else would share the bottle with him. It served the purpose and relaxed him to the point of not caring if we were in the mountains or the plains. He was a happy man when he was under the influence which didn't happen very often. It made the trip quite interesting and sometimes embarrassing for Kathy's mom, Edith. He was a shy, conservative man who would easily embarrass. When he had a drink or two, he wasn't quite so shy and proper which provided me with many laughs but his wife and daughter were not always so amused. Sometimes they couldn't help but laugh, even if they were embarrassed. I enjoyed him as a traveling companion and as a person with many attributes more of us should have. He was a great father-in-law.

My Mother-in-law, Edith was a saint. She was kind and compassionate to a fault. She was also a miracle worker. Times were tough when they were raising a family and often times there was barely enough food for the family let alone the rest of the neighborhood, friends and relatives. It seemed to me, people flocked to their farm at meal time. They didn't have a telephone so people just dropped in. Edith was a wonderful cook so these people would appear at meal time. Edith would go into the pantry or down the basement where the canned goods were kept and would always come back with something to feed the multitudes. She had the ability to make something delicious out of practically nothing. Her home baked bread and canned pickles could make a meal by themselves not to mention her canned tomatoes. The best restaurants couldn't compare to her cooking. I was accused of keeping her daughter out all night, just so I could partake of breakfast. There may have been some truth to it, although spending time with Kathy was not really a burden or a task but a genuine pleasure. So it was a win-win for me.

Anytime anyone needed a bed to sleep in or a meal, Edith would provide both. It made life interesting around the Hoffman farm because as a child, the kids never knew who they would be sharing their bed with. Wester was not always so eager to share his food and home as his wife. He would refer to all the strange kids running around as "Army Worms", eating all his grub. Lucky they lived on a farm and milked cows to provide milk for all the army worms. Edith would take in other people's children for an extended period of time for any reason and treat them all like her own children even though she had seven of her own. Edith and Wester were hard workers and provided a good wholesome life for their children and many other children. Their wealth was their children and the wonderful people their children became because of their upbringing on the prairie of North Dakota.

Kathy and Siblings; Mike, Vivian, Larry, Lynn, Kathy, Roger

Edith and Wester lost their first child, Elaine Faith as an infant. Any loss of a child is heartbreaking and devastating to the parents but Edith turned to her faith for comfort and solace and prayed for healthy children in the future. That was the way of coping with the hard prairie life. Your faith and don't dwell on the past but live in the present and build for the future. God heard Edith's prayers and they soon had a set of twins, a girl, Vivian and a boy, Vincent. While these two were still in diapers, Edith had another set of twins, this time two boys, Lynn and Larry. Now Edith has four children in diapers. This was before God helped man invent disposable diapers so Edith had cloth diapers for four babies to keep clean in addition to the care and feeding of four babies. Of course she also had a husband to care for and he was busy trying to make a living on the ND prairie, farming. This was a time when farming was daylight to dark hard labor and all your work could be wiped out by mother nature in the form of a hail storm, draught, flood or prairie fire not to mention the crop diseases and pests such as grasshoppers. Just when you thought you were having a good crop and the income with it to live another year, the weather would turn wet so it couldn't be harvested and would rot in the field. To add to this stress and worry, Edith and Wester did not have a well on the farm they lived on so Wester had to haul all the water for cooking, cleaning and the animals they raised such as horses, cows, chickens and other farm animals. Sometimes in the summer if the sloughs had water in them the animals could fend for themselves with that water. In dry periods or winter, all the water had to be hauled. A full time job by itself without the other farm chores. Add to this the hand washing of diapers for four babies. If you think our parents didn't work harder and worry a lot more than their children, you don't know the facts and have no imagination. They indeed did make a better life for their children and at the same time, by example, taught a work ethic and built character in the personalities of their children. They may not have left financial wealth for the children to fight over after their demise but they gave us a much better gift that can't be squandered away and we will always have, our character, integrity and work ethic.

Edith probably had a direct prayer line with God and may have been asking to stop with the twins already. I know I would have. Weather she did or not, the next birth was one boy, Roger followed several years later by one girl, Kathleen who was destined to become my wife because I would not take no for an answer. Also, she fell in Love with me. Well, falling in love with me may not be the correct terminology, I may have pushed her, begged, brainwashed and cajoled her. I like to believe, it was a fall.

Aunt Elsie (Knuth) Chole Kofstad History

The Knuth Sisters; Elsie Chole Kofstad, Lillie Kriedeman, Elizabeth Knuth

Written by Elsie (Knuth) Chole Kofstad

The following is an account of the history of her life and her parents and grandparents, in her own words, just as she wrote it. All of the account was written by her except when there are comments by me in *Lucida Calligraphy.*

Knuth Family History as told by Elsie (Knuth) Chole Kofstad.
Family History of my (Elsie's) Grandparents
Christian and Wilhemina Knuth

This Dummy Pulls His Own Strings

This is what I remember what my parents mentioned about their parents, which are my grandparents. We didn't have the joy or happiness to have our grandparents living near us. They did not come to America, so we did not get to know them. We can only say that we loved them as all grandchildren love their grandparents.

Our grandparents were not rich, but were hardworking people. They worked hard for a living and the necessary things they needed.

In Germany they didn't live on farms as we do here. They lived in little villages, I call it. They had garden plots and the men went out to the fields from the villages to work. In those days they cut hay and grain with a scythe. My mother mentioned more than once how early they started to go to work in the morning when she walked two miles to dig potatoes. Most likely they have machinery now that makes life easier.

My father's parents, Christian and Wilhemina Knuth were born in Germany. They lived in the province of Brandenberg. They were the parents of eight children.

Charley, the oldest, came to America before he was 21 years old. The reason he came before he was 21 was because in Germany, at that time, they were called for training when they were 21 years old whether there was war or not. He didn't want to go for training. He came to Vinton, Iowa. There is where he lived on a farm, with his wife Margaret McGinity. They had six children, Edith, Clara, Ervin, Grace, Fred and Annie.

Second child, Herman, stayed in Germany until 1894. He was married in Germany to Justine Umberg. Their children were Paul, Elizabeth and Martha. His two oldest children were teenagers when they came to America and they were the only three that got to know their grandparents.

Their third son was William who married Amelia Nehls. The following excerpt was taken from the family Bible.
Married: April 14, 1884
Julius Christian Wilheim Knuth and
Augusta Emile Johana Nehls
They were the parents of ten children. Paul was born in Berlin, Germany. His grandparents got to see him but Paul would not

remember them, as he was a baby when my parents came to America. Elizabeth, Louis, William Jr., Fredirick, Lillie, Herman, Charley and George were all born in Iowa, Plymouth County near Lamars and Elsie was born in North Dakota on their homestead.

Their fourth child was a daughter, Whilhemina. She was married to John Bartels. They had four children, Martha, Bertha, Minnie and Amelia. Her second marriage was to Joseph Marsh. They had a son Joseph Jr.

The fifth child, a daughter, Bertha, married Louis Buse. They had four children, Paul, Frieda, Lydia and Herman.

Sixth child, a son, August, married Anna Pipenbush. They had one daughter. His second marriage was to Carrie Rumbolg. They had four children, Mabel, Willie, Esther and Ervin.

The seventh child was Fred. He married Dora Barte and they had three daughters, Monica, Annie and Helen.

The baby of the family was Louis. He married May Kriedeman. They had no family.

We knew all our Aunts, Uncles and Cousins from grandpa and grandma Knuth's family and had many good times together. Our Aunts and Uncles sort of had to take the place of our grandparents.

Grandpa's first wife died when the youngest child, Louis, was a year old. Grandpa's second marriage was to Mrs. Wodrig, a widow. She had a son, Carl and a daughter Lena. This gave a stepsister and a stepbrother to the six brothers and two sisters already in the family.

We never thought of them as our step Aunt or step Uncle. They were Aunt and Uncle like our other Aunts and Uncles. Carl was married to Bertha Kriedeman. They had two children that died in infancy. Aunt Bertha was a good cook and John always said the coffee she made was the best. Having coffee at her house was an every time affair at her house. Aunt Bertha worked hard when they lived on their homestead. Uncle Carl lost his left arm. It was off up to his elbow and she helped dig fence postholes and helped him in many other ways. Uncle Carl surprised many when they saw the work he did with one arm.

Aunt Lena was married to Jacob Bartels. They had four daughters, Martha, Annie, Katie and Hattie. They lived in Minnesota.

This Dummy Pulls His Own Strings

They came to North Dakota to visit their two daughters, Mrs. Fred Kriedeman and Mrs. Louis Schucka. She was a kind and loving person. George and I always looked forward to her coming. She always had candy for us. Her husband, Jake, as we called him, was a brother to John Bartels who was married to grandpa's sister Minnie. We never called her Wilhemina.

Grandpa and Grandma Knuth's children all came to America when they were young. Herman and William and Uncle Carl Wodrig were married in Germany. Uncle Herman and his family come nine years later to America, then my parents. I don't know whether our grandparents were still living or not when they came.

There were none of the children that made a trip back to Germany. The first farewell was the first and last.

Imagine saying goodbye to your parents with the knowledge that you more than likely will never see them again. Imagine the emotion of the parents saying goodbye to their children also thinking they will never see them again. That must have taken real courage and fortitude.

History of my grandparents, Carl and Henrietta Nehls. Written by Elsie (Knuth) Chole Kofstad

This is what I remember from grandpa and grandma Nehls, my mothers parents.

If my memory is correct, their names were Carl and Henrietta Nehls.

They were the parents of four children. They too, lived in a village like place. Only two of the children came to America. My mother was the first one to leave. Her parents died while she was still in Germany. She bid farewell to her two sisters, Bertha and Fredrica and brother William.

After several years, her sister Bertha and her nephew Frank came to America. I think my parents helped them with the fare. They came to Iowa where my parents lived. Bertha married John Dohrman and they lived in Iowa until they entered a home for the aged in Lincoln, Nebraska. They had no family. My older brothers and sisters knew aunt Bertha but I didn't get to see her only on a picture that I have. Mothers brother and other sister married and had a family. I don't know how many children they had and being I didn't know them, I don't know who was the oldest of those two.

Frank Nehls, our cousin was the only relative that I got to know from my mother's family. He often told me, "you look like your mother". I know he thought a lot of my mother. After my mother was gone I often caught him just setting and looking at me and he would say, "you look like your mother".

Frank married Lain Walz in South Dakota or Iowa. She was a sister to Aunt Francis dad. Frank and Lain farmed at Wibaux, Montana. When they retired they moved to Beach, North Dakota. There is where they are both buried. I visited their graves twice when John and I visited in Beach.

Grandpa and Grandma Nehls were hard working people. Grandpa was sick much of the time and wasn't very old when he died. Grandma then got a job in a factory where they wove cloth. After her death my mother took the job and worked there until she got married.

While working there she lost half of her little finger on her one hand by accident. The part she lost they took to the cemetery and buried it on her mother's grave. So a little part of her body was buried in Germany before she came to America.

My mother had no picture of her parents. I often wish she had. She did have a picture of her oldest sister and nephew Frank. I do have a picture of my grandma Nehls grave.

Family History of our parents.

Our parents, William Knuth, born June 13, 1858 and Amelia (Nehls) Knuth, born Dec. 13, 1858 in Germany and grew up in Germany.

They were united in marriage April 14, 1884 in St. Johns Lutheran church in Berlin, Germany. Here they made their home until they came to America.

This Dummy Pulls His Own Strings

I do not know what kind of work my father did in Berlin. But wages were only enough to make a living. There was not enough to have much savings laid aside.

Their oldest son, Paul, was born in Berlin. When he was six or seven months old, my parents received a letter from my father's oldest brother Charley, who had come to America before he was twenty one years of age. His brother offered to help my parents come to America by sending them the money they needed for fare.

My parents accepted the offer and in the summer of 1885 they bid farewell to their native land, to their parents and other loved ones and friends and came to America, to Vinton, Iowa where brother Charley was living on a farm.

They landed in New York. There was no one there to meet them and no one that spoke German and my parents could only speak German. At Vinton, Iowa my father got a job on a farm and mother did house work for other people taking Paul with her. When they had enough cash earned to pay back the fare to brother Charley, they kept on working until they had enough money to take another journey. This time they went to Plymouth Co., Iowa near La Mars. Why they came to this area near La Mars I do not know. They must have come to Plymouth Co., Iowa near La Mars in 1886 because their second child was born on the 16th of Dec. in 1886, a daughter, Elizabeth.

Here they started farming and worked hard. They had to pay cash rent as they did not own their own land. There was enough to eat but lot of this food was raised on the farm. They farmed in Plymouth Co. from 1886 to 1901.

After their daughter, Elizabeth was born, there were seven more children born in Plymouth Co., Iowa., Louis, William Jr., Frederick, Lillie, Herman, Charley and George.

They heard about the homesteads that could be taken in North Dakota so father and two of his brothers came to North Dakota to look at the land. It was satisfactory and they each took a homestead which consisted of 100 acres. *(Aunt Elsie was not born yet when they emigrated to ND so it's* *possible she got the acres above wrong. The Homestead Act signed into law by Abraham Lincoln on May 20, 1862 gave homesteaders 160 acres free if they lived on it and farmed it for 5 years. It also gave them all requirements for citizenship. After 6 months, if you wanted to, you could buy your homestead for $1.25 an acre, a total of $200.00 for 160 acres. In 1873 the Timber Culture Act allowed you to add another 160 acres to your homestead, free, if you planted 10 acres of trees. I'm sure my grandfather took advantage of both acts and Aunt Elsie mentions adding land so they needed more horses. My Father once told me Grandpa gave each of his children land and even if he only gave them each 80 acres for 8 living children that would be 640 acres. He was quite successful at farming and not only had a lot of land and horses, he owned the only threshing machine in the vicinity. All the farmers would get together to thresh the grain and use grandpa's threshing machine, going from farm to farm. I'm not sure if the other farmers, mostly relatives, paid grandpa for the use of his threshing machine or if there were other arrangements made.)*

So there was another move to plan for and they moved to North Dakota in the spring of 1901 and settled on the homestead with their family. My father's uncle and his wife were with them. They lived in the granary the first summer. The granary was built on to the barn so they could save the expense of one wall.

My father, Paul and Louis came by immigrant car. They were the two oldest boys and were able to help feed the cattle and horses in the cars. *(This was an Immigrant train much like a freight train for transporting immigrants with their farm implements and livestock. Those immigrants moving from one location to another, often used a boxcar. Historian Everett Dick says Farming equipment and household goods were stored in one end of the car, and the other was left open to accommodate the livestock, particularly favorite draft animals and perhaps a cherished milk cow. Hay and grain were stored near the stock, and a small space in the middle of the car was left for the family's living quarters during the several days en route. In this cramped space, makeshift sleeping quarters and cooking accommodations were set up. In mild weather a door would be pushed ajar to provide light, and the near proximity of the animals guaranteed good care for them. The wagon, which had been dismantled and packed as close to the door as possible, was taken out first and set up where it could be loaded with the farming and household goods.")*

Father's brothers August and Louis Sr. were also in this group, for they too had taken a homestead.

The women and children came by passenger train to Balfour, North Dakota. Mother packed enough food to last until they got off the train. All the children that were old enough to carry a box had to help carry the food boxes. I often heard them talk about when they got on the train in Iowa and wondered what the people thought, what they had in all those boxes. Lizzie was the oldest of the children in the train so she carried the largest box. It was a round box that cheese came in when it was shipped to the store. Aunt Mary used to laugh about the cheese box. Lizzie would say, "they wouldn't catch me carrying it now".

The trip was made and now to get out to the homestead on the barren prairie. I missed out on all this moving, packing and unpacking and riding over the prairie trails. I was born too late. *(There were no trees growing on the prairie when they homesteaded. There was only barren prairie covered with grass.)*

I often wondered how my mother managed with the big family and then bringing father's uncle and aunt along to live with them and gave them a home. She suggested to bring them. "Reason". Father's uncle had helped my parents when they were hailed out and no crops to harvest. The cash rent had to be paid or they would be evicted. My father's uncle mortgaged their home to take a loan to let my parents pay the rent. My mother was so grateful they could stay on the farm as they would have no place to go. So she wanted to do something good in return.

My parents repaid the loan to uncle as we had called him. He sold his house in Iowa and came along and lived with us. His wife for three years and uncle thirteen years before their death. They are both buried in the little cemetery on highway # 14 where our country church stood. *(Their names were Carl Theodore Knuth and Ragina Knuth.)*

They arrived safely to the homestead and life on the prairie had begun. There were many things to do. What they did first, I would like to know.

These are some of the things I heard them mention, that they had to haul water for drinking and cooking from the G.J. Nehrenberg place. Myron Knuth now owns the farm. There was water in the sloughs that the cattle could drink. I'm sure they dug a well as soon as possible. They built a house during the summer. They only planned on building a kitchen, bedroom and pantry downstairs and two rooms upstairs. But uncle said, "as long as this will be our home, I will build a room too and when we are gone it can be yours", which was done. My parents added the room upstairs above uncles room. The room uncle built became our living room after he was gone. William Conrod built the house on the farm. They broke up some land for flax and for to raise some feed. They also worked up ground for a garden. Mother had help working in the garden. Uncle loved to be out there helping in the garden. He had a small hoe that he used in the onion patch because it wasn't so wide. Lizzie used it a lot in the flower garden. *(I have that hoe and use it.)*

Those that came to their homesteads had no wood to burn in their stoves. There was only the bare prairie. Most people went to the sand hills for wood and I suppose that is what my parents did too. This is what I missed out on, to see the farm without trees. By the time I could remember there were trees growing. They also used cow chips. I wasn't born when they first used them. But, I remember after I was old enough, I helped pick. My brother George and I had to pick them. We put on a pair of gloves, took some sacks, filled them up and tied the sack shut. We kept on picking until all the sacks were filled. Then (papa), this is what I called him as long as he lived, would hitch a horse to the stone boat and gather them in. They would put them where they would keep dry. They took the place of coal, gave good heat and every one used them. They were there for the picking.

The boys had to herd the cattle during the summer months. One day when Herman and Charley were herding cows, my mother had baked bread. When the bread was baked and she was taking it out of the oven, she took the first pan of bread to the pantry. She left the oven door open because she didn't see me around. But when she got to the pantry, I came into the kitchen and sat on the hot oven door and you can guess what. I got burned and cried. I was only about three years old. George heard me cry and came in the house. He got scared and ran out to where Herman and Charley were herding cows, crying and told them what had happened. They rounded up the cows and came home to see what had happened. That was the end of herding cows for that day.

We had a straw barn in the pasture where they kept some of the young cattle in. The frame barn was only big enough for the milk cows and horses. *(A straw barn is a structure that is built from straw. Straw had many uses. It would be used for bedding for the animals and sometimes for stuffing for a mattress (straw tick) for humans. There was more straw than could be used so eventually what was left of the straw pile would be burned to get rid of it. Often times this was a social event that neighbors and friends and relatives participated in. Sometimes there would be singing, usually church hymns, and in latter days when I was a child, hot dog and marshmallow roasting. The kids would climb to the top of the straw pile which was often 20 to*

30 feet tall or more, and slide down. We would also burrow into the straw. I often heard my dad tell of traveling away from home by horse and when night came would find a straw pile to sleep on if the weather was nice or inside if it was cold or inclement weather. The problem was, wild animals also used it for their homes. Animals such as skunks, badgers, mink, mice etc. There was an abundance of straw so the farmers would use what was known as pig fence to build to squares of whatever size you wanted or could afford or needed. This fence would consist of fence posts or poles whatever height you wanted your straw barn to be, in a square or rectangle. They would then put up posts in another rectangle a couple feet from the first and put the pig fence all around the two rectangles leaving an opening for a door. These two rectangles of poles and fence would then be filled with straw so you had a two foot wall of straw. They would stretch the pig fence across the top for a roof with whatever support was necessary and put several feet of straw on for the roof and more pig fence on top of this layer of straw to keep it from blowing away. This provided a place for the stock to keep out of the wind and weather and the heat from the animals kept it warm in the winter. Often times the door would just be an opening that allowed the stock to enter or leave as they pleased. Of course if you wanted to keep the stock in you would have to devise a door or gate that could be closed but then you would need to feed and water them so most times it was just used for the stock to come and go as they pleased to get out of the sun, rain, heat, cold, wind or blizzards.)

Uncle August and Uncle Louis came to North Dakota when my parents came. Uncle August homesteaded three miles from us and Uncle Louis homestead was two miles from us. So when ever there was some spare time they would work together to put up sheds for winter use for the hogs, chickens and a shed to keep the coal in, which we also used to smoke hams and sausage in.

They had to haul the coal from Balfour also the groceries. When they had grain to haul they would take a load of wheat to the elevator and bring back a load of coal.

There were no phones and there was no mail service on the route. They only got their mail when they went to Balfour.

Papa was a good provider. Since I could remember, he always brought enough flour home to last all winter. We stored it upstairs. He also bought a hundred pounds of sugar. Those years apples could be bought in a barrel. He would bring a barrel of apples to put in the cellar. We didn't have full basements as they do now. The apples in the barrel were mixed sizes which was good for our family because the younger children liked the smaller ones.

All this food that was bought, the homemade sausage, home smoked hams, smoked beef, smoked goose and duck breasts and home grown vegetables gave us good nourishing food to eat. I don't remember that I ever had to go to bed hungry. I don't think the rest of the family ever did either. If we were hungry we could always make a sandwich, even if it was before we went to bed.

We always had lots of company and would have coffee and lunch together. During the winter months if neighbors would come to spend the evening, or we would go to their house, we always had lunch before they went home or when we went home. We would have some of the duck breasts or sausage that we made. They all made homemade meats. The men knew how to cut up the meat. This is not so anymore. Now most of them don't do home butchering any more. If I had some of the home made sausage that my mother made, I would eat my share. Mother was a good cook. The roasts, ducks, geese and sausage always were seasoned just right.

Another treat for us was when she baked bread, she would take a piece of bread dough and sort of flatten it to the size of a sauce dish or perhaps a little larger and deep fat fry it like doughnuts, then she would roll them in sugar. It took quite a few of these for our family. Uncle always asked for potato pancakes for his birthday and he liked them so much. Mama always granted his wish which made him happy.

We had nothing modern in those days. We had to carry in all the water for washing clothes and carry it out when we were through, carry all the water for drinking and cooking.

We had to carry in the wood to fill the wood box and carry in the coal. We all had our chores to do but we didn't mind. It kept us out of mischief. We had plenty of time to play anyway.

Those days when we made ice cream we used a gallon syrup pail, put it in a larger pail and packed ice around it. The syrup pail had a handle on it and we took turns turning it back and forth, until it was ready to eat and it tasted so good. It took a long time but there was enough to change off. Later we had an ice cream freezer. *(An ice cream freezer was much like Aunt Elsie described the syrup pail method. The early ones like the one we used had an outside container made of wood staves much like a barrel. The inner container was made of metal with a metal/wooden paddle from top to bottom. There was a gear on top on the outside and the paddle extended through the metal lid into the gear which was attached to a handle on the outside of the outer container. When you cranked the handle, the inside paddle inside the inside container turned which is where the cream recipe resided. Ice was packed between the two containers and salt was sprinkled on the ice to help it melt as you turned the cream recipe. The cream recipe hardened slowly and when it was hard to turn, you had a soft ice cream. My job, as a child, was to sit on the ice cream freezer while the adults took turns turning the handle. They generally put a coat or two on top of the freezer to make it softer and to keep my butt from freezing from the ice below. This was the best ice cream ever made, probably because as a child we seldom bought any ice cream from a store until we were older. Even then, the home made was better. The youngest toddler that was present generally got to sit on my father's lap while they held the paddle from the ice cream freezer on a large plate and they scraped the ice cream from it and ate it. In the early days, there was no electricity or freezers so when ice cream was made there were generally lots of people there, probably a dozen and we would all sit around the table eating ice cream until it was gone. If by chance there was some left over, they would take it out to a snow bank and bury it inside a wooden box so the animals wouldn't dig it up and eat it. It wasn't often that we needed to bury the leftovers.)*

My Mom & Dad (George & Margaret Knuth) making ice cream and pulling the paddle from the ice cream bucket with my niece Linda Knuth Zeller looking on in anticipation of cleaning it off, sitting on Grandpas' lap.

It was even fun to stuff the straw ticks. We used oats straw. When the thrashers left, the straw ticks got new straw in them. We had a feather bed for each bed. *(The feather beds were made of goose down.) The feather bed was on top of the straw tick and when we would sink into them we were warm. (On the early homesteads, there generally were no furnaces or heat piped to each room of the house. The only source of heat was the cook stove and/or fireplace if you had one. The bedrooms were generally upstairs and the only source of heat was the stairway and/or holes in the floors upstairs rooms that had metal grates in them to let the heat into the room from the first floor. Often times it was cold enough upstairs to freeze water in a drinking glass beside your bed. The feather beds combined with wool quilts kept you toasty warm especially if you wore a night cap to keep the heat from escaping your body.)*

Then after there was more money for better things we had a mattress on all the beds and we couldn't have fun stuffing the straw ticks any more.

There was a time that there were three families living in our house, our own family and papa's uncle and aunt living in the room that later was our living room. They did no cooking, they ate with us. Uncle Louis and Aunt Bertha Buse lived in one room upstairs. Lydia (now Kriedeman) and George used to play together. I was a baby when they lived with us and I don't know how long they were with us. I think Uncle Louis and Aunt Bertha lived on Uncle Fred's homestead for awhile which is where Monica and Emil lived. *(Monica is the daughter of Rev. Fred Knuth and Dora Barte. Fred was a brother of Grandpa William Knuth.)*

Here I will make mention that my parents worked hard as did the other families but they had time to help build our country church which was built in 1902. Before the church was built, they had church in the homes. Not any of the families were rich but they wanted a church to worship in. Their labor was donated, only the carpenter was paid. No doubt he donated some work too as he belonged to the church. Uncle Fred Knuth was the first pastor. Services were in German. Sunday School was German too. I memorized German Bible versus. Devotions in the home were German and if we sang a chorus it was in German. Later on in church, we had no German services because we had pastors that couldn't speak German.

We enjoyed the church activities. We had ice cream socials, basket socials, grab bag, fishing ponds and church picnics. *(A basket social was a social event as well as a means to raise money for specific causes. The members of the female persuasion would pack a picnic basket. These picnic baskets would be auctioned off to the highest bidder of members of the male persuasion for the privilege of eating with the female that had packed it. The picnic basket packers/owners were supposed to remain anonymous but sometimes the ladies would give hints to certain young gentlemen that they were interested in. Sometimes there was trickery involved, which made it fun and interesting. Generally this was done by the single males and females but I suppose it could have been done by everyone and may even have raised more money.)* We had Christmas and children's day programs. Sometimes we would have a Thanksgiving program too. I sang my first solo in church at a Thanksgiving program when I was seven years old.

Other activities after we were older, the boys would play ball evenings with neighbor boys. They also played croquet and horse shoe. During the winter months we had parties in the neighborhood. We didn't go far from home in horse and buggy days. *(There was another mode of transportation in the winter using horses. It was called a stone boat because in the spring it was pulled around the field by horses and stones and rocks would be loaded onto it and then hauled to a rock pile. It was timbers or logs attached together which made it quite strong and low to the ground so you could heave large rocks onto it without lifting. It also had to be strong so it wouldn't break under the weight of the rocks. These same stone boats could be dragged over the hard packed snow in the winter. In North Dakota the wind blows all winter long and makes the snow banks hard as rock. Hard enough to hold up a team of horses and a stone boat. The wind also blows the fields bare in some places so the stone boat could be drug across these patches of bare field also. When roads were blocked by blizzards and snow banks, the stone boats were sometimes used for travel. It was a rough, cold, slow ride but it got you there.)*

After we got the piano we spent time singing hymns and folk songs. Other young people would come and sing too.

Mama and uncle had their own pastime. They were a team. We had sheep, mama would spin wool for stockings and uncle did the knitting. They really enjoyed doing this. Both were good at this work. Uncle knitted for many other people but they furnished their own yarn.

We three sisters learned to crochet and embroider when we were real young and we did lot of this work evenings. Mama never learned to crochet. When she was young she didn't have time for it as the big family kept her busy. When the children were grown and she didn't need to work so much she spent her time reading in spare time.

When times got so there was more money, a new barn was built. The boys were old enough to help with the work. Then papa bought more land and the boys helped work in the field. We needed more horses now that the boys helped with the farming, so he bought enough horses so he could use two gang plows and could drag or seed. We had eighteen horses. When they used the drag the men walked behind it the first years but papa bought a cart to put on the drag so they didn't need to walk.

Some times when the weather would be chilly the men would hang the lines on the lever of the plow and the horses followed the furrow The men would walk behind the plow to keep warm.

This Dummy Pulls His Own Strings

Herman and "Bill", as his brothers and sisters called him, his parents called him "Willie", worked for other farmers much of the time as they weren't all needed at home.

Uncle had a buggy horse named Beddie, also a single buggy. He would visit with relatives or friends three and four days at a time. He also hitched Beddie up and got the mail. He would take George and me along for a ride. The mail box was one and a half miles away from our house. We always liked to go with him and he was always so kind and good. Never once did I see him angry or upset over anything. We have nothing but good memories of him.

When the children were grown, of course, they one by one left to establish homes of their own.

Paul was the first one to marry. He married Anna Kriedeman. They had five children, Henry, Mabel, Verna, Wesley and Delores. Elizabeth never married. Louis was called for service during World War I. He was home for furlough when he got the flu and pneumonia and passed away Nov. 6, 1918.

William married Francis Walz. They had four children, Alvin, Verdell, Orlin and Glory Ann.

Frederick died in infancy.

Lillie married Paul Kriedeman. They had three sons, Tyler, Lloyd and Delos.

Herman married Nettie Fairchild. They raised foster children, James Muldoon and William Benbow. After Netties death he married Theresa Krenetz, after her death he married Mercedes Conister.

Charley married Lizzie Schwede. They had eight children, Arlene, Vernita, Videll, Marlen, Elvera, Willis, Donald and Carolyn.

George married Margaret Valentine. They had four children, Dorel, Verla, Fern and Dwight.

Elsie married Walter Chole. They had one son, Eldon Dwight. After Walters death she married John Kofstad.

We had a good home, good parents, a good childhood on the farm. I don't think any of the children had a regret for being raised on the farm.

There was work, there was fun, there was laughter. We always had enough to eat. I don't think any of us went to bed hungry.

Dwight E. Knuth

God was good to us. God left us have our parents until we were grown up. I have been thankful for this many times.

The homestead was sold. It stands forsaken and forlorn as no one lives there. If the buildings could talk, they perhaps would ask, where are the former owners? Don't they care? All have passed away. I am the last one of the family living.

And I care.

The summer of 1988 was very dry and hot. The grass was burnt from the heat. On June 25, 1988 someone drove on the yard in the grass and a spark from the exhaust set fire to the grass which traveled to the buildings and all were destroyed by the fire.

This is my Life

I, Elsie Dora was born March 24, 1902 to William and Amelia Knuth. The only one of ten children born on the North Dakota homestead.

I feel somewhat proud that I was born on the homestead and grew up there on the farm.

I have good memories of my home where I was raised with brothers and sisters and my parents. I am eighty six years of age as I am writing this chapter and I am thankful for having my parents until all the children were grown up and we were able to take care of ourselves.

I don't remember that I ever said when I was a child that I don't know what to do. Where there is a big family, there are few dull moments.

One thing I remember is before I was old enough to comb my hair, Lillie always combed my hair. When I saw her go to get the comb, I would take it on the run, so she would have to run after me.

Also, when I was three years old, I didn't want to sleep down stairs any more. I wanted to sleep up stairs with Lillie and Lizzie. The only heat that got up the stairs was by having the upstairs door open. Mama thought it was too cold for me but finally she

This Dummy Pulls His Own Strings

made a night cap for me and left me try it. I slept between Lizzie and Lillie and with my night cap on I was warm and slept upstairs ever after. I was a winner again.

I attended a country school which was two miles from home. We had good teachers and I remember the first solo I sang for a Christmas program when I went to school the first year.

When I was seventeen years old I started to do house work for others. For two falls, I picked potatoes at Des Lacs. The first two days it was hard on the back and legs. But, after I got used to it I didn't mind. I made as much in one day as I would make in a week of house work. This sounded good to me.

In the spring of 1921 Walter Chole and I started to be rather friendly together which led to courtship. In the spring of 1922 we were engaged. In November 1922 on the twenty second we were united in marriage at a home wedding with the families present. Brother George and his wife were our attendants. Pastor Agte performed the ceremony. I have all the beads that were on my wedding dress.

The day after we were married we took the train from Balfour to Minot and had our wedding pictures taken, then we took the train back to Balfour and went to the farm that Walter had rented south of Balfour and had batched one year before we were married. This was our home for another two years.

We bought only the necessary furniture that was needed to keep house. But it was home. We had no car but had a buggy horse named Prince. I could harness him, hitch him to the buggy and go to town and Women's Missionary Society any time I wanted to. He was really a Prince.

After living two years on this farm, we moved north to what was the Charles Kriedeman farm and lived on it two years.

Then we moved to my parents farm which was across from them. This is where brother George and Margaret lived when they got married. We lived here five years.

In 1930 Walter had surgery in the fall. All things seemed to be doing well until the fall of 1931 when he became seriously ill with obstruction of the intestine. Surgery was performed. At that time there was no penicillin to fight infections and peritonitis set in. He was in the hospital a week and passed away October 30, 1931.

On May 12, 1931 we had lost our infant son, Eldon Dwight.

It is natural when one is young, we look forward to a long life together and one wonders why did this happen to me? But there are many things we don't understand here in this life and God makes no mistakes because he is all knowing.

I couldn't farm so I sold the machinery, cattle and horses. I moved some furniture over to live with my parents. This is what Walter wanted me to do. Some furniture I stored. I did house work when I was asked. Wages, $2.00 a week. The most they payed was $2.50. This was not very often they paid that much. I also helped pick corn for 3 cents a bushel, another big wage. But these were the thirties.

In 1936 in November, I stayed at the hotel in Guthrie while Herman and Nettie were holding meetings at Coleharbor. I did the cooking and kept things going. John was boarding at the hotel, also a man by the name of Peter Dahl. He was from Kent, Minnesota. He was finishing six months of work as section boss. His wife didn't move to Guthrie because of only the six months of work. He was a good friend of John's and he became a good friend to me.

One day when he was visiting with John, he said, "John, if you are thinking of marriage, our cook would be a good wife for you".

Then on Easter, I received my first card from John. I still have the card. During the summer of 1937 he drove past our place several Sundays wanting to take me out riding but at Grandpa and Grandmas' house there was always lots of company on Sundays and he hesitated to stop. But, in the fall he asked Herman and Nettie if they liked lutefisk. Well, they had never tasted them. Neither had I but I didn't wait to say yes when he asked whether I would go along with him to the lutefisk supper at the Lutheran church in Balfour, so the four of us went. Those old timers really knew how to make fattigman and lefse. On that night I also received my first box of candy from John.

This was the beginning of our courtship. The people in and around Guthrie really kept an eye on John from then on. Mrs. Benedict, the depot agents wife told him one day, John, you are on the front page of the news every week.

In March 1938 we were engaged and we got married on the fifteenth of June 1938. We were married at Herman and Nettie's house. We had wanted Lillie and Paul as our attendants but they had small pox at their house. So we chose Bill and Frances. We just wanted to have Herman perform the marriage ceremony but Nettie thought we should have supper together.

The next morning after our marriage we went to Minnesota for our honeymoon. There I met his youngest sister and his cousins. We were gone for two weeks and we had a good visit and I was received as a relative. They really didn't believe John when he wrote and told them he was coming and bringing his wife along. John was his aunts favorite.

When we got back from our honeymoon, we lived in the house where his mother lived in. In 1940 we bought Benedict's house, when they left Guthrie. In 1963 we moved this house to Drake.

John passed away March 10, 1967 after surgery. Lacking three months we had twenty nine good years together.

I continued to live in the house until 1979, then moved into the apartment where I am living at the present time.

I was once asked which one of my husbands I loved most. There is no such thing, who I loved most as I loved them both equal. They were both a part of my life and all I have left are memories until we will be reunited where there will be no farewells.

And as I am the last one of the ten children living, I look forward to the reunion with my parents, brothers and sisters.

This is the story of my life and until then I look forward to meet them. Not by my time but God's time.

End of Aunt Elsie's history.

10

Health

If you don't think each day is a good one, just try missing one.
                                    Robert Cavett

I wrote this chapter as a sleep aid for those of you that are healthy. Some of my ailments are genetic so if you are a descendent of mine and have some of the same ailments, you might want to stay awake. If not, use it for its intended purpose and go to sleep. It should cure most insomnia. Should you not be able to sleep, I hope my experiences with my ailments can help you cope with yours.

From the time I was a child, I have struggled with health issues. When I was 5, Jan. 28, 1947, according to my fathers' record book of income and expenses, I was circumcised because of repeated infections. The cost of the operation and stay in the hospital was $30.00. Being only 5, I don't have much of a memory of the procedure, only that it was painful both during and after, through the healing process.

I remember being plagued with headaches as a child. I would be playing with my friends and have to go lie down and cover my head with a pillow. The Drs. said they were migraines and I had them all my life until I retired at the age of 58. Suddenly they were gone. I attributed the migraines while I was working and going to school to stress, being a somewhat nervous child and adult. After re-evaluating and giving it considerable thought, I now believe they were caused by insufficient sleep. Even as a young child, I fought going to sleep and as an adult believed 8 hours of sleep to be wasting time. My usual routine was going to sleep at midnight and getting up at six AM, six hours of sleep. I was at work by seven and got off work at four PM. Toward the end of my career I would come home at noon and take a half hour power nap which would help.

When I retired, I still had stress in my life as everyone does. What changed was, I now was getting as much sleep as I needed. I didn't have to set an alarm so therefore I slept until I woke up on my own, when I had enough sleep. Whenever I got a migraine, I would have to go to bed, cover my head, actually my eyes, with a pillow to shut out the light which would allow me to sleep. Generally when I woke up, the headache was gone. If I had been smart enough to realize this before I retired, I may have been able to live a migraine free life and the only headaches I would have had to endure would have been the self-inflicted ones from a hangover. I often wonder how many migraines that people have are caused by insufficient sleep. In my unprofessional opinion, the migraine triggers probably would not go off if the sleep was sufficient. Sometimes we are our own worst enemies.

I was 7 when I had my tonsils removed at the Harvey Hospital. According to my Fathers' meticulous records it was Dec. 17, 1949 and the cost was $45.50. I'm sure it was the start of Christmas vacation so I wouldn't miss school. I had been sick a lot and the Dr. didn't know the cause so thought if I had my tonsils removed, my health would improve. My cousin Meridith Beutler Shaide and I both had the procedure at the same time and we shared a hospital room. Merideth was a year older than I and prior to her starting school we were daily companions and playmates. We lived next door to one another so it was a short trip to find a playmate to ride stick horses, make mud pies, play with paper dolls or real dolls or in the winter, play in the snow. The Sisters at the Catholic hospital were always getting after us because we wouldn't stay in bed but would get up to play. Being a protestant of the Baptist denomination this was my first exposure to nuns and my opinion was that they were a grouchy bunch of females with no sense of humor. I probably sustained that opinion until I saw the movie, "The Sound of Music", one of my all time favorites. Who knew the hills were alive.

The tonsillectomy didn't improve my health and following it when I was 8 years old, I was still sick all the time. My parents had to take me to Harvey to the Dr. once a week for a penicillin shot. They gave the shots in the butt back then and one week they broke off the needle in my butt. I imagine it broke off because the needle hit a bone. Maybe it was because I was so little but it seems to me they used longer needles back then, at least it looked huge to a skinny 8 year old . I can tell you, it didn't hurt to have the needle in my butt, however the procedure the Dr. and nurse used trying to retrieve it, which involved a pliers, was a bit painful. They had to push the skin and flesh in so the broken piece of needle would stick out and then grab it with a pliers. After several weeks of these trips the Dr. finally told my Mother that I was not a well child and she would never raise me to be an adult. I guess the Dr. was right. I don't think anyone can or will accuse me of being an adult despite my advanced years. Try as she might, sadly, my mom failed. I doubt I will ever act like an adult. When Kathy married me my Mother told her she had to finish raising me. I think it may be too late to become an adult at this stage of my life.

I'm a strong believer in prayer and have witnessed several miracles in my life as the result of prayer. My being here, living long enough to make everyone I love miserable, after the Drs. said I wouldn't live past childhood, is one of those miracles. My mother took everything to God in prayer and prayed without ceasing. She was in a constant conversation with God, sometimes silently and sometimes not. I believe it is her prayers that kept me alive through my childhood and young adult life, in spite of my reckless, ill spent youth.

They finally diagnosed me with rheumatic fever and sent me home for bed rest. The teachers sent my school work home and I stayed in my parents bed during the day so Mom wouldn't have to run up and down the stairs. This was before God invented television, at least in our home, so they set up the only radio we had beside my bed and I listened to Oxydol's own Ma Perkins as well as other radio programs such as Roy Rogers, The Lone Ranger, The Shadow, People are Funny (Art Linkletter), Father knows best, Baby Snooks, Groucho Marx, Straight Arrow and many others. Ma Perkins was radios version of a TV soap opera. I would guess that is how they got the name of soap opera because they were all sponsored by some type of soap commercials, usually laundry detergent. I still have that old tube radio that kept me company for many hours of bed rest.

The Dr. told my parents that my feet should not touch the floor so they carried me to the bathroom or from one bed to another. In other words, total bed rest but they took him literally and my feet never touched the floor. I'm not sure how long this went on but I remember spending one Christmas Eve alone, at home, while the family went to Church. My Mother and I think my sister, Fern, offered to stay home with me but I told them to all go to church and I would be OK. The up side was I didn't have to be in the church Christmas program that year and memorize my part. I also remember opening my Christmas presents lying down on the couch in my pajamas and a bathrobe and not being able to play with my new toys on the floor. I got a lot of nice presents that year. I suppose it was because everyone thought I was dying and perhaps this was my last Christmas. My Mother could have told them I was too stubborn to die. I remember watching my friends playing ball on the street outside our house in the spring so I would guess it was about 4 to 6 months I spent in bed. My parents had a picture in their bedroom that showed a little boy lying half in and half out of bed like he was ready to fall out and an angel watching over him. I would look at that picture and wonder if I had an angel watching over me. I believe I did and God sent my angel because of my Mothers prayers. I now have that picture hanging on my bedroom wall and still believe I have an angel watching over me.

I think I was supposed to have bed rest for 6 months but they said I could go back to school in the spring before the 6 months had been reached. I had been doing my school work at home. My sister, Fern, or one of my classmates would bring me my assignments and pick up my work. I passed my grade that year in spite of missing close to 6 months of school. This might have been the start of home schooling. I remember when I returned to school, one of the high school girls stopped me in the hall and asked if I wasn't the little Knuth boy that had rheumatic fever. When I said I was, she wanted to know why I was in school. She seemed genuinely concerned. Whatever it was and I say that because I'm not convinced it was rheumatic fever, the bed rest and the prayers on my behalf seemed to take care of it because from then on I was generally healthy except for an occasional migraine. After I could return to school, I had no restrictions on my activities. I played all sports in all seasons and enjoyed my childhood to the fullest. I was in good enough physical condition to join the Army National Guard at 17, the Navy at 20 and boxed on the Golden Glove Boxing team and lettered in the sport in high school.

About the only illness I had were the usual kid ones such as measles and mumps and an occasional pink-eye, impetigo, cold and flu. When I entered my teen years and through my early twenties, I suffered many self-inflicted headaches and had many conversations with Rolf, the big white bowl dude.

I was in my early 30s and I was in Chicago on business. I was in great pain and eventually passed out. I regained consciousness on the floor with several people kneeling over me and my pants unbelted and open. They called an ambulance for me and took me to the hospital. One of my co-workers rode up front in the ambulance and he said he never was so afraid for his life. I guess they whipped through the Chicago traffic like they were the only ones on the road. They suspected a kidney stone was causing the pain but would not give me any pain killers until they did x-rays and confirmed that. After the confirmation, they gave me drugs and everything was rosy. I guess in Chicago, it was not unusual for drug addicts to fake a kidney stone attack to get drugs. They told me to drink lots of liquids which I interpreted as beer and sent me back to my hotel room.

When we got to our hotel, we had to check in again because we had already checked out in anticipation of flying home that day. We had missed our flight home so rebooked for the following day. I went to my room and immediately called my wife before doing anything else to let her know I was OK. My fellow worker had called to let her know I had been taken to the hospital by ambulance. I was on drugs for the pain and not tracking real good but while talking to Kathy, noticed lady's garments around the room. I mentioned this to Kathy which kind of sent her into panic mode. She wasn't sure if I was hallucinating or something else was going on. She told me to get off the phone and call my fellow worker in another room, which I did. It turned out they had assigned me to and given me the key to an occupied room. I got a different room and all was well.

I continued to follow Drs. orders to drink a lot, specifically beer. It turned out that was the right thing to do because I passed the kidney stone. The actual passing of the kidney stone was not painful at all. Perhaps it was all the beer supplemented with drugs that made it painless. It is very painful when it first starts the journey and one Dr. told me it is the closest a man will come to the actual pain of childbirth. For me it was painful enough to cause me to pass out. Guess I'm a wimp compared to the women who give birth. Some of you do it repeatedly. Slow Learners?

In my late twenties and early thirties I started noticing blood in my stool. I thought I had cancer until my sister Verla told me she has it all the time and they had done many tests and found nothing. At this time, I wasn't aware that beer exacerbated the symptoms so I continued to drink beer like a sailor. By the time I reached my forties, I was having severe symptoms. One Christmas I became dehydrated and was hospitalized. The medical Drs. consulted with Mayo Clinic in Rochester, MN and diagnosed me with Ulcerative Colitis. They pumped my stomach and fed me with an IV for a couple weeks. No food entered my stomach through my mouth and they had a tube up my nose and down my throat to my stomach to remove the stomach acids etc. After a couple of weeks they started me on a protein drink along with the IV but no solid food. They also had me on steroids the entire time. It was a diet guaranteed to lose weight. Kathy, my wife, finally was at the end of her patience with the treatment I was receiving and consulted with Dr.Talsness, the Boise Cascade paper mill Dr. where I was employed. He told her to get me out of the local hospital and down to Mayo before they killed me. The local Drs. were already consulting with the Mayo Drs. so I was not convinced that going to Mayo would have any benefit.

They finally discharged me from the hospital after about a month and told her to take me home and fatten me up with pies and cakes. I had complained while in the hospital of changes to my eyesight but they just shrugged and said they had no clue what that was about. Also at one point, my white count was extremely high but they couldn't find a reason for it. I kept losing weight even though I was eating a lot and so went to the Dr. They diagnosed me with diabetes and put me on a pill, assuming it was type 2 diabetes which is also referred to as adult onset. They assumed I was an adult, so therefore adult onset diabetes or type 2. Again, my wife could have told them I'm not an adult. Type 1 diabetes is when your pancreas doesn't make insulin to keep your blood sugar in control. Type 2 diabetes is when your pancreas still produces insulin but your body doesn't use it efficiently, sometimes because you are overweight and/or lack of exercise. After lying in a hospital bed for a month, I was too week to exercise but I definitely was not overweight after not eating anything solid for that same month.

They were treating me for type 2 diabetes and the pill was not doing the job and I continued to lose weight which happens when your blood sugar is high. This is not a recommended weight loss program. The pill is designed to help your body use the insulin the pancreas is making more efficiently. Because my pancreas was not making insulin, there was no insulin to use more efficiently. Thus high blood sugar and weight loss because your body burns fat and muscle instead of the food you eat when there is no insulin to process the sugar your food is converted to. Finally, with my wife's insistence, they sent me to Mayo. Dr. Roger Nelson of the

This Dummy Pulls His Own Strings

Mayo clinic diagnosed me with type 1 diabetes and put me on insulin and brought my blood sugar under control. His theory was that the steroids they were giving me to treat the ulcerative colitis caused my body to start attacking itself, specifically the pancreas and the islet cells that produce insulin. By destroying these cells, I had no way to produce insulin to keep my blood sugar under control, therefore I had type 1 diabetes, adult onset, even if I wasn't an adult. So I got diabetes because of the treatment for another health problem, there goes the Hippocratic oath of, first do no harm.

Dr. Nelson also strongly suggested I be admitted to St. Mary's hospital in Rochester for a week of intensive training on diabetes, controlling it and living with it. There were classes for the whole family because the whole family lives with the diabetic and should know what is happening and how to live with it. The kids had come along with us so we just stayed in Rochester while we learned how our lives would change forever. They brought me an orange and a syringe to practice giving myself injections. Kathy was with me at the time and she had to leave the room. I guess the realization hit her that I would have to give myself 4 shots a day for the rest of my life and it overwhelmed her. The thought of it was far worse than the actual doing it. The mind is a strange organ. I remember as a youth when my aunt Nettie had diabetes, thinking, of all the diseases there are, diabetes would be the worst one to have because of the injections. So what do I get, diabetes. I've since learned, there are worse diseases than diabetes.

The injections are relatively painless, about like a mosquito bite. They are of the least concern and become routine. The routine is the hard part. It's the constant repetition of it and not being able to eat a meal without first checking the blood sugar level and taking a shot, that is depressing. Never eating a snack or anything ever without first thinking how it will affect your blood sugar. Always having to take your insulin with you when you will be gone for a meal and planning ahead. You never get a vacation from diabetes. Trying to estimate how much you are going to eat and how it will affect your blood sugar so you can estimate the amount of insulin to take. Entering into the calculation is how active you are and how much exercise you will get because that also affects your blood sugar. Too much insulin and you have an insulin reaction, which makes you feel as if you have been drinking and can't think clearly. Kathy was afraid that I would not be able to detect an insulin reaction, because it was a rare occasion I thought clearly. I even think she said to the Dr., "How will he know". Eventually, without treating the insulin reaction, you will lose consciousness and die. Not enough insulin and your blood sugar will skyrocket which is bad for your organs and it also can cause you to pass out but not as quickly. All this is what will put you in depression, if you allow it. I fight this tendency by remembering all the people that are a lot worse off than I am. The ones that are terminal or confined to bed or a wheel chair. All things being relative, I am extremely blessed. If on occasion, I allow myself a "pity party", I go to the shower and let the tears wash down the drain with the dirt. Get it out of my system so I can go on enjoying the day and the life God has chosen for me without depressing everyone around me.

Let me try to describe a severe insulin reaction, which I have had several, even passing out once. I am one of the lucky ones because I usually have symptoms that tell me I am having an insulin reaction. At first I begin to feel a bit strange or woozy. The thought process slows down and for me my vision changes. I may break out in a cold sweat and may stumble if on my feet. It is kind of like if I have one or two drinks too many. In some people, their speech can be slurred or slow. I'm one of the slow talkers of America so that is my usual speech pattern. If not treated with some sugar that gets into the blood stream quickly, like soda, juice, frosting or an IV with sugar, the symptoms increase until you appear to be a falling down drunk and eventually pass out. I can remember on one occasion, I knew I was having a insulin reaction and needed to get some sugar. My mind was still working but my body didn't do anything. People would ask me questions, I would know the answer to but I wouldn't answer. It's kind of like you are operating in a fog. Even when I was a drunken sailor, I would pass out before I got to this state. Now I just walk around like a drunken zombie. I guess you could call it being passed out on your feet. One time when they called the ambulance for me and the EMT's checked my blood sugar to confirm it was an insulin reaction, when he found out my blood sugar level he told me most people pass out when their blood sugar is that low. I guess I'm just too stubborn to pass out.

Because of the Ulcerative Colitis and the greater risk of colon cancer, I have a colonoscopy every three years. In this procedure you are given an intravenous sedation. Sometimes they give me enough so I am out, other times I can watch the procedure on a screen as they thread the scope through the large intestine (colon). They insert a lighted scope with a miniature camera that transmits a picture to a video screen. They explore the colon and remove any polyps as they go. Fascinating to watch especially because it is painless. They can also do biopsy specimens, inject solutions and cauterize tissue. It takes from 15 to 60 min. By doing this procedure every three years they can remove the polyps before they turn cancerous.

I can tell you the procedure is a piece of cake. It is the preparation for the procedure that practically kills you. It involves drinking a gallon of solution that cleans out your colon so they can view what is there. I can tell you from watching the procedure on the screen that it really does clean out the colon. There is nothing but pink colon that is completely empty and clean as a whistle. It is quite difficult to drink a gallon of liquid unless it is beer you're drinking. In this modern scientific age why can't they make that gallon of solution you have to drink taste like beer? Talk about a colon cleansing, this is the ultimate. After several colonoscopies, they informed me that I have crohn's disease, not ulcerative colitis as they originally diagnosed. However, the treatment remained the same for both. Sometimes they find polyps and remove them and sometimes they find nothing. Living with crohn's disease can be a bit of a challenge even if it is well controlled. When it is out of control it is a nightmare. Crohn's can go either way, constipation or diarrhea. I've never experienced the constipation side but have had the diarrhea side several times. When that happens, you need your own bathroom 24 hours a day and traveling anywhere is out of the question. Sometimes traveling to another room other than the bathroom is a risk. Crohn's is a disease that is genetic and it is not unusual for more than one member of the family to have it, especially for siblings. My brother had it, his grandson and I'm sure my sister Verla also had it although they never diagnosed her with crohn's they did tell her she had ulcerative colitis which is a close cousin to crohn's and often times crohn's is misdiagnosed as colitis. It is best to get an early diagnoses of it and get it under control because it can make life miserable for you and eventually can and will kill you.

By keeping your blood sugar as close to normal as possible, you avoid damaging your organs such as your heart, kidneys and eyes. When you try as hard as you can to keep your blood sugar under control and you are unsuccessful, it is quite easy to get depressed. You have to learn to do the best you can with the knowledge and experience you have and continue to learn from your failures.

There are insulin pumps now that make it easier to give yourself insulin more often without multiple injections a day. My Dr. at Mayo, Dr. Roger Nelson, says I am the poster boy for controlling diabetes and thinks I am doing such a good job of controlling my diabetes he doesn't think it would benefit me that much. He always says, " if it isn't broke, don't fix it ". I tend to agree with him. You still need to check your blood sugar each time you give yourself insulin, weather it is with the pump or an injection. The checking of the blood involves sticking yourself in the finger to draw blood which you put on a strip that is inserted in a monitor that tells you how much sugar is in your blood. The sticking yourself in the finger is more irritating than the injection of the insulin with a syringe. The fingers get sore from the multiple finger sticks a day, a minimum of four and often times many more. You also build up calluses on your fingers so it becomes harder to get the blood.

One night I woke up in the wee hours of the morning and there was a fully dressed female whom I did not know on the bed next to me. The lights were on and I looked around the bedroom and thought I was having a nightmare. The room was full of uniformed policeman, all looking at me and the lady on the bed. There was at least four officers and a couple other guys, none of whom I recognized. I was thinking this must have been some party or what in the world have I done now. There were also red stains all over the sheets which at first glance appeared to be blood and my wife was not within sight. It didn't look good but everyone seemed to be concerned for my welfare.

They started asking me questions. My first thought was perhaps I should have a lawyer before saying anything but they were questions like, what year is it, who is president, so I didn't see how that could be incriminating.

I take insulin before each meal and this insulin is to keep my blood sugar down after eating. It is what they call regular insulin and should not be taken unless you eat something. At night before I go to bed I take what they call long acting insulin which stays in your body a minimum of 24 hours and slowly lowers the blood sugar. It helps keep the blood sugar level during the night.

This night I wasn't paying attention to what I was doing and took the wrong insulin, the insulin that is for ingesting food rather than the long acting insulin. Because I didn't eat after taking this insulin, my blood sugar plummeted and I went into insulin shock and lost consciousness.

I generally go to bed, read a few chapters in a book and go to sleep. Kathy follows me and has pretty much the same routine. Sometimes, I'm asleep before she gets to bed and sometimes we read together. This night I was asleep when she came to bed. She proceeded to read her book and my arm suddenly came across her body. Normally she would say, go to sleep you old fool but I was already sleeping so she took my arm to move it. My arm was cold and she checked the rest of my body and it was cold and my face was white except for my lips which were blue. She suspected I was in insulin shock because she couldn't wake me. We have glucagon for just such an occasion. The process to administer glucagon is to take the syringe, insert it into the bottle of liquid, fill the syringe, remove it from the bottle of liquid, insert it in the bottle with two pills in it, dispense the liquid in the syringe into the bottle with the pills (Glucagon) in it, shake up the bottle until the pills dissolve, fill the syringe with this liquid, remove the syringe from the bottle and stick the syringe in me and depress the syringe plunger until the syringe is empty. This would then bring a person out of insulin shock.

Kathy, in her panic, forgot the first step which was to remove the hard plastic cap from the bottles. She tried to put the syringe into the hard plastic capped bottle of liquid and of course the needle bent. The kit only comes with one syringe so it was of no use. She had already dialed 911 but they hadn't arrived yet. Normally if I'm conscious, she gets some sugar in me to bring my blood sugar up. She decided to try to get some sugar in me in the form of grape juice. She got a glass of grape juice and a straw and slapped me around a little to try to wake me up and somehow got me to a partially sitting position in bed, propped with pillows. She then put the straw in my mouth and told me to suck. I guess I did take a few straws of juice but then wouldn't suck anymore. She sucked up the grape juice to fill the straw and then stuck it in my mouth and let gravity take it into my mouth. Of course there was more grape juice on the bed than in my mouth. Thus the crime scene look when I came to.

When the ambulance arrived, none of the guys wanted to crawl in bed with me and give me a shot of Glucagon so the female attendant did it. How about that, I can get a female into bed with me but only if I'm unconscious. This is when I regained consciousness while she is still on the bed next to me after giving me the shot. They then loaded me on a stretcher, put me in the ambulance and took me to the hospital to check me out. I was only there for a couple hours of observation and then Kathy got to take me home to my grape stained sheets.

These are all things you can live with. The biggest danger is allowing yourself too many " pity parties " and depression. You must accept what life throws at you and learn to deal with it the best you can. As a boxer I always say, learn to roll with the punches. Educate yourself about whatever it is you have and the treatment of it so you can live a productive life. In this age of technology and information, there is no reason not to educate yourself about anything, especially your health or lack of it. Life is too precious and exciting to waste it feeling sorry for yourself or feeling that life isn't fair. You're as happy as you decide you want to be. It's a matter of mind over matter. If you don't have a mind, it doesn't matter.

I can always find many things to be grateful for. Just a short list.... I am not blind, I am not confined to a wheel chair or worse, bed, I have people that love me and that I love, my parents taught me about God and having faith in God and prayer and instilled good moral fiber in me. The list goes on which often makes me speculate, life isn't fair, why was I blessed with all these things and many others were not. Why do I have the thought processes and ability to keep a positive attitude and be happy while many others don't? Life is not only unfair, it is a mystery. " Now we see through a glass darkly, but then face to face ". King James version of the Bible, 1st Corinthians 13, the love chapter.

Diabetes, even diabetes that is under good control, takes a toll on the body. It can do damage to all of your organs and more often than not does. Especially the heart, kidneys, eyes and liver are susceptible to damage from diabetes. Also the blood circulation is inhibited and loss of feeling in the feet is common. Because of the loss of feeling in the feet, many diabetics injure their feet without knowing it and they become infected and ultimately they lose a foot or leg. With diabetes, high blood pressure is common as well as uncontrolled cholesterol.

Heart Attack

I also have acid reflux and have had it for many years. I take medication to control it and removed things from my diet that cause it to flare up such as sodas. Some of the symptoms are heartburn, gas and burping. In 2010 I was doing some landscaping work for my daughter, Kim, at her newly acquired first home. I was making flower beds with landscaping blocks and straightening her sidewalk that had frost heaves in it. In the process of making the raised flower beds, dirt needed to be hauled into them and I hauled two truck loads, one shovel and wheel barrow at a time. It was heavy work and I had trouble keeping my blood sugar from dipping too low and going into insulin shock.

When I felt my blood sugar drop, I would stop and eat a candy bar to bring up the blood sugar so I could keep working. This seemed to work pretty well but then I noticed I was getting a lot of heartburn and gas. I attributed this to the acid reflux and the sugary candy bars causing the acid reflux to act up in spite of the medication. When this would happen, I would go sit down and rest for a few minutes and burp and when it was better go back to work. I was taking a lot of anti-acid medication like Tums and Rolaids. This went on for several weeks and seemed to get worse so that I was having problems at night with it also.

Kim had rented a house in Duluth on the waterfront for a weeks vacation and invited Kathy and I along. We were only there a couple days when I had to get up in the middle of the night with what I perceived to be acid reflux. I was about to call 911 when it got better, so I went back to bed. The next day I told Kim and Kathy I needed to go to urgent care and get whatever was going on resolved. I thought perhaps I needed stronger acid reflux medication. Kathy and I went to urgent care and I explained what was going on and they immediately sent me to the emergency room.

The Dr. there did tests of every nature and informed me that I had a heart attack but there didn't appear to be any damage to the heart. They admitted me to the hospital and scheduled an angiogram for the next day. The angiogram showed several blockages, one of which was 99% and one 95%. They informed me that I couldn't have stents inserted because the medication they give you after they insert stents causes crohn's to become active. My only option was bypass surgery. This was before they started doing the not so invasive surgery. They scheduled it for the next day. They cut my ribs open from top to bottom and open you up exposing your heart. They remove a vein from your leg to use in the bypass procedure to go around the blockages. They did a triple bypass on me.

My Grandson, Jack was two years old and was spending a lot of time in the hospital with his mother, grandmother and me. He had a little rubber frog that he loved and carried with him everywhere. When he and his mom were leaving the hospital for the night to go back to their rented house, he would come to me and give me his frog to stay with me so I wouldn't get lonesome. Knowing what it meant to him and how hard it was for him to be parted from it, I would tell him to keep it and I would be ok. He would insist and would appear to be disappointed that I didn't want his frog so I thanked him profusely and accepted it. Strangely enough, it did give me comfort and kept me from getting lonely and made my newly repaired heart smile when I saw the frog and thought of his generosity. His mother did a good job of teaching him to share and to care about those he loved not to mention the thoughtfulness of a two year old.

The heart surgeon told me I have a strong heart that performed admirably during surgery, never missing a beat. He also said I didn't need any transfusions during surgery or after. He told me once I am healed, I could do anything with no restrictions. I had very little pain after surgery and took very few pain killers. Part of that was due to the good physical condition I was in when they did the surgery. From all the landscaping I had done, my muscles were well toned and in good shape. I spent three days in the hospital after surgery and they said I could go home the next day if I had a bowel movement. I was afraid that wasn't going to happen so they gave me prune juice. That resolved the problem and they sent me home to my wonderful nurse and wife, Kathy.

Because of my service in the Army and Navy, I get all my medications from the VA (Veterans Administration). There is a small co pay but it is much less than any insurance plan including Medicare. The problem with the VA is it is run by the government and therefore, for whatever reason, they tend to change medications for no reason whatsoever as far as the patient is concerned. I suspect it is to reduce cost. Imagine that if you can, the government trying to save money. I imagine that is because the VA is underfunded. They send me my insulin through the mail and usually it is in an insulated container to keep it cool but also keep it from freezing. I live on the Canadian border and it can and does get 40 below zero in the winter. If the insulin is on a mail truck the insulin could freeze solid. I have received some that was frozen solid. My daughter belongs to a wine club and one winter a shipment of wine froze and the bottles broke. Because it was our daughters package, we didn't open it and had no clue that it had frozen until it started leaking wine all over the floor when it thawed out.

One time my insulin came without being in an insulated container. I called the VA to complain and they told me they had no control over it because they were now getting their insulin from Canada. This was when the Government would not allow us, private citizens, to buy drugs in Canada legally, yet the Government bought them there and shipped them to us. Go figger.

Hospital stays & Care

Hospital care is changing constantly. When I was a child and in the hospital, the Dr. was the ultimate authority and anything he/she said was almost like gospel to the patient. We still listen to what they say but lots of times, not without question and understanding the reasons for their instructions. We've kind of evolved to where we question anything the Dr. or Nurses say or do to verify that it is correct and right for us. There is good reason for this. These professionals are human and make mistakes just like the rest of us and there is a lot of knowledge to retain so it needs to be verified that the knowledge and instructions are being applied correctly. Mistakes can be very costly and even deadly so it is in your best interest to question all procedures and medications.

Medications are generally dispensed by the hospital staff. Some facilities even mandate that over the counter medications are dispensed by the staff so they are aware of everything you are ingesting to prevent an overdose or adverse reaction. My Dr. at Mayo clinic told me when I am hospitalized to insist I keep my medications and take them myself. He said they sometimes aren't timely about the giving of the medications and have been known to dispense the wrong medications or dose. Kathy and I have both experienced all of those things. Always question what they are giving you and in what dose and why. You can refuse any medication. Sometimes, that will get you a visit by the Dr. ordering it, to discuss it. That is not necessarily a bad thing. Some facilities are of the opinion that one size fits all which is not true at all. Most of us are different sizes and our metabolism is different. We know our bodies better than anyone so are in a better position to know the effects of some medications. Many times when you are hospitalized, you are on pain killers and are not capable of thinking clearly so you need someone with you to help you with your medications and making choices and decisions about your care.

After my heart attack and bypass surgery, my heart surgeon told me I should take an aspirin every day. I told him my Dr. at Mayo clinic told me never to take aspirin under any circumstances because of my crohn's disease. He said it will cause a flair up. My heart surgeon said heart disease trumps crohn's so take the aspirin. I tried it and sure enough the crohn's flared up so I stopped taking the aspirin and got the crohn's under control. To this day I do not take an aspirin and kind of enjoy ignoring my heart surgeons orders. See how I am.

Kidney Stones

They did x-rays of my kidneys at Mayo about 40 years ago and found a huge kidney stone. They told me if it ever starts to move get down to Mayo so they can bust it up because it could not pass whole. About six months ago I started having some back pain like I've had with previous kidney stones, some blood in my urine and sometimes not being able to urinate when it felt like I needed to. I've passed several kidney stones so I was pretty sure that was what was happening. I was just hoping it was not the huge one. I was in Bismarck at the time I started having symptoms so I started paying attention to hospital signs. When the pain starts you want to know where to go to get pain killers. The next day we started home and again I watched for hospital signs in towns along the route. I wasn't in any pain to speak of and when there was any pain I would take Tylenol and that would take care of it. We made it home and the next day there was some blood in my urine but again very little pain. I thought perhaps I have a bladder infection and decided I would probably have to go see the Dr. The following day I was going to make a Dr. Appointment but before I got around to it I gave birth to a kidney stone the size of a large kidney bean. Again, there was no pain with the kidney stone passing and all the other symptoms disappeared. This is the stone that Mayo had found years ago and warned me about. It appears the kidney stone was tired of the abuse I give my body and decided we should part company. It must have become fond of me because it stayed around for 40 years. Because of our relationship, it was very charitable with me in the pain department when it was time for it's exit. I'm very thankful for that.

General Health Care

I try to stay active and moving and get enough sleep. By getting relatively the same amount of exercise each day, my blood sugar is kept under better control. In the winter when I don't exercise shoveling snow, I do exercises such as sit-ups, pushups, deep knee bends, touch the toes and walking on a Walk-fit, Gazelle or other non-motorized walking device. I start out at the beginning of winter with just a few repetitions of each, daily, and a few minutes walking. I daily increase the repetitions and time walking. Sometimes by the end of winter I am up to 100 repetitions and a hour of walking. This also tends to keep the muscles toned and the weight down. I have a TV in my shop where I exercise so I can watch a show I enjoy such as The Price is Right or a fishing, hunting or sports show. If I tire of the TV, I can always listen to music while exercising.

Migraines

I'm not sure if the migraines disappeared when I retired because of the lack of stress or if it was because I'm finally getting enough sleep or perhaps the combination together. On occasion, I may get a sinus headache but they are few and far between. The migraines have magically vanished, for which I am grateful. Because I have given up alcohol because of the diabetes and chrons disease, I've eliminated the self-inflicted headaches.

As everyone knows, your physical health is an integral part of your mental and emotional health. It is important that you pay attention when your body is speaking to you and trying to get your attention. Exercise and diet are important to your general health. Education is also important, especially when you are being treated for any illness or anything that is not normal for your body. The medical profession is not always right and no one knows your body better than you. Don't blindly follow the advice of the medical profession but find out if it is the right advice for you.

11
Work

Work keeps us from three great sins; boredom, vice and poverty.
>Voltaire

He who is working all the time, busy as a bee, often finds someone else is stealing his honey.
>(Author unkown)

Too many people spend money they haven't earned, to buy things they don't want, to impress people they don't like.
>Will Rogers

Success at anything requires two vital ingredients: enthusiasm and perseverance.
>Norman Vincent Peale

Opportunity is missed by most people because it is dressed in overalls and looks like work.
>Thomas A. Edison

Well begun is half done.
>Aristotle

He that can have patience can have what he will.
>Benjamin Franklin

This Dummy Pulls His Own Strings

Keep cool: it will all be over 100 years hence.
                    Ralph Waldo Emerson

The world is moving so fast these days that the man who says it can't be done is generally interrupted by someone doing it.
                    Harry Emerson Fosdick (1878-1968)

I lived during an interesting period of time where we transitioned from out houses to indoor plumbing. From using horses for work and transportation to traveling by jet aircraft and spacecraft. From reading by kerosene lamps and candles to electric lights and all the conveniences that came with electricity such as radio, TV, computers and the internet. From men exploring the last geographical unknowns of the planet earth at the north and south poles to exploring other planets in space and walking on the moon.

As I begin the September of my life while looking back, I see that it has been an interesting and enjoyable journey. A journey blessed with friends and family helping during rough patches and celebrating the good times. I have accomplished very little in terms of making the world a better place. My greatest contribution to society is my children and grandchildren and the great and great great to follow. They were all cute and smart as children and are becoming adults of varied talents and much smarter and educated than I could ever claim to be.

My parents were hard working farmers who were pretty much self-sufficient. They instilled a strong work ethic in all their children and taught us the value of a job well done. We learned that there is pleasure to be had in work, the accomplishment of goals and the feeling of self-worth that comes with a job well done. We learned the rewards of hard labor, both while you are doing it and when you are finished. Rest is appreciated more after hard work.

My parents raised, grew and processed just about all their food most of their lives. They raised cows, milked them, churned butter and sold cream to buy things they couldn't or didn't grow themselves such as coffee, sugar, flour and a few other staples. They started out farming with horses and later used a tractor and other mechanized farm machinery. There was always plenty to eat and we never went hungry while living under their roof. They raised all the normal farm animals such as horses, cows, pigs, chickens, ducks, geese, turkeys and sheep. All the farm animals were raised for food or cash crops except the dogs, cats and horses. Even these animals contributed to the farm. The dogs were used for herding cows and bringing them in for milking and sometimes for hunting. The cats job was to keep the mouse and gopher population in control. The horses were used to pull farm implements and transportation and sometimes for hunting. My parents planted and harvested large gardens of vegetables and fruits. The produce would be canned or stored for use during the winter. Sometimes if there was an over abundance, it would be sold or given away.

As kids we shared the chores of caring for the animals and gardens as our age and size allowed. We were never paid for these chores but it was expected of us as a member of the family and as a learning experience. Sometimes, if I did work for others, I would get paid and was always allowed to keep whatever I earned.

One of the jobs I remember getting paid for was pulling weeds in my sisters', Verlas' garden when she was married and had her own family. I also was paid by my uncle, Rev. Herman Knuth to pull weeds on his farm in his trees. Before I was old enough to own a BB gun, probably 7 or 8, I trapped gophers on the farm and was paid one cent per gopher tail by the county. When the county quit paying a penny a tail, my mother continued to pay me. I would set traps to catch them and remove the tail. There were colonies of these rodent pests in the pastures and it was not unusual to have one hundred or more gopher tails at the end of the summer. When I was finally old enough I acquired a Red Ryder BB gun and I could then lay in the pasture for hours shooting them with BB's. You had to be a fair shot and hit them in the head or you would only wound them. As I write this, it sounds cruel, even to me, but those were different times. I went along with my Father as a young boy to check his traps in the winter time to trap mink, weasel and muskrats. He would skin the animals, dry the skins and sell them. It would provide extra income to supplement the household income.

I remember my dad telling me about his sister Elsie and he, as children, picking up dried cow chips (manure) from the pasture for fuel for the cook stove. We never had to do that as children because we used corn cobs, wood or coal in our cook stove and furnace.

In the big city of Drake I would rake leaves in the fall for the bankers and business people who would hire me. I never charged a fixed rate but would let them pay me whatever they thought my work was worth. In the winter I would shovel sidewalks for these same people. I didn't mow lawns because we didn't have a motorized lawn mower. We had the reel type push mower. We had a large yard and just mowing our yard with the push mower was more mowing than I wanted to do.

As I got older, in the fall, we would pick potatoes for the potato growers in the area and I was allowed to keep whatever I earned. I sold greeting cards, garden seeds and the weekly newspaper Grit to make spending money. Back then the Grit newspaper was a weekly paper not a magazine as it is now. I would get a package of about thirty newspapers on Saturday. I had about 20 regular customers that bought the paper every week and the rest I would try to sell on main-street. Saturday night was the night all the farmers would come to town and buy their groceries for the week. Many of the men would go in the bars for a drink or two while their wife did the shopping. There were three bars in town and I would go in each one and walk up and down the bar. Some of the customers would invariably buy a paper and if they had consumed a few drinks and were in a good mood or wanted to show off to their drinking buddies, often gave me a nice tip. I used my spending money to buy dime comic books, malts, hamburgers, ice cream cones, candy and sun seeds. Grit would also give prizes for increased sales. One of the prizes I earned was a Wilson first baseman's baseball glove. I still have that glove today and use it on occasion to play ball with my grandkids. On these summer evenings, the town would be full of people on main-street visiting with one another. The kids would be running around playing and of course the teenagers flirting or holding hands and going for a walk or to the movies. It was a Norman Rockwell lifestyle. Good times.

There was the drug store with the soda fountain counter and high back booths if you wanted more privacy than the counter for cherry cokes or malts and sundaes. There were two hotels and cafes and a coffee shop for hamburgers and fries and there was a movie theatre. I seldom went to the movies but when I did go, my friends and I would sneak into the movie. There was an exit door on each side of the movie screen at the front of the theater. These doors were locked but had push bars on the inside to allow use in an emergency or if it got too hot and stuffy in the theater they would be propped open to allow air exchange. There were no alarms that went off if you opened the door. Generally there was only one person that sold tickets, took tickets, sold popcorn etc. at the movie. About 4 or 5 of us would pool our money to buy one ticket for the movie. We were between the ages of 8 and 12 years old during this period of our ill spent youth. The ticket price was 25 cents and sometimes for special movies 35 cents. After the person who purchased the ticket entered the theater, he would go sit in the front row. If he was the only one in the theater, he would walk to the exit door and press the bar to open the door and wedge something in it so it wouldn't close. If there were others in the theater, he would do this unobtrusively like he was throwing something out the door. The rest of us would enter the theater one at a time crawling on our hands and knees and when we got to the seats would stand and take a seat. We never got caught but if we wanted popcorn we would have the guy that bought the ticket go get it because we figured in a small town the movie employee would remember she/he never sold us a ticket.

When I was a boy the circus would come to town just about every summer. This was the time in history when the circus was a big deal and it was usually a three ring circus with the big top. There would be elephants, horses, tigers, lions, performing dogs and of course the tight rope walker and flying trapeze with the scantily clad pretty girls. Prior to the first show they would have a parade through town. Several weeks prior to the circus arriving, there would be posters in stores and on telephone and electric poles around town. This would build the anticipation and excitement and everyone would be talking about it and inquiring if you were planning on attending. It was an exciting time but times were tough then and we didn't always have the price of a ticket. One year, one of my friends, David Jans and I heard they were hiring kids to help set up the circus. I think the pay was somewhere around one dollar an hour and there even may have been free admission included. We got our parents' permission to go see if they would employ us. We were successful at getting the job along with a bunch of other kids. I don't remember what the job entailed but helping get the big top up was part of it. They used the elephants for the heavy pulling and as I recall we did very little. It was exciting just to be there and watch the set up. We hung around after we were no longer needed because there were some pretty young girls about our age or perhaps they were teenagers, that were part of the flying trapeze act. One especially caught the interest of both David and I. It seemed like David and I had the same taste when it came to girls. Perhaps the common denominator was female. We engaged the young ladies in conversation and stuck around to watch them practice their act. I can remember being in love for several days while the circus was in town. This was one job that was not about the money. I would have worked for nothing just to be near the lovely trapeze girls.

While I am thinking about the circus, it brings to mind the Minot State Fair. One summer after I had my driver's license, my friends, Charlie Toy, Mike Toy and I believe Dennis Hinsz and I went to the fair on a Saturday night, the last night of the fair. They always had a huge carnival with all the latest rides, games, freak shows and the strip tease shows. We, of course, did all of it and we had a few six packs of beer for a courage booster and to make it more enjoyable. We stayed until it was time to close up and they were advertising over the loud speakers they needed young men to help tear down the carnival rides and pack them up on their trucks. We all applied for the job and we all were hired. I think the only qualification was that you were upright and could walk. As I remember, we worked all night tearing down the rides and packing them up. I remember the sun coming up Sunday morning while we were driving home. At least the work sobered us up so we made it home safely. It was not easy work and we were sweating most of the night. It provided insight as to how the rides were put together and caused me to pause and reflect on that experience before riding carnival rides that were not permanent.

When I was about 13 I got a paper route delivering the Minot Daily News to about 100 customers. I did this for about two years. It would take about an hour to deliver the papers each evening except Sunday. The bus would bring them about six PM and I would be done shortly after 7 PM. In the winter I would ride my bike delivering until the snow was too deep and then I would have to walk. I was one of the few kids in town that could ride a two wheel bike without using any hands to steer or balance. All my customers wanted their paper delivered to the house inside the screen or storm door so there was no throwing of the papers on the steps or lawns like in the bigger cities. Many customers tipped me for this service. Others thought it was part of the job. I can remember delivering papers in blizzards where I couldn't see from one house to the next. I would head in the general direction of the next house on my route and keep walking until I physically bumped into the next house and then would work my way around to the door and could usually tell who lived there and if they were one of my customers. Houses in Drake were unique. There were no cookie cutter developments where all the houses look alike.

Most people who lived in town were my customers but some had the paper delivered to their post office box because it was cheaper. When delivering papers in a blizzard I would be extra cautious when I got to the edge of town. If I missed bumping into a house and wandered out of town onto the prairie I could have become hopelessly lost and frozen to death. I remember hearing

This Dummy Pulls His Own Strings

about an eight year old boy in Minnesota who lived across the street from the school and after school there was a blizzard raging . I guess the teacher thought the kid could make it across the street to his home. Whatever the reason, the kid headed for home but never made it. They found him the next day eight miles from home frozen. Even in the middle of town, there was the possibility that you might wander onto a street and out of town. I can recall getting very anxious and afraid when I didn't run into a house after taking a pre-calculated (guess) number of steps from one house to the next. I got pretty good at guessing and when I hadn't bumped into the next house it was usually because I had veered off course while trying to keep my face from freezing. There is nothing like a North Dakota blizzard for making you doubt your sense of direction and getting you turned around. In town, like I was, you could usually stand still for a few minutes and the wind would let up enough for you to catch a glimpse of some building so you could get oriented. Until that happened, there would be some anxious moments that were near panic.

I can remember my mother-in-law telling about walking home from the one room rural school in winter and a blizzard developed. It was her and some of her siblings and they got lost but ran into a fence and followed the fence until they came to the farm. If a blizzard began before the bus that brought the papers arrived, many times the bus wouldn't come and then I wouldn't have to deliver the papers until the next day when the bus finally arrived.

I had my paper route for two years and never failed to deliver the papers as soon as they arrived, even when I was sick. Some of my customers were not as prompt with the payment when I would collect for it. Partially because of this and partially because of bad money management I got delinquent in my payments to The Minot Daily News. The paper never complained or threatened me even when I was delinquent for months at a time. This seemed to me as a good way to acquire a loan if I needed money for other things. Over time I accumulated a sizeable debt. I devised a scheme to get out of debt by giving the paper route to someone else and then after they took over, collect one more time for the next week. I thought this would work because that is what the previous route carrier did when I took over the route. They claimed it was the way it had always been and the way it was done. I believed them and was afraid if I didn't agree to it, they would find someone else to give the route to. I didn't classify it as dishonest, just the way business was done. We can generally justify any of our sins, at least in our own alleged mind. The fellow I turned over the route to was smarter than I and was not going to allow this to happen and it didn't. I was informed in no uncertain terms by the newspaper that the debt was my responsibility and I would pay it. I went to work picking potatoes and turned my earnings over to the paper. It was an important lesson of honesty and responsibility that shaped my future both personally and financially.

After I relinquished my paper route, I would take whatever work I could get for whatever they were paying. I picked rocks out of the fields for farmers, picked corn in the fall and one summer worked for my brother, Dorel, who was farming. While working for Dorel I helped with making hay for the animals. I would use a team of horses to cut grass or alfalfa for hay, rake the hay and haul it in a hay rack to the farm. I also milked cows by hand, slopped pigs and did odd jobs and occasionally got to drive the tractor.

I also worked for my brother-in-law, Clifford Kummer, on the farm whenever he needed me. He had me work the summer fallow with a John Deer tractor and what was called a duck foot. So named because the cultivators looked like a ducks foot. This was done to keep the grass and weeds from growing and let this piece of land lay fallow for a year so that it would grow a better crop the following year. This was how you kept the weeds under control before chemical weed killers or Genetically Modified weed resistant seeds were available and used. If you planted a crop in a field every year you would soon deplete the nutrients and wear the soil out. Now the farmers fertilize the field with chemicals to replenish the nutrients and to provide a better yield. It was a boring job going up and down the field all day long and when you finished one field it was on to the next one. Many of these fields had large mud puddles in the low areas or as they are referred to in North Dakota, sloughs or pot holes. Of course if you get too close to the slough, you would sink in the mud and get stuck. To make the work more interesting, I would try to get as close to the slough as possible without getting stuck. One time I got too daring and sunk that John Deer up to the axels. I think it took Clifford an entire day to get that tractor out. He was as pleasant and nice to me and never scolded or reprimanded me. He did mention that perhaps, I should not get so close to the sloughs in the future.

At harvest time I would drive his pickup truck to the combine to unload the hopper of the combine. I was only about 7 or 8 and couldn't reach the clutch and brake from the seat. I would sit in the pickup at the end of the field and Cliff would combine until the hopper of the combine filled up with grain. He would stop the combine and wave to me. He had left me with the pickup in first gear and I would stand up behind the steering wheel and push in the clutch and turn the key to start the pickup. I would then let out the clutch and slowly proceed down the field until I got to the combine, never shifting out of low gear. At this point I would simply turn the pickup off and Cliff would come and drive it to the combine and unload the hopper. We would repeat this procedure all day or until the field was finished or the pickup was full of grain at which time Cliff would drive it to the granary and unload it.

When I was 15 I went to Plentywood, MT to spend the summer with my sister Verla, her husband Cliff and my nephews Douglas and Dean Kummer. By this time Cliff had given up on farming and worked construction, building steel buildings. I wasn't old enough to get a job with Cliff but we thought I might be able to get a job in town as a stock boy or waiter or whatever was available for a 15 year old boy. I went to all the grocery stores, restaurants and businesses that might consider my employment such as Coca Cola bottling, lumber yards etc. I soon learned that looking for a job was a lot more work than actually working. It got very frustrating and discouraging being turned down over and over. I finally resorted to going up and down the street for about a mile, stopping at every business on the way. I had about a half mile left to go when I stopped at a site where they were shingling a Lutheran church roof. It was an A frame roof and quite high but I was ready to do anything at this point. My thought process was, I'm getting used to being rejected so nothing ventured, nothing gained. My communication with prospective employers was improving and I was learning and retaining what to say and what not to say. Most of the time it was advantageous not to give more information than was asked for. The Foreman asked my age and if I was afraid of height and I told him I was 15 and not afraid of height. I may have lied a little about not being afraid of height. I found fear is relative to the amount of money being paid. He said well, we're looking for workers, you are kind of young but we can give you a try. Show up tomorrow morning at 7AM with a hammer and we'll see how it goes. My perseverance paid off and I finally had a job. I showed up the next morning with my hammer and a nail apron and went to work.

There were some older guys who showed me the ropes and before long I was pulling my weight and shingling with the rest of them. One day while shingling about halfway up the roof, some other workers were installing scaffolding above our heads near the peak of the roof. This was an A shaped roof that was very steep. When you were standing on the scaffolding the roof was only a foot or two from your shoulders. The guys above our heads were standing on scaffolding they thought was secure, directly above me. I looked up and saw the scaffolding begin to come loose. I hollered at my partner and he jumped down to the next level of scaffolding, below us. I stayed where I was and layed against the roof with my hands extended over my head. The scaffolding above slid slowly down the roof until it was stopped by my extended hands over my head. I of course had my arms locked and my body stiff and surprisingly it was not difficult to hold, even with two men on it. Once the scaffolding had stopped sliding down the roof, they jumped down to the scaffold I was on and we lowered the loose scaffold.

Everyone was congratulating me on my quick thinking and action. In reality, I didn't think about it at all, I just raised my arms to protect myself and it turned out it was the right thing to do. I worked for a couple weeks until Cliffs' job in Plentywood was finished and they were moving on to Glasgow. In Glasgow I thought I would have to repeat the process of looking for a job all over again and in fact started to. This time I went to construction and building sites because now I was an experienced construction worker. I went to several job sites with no luck but one or two told me to check back later. In the construction trades, workers come and go on a daily basis so you never know when a job will become available. In the meantime, Verla, my sister, found out my Uncle Herman (Dad's brother) who was a minister in Circle, MT was helping build a church in Glasgow. They were building it with all volunteer labor. I was looking for a paying job but I thought I would stop and talk to my uncle and perhaps he could steer me to a paying job. I went to see Uncle Herman and he offered me a job and paid me out of his own pocket. This was a one story church and they were in the process of putting on the roof boards. So again, I am on the roof of a church but his was a one story building with not a very steep roof. I guess I thought this was one way to get closer to God. I worked there for several weeks until we finished the roof and Uncle Herman was heading for Drake, ND on vacation to see his relatives. He offered me a ride home, which I accepted.

Our church, First Baptist of Drake, didn't have a permanent janitor. They would pay $20.00 a month to a member for cleaning and everyone would take their turn. Most of the members would take the $20.00 monthly pay and return it to the church. I offered my services as a full time janitor for the same pay only I kept the money. A guy had to have cigarette and beer money. The job involved dusting and sweeping the main sanctuary and the basement which was used for Sunday School and any scrubbing when required on a weekly basis. It also involved turning up the heat prior to services on Wednesday and Sunday and in the cold months keeping the coal stoker full of coal on a daily basis. I did this for a year or more and sometimes when my social life was very busy, I ended up cleaning the church at midnight on a Sat. night.

Truth be told, some of those late Sat. nights I wasn't completely sober but I got the job done. Sometimes while cleaning, it was a good opportunity to speak with God in his house, sober or not. I came to the conclusion that God loves sinners, even drunks. Wouldn't God be out of a job if it weren't for us sinners?

I remember one occasion when one of my classmates was putting gas in a farm implement and was smoking and the gas caught fire. He was burned quite bad and there was some question if he would live. While I cleaned the church, I asked God to spare his life and heal his burns. I know, I was not the only one speaking to God with the same request. Our prayers were answered and he made a complete recovery. When I left town for the summer to pursue summer construction work, I obviously had to give up the church janitor job.

My next job was in Hunter, ND installing sewer pipe in the village. It was very hard work that helped build a lot of muscle and endurance. They found a shovel that fit my hands perfectly and I had it in my hand most of the day except when I was lifting clay sewer pipes or unloading a semi-truck of them. I was one of the guys that would hand shovel gravel into the trench when it required gravel under the sewer pipe to bring it to the right elevation so the sewage would flow properly. Usually I was on the top of the trench but occasionally I would have to go into the trench to help remove excess gravel in the installation process and help level the pipe. We also had to back fill the sewer pipe by hand, shoveling so the clay pipe wouldn't get moved or broken by backfilling with the backhoe. Sometimes when shoveling you thought your arms and back would break and other times you were just leaning on your shovel while the pipe laying and leveling were taking place by other workers.

I got the job through my Dad. Our church's minister was gone for a Sunday so they asked a fellow from Minot to come and preach for our Sunday service. His name was Rodney Kephart and he was a World War II veteran and prisoner of war. He was the author of a book titled "Wake, War and Waiting" about his war and prisoner experiences and how God had spared his life several times in certain death situations when others were dying. As my parents always did, when we had a visiting speaker, minister or missionary, they invited him to break bread with us for our Sunday noon meal after church. We referred to this noon meal as dinner. He accepted the invitation and in the course of dinner conversation, Dad inquired as to what he did for a living. It turned out he was an accountant for a construction company. Dad asked him if they were hiring and if they were, how I would go about applying for a job for the summer construction season. He told us they were not hiring at the time but when they started, he would give Dad a phone call and let him know.

Shortly after school was out for the summer, he called and told Dad that he had a job for me and I was to start on Monday morning. The job was at Hunter, ND not far from Casselton which was close to Fargo and if I needed a ride he would arrange for a fellow from Garrison to pick me up on his way. I did need a ride and the fellow from Garrison who was driving a brand new 1958 mercury picked me up and we proceeded to the job.

Hunter was a very small town with only one café and no hotel or motel. All the construction workers either drove to Hunter daily for work from lodging elsewhere or stayed in private homes that had beds for rent. I and several others rented a bed at a farm just a little ways out of town. My bed was a cot in the hall. We would eat at the local café and put our meals on a tab until payday and then pay our bill. In the evening after work and supper, the other guys who were all of drinking age would go to the bar and pick up several six packs and we would take them out to the farm and drink a few beer. I was 16 years old.

On Friday night there was a barn dance just a few miles out of town. One of the guys I was working with was from Fargo and was a few years older than I. He drove a 56 Oldsmobile convertible and was a bit of a lady's' man. He and I would go to the barn dances known as Herbs' barn dance. There was a young band playing there that was quite popular in the Fargo area. The lead singer was Robert Velline but latter became famous as Bobbie Vee. In his career as a rock and roll recording star he had 38 top

Dwight E. Knuth

100 hits and 6 gold records. To name a few, "Take Good Care of My Baby", "Rubber Ball", "Devil or Angel", "Run to Him", "Please Don't Ask About Barbara", "The Night Has a Thousand Eyes", "One Last Kiss", "How Many Tears" and "Be True To Yourself". The Beat goes on voted him 1991-Best American Act, 1992-Best Live Performance, 1993-Favorite Male Singer and in 1994- Runner up to Paul McCartney in the category of most accomplished performer.

Years later when I was married and living in International Falls, Bobbie Vee came to Fort Frances, Ontario Canada for a concert. Fort Frances was just across the Rainy River which separated International Falls and Fort Frances. During the concert we could dance and Kathy and I danced up to the stage where he was singing and after the song finished, I engaged him in a conversation and invited him to join us at our table after the concert for a drink and more conversation. This he did. We talked about his days before he became famous and when he was playing at Herbs' barn dances at Hunter, ND. The governor of North Dakota awarded him The Theodore Roosevelt Rough Rider award and said he was a kind, good and humble person. In the brief time I spent with him and visited with him, I found that to be true. He seemed to be comfortable with me and my wife and friends sitting around a table discussing the good old days as if we were old friends. He would only drink non-alcoholic drinks but didn't mind that the rest of us were imbibing. As I remember it, he stayed at our table and visited for quite some time, longer than I expected he would. I got his autograph, supposedly for my kids. I also remember discussing how similar his style was to Buddy Holly and how he was hoping to get the role to play Buddy Holly in the Buddy Holly story. I wasn't aware that he had filled in for Buddy Holly in Moorhead, Minnesota after the plane crash that killed Buddy Holly, Ritchie Valens and "The Big Bopper". The day that music died. He was fifteen. That concert was the start of his road to fame because of his style and the way he sounded like Buddy Holly. They hadn't picked a name for the band at this time and when the announcer asked him the name of his band, he blurted out "The Shadows". His real name was Robert Velline but after this appearance his band became known as Bobby Vee and The Shadows.

At one time, Bob Dylan played piano for and with The Shadows. He was going by the name of Elston Gunn at the time. He didn't stay with The Shadows long because they were playing in little towns in North Dakota that all seemed to have out of tune pianos. He couldn't stand playing the out of tune pianos so he parted ways amicably with The Shadows. Sadly, in 2011 Bobbie Vee was diagnosed with early Alzheimer's Disease.

Meanwhile back to Hunter and work. The guy with the convertible and I became friends and actually were working side by side, as a team . The fellow from Garrison and I also became friends and while I was working on top of the trench, he was down in the trench most of the time. This was before OSHA and all the safety rules. We did wear hard hats but there was very little shoring of trench walls and occasionally one would collapse. Generally when this happened you could see it was going to collapse and everyone would hightail it down the trench away from the collapsing sides, or scurry up the ladder. One day it was too fast for my friend from Garrison and he was completely buried alive with several feet of earth over his head. We knew where he was buried, just not how deep he was. We didn't know if the collapse had knocked him off his feet and if he was lying on the bottom of the trench or if he was standing up, buried. They had the back hoe gently move some dirt from where we knew he was and then we started digging somewhat frantically but gently with our shovels. It seemed like forever before we got to him but in reality, I imagine it was just a few minutes. He was unconscious when we uncovered his head and he was still standing. His hard hat was still on but had slid down over his face and had trapped some air in it. As we proceeded to dig out his body, he regained consciousness and seemed fine other than a bit panicky not being able to move. He was fine other than sore muscles and they gave him a couple days off to recuperate.

My friend with the convertible and I were working side by side on top of the trench one day and had been working really hard and were exhausted. Something happened down in the trench that was going to require some time to fix. We had some bosses that roamed the construction area and made sure everyone was giving a full day's work for a day's pay. They didn't like to see anyone leaning on a shovel. Our foreman was a good boss who expected you to work but knew in reality that you also needed a break to keep going. If he thought you were sluffing off he would tell you to get to work but he could also tell if you needed a break. He had been watching my friend and I working hard and thought we should have a break but also knew if some of the bosses saw us leaning on our shovels, they would find other work for us and reassign us. Our Foreman considered us two of his best workers and didn't want us to be reassigned and lose us for the day. He told us to take the pickup and get a load of gravel from a few blocks away where they had a gravel pile. This involved loading the pickup by hand with shovels but could be done at our leisure rather than in a hurry like most other shoveling. In other words, it was basically busy work so we wouldn't get assigned somewhere else. We did this and had the pickup almost filled with gravel and were taking a break, leaning on our shovels and conversing. One of the roaming bosses came along and told us in no uncertain terms to get back to work. There may have been some name calling and swearing involved on his part out loud and by us under our breath. Neither of us were sluff offs and we had been working diligently as you could see by the loaded pickup so this reprimand did not set well with either of us.

    We started talking about quitting the job and what we would do if we did quit. We had been working for about a month and had saved most of our paychecks so had some money. My friend thought we should head out to California for the rest of the summer and be beach bums and pursue bikinis. This was the era of beatniks and flower power. At the time, that sounded a lot better than laying sewer pipe and being reprimanded for not working hard enough. What did I know about life and reality, I was 16. So we threw our shovels in the pickup and drove back to our foreman and told him we were quitting. He tried to talk us out of it and even called over the roaming boss that had hollered at us. He chewed him out and told him we were his two best workers and he had no right to interfere but we had already made up our minds.

In retrospect, I think we had been scared by the cave in and near death experience of our friend and were looking for an excuse to flee the scene. We went to the office and picked up our pay that was due us, paid our outstanding restaurant bill and headed to Fargo. My sister Fern and her husband Clarence were living in a trailer park in Fargo so I had him drop me off there. He was going to go home and talk to his parents and if everything worked out we would head to California. I never heard from him or saw him again. Another life lesson learned, don't be too hasty in your decisions and don't rely on casual friends or believe everything that they say.

After a few days I hitchhiked back to Drake where my friends were bored and wishing they had a job to make some money. One of these friends was Gary Richards from Tacoma, WA who was staying with another of my friends, Charlie Toy. I told them about my experience and told them I was pretty sure they could get a job there. They hitchhiked to Hunter and were hired. They later told me that I could have had my job back if I had wanted it and my foreman spoke highly of me and my work ethic.

In my work as a computer programmer and system analyst, I helped keep the planet green by writing programs to grow trees. This was before the environmental concern, recycling and global warming. We named these programs I wrote, "Continuous Forest Inventory" or CFI. Sometimes, for whatever reason, we referred to it as, CFI care. The company I worked for was Boise Cascade and was in the business of making and selling paper and wood products. To be successful at that, trees are needed and harvested just like any other farm crop. Trees are a renewable resource. Forests regenerate naturally if the trees are not harvested. Trees die due to disease, pests or overcrowding and new ones start from seed. If trees are harvested at their prime or clear cutting is involved, the forests sometimes need help in regeneration.

The company hired foresters to study and analyze the forest and determine how to best help generate growth. More trees and growth equal higher profits.

They would do this by setting aside plots of trees one tenth of an acre or in Canada one tenth of a hector. All the trees in this plot would be numbered and every 7 to 10 years each of these trees would be measured and recorded. The species, tree height, diameter at breast height (DBH), age, diseases, mortality cause if dead, were all recorded. The description of the plot was also recorded such as soil type, density of trees, dominate species etc. My Navy buddy, Jim Gulbranson and I would write the programs to calculate the growth of the trees between measurements so the forester could plan what would grow best and fastest in the soil type and location.

In the early days of computers, IBM was the leader and had devised a system of holes punched in cards to record information on. These cards could then be read by the computers with electrical impulses and programs could make calculations and print results and store the information on tape. These programs also allowed the foresters to determine when trees should be harvested and the species to be planted to regenerate the forest.

Boise did such a good job of managing their forests that the federal government wanted their forests to create a national park. They were eventually successful in that endeavor. This is the park on the northern boundary of Minnesota with Canada called Voyageurs National Park. Boise believed and practiced multi-use forestry. They allowed hunting and fishing on their land and even encouraged it. They would allow private citizens to build hunting cabins on their land. They built boat landings and access roads to the lakes in their forests and built camping areas complete with fire pits, tent pads, outhouses, fish cleaning stations and hiking trails in the woods. They did all this with no financial help from the government and maintained these facilities for the use of the general public, not just their employees. They also built and maintained cross country ski trails and snowmobile trails on their land. It was already a park like forest when the government took it over. I was the programmer that was assigned the task of creating the programs to calculate the value of the land to sell to the government. Boise sold it for way less than its value in my opinion. When I inquired why, they said they didn't want a prolonged legal battle and media attention over it. That would possibly give the company a bad public image and be bad for business. It turns out the decision makers were right in what they were doing. If Boise had retained the forests there was no guarantee that the same policies and procedures that took such good care of their forests and land would continue into the future. Corporations come and go, buy and sell and their executives change and goals and policies change. With the federal government in charge, there is a better chance it will be preserved for generations to come.

Programming and Systems Analysis was interesting, challenging, rewarding work and could be frustrating when the computers were malfunctioning as they often did then. The early computers were prone to break downs that caused computer programs to give erroneous results. The other problems were the computer programmer not programming correctly or the information being fed to the program being in error. We had a saying, garbage in, garbage out (GIGO).

Back in the 60's, computers took up whole rooms and the rooms, oddly enough, were called computer rooms. We weren't very imaginative, just called it as we saw it. One of the problems with these old computers was that they used tubes and were huge and produced a large amount of heat. If the computer got too hot it would cease to work. Therefore the computer rooms were air conditioned, so we were some of the first office workers that worked in air conditioned offices, year round. Most computer rooms had raised floors that were raised about one to two feet above the original floor with a removable floor. The raised floor was set on aluminum risers and was made of heavy aluminum squares about 18 to 24 inches square. This allowed for the thick electrical cables that hooked the disk drives, tape drives, printers and card readers to the central processing unit. Without the raised floor we would be tripping over these very large cables.

The raised floor also allowed for the air conditioner to blow cold air under the floor and into the individual components to cool them. Because of the raised floor, most computer rooms had a ramp leading up to the room.

    I credit my sister Verla with pointing me in the direction of computers and computer programming. I was working for her husband and my good friend and boss, Clifford, doing construction work out of Williston, ND. We built steel Butler buildings which were used mainly as grain storage or farm machinery storage and sometimes we built a few bomb shelters on farms. During this time in History there was what was referred to as "the cold war" between Russia and the US. It was the time of the bomb and inter-continental ballistic missiles. All over ND and MT there were missile silos which were underground silos with missiles in them aimed at Russia. In the case of an attack by Russia on the US, the tops of the silos would be opened and the missiles fired at Russia. It was a deterrent to keep Russia from attacking us. In school we would practice ducking under our desks in case of an attack. Now I'm not too sure how much protection a desk is going to be in a nuclear attack but I suppose it could give some protection from falling ceilings and bricks. While constructing machine sheds and grain storage, many farmers had us dig holes in the ground, usually about 12 X 12 and pour cement on all four walls, floor and ceiling and cover it with dirt. It was then supplied with fresh water and food that would not spoil such as canned Spam. I think Spam has the same half-life as uranium. Some farmers would put cots and blankets in them. The idea was that they could be used as a bomb shelter in the event of attack. They also doubled as a tornado shelter.

    The grain storage bins and buildings were made of steel. The steel would get burning hot in the summer and freezing cold in the winter so it wasn't pleasant material to work with. We also installed grain augers on top of the grain bins which were round bins sometimes nearly as tall as the grain elevators they sat next to. In ND almost every town had a grain elevator for grain storage and this was the tallest building in town, often times almost as tall as the water tower. We would generally build a row of two to ten of these round storage bins next to the elevator and then install a grain auger running from the top of the elevator along the top of the grain bins. Back then there was no OSHA to protect the worker and insure we were doing the work properly and safely. In fact we were not even union employees. The grain bins sat about three to four feet apart on the ground. It was a big job to climb up the ladder to the top and in the process of installing the grain augers you often needed to go from one grain bin to the one next to it. Rather than climb all the way down the ladder on the side of one grain bin and climb back up the ladder to the top on the next, we would run down the slanting roof of the one we were on and jump the gap between the grain bins and walk up the slanted roof to the top of the next one. The gap at the top was only about 2 to 3 feet because there was an overlap of the roof on each one. It wasn't the gap at the top that worried me. It was the distance to the ground which could be anywhere from 40 to 70 feet. No one ever slipped and fell, that I am aware of.

One of the fellows I worked with fell out of a Bo Swains chair while he was working on the outside of a grain bin close to the top. A Bo Swains chair is kind of like a seat of a swing that is attached to ropes and lowered over the side. You can pull yourself up and lower yourself to position yourself wherever you need to be. As I said before, this was before the days of OSHA and this employee was probably not secured properly. I don't remember exactly what caused the apparatus to fail but he fell onto the roof of a lean-to on the elevator, slid down that roof and ended up on the ground. I think it was about a 30 to 40 foot fall. He lived but broke so many bones in his body I can't remember how many or which ones. He did eventually return to work but I think it was a year or more later.

Many times we would have an audience while performing our acrobatics of jumping between grain bins. There wasn't much entertainment in small town America back then so the village people would gather to watch. If there were some pretty girls watching, we might make the trip more often than necessary, just to show off and show how brave and masculine we were. It never hurts to impress the local ladies just in case you want to date one of them. I'm sure OSHA would not approve of this practice.

Although this was interesting work and at times challenging, as you might imagine, it could be dangerous and often times the weather made it uncomfortable. The summers were stifling hot and the fall and winters were freezing cold. When it became too cold or we had too much snow, operations would be suspended until spring. There goes the paycheck. It was the late fall, when it was really cold, with the wind blowing and your fingers too frozen to hold onto the frozen steel so the wind wouldn't blow you away on top of grain bins and buildings, that I concluded there must be a better way to make a living. I had the best boss I have ever had and he wouldn't fault you for going to the pickup to warm up. He was the kind of boss that would work right along side you and would not ask you to do anything that he wouldn't do himself. In fact he would do things himself that he would never ask his men to do because he considered it to dangerous or above your skillset. He was also very tough and could do anything and withstand any pain or discomfort. So if you went to the pickup to warm up, he was still out in the elements working and even though he would not say a word to me about it, I would feel guilty.

This boss also happened to be my brother-in-law, Clifford Kummer, married to my oldest sister Verla. He only had an eighth grade education in a one room country school but he could read a blueprint or devise a method to do anything and sometimes even make the tools to do it. To observe him and his talents, you would think he had a degree in engineering. He had a fine mind and used it to solve problems even though he had a limited formal education. He had the advantage of being married to my sister who was also a school teacher so if he had a problem to solve but not the level of education necessary, he would ask his wife and she would teach him what he needed to know. He wasn't afraid to ask questions or learn. He also was way ahead of the industry in human resources and how to treat his employs and make them enjoy their work and do a good job. He was very much in demand to do the jobs for the farmers and business people because he had a reputation for doing a good job that was done right and always being honest with you. I never had to ask for a raise from him and always got one when I was eligible and deserved one. He would fight upper management for his employees and generally won because they didn't want to lose such a valuable employee as he was. As much as I hated to leave his employee, I wanted to branch out and look for other opportunities in other fields than farming and construction which was my exposure at this point.

After some education in the computer field at the College of Automation and in the Navy, I started my civilian career as a computer programmer. When I started work as a computer programmer, the computers were huge and had less memory than our phones have now. A computer took a whole room to house it in. The memory was probably 8 to 64 megabits and we programmed them in what was referred to as machine language or binary code. I remember programming on a 8 megabyte computer and having it upgraded to a 16 megabyte computer. At that time we said this is all the memory we will ever need.

We upgraded memory as well as storage devices from magnetic tapes to disks larger than bread boxes to eight inch floppy disks to hard plastic 3 ½ inch disks to memory storage sticks.

One of the first methods of recording data and feeding information into the early computers was IBM's 80 column punched cards. You could store 80 characters of information in one card. Each column of the card could have one character of information. There were 12 rows across the 80 columns of the card. The top three rows were reserved for what was referred to as zone punches to form letters and special characters. The top row or 12 zone was used in combination with numbers 1 – 9 in the same column for letters A – I. The 11 zone directly under the 12 zone was reserved for letters J – R. The 10 or zero zone was reserved for letters S – Z. If the first column had a 12 zone punch in combination with a 1 punch, it was an A.

When I started my adult career as a computer programmer, it was shortly after computers were being used in business applications, record retention and information sharing or as it was referred to at the time, data processing. In the Navy our job description was "Machine Accountant". Up to that time computers had been primarily used in scientific applications and the languages used for those applications were Fortran, Assembler and Machine language or binary code. With the added business applications came the computer languages for these applications such as RPG, (Report Program Generator) COBOL (COmmon Business-Oriented Language), PL1 (Program Language 1), Autocoder, (used for IBM 1401) and Assembler. I wrote in all of these languages. You could say I was multi-lingual in computer languages and wrote programs in six languages.

In the Navy, our uniform of the day for work was generally like our dress uniform but without the piping and stars on the flap. The summer whites were a short sleeve button up the front shirt with white bell bottom pants. If we were doing physical labor like swabbing the deck, we would wear dungarees, bell bottom denim and cotton blue button up shirts. We were not allowed to keep pens in our shirt pockets but kept them in our pants pocket and sometimes in the v of our jumpers.

When I became a civilian and started work for the bank, suits and ties were mandatory. Generally I would have a plastic pocket protector for my shirt pocket for my pens. After wearing a suit and tie for a while, it became normal and you would feel somewhat undressed without one. Also working in an air conditioned environment year round, it felt comfortable with the suit jacket to keep you warm. When I went to work for the paper company as a programmer, the dress code was basically the same but we could take our jackets off while working at our desk. Others sometimes would view your attire as uncomfortable and urge you to take off your tie and coat. I think it made them feel uncomfortable and they would continue to harass you until you complied and removed the tie and suit jacket. After a decade or more of the suit and tie culture, restrictions were reduced and we were allowed to wear dress slacks and dress shirt without the tie and finally even jeans and casual shirts.

This Dummy Pulls His Own Strings

I guess the transition from computer programmer to author is somewhat of a normal transition. I was writing programs for computers most of my adult life and now am writing stories and history for humans. Still putting thoughts into words only words for humans rather than computers. Writing computer programs for computers, for me, was almost like reading a good book. I was totally involved in the execution so time would fly and before you were ready, the day was over. When a problem that seemed to be unsolvable appeared, I would put it aside and go on to other things, keeping the problem in the background but not focusing on it. I would go to sleep with the problem still unsolved and often times when I woke up in the morning would have the solution to the problem. I guess my subconscious was a better problem solver than my conscious self. There probably was better focus in the sleeping subconscious than the awake conscious. When you successfully complete writing a program, like reading a book, you were sad that it was over but like a book, there was always another book to read or program to write.

Writing a computer program is just telling the computer, in a language it can understand, what you want it to do or accomplish. It could be interpreting a math formula to arrive at a conclusion. It could be placing information in a certain format to make a graph, spreadsheet, bill, statement or whatever the application called for. You needed a logical mind to write the instructions in the proper order to produce the desired results. Often times, when a program was somewhat complicated, we would draw a flow chart, prior to writing the program, so we could insure the steps were in the logical order needed for the desired results. Sometimes, a person other than the programmer would draw the flowchart. This person was referred to as a systems analyst. That persons' job was to analyze an application and determine the flow of it and what was needed to transition that application from a manual procedure to a computer application. I did both jobs, systems analyst and computer programmer, sometimes for the entire application. I preferred the actual program coding but both were challenging and interesting work. The advantage of having two people do the two different jobs is that you have two points of view and a disagreement of how it should be accomplished. This is an advantage because you discuss your differences and generally come up with a better solution. The disadvantage is that it may take longer with this approach.

As is common in business, when you do a job well, it is assumed that you want a promotion and that if you are doing your current job well, you will do the next job up the ladder well. This is called, promoting you to the height of your incompetency. This happened to me. I was promoted to Manager of the Data Processing department or as it is called now IT (Information Technology). This was a position that I did not want nor aspire to but there was a need and I accepted the challenge and the position and filled it for several years. Although I like to tell people what to do, I found as a manager, it is not always that pleasant. For the most part, I had good employees and I tried to treat them with respect, honesty and integrity. My philosophy was if you give your employees the tools to do the job and make the environment one which is enjoyable, the employee will like their work and be happy and a happy employee is a productive employee. I had not been trained in managing people other than in the Navy and that is a much different environment than the business world. In the Navy, you give orders and whoever receives them, obeys them generally without complaint or question. In the business world, often times to get an employee to do something, you need to make them believe it is either their idea to do it or in their best interests to do it. Sometimes neither of those approaches work. Sometimes, you use a reward system to encourage cooperation. As in, I will go to bat for you in whatever manner if you do your job well and follow the rules and do what I ask of you. Going to bat for you could be but is not limited to, getting you a raise, giving you time off when you need it for whatever you need it for, recommending you for promotions and generally making your work environment pleasant for you.

On the other hand, if you are one of those people who have trouble following the rules or taking orders or executing them, you might not get the cooperation from me when you are in need of something such as time off, pay raises, promotions, overtime or whatever I have control over. Some employees would refer to this as, sucking up to your boss. I would refer to it as self-preservation or looking out for number one. There are employees that will do anything you ask of them and do it cheerfully and with grace. There are other employees that fight you every step of the way and complain about everything. For example, an employee complains that they are having financial difficulties and would appreciate more overtime. You rack your brain for some overtime work to give to that employee and tell them what it is. The employee refuses to do it because they say it is not their job or part of their job description.

So, not all of us are cut out to manage people and some people are not manageable.

In addition to having an employee that was not manageable, at one time, I had a boss that in my view was not a good manager. He was from the corporate office and had dotted line control over my boss. My boss reported directly to a local boss so it was as if we had two bosses. I suppose my opinion of him was lowered because he went to the local boss and asked what he would do if he fired my boss and me. The local boss told him he would just re-hire us so that put an end to that. I never did find out why he wanted to get rid of us and we weren't supposed to know that he was trying to but there are very few secrets in a small town. He always gave me good reviews in my performance reviews and generally I got a raise. He never raised an issue with me in my performance reviews and if he didn't think I was performing up to par, that would have been the time to address it. It is possible, he wanted to hire someone else to replace us and just wanted to get rid of us. He may have thought I wasn't productive enough.

As a child, my parents taught me that any job worth doing is worth doing well. That is how I approached every task I was assigned. I am somewhat of a perfectionist which sometimes slows you down. I had another one of my managers tell me if he needed something done right, he would give it to me but if he was in a hurry for it, he would give it to another employee. I think his description included, slow and methodical. Sometimes there is a need for speed and just get er done. We can always go back and fix it later or do it over. I'm not very good at that. Whatever his complaint, he didn't make it known to me, even through the grapevine. There were other qualities of his managers style that were not so good. Whenever he would come to town, the whole department would be nervous and under pressure. He governed with anxiety and the fear factor. I have been in meetings with him where he has chewed out another employee up one side and down the other in front of all the other employees. In my mind, I didn't think it was justified and even if it had been, it should have been done in private, one on one or with the HR manager present. I traveled on business with him on several occasions and did not find him to be a pleasant person or one that cared about anyone but himself. I guess I would describe him as an egotistical, selfish, uncaring person. He was my worst boss and I can't recall another boss I disliked. I would have quit and found another job but I believed that was what he was trying to accomplish and was advised to just hang in there and eventually he would either get enough rope to hang himself or get promoted out of our lives. He eventually was promoted and in time left the company.

I've found if you treat people with respect and dignity, they generally reciprocate. I've had several bosses that were exceptional. One was my first boss who was also my brother-in-law, Clifford Kummer. A man with integrity and morals. He treated everyone fairly and I didn't receive any special treatment because I was his brother-in-law. He wouldn't ask you to do something that he wouldn't do himself. If the ND weather was not so extreme and the pay better, I would have probably remained in his employ and worked construction as long as possible.

Another of my favorite bosses was my boss when I was manager of Data Processing, Bud Larson. He has a great sense of humor on top of all the qualities that made him a great person and a good boss and manager. His sense of humor was unique and perhaps some didn't appreciate it as much as I did. Kathy also enjoyed and appreciated Bud's sense of humor. Bud once told Kathy she would never have to worry about me losing my job because he couldn't find anyone else to work as cheap as I did. She had a quick reply of something to the effect of; don't I know it? Bud was great at left handed compliments. You sometimes had a hard time distinguishing the specific part of the anatomy he was getting at, whether he was patting you on the back or giving you a kick in the butt and sometimes it was both. When he announced his retirement, I heard from many of his peers at the corporate office who were expressing their sympathy that I was losing such a great boss. They said he was the most respected of all the mill controllers in the corporation. I also heard the sentiment that he is a very nice guy, repeatedly. He has what I refer to as un-common sense because it isn't very common any more. He always tried to make his employees happy and make their jobs enjoyable. He once told me when I sought his counsel when I was manager, anytime you can do something good for an employee or make that employee happy, choose that route. It was a pleasure to come to work and that made the work enjoyable and when the work is enjoyable you are more productive. Whenever possible, he gave his employees the tools and means to do their jobs more efficiently and effectively. He was a rare boss and manager and an even rarer human being.

There are a few men that I have known in my life that I strive to emulate. One is my Father, one is a former pastor, Rev. Virgil Anderson and the other is my former boss, Bud (Albert) Larson. They all shared the qualities I most admire, a good sense of humor, they didn't take themselves too seriously yet they had a good self-image and confidence, they were tough and yet gentle beings in the right proportions at the right time, had a great attitude, were kind, caring, respectful and good natured. People you want to be around and learn from.

A boss and friend that I would be remiss not to mention was Joe Melin. He was also a person with a good sense of humor, fairness and integrity. A good and kind human being and an easy to work for boss who made coming to work a pleasure. I could write much about Joe but he is a very private person so will say no more other than he moved out of town when he retired and we lost touch.

I was pursued by several head hunters when I was a manager. I don't know how they acquired my name as a candidate but somehow they found me and thought I would be a good match for the position they were trying to fill. I was happy where I was, at the time and was not looking for another job. Perhaps it was from a company task force I was chosen to participate in that was evaluating the integration of business applications with process applications for a more efficient operation. I spent one summer on that task force where we traveled all over the US, not only to the Boise mills but also to firms that had already accomplished what we were considering, such as the General Motors plant in Michigan. I was also known to other Boise mill locations and their data processing departments as well as Human Resources and other departments. I knew many of the IBM repair and Sales people and had visited their plant in Rochester, MN as well as the data processing department at Mayo Clinic in the same city. So it wasn't as if I was a recluse. It's a small world.

No matter how they acquired my name, they called me at work and wanted to set up a phone interview with me to see if I was a good match for the position. I resisted at first because these things are time consuming and I had no interest in changing jobs or locations. As head hunters do, they continued to call to see if I had changed my mind or if my situation had changed. I had been through several downsizings at Boise where it was almost certain I was going to be eliminated or at the very least have to move to Canada to work at the paper mill across the river. I survived all of those downsizings. Many of my co-workers were not so fortunate. I was re-thinking my position and concluded that this might very well be good experience to go through for future downsizings and the headhunters would have my resume and I would be better able to find a job if that occurred again. So I gave the go ahead and we started with the first step which was the phone interview. They had a particular location and position in mind for me which was the head of the Data Processing for the St. Joseph's Indian School in Chamberlain, South Dakota. This appeared to be doable for me and my wife agreed. It was about the same distance to our childhood home in ND where her parents still lived but were elderly. We wanted to be within a day's drive if they needed us and to visit on holidays. The only problem that was evident to me was this is a Catholic school and we are protestant Lutherans. They assured me this was no problem for them if it wasn't a problem for me and that they had other non-Catholic employees. Wanting to give them full disclosure I informed them of my known chronic diseases, type 1 diabetes and crohns. They again assured me this was not a problem and had another employee with diabetes and were aware of symptoms and needs to accommodate it.

After the phone interview they wanted to proceed with a face to face interview. The head hunter told me where she was located and asked if we could meet somewhere halfway from her location and mine. I had relatives living close to Barnum, MN and we were planning to visit with them the following weekend. She was located in St. Paul so the Barnum restaurant was chosen as the meeting place for the face to face interview. We exchanged information, and answered each other's questions and visited over a cup of coffee. Several days later she called to inform me that the staff at the school and the person I would report to wanted to meet me and my wife and visit with us and show us around the area, introduce us to a real estate agent and see if we were interested in relocation.

They set up a date that was mutually agreeable for us to fly to SD and proceeded to book us a flight and rental car. In the meantime, I was concerned for my health insurance and was trying to insure that they would and could insure me with my pre-existing health conditions. They assured me that this was no problem so the plans went forward. I guess my concern about health insurance alerted them and they began to investigate further. They discovered that I could not be insured until I had been employed by them for one year because of my pre-existing health conditions. It didn't make sense to either of us but said there was nothing they could do about it. The previous year, my insurance had paid out over $10,000.00 for my care and this was an expense I did not wish to have. They did not know how expensive my care was at this point and offered to have the school pick up the bill for it. I gave them the previous year's figure and that it could be more depending on if I needed hospitalization or more extensive care than the previous year. I told them I would need something in writing to insure I was not saddled with large health care expenses. I guess, after discussing it with their lawyers and financial people they concluded and I concurred that my employment with them was not a good fit.

    I was both disappointed and relieved. Anytime you change jobs or locations, it is stressful. I liked the boss I had and the job. I was warned that in my new position at the school, there were employees that might be difficult to work with or manage and I may find it necessary to discipline or fire an employee or two if they would not accept me and my manager style. They supposedly were good employees but had conflicts with previous managers which is why they were looking for a new manager. These employees had created a hostile work environment for the manager so the manager quit. I was hopeful that I could work with them, make them happy in their jobs and thus have their cooperation.

    If not, I had the authority to get rid of them which sounds easy but in reality is not. In a small town, gossip is abundant and not always favorable and it does affect relationships at work and personal relationships with friends and neighbors. So that was a concern for me and I also was concerned about the politics at the office and my peers and superiors. They assured me that because it was a Catholic school, that politics was not a concern but in my experience, politics is always a concern. I'm not very good at office politics and when I see something that needs fixing, am not good at keeping my opinion to myself.

    The next job offer, from a different headhunter was in Door County, Wisconsin not so far from Green Bay and the Green Bay Packers football team. This time I brought the health issues

This Dummy Pulls His Own Strings

to the table before we got too far into the interview process. Again, the insurance issue was a problem so we terminated the process. It appeared I could have had this position also as they told me I was the number one candidate. Apparently there is a network of headhunters and candidates because after this offer, the headhunters quit bothering me so I must have been flagged or removed from their list.

In my career, change was the only constant. The advance of technology made changes to hardware, software, programming and the way business and manufacturing was done necessary. You barely had a chance to become proficient on the hardware and software before it changed and you had a whole new learning experience. This made life interesting and challenging but also accelerated burn out. It seemed we were always going through some sort of a conversion whether it be an application conversion, software or hardware. In addition there were the changes to the business and manufacturing and the constant threat of downsizing workers. This made one begin to consider retirement and actually look forward to it and hope your business would be swallowed up by another conglomerate that would offer early retirement packages.

Boise Cascade offered a good 401K plan that the company contributed to quite generously if you also contributed. I was convinced from the start of it that this was a good plan to be taking advantage of. We could select the type of investment for our contributions as well as the companies' contribution that would be the best fit for our situation. Kathy and I, together agreed at the outset to invest in the stock market with a lesser portion in bonds. Kathy did research on investing and I tracked specific stocks daily over a long period of time to find out if they were cyclical and if they were, when was their typical high cycle and their typical low cycle. This would allow us to buy low and sell high which worked out about 80% of the time for the cyclical stocks. Others, we found, were just a guess as to when to buy and sell. We were allowed to buy and sell anytime in our 401K plan or to switch between stocks and bonds which we also did from time to time depending on the economy and forecasts. It was a lot of work and took a lot of diligence, probably more from Kathy than myself. She would watch the stock market daily and knew if it was going up or down and would be concerned or elated depending on the circumstance. We had accumulated a sizeable nest egg in our 401K and I was feeling the pressure of my health issues and work related burnout so we were looking at retirement and if we could manage an early retirement. I was only 58 years old and Kathy was 53 but we looked at our estimated income from 401K, my pension plan and farm income until my social security kicked in and our estimated expenses. We determined we could live comfortably, not in opulence but comfortable if we were frugal as we had been all our life. We even thought we could manage a little travel to Europe and Hawaii if the stock market cooperated a little. Our biggest concern was our health insurance which was around $1000.00 a month for each of us so about $24,000.00 a year total. Not a small chunk of change.

However we were pretty much debt free, no credit card debt, home paid for, vehicles that were reliable but not new so we decided to pursue it. We thought, perhaps if we would retire, we should have our nest egg managed by a professional instead of doing it ourselves as we had been doing. As I said before, when we were doing it, it was a lot of work and worry. I wanted to be free to pursue other interests, like sleeping in and getting fat which I might add, am very successful at.

I knew a stockbroker who used to live in International Falls and attended church with us. I had even served on the church board with him so knew his character and a little of his moral fiber. He also was a business man in town before moving to Rochester, MN to become a stock broker for Merrill Lynch. His name is Frank Fawcett. On my annual pilgrimage to the mecca of health care at Mayo Clinic, I scheduled a visit to his office to have a conversation with him about acquiring him for our broker. We had the conversation, asked the questions, exchanged information and discovered that we still liked and trusted him. The trust part was the big part of it for us in this society where you can barely

This Dummy Pulls His Own Strings

trust yourself, much less anyone else. He was of the same opinion as us, that we could retire on our 401K and pension and live comfortably until the social security kicked in for me and then later for Kathy. He also agreed to take us on as one of his clients.

Things were going south at work. I had to terminate an employee because of downsizing and of course the employee was not happy about that. Some former friends would no longer associate with me. I never pursued it to find out why. I thought if they are that shallow to not bother asking me about it and just accept the gossip in the air, they may be doing me a favor by terminating our friendship. I never was one to be in the popularity parade, I pull my own strings.

I told my boss, I wasn't enjoying the manager position but would continue in it until they found a replacement or my retirement, whichever came first. The company was looking to join the business data processing with the manufacturing computer processes so this was a good opportunity for them to find a new combined manager which they did and to whom I reported. He was a very intelligent young kid who actually did a good job considering what he inherited. I was allowed to keep my salary but not my title and of course was assigned different work. Some of it was interesting and some not so much. There was so much change and learning and I found I was not as good at retaining knowledge as I was earlier in my career.

Perhaps it was because I was not as interested or trying as hard. My new boss then demoted me another position and promoted one of the employees above me. He told me he was doing it for my health but had never asked me if this is something I wanted or would accept. I had an insulin reaction at work one day where I became very confused and didn't know where I was or what I was doing. My fingers knew my phone number and called my wife who immediately got another employee on the phone who got some sugar in me. Other employees took me home and brought my car home for me. I think this incident may have scared my young boss, who was unfamiliar with diabetes and insulin reactions and he probably was hoping I would not accept the demotion and leave. It seemed in office politics there was always an ulterior motive to every decision. It never was what they said it was. I actually preferred reporting to the person who was promoted above me rather than the boss who had demoted me but of course was not that happy in my work anymore. I'm sure that was evident in my production and attitude.

I was given the assignment to insure the department and all our applications in the mill were ready for the change to the year 2000. This was predicted as a disaster because many computer applications only use a two position year such as 98 instead of 1998. If you continued to do this after the year 2000, when you subtracted any 1900 date such as 1956 from 2000, you would arrive at a negative number as in 56 subtracted from 00 equals negative 56. However when you subtract 1956 from 2000 you arrive at 44. It was decided by the computer industry, rather than program around this by doing your math in a work area and automatically expanding the date to include 1900 and then subtracting or any time a year comes up negative you could subtract the two digit year from 100, in this case, 56 subtracted from 100 equals 44, it was decided to change all years in all applications to a four digit year which should eliminate any problems in the future.

It was my job to be sure that this happened in all our "home grown" applications and those we purchased either for the business computers or the manufacturing process control computers. They all had to be tested and proven to work which required running them in a test environment with the year 2000. It was referred to as Y2K conversion. Our company alone spent hundreds of thousands of dollars in the conversion and testing as well as the prevention of disaster such as renting generators in case the public utilities shut down and there was no power. The disaster, as it was forecast, never came about, partly because we did a good job of averting it and partly because the predictions were overblown.

I gave my notice of retirement and this was my last assignment. I had enough time off accumulated with vacation etc. that I didn't need to come into work in 2000 but my retirement date was

March 17, 2000. There is another chapter that is strictly about my retirement, oddly enough, titled "Retirement".

Boise Cascade, now Office Max was a great company to work for. They compensated and rewarded you for your hard work and dedication. They were always willing to send you to school to make you a more valuable employee and further your career with promotions and advancement. I traveled a lot while employed with Boise and often took my wife along with the company's knowledge and blessing. I paid for her airline tickets and meals but the company would pay all my expenses and provide us with a nice hotel room. Often we would incorporate a business trip with an opportunity to visit with relatives or friends in the area.

Boise provided you with the tools necessary to do your job. Most of my bosses were caring, reasonable people who would go out of their way to help you do your job. They had a good employment package that included a pension, 401K plan, health and life insurance and holidays off with generous vacations. They tried to compensate you If you had to be away from home for school, meetings or business by being generous with their expense accounts. I was told by one of my bosses that because the company took me away from my family for whatever the reason, he felt I should at the very least be fed well and even enjoy a few drinks. Because I didn't drink alcoholic beverages latter in my career, he suggested that I order something special that I ordinarily didn't buy myself like Oysters Rockefeller or Escargot, which I often did. I enjoyed my career with Boise Cascade and appreciate the caring and kindness I received while employed there.

Data Processors do it Bit by Bit.
IBM users do it at high speed.

12

Friends

Common-looking people are the best in the world: that is the reason the Lord makes so many of them.
Abraham Lincoln

Nothing is ever lost by courtesy. It is the cheapest of pleasures, costs nothing, and conveys much. It pleases him who gives and receives and thus, like mercy, is twice blessed.
Erastus Wiman (1834-1904)

I fear the day that technology will surpass our human interaction. The world will have a generation of idiots.
Albert Einstein

I started school when I was six years old as a first grader. There wasn't any kindergarten or pre-school. Before I was of school age when I was four years old, I would play with my cousin who lived next door to me. Her name at the time was Meredith Wentz and later when her mother remarried, her step dad adopted her and she became Meredith Beutler and when she married became Meredith Shaide. She had three name changes in her life which, I would think, makes it difficult to maintain an identity. In early society, females seemed to disappear when they had a name change. When trying to locate former friends and acquaintances of the female persuasion, I have had a hard time tracking them down because of name changes. Not so with the males. This is a subject that probably would be better addressed in another chapter but here I am, writing about it. I pull my own strings.

Getting back to my childhood friend, cousin and playmate, Meredith, she was a year older than I so she was much more mature and sophisticated than I. Meredith's Grandfather was Rev. Fred Knuth, a missionary to ND and the first minister of the country church on highway 14 east and north of Balfour. Meredith started school a year before me leaving me to fend for myself.

We played with dolls a lot and she would be the mommy and I the daddy. We both had tricycles to ride and we rode stick horses when playing cowboys. We had sidewalks out front of our houses and would play hop scotch. We had roller skates, the kind that attached to your shoes and you used a key to attach them. We made a lot of mud pies in the summer and in the winter would pretend we were in Alaska hunting polar bears and walruses. These were the days prior to TV and the World Wide Web or internet so we had to be inventive in our play. The snow bank between our houses was generally 15 to 20 feet high. Meredith's big brother Bob, who was in high school, and his friends would dig tunnels in it that we could physically stand up in. Of course we were much shorter then, about half size. The snow was so hard packed from the wind that there was no danger of it collapsing or caving in except in the springtime when it started to melt. We were smart enough to stay out of the tunnels then.

When we went to the post office with one of our parents, the postmaster would put some junk mail in a broken post office box and tell us it was our mail. He told us that was our mail box so every time we would go to the post office we would check it for mail and he often saw us coming and filled it with junk mail. Meredith's sister, Dorothy was in high school and was very good at playing the piano and was a piano teacher who gave piano lessons. I guess that is self-explanatory, what else would a piano teacher do? Both Meredith and I took piano lessons from her. One year for the recital, Dorothy had Meredith and I push a toy baby buggy onto the stage, side by side, stop by the piano and both of us took a seat on the piano bench and proceeded to play a duet. I don't remember exactly what we played but I believe it was a lullaby.

When Meredith started school, that was pretty much the end of our playing together all day long. I was quite nervous and stressed about losing my soul mate and play mate to school and about having to go down that same path in a year. Some of my friends started teasing me that I played with girls and with dolls which didn't really bother me that much (I was pulling my own strings even then) but she had new friends from school so we drifted apart.

Another cousin of mine was Billy Brieher. He was the son of a preacher man. His Dad, Uncle William, was a kind, loving, forgiving gentleman. He was the minister at the EUB (Evangelical United Brethren) church in Martin just a few miles up the road. Billies' mom and my mom were sisters. I would sometimes stay with them while my parents shocked grain for a farmer or picked potatoes. They often came to our house to visit and his Dad and mine were good friends and liked to go fishing together. Sometimes they took us boys along. Billy was a year older than I so was more worldly. He knew that China was on the other side of the globe. We figured, that being the case, if we dug a hole deep enough we could get to China. We thought my parents garden was a good place to start this experiment. I think we had a pretty good start before one of my parents discovered what we were up to. Of course, that ended that experiment.

I had an all black cocker spaniel dog. It was really my Dad's dog and was trained as a hunting dog. He was really good at retrieving ducks and pheasants and chasing pheasants up. He was also very protective of all of us but especially my Dad. Another form of entertainment for Billie and I was harassing my dog, Butch. Dad kept Butch tied up on a chain when he was outside so he wouldn't try digging to china in the garden or bother the neighbors. Dad had made Butch a dog house from a metal barrel cut up the side, with the split side spread apart and attached to a flat wooden platform for the floor. This made a Quonset hut shaped dog house. It was placed at the end of the chain so butch could go in and get out of the rain but he couldn't go around it and get his chain tangled. Billy and I would sneak up behind it when butch was sleeping inside and jump up on top and start pounding on the metal top. Butch would wake up and come charging out at full speed until he hit the end of the chain and then flip over backwards. Of course we never did this when there was an adult around to witness it.

Billy and I had great fun with fire crackers around the fourth of July. One of the favorites was putting a firecracker under an empty inverted tin can and seeing how high we could make the can go in the air. Another was putting the fire cracker in an ant hill hole and blowing up the ant hill.

We also had cork guns which we used to hunt and shoot humans, usually our older siblings and on occasion our parents. The guns didn't have much power but the corks could sting a little if you got hit. Occasionally we would hit an innocent adult bystander and of course get into trouble. I think sometimes we hit them on purpose but claimed it was an accident. Eventually the cork guns would get confiscated.

Our families often went places together with two cars following each other. One winter we were on our way back from Minot which is fifty miles from Drake and we got caught in a blizzard. It got so bad you couldn't see the road anymore. Our Dad's were driving but would stop frequently to talk to one another and put a plan together. They decided they couldn't be too far from Voltaire and they would drive slowly until they got to Voltaire and re-access the situation. I think at times one would walk along the road while the other drove to make sure they stayed on the road. They would then walk back to the other car and do the same with it. They finally arrived at Voltaire and decided to park the cars on the side of the road and walk across the ditch and railroad tracks to the train depot to see if there was a passenger train coming that we could ride to Drake and Martin. They did this while the rest of us stayed in the car and the mom's and older kids worried that our Dad's would get lost in the blizzard. I wasn't worried because

I knew my daddy would find a way to get us home and protect us. I was probably four or five years old.

Eventually they returned with news that a train was coming and we could take the train home. However, we had to walk to the train depot. Back then we dressed for the weather and everyone was dressed for the winter weather, probably in anticipation of things like this and because the car heaters weren't that productive, heating. I had purchased a pink piggy bank at F.W. Woolworths in Minot and I insisted that piggy bank had to come with me. The snow was as deep as I was tall so there was no way I could walk. Dad carried me and my piggy bank to the depot and when the train came we all boarded and made it to Drake. Of course when we got to Drake we had to walk home because our cars were still in Voltaire. It was about three blocks but somehow we managed to make it. I'm not sure if Briehers stayed with us that night or continued on to Martin on the train. My recollection is that they proceeded by train to Martin. The next day when the blizzard subsided, Dad and Uncle William took the train back to Voltaire and got the cars.

The Dieterle's lived about a block from us on a farm. Our house was on the west edge of town. Their farm was like most farms in North Dakota and had at least one slough. So we would build rafts out of dead trees and go rafting in the slough in the spring time when the snow melted and filled up the sloughs.

They had three boys, Wayne, a year older than me, Dwight, a year younger than me and Robert (Bob) several years younger. We went to the same Sunday School and Church together and their mother, Ida, was my Sunday School teacher. We became fast friends and played together nearly every day. They had lots of great toys and a new house with a basement to play in. They were also one of the first families in the neighborhood to get a TV when I was about 12.

We played basketball a lot, out in the farm yard where the chickens would dig out dusting holes to lay in the cool dirt. This did not make a very good court for dribbling the basketball but it improved our passing game. In addition to the dusting holes

This Dummy Pulls His Own Strings

the chickens created, they also defecated wherever they felt like it, as animals and birds do. If you dribbled the ball in it you would more than likely end up with it on your dribbling hand. Talk about a greasy ball.

It was a dairy and grain farm so the boys would have to quit playing at chore time and feed and milk the cows and clean the barn. Usually the rest of us would be sent home when it was chore time so we wouldn't distract the boys from their chores. Once in a while we would be allowed to stay and help with the chores. What boy doesn't want to shovel manure or climb the silo? We played in the hayloft of the barn in the hay bales and climbed the silo. I probably played with Dwight more than Wayne and Bob because Dwight and I were closer in age and we both liked to get into trouble. When getting in trouble, we could always say Dwight did it even if we were referring to ourselves.

One time we found more trouble than we wanted. It was common back then, in the spring, to burn areas of tall dead grass, especially along the fence line which usually had an accumulation of dried Russian thistles stuck in it. The fire cleaned up the tall grass and thistles and rubbish that had blown into the fence over the winter. One spring day, Dwight's mom, Ida, was burning the fence line at the border of the pasture just about a half a block from my house or between their house and ours. Dwight and Dwight wanted to play with the fire and "help" her with this task. We were about five and six at the time. Mrs. Dieterle told us we were too young to be playing with fire and chased us away to go play.

Dwight said he knew where his mother kept the matches in the kitchen and we could get our own matches and make our own fire. I remember we had to get a chair to reach the match dispenser which held the wooden matches and then we still couldn't reach it because it was attached to the wall high up out of the reach of children. We proceeded to get something to stack on the chair so we could reach them, probably Sears and Montgomery Ward catalogs which were several inches thick. These catalogs had many uses back then and were even used in the outhouse for toilet paper.

After acquiring the matches we then went out in the pasture down by the barn where there was a hayrack full of hay out of sight of Mrs. Dieterle. We took a couple hands full of hay away from the hay rack on the ground and tried to light it on fire with our matches. It was a little breezy and the wind would blow out our matches before we could get it burning. After many tries and when we were almost out of matches we moved closer to the hay rack and piled lots of hay on the ground. The hayrack sheltered us from the wind so the match stayed lit and caught the pile of hay on the ground on fire and in a flash it was burning with gusto.

Not only was the hay on the ground burning but the hay in the hayrack was also burning. We both took off running for our respective homes. On my way home I was hollering for help and our neighbor, Mrs. Jans, was in her back yard getting clothes off the clothes line. That tells me that it was a Monday because everyone washed clothes on Monday and hung them outside on the clothesline to dry. She asked what the problem was. I told her to call the fire department because Dieterle's barn was on fire. That wasn't exactly true but the hayrack was sitting close to the barn and the way it was burning, I was sure the barn would burn also. I proceeded to go home and to my room, afraid to tell my parents what we had done.

Drake had a volunteer fire department but it didn't take long before I could hear the fire whistle and the fire truck heading for Dieterle's just a block away. I was too scared to go watch the excitement. I didn't know what would happen to me once they found out I helped start the fire and I probably thought they would haul me off to jail, so I stayed away. You probably can remember that sick feeling in your stomach when you knew you had done something that was wrong and you couldn't fix it no matter what you did. I had that feeling. The fire department did an excellent job. The hayrack and the hay in it were a total loss but they saved the barn.

They couldn't locate Dwight Dieterle for some time and when his parents found him he was in the house hiding under his bed. I don't remember what our punishment was but I'm sure Dwight

Dieterle's punishment was greater than mine. We didn't learn not to play with fire either, because as teenagers we both smoked and Dwight would take cigarettes from his Dad's carton behind the seat of his pickup. His dad probably hid them there because as a Baptist he was not supposed to smoke, either.

I quickly learned that about Baptist's as I grew older. They are human just like everyone and temptations are no stranger to them. They seemed to consider more things sins than other Christian denominations but did them anyway. Their rules were too hard, even for them to follow. Drinking alcohol was a sin for most Baptists. They used grape juice instead of wine for communion. When I would go into a bar to sell newspapers, there were a lot of Baptists, belly up to the bar. They would ignore me and pretend that I wasn't there. The old ostrich, head in the sand syndrome. If they don't make eye contact with me, I didn't see them, must have been someone else.

Of course they wouldn't buy newspapers from me either because that would confirm that they were there. As I got older and went in bars as a customer, these same Baptists would be in there and still ignored me, even though we were both Baptists and drinking, against our religions rules. I also noticed, most of them came and went through the back door. My parents were not like that. If they preached something, they lived it. They walked the talk.

Sometimes someone would come to ask my Dad to come get their husband out of the bar. Dad would be reluctant to do it because he didn't want to be seen in the bar. He thought if he was seen in the bar, people would get the wrong impression and he would be setting a bad example. He did extract a drunk or two but didn't like it. Later when my parents were older, the Dr. suggested they should be drinking a glass of wine a day. They wouldn't do it unless I or one of my siblings would get the wine for them because they didn't want to go into a bar or liquor store to buy a bottle. North Dakota didn't sell any alcoholic beverages in grocery stores.

As a youth I was a good student and brought home almost straight A's on my report card. I always liked school and even liked studying and learning. That changed in my teenage years when I became a D student and even a few F's. As a teenager, I thought school was just a means to socialize. Many of my high school teachers told my parent's, Dwight isn't working up to his ability.

We played many different games at recess time and after school, depending on the time of the year. Spring was the time for playing marbles and stretch. All the boys had jack knives and we would play a game called "stretch". You would stand facing your opponent a foot or two apart and throw your jackknife a few feet to the side of your opponent and make it stick in the ground. He would then have to stretch one foot out to where your knife stuck in the ground. Then it was his turn to throw his knife into the ground and you would have to stretch out to where his knife was sticking. Because he was already stretched out he could reach farther when sticking his knife in the ground. If the knife didn't stick you lost your turn. The object was to try to make your opponent stretch farther than the legs could.

We also dug wild onions with our jackknifes and would eat them, much to the disgust of the girls and teachers who would eventually make that off limits. Not ever, did anyone get stabbed by a jackknife, by accident or on purpose. The thought never crossed our minds to use them as a weapon. If there was a fight, it was always with fists. Sometimes the blood would flow but usually it was from the nose.

Much of the school property didn't have grass and was just dirt. We would draw a circle in the dirt and each player would deposit a marble within the circle. We would then walk away from the circle about 10 feet and throw a marble at the circle. The closest one to the circle would get to shoot his marble at the marbles in the circle and knock them out of the circle. When you knocked one out you got to keep it and got to keep shooting until you missed another marble. There were other rules which I don't remember but it was great fun. It was kind of like playing pool without a pool table or ques. Another way of playing the game was to dig a hole and deposit a marble in the hole and then throw your marble at the hole. Whoever landed in the hole got all the marbles in the hole. If you both missed getting into the hole you deposited another marble until someone landed in the hole and won all the marbles. Our form of gambling.

Dennis Hinsz was a classmate and good friend of mine in grade school and high school. We would make things out of wood scraps from his uncles lumber yard such as wooden swords etc. We both had flyer sleds so did a lot of sledding in the winter after school and on weekends. On occasion when we were sledding on the streets which were gravel, packed with snow cover, a car would go down the street. We would step to the side of the street to allow the car to go by. Once it had passed, we sometimes would catch the back bumper and slide along on our feet with our knees bent so the driver wouldn't see us.

We also had ice skates and would skate on the rink when they made one on the school grounds or on Dieterle's slough when they didn't. Usually the ice skates were not the right size but had been one of my older siblings. We would put on more socks until the ice skates fit. This did not give very good support and I was usually skating on my ankles. Thus, I was not a very accomplished skater and didn't like ice skating that much, other than the social aspect, flirting with the girls and the bon fires.

Later in high school, both Dennis and I played the trumpet so we would, on occasion, practice the trumpet, together, usually at my house because his parents ran a dry cleaning business and lived at the back of the business. If we practiced at his house, we might have chased all the business away. As I recall, he was better on the trumpet than I was and played first trumpet in the band while I played second trumpet. I couldn't have been too bad because I was in several bands whose participants were picked by the band leader. Maybe I was chosen because I was the only one that was available. I was in the pep band, the marching band, the orchestra and a jazz band.

In our high school days, after we acquired our driver's license, we would find an old car hood, tie it behind the car with a rope and use it as a sled or toboggan. Dennis was the one that taught me how to hot wire a car with a gum wrapper of tin foil and disconnect the speedometer cable. If you disconnected the speedometer cable, no mileage registered on the car so it appeared that the car hadn't moved. That way when my parents weren't home but the car was because they rode with someone else, I could use the car, without permission or a key. I would have asked but no one was home to ask. Dad eventually found out because I didn't get the speedometer cable hooked up correctly one time and he took it to the garage to have it fixed. The mechanic told Dad someone disconnected it and didn't hook it back up properly. When he confronted me with this, I confessed to what I was doing, including the hotwiring. He just told me not to do it anymore. In fact he had me show him how I did it and I think he thought it was kind of cool and may even have been a little proud of me for my ingenuity. Of course I didn't tell him I learned it from Dennis. You just didn't rat out a friend.

In the early grades when we had recess, we went outside to play games such as, pump, pump, pull-a-way, red rover, tackle football, kick ball, tin can alley, king on the mountain and various other games we made up. There was no supervision from adults probably because most of the teachers were in the teachers smoking lounge. There was bullying, fist fights and occasionally someone would go tell the teacher when someone was doing something they shouldn't. Most of the time we got along fine and had a good time. I've been reading articles that are saying we need to get back to that type of play for our children. With all the rules and supervision by adults, we are taking away the ability of children to learn to make choices and take risks as well as problem solving. They don't learn which risks are minimal and which should be avoided. Later in life, they still haven't learned to be healthy risk takers and make bad choices, like texting and driving. Some schools are going back to the old way of eliminating the rules. One of the benefits they say is less bullying. Perhaps, kids learn to stand up for themselves and others when there are no rules or supervision. If they don't handle the situation, there is no one else to handle it.

This Dummy Pulls His Own Strings

Those games we played at recess in grade school, we also played in our neighborhood on spring and summer evenings. We would get a bunch of kids from the neighborhood together and play until dark and sometimes after dark, especially moonlight starlight. The neighborhood kids were the Dieterle boys, Wayne, Dwight and Robert, the Shink boys, Edward and Henry, the Ritzke boys, Alfred and Ronald, the Ziegler girls, LaDonna and Linda, The Jans kids, David, Dennis, Donald and Debbie. Emery Suckert and his sister Gracie, The Schmitgall girls, Meredith Beutler, Audrey Drake, Ruth Ann Christianson and Gary Hoffer are the ones that come to mind. If we got a game of street baseball, softball or 500 going sometimes the older kids like my sister Fern, Ailene Jans and others that happened to come by would join in. It was great fun and we seldom had any serious disagreements or fights.

When I was in 7th grade, Jerry Hordinski and I became friends. He lived about a half a block from me as the crow flies. His Dad was the local Dr. and a very good one. See the chapter on "My Hometown" for an article on the good Dr. People would come from all over the state and even out of state for his medical expertise. Jerry had all the toys a lad could dream of. We spent many summer days playing ping pong or the board hockey game with the levers and slides. While watching "The Price is Right" not long ago, they had the same hockey game as a prize and it's price today was in excess of one thousand dollars.

Jerry had a better income than I did so he often would treat me to cherry cokes or malts at the local drug store soda fountain. Jerry also collected stamps and coins and he convinced me to do the same so we spent many hours trading and filling stamp books or coin books. We were the same age but Jerry had skipped a year in school so was a grade ahead of me. I was in 7th grade and he was in 8th grade. In our school, they often put two grades in one room with the same teacher. That was the case with our 7th and 8th grade class.

His genius and study habits didn't rub off on me. The 7th grade was the first year I ever got a D or F on my report card. We had some classes that both the 7th and 8th grade combined for and some such as math that were separate. Jerry got straight A's and seldom got any questions wrong on a test. When he got a test question wrong, he would argue with the teacher and tell the teacher which page, paragraph and sentence the answer was on in the textbook and he usually was right. The teacher would have to give him credit for it and stand corrected, which pleased everyone but the teacher. One time Jerry was wrong and got one wrong and there were tears shed. It was a trick question designed just for Jerry because the teacher probably was getting tired of being wrong and losing arguments to Jerry. It was probably Jerry's fault I was doing so poorly that year. With him getting 100 percent right all the time, it made it difficult to grade on the curve. Or I should say grading on the curve made my papers failing.

I often went to his home with him after school and he would do his homework while talking to me, listening to the radio and reading the textbook. He could recite the textbook, comment on the radio program and carry on a conversation all at the same time. He was remarkably smart with great learning and memory skills. We were only friends the one summer and one school year because the next year Jerry went away to military school because the local school probably would have held him back from achieving his full potential.

He later became a medical Dr. and scientist who was the Space Lab Mission medical officer for NASA where he designed experiments for the space program. I visited with him after we were both adults and married when he was home visiting his parents and I was home visiting mine. It was interesting visiting with him about his work and recalling the good old days but we had little in common, anymore. At the time, as I recall, he was doing experiments in space on the effect of space on the human eye. In 1974 he was aboard the U.S.S. New Orleans to check out astronauts Gerald Carr, William Pogue and Edward Gibson after their 84 day space flight. He and his Father were the most intelligent people I have ever known on a personal level.

In the 8th grade, I was missing my good friend Jerry Hordinski so I started hanging out with my friend Charlie Toy, his brother

Mike Toy, classmates Wayne Anton and Dennis Hinsz. Other friends and occasional partners in crime were David Traiser, Danny Schafer, Glen Krueger, Emery Suckert, Dennis Schiele, Jim Martin and on occasion, Gary Hoffer, Edward & Henry Shink, Alfred & Ronald Ritzke and Robert Schmitgall. I also hung out with my class mates and kids that were in my church and BYF (Baptist Youth Fellowship), the Dieterle boys, Jans boys and McCartys. This was when I first experimented with smoking and started smoking as a regular thing. Ralph Cushing ran around with us for a time and also experimented with alcohol with us.

There was another Dieterle family that lived on a farm south of Drake, Dave Dieterle. They had three children, Brian, Janet and a younger girl whose name escapes me. Brian was a year older than I, Janet was the same age and a classmate of mine in high school. All of these kids attended a country one room school through the eighth grade and then came to Drake to High School. When I was in eighth grade, Brian was a freshman. Drake was not using school buses at the time to bus students. Each family had to get their kids to school with private transportation. Most high school students drove themselves to school and home. Brian's parents asked my parents if Brian could room and board at our place during the winter when the roads were snow covered and there was a danger of blizzards. My parents agreed as they could use the extra income and it really wasn't much trouble for them. For me it was like having a big brother. Of course Brian and I had to share a room and a bed. Brian was a well behaved, intelligent youth who was popular in high school and fun to be around. He only stayed with us his freshman year because the next year his sister Janet was also in high school and he either drove to school or the school started busing. I wouldn't have protested if they wanted Janet to stay with us but it was not to be. I believe both he and Janet pursued education beyond high school and both had their Drs. degrees in their respective fields. It's possible their younger sister did also. A family of Drs.

Robert Schmitdgal was the son of the local Ford dealer. He was a year older than Charlie Toy and I. He was the first one of our acquaintances to get a driver's license and a car of his own. No surprise, his dad was part owner of the local Ford dealership. The year was about 1955 or 1956 and he had an older Ford with the humpback. Probably a 1940's vintage. It may not have appeared to be a chick magnet but back then, anyone who had access to a car, usually could find a girl that was willing to spend some time with you. Sometimes you could even convince her to part with some money for gas. Gas back then cost somewhere between twenty five and thirty cents a gallon.

    The car didn't have much of a working heater which sometimes worked to our advantage as the girls would snuggle a little closer, not because they liked us but trying not to freeze. In ND in the winter with the temperature close to zero and sometimes below zero, with the wind howling, it's difficult to keep from freezing. We had blankets to put over our legs and warm coats but of course we never wore a hat of any kind as it would mess up our hair. The girls were a little smarter and sometimes wore a scarf over their head. The boys would wet down our hair before going out for the evening and comb and style it and when we stepped outside, it would freeze solid, almost instantly. It was a good way to make your hair wavy, at least until it thawed. It was kind of the same principle as curlers. The down side was the girls seldom, if ever, ran their fingers through your frozen hair.

    We would go to out of town football and basketball games, three guys and three girls. With that combination, there was usually two guys and a girl in the front seat and two girls and a guy in the back seat. Robert always had whoever his present girl was, beside him and I was usually the odd guy in front riding shotgun. Generally, as I remember it, Charlie or Mike Toy was in the back seat with whoever the other two girls were.

    We all smoked, including most of the girls and when we could find any, would drink beer or whatever alcohol we could find. At this point, obviously, none of us could get served in a bar so we would have to convince an adult to buy our alcohol. It wasn't always that difficult because we knew some adults who were cheating on their spouses so we could always resort to blackmail if no one was willing to buy our alcohol for us. The hard part was finding the money to pay for it.

Sometimes, there weren't any girls or alcohol involved and we would just drive around smoking cigarettes. Robert liked to drive on the country gravel roads and spin doughnuts or drive down the ditch and back up on the road. He was a fairly good driver and even though I was a bit apprehensive, don't recall coming close to rolling the car. I think some of the older cars were made for driving in fields and ditches because back then many of the roads weren't much more than tracks in the field. Our biggest concern was that we would hit a large rock sticking up and put a hole in the oil pan and drain all the oil out.

My freshman year in high school our class was expanded considerably by all the farm kids that were previously attending school in one room schools in their respective townships. In those country schools, one teacher taught all eight grades and all the students were in one room. While the teacher was spending time with one grade and teaching the student or students in that grade the other students would be working on their assignments. It helped heighten your concentration. If you weren't concentrating on your work, you could listen in on the other classes, especially those that were ahead of you and get a head start on the upper class lessons.

Both my sisters taught in one room country schools. All these new students in the high school gave us the opportunity for new friends and companions and especially girlfriends. One of these new friends was David Traiser. He was in my freshman class and we had a lot of the same interests. I believe David stayed with Danny Schafer the first year or two until he got his driver's license or until his sister, Faye started high school. Seems like kind of a pattern, the guys room and board in town until their younger sister starts high school.

Danny Schafer lived next door to Charley Toy, my best friend since first grade. Danny was friends with Charley and Mike Toy and soon became a close friend of mine and of course because David was staying with Danny, David became a close friend also.

In addition, David and I were classmates and took many of the same subjects so we studied together both in school and after school on rare occasions. I visited Dave and his wife Suzie last year and we still have a lot of the same interests. Another of these new high school friends was Allen Volmer who became another partner in crime and drinking buddy with transportation. My cousin Donald Knuth, who is my age but not in my school, also became a drinking buddy with transportation.

After high school graduation, I had friends where I worked. Some of these friends I spent time with after work, hunting ducks and deer, bowling, drinking or riding home to Drake on weekends and back to work at Williston.

When I joined the military, I made new friends both in the Army and Navy. When you live in a barracks with a bunch of guys, you have lots of friends, weather you want to or not. You do get to pick who you hang out with and how much you hang out with them. As I recall, there were a lot of movies, USO concerts and activities, beer drinking, sightseeing, skirt chasing, bar hoping and a great quantity of shooting the bull and philosophizing. There always seemed to be a card game or chess game in progress in the barracks. I found it quite interesting to socialize with guys from all over the country. From the hills of Tennessee to Alaska, Brooklyn, Bronx, Maine, Alabama and even Canada. Not only did they have different lifestyles but many of them spoke differently with different accents and local styles and sayings. This in itself was an education, especially when I would be invited to go home with them for the weekend.

I didn't make many lasting friendships in the Army, probably because we were together for a shorter period of time. In the Navy I made many close friendships, several of which I maintain today. John Dempsey, Lloyd Henderson and Jim Gulbranson come to mind although I have lost touch with Jim. Alan Leavy, my good buddy from Brooklyn and I had plans to go to Australia and pursue the fair maidens there after our discharge from the Navy. I chose to go to exotic North Dakota for the same reason and Al and I never pursued the beauties in Australia.

This Dummy Pulls His Own Strings

Other names that come to mind and bring fond memories and a smile to my heart are: Richard Dingler of Maine, Rick Alm of Minot, ND, Gustav F. Kropa of Tonkhannock, PA, Serafin Maldonado of San Francisco, CA, George Mount of Maine, Michael Ochs of IL, Warren Otis of Lapeer, MI, Fred Thorne of the Bronx, Ray Grams of MN, Charlie Hauff of Fort Wayne, IN, Ken Fluhrer of MN, Bert Pellinen of Duluth, MN, Skip Miracle of KS, Billy Warr of Boise, ID, Duane Martian, Norman Schimke and Tiny Hirschcorn all of Harvey, ND, Marion Moore, Danny Tonnies, George Duffy, Bill Allen, Angelo Olivo, Ron (Pappy)Papaleoni, Jim Dupre, Bob Sutton, Tom King, Duane Roberts, Bob Foster, Roger Gibson, Emil Hirselj, Ronald Johnson, Ed Kotkiewiez, William Morgan, Huey McCloud, George Rieger, Art Kincaid, Edward Thorpe, Ellsworth Woodruff, and many more, some whose name escapes me. I lived with, worked with and respected all of these fine gentlemen and enjoyed their company. Some were part of the PAMI Animals, some were drinking buddies, some barracks buddies but all were friends that enriched my life. Many are on my email list or facebook friends, still enriching my life.

Later when I moved to International Falls where my Navy buddy Jim Gulbranson lived and worked and was instrumental in finding me employment with Boise Cascade, we made new friends. Most were guys I worked with and their wives. Terry and Marlene Bunnis, Tim and Marsha Shuff, Robbie and Laurie Trompeter, Mike and Karen Nolan, Dan and Kay Larson, David and Amber Chute, Jim Peterson, Ed Bernath, Don Johnston, Lee Dornhecker, Joe Melin, Ron and Linda Eply, George and Bernice Englund, Verne and Jackie Larson, Skip Scott, Monty and Joann Bokovoy, Guy Leolich, Gary Bowman, Brett Bartlett, Tom Fairhurst, Wally Glatz, Linda and Brad Carlson, Ann Bzdok, Mary Sether, Velva Cassibo, Mabel Cantrell, Vivian McMickken, Dan and Joyce Einichner, Dick and Elizabeth Forsythe, Jim & Gloria DeMuth, Riley & Mary Dunn, Paul & Peggy Curan, Ray & Arlene Julien, Gordy and Pat Ettestad, Ed Kuldanek, Kirk Skallman, Robert Myer, Hilliard Devlin, Arnold Johnson, John Hubbard, John Budris, Ken and Neica Neize, Bud and Jean Larson, Norm Boyum, Wilbur Tveit,

Tom and Jean Fisher, Larry and Ruth Lewis, Dale Johnson and the list goes on and on.

The guys from the data center would get together to race little hand held remote controlled cars, go to football games, go to bars, supervisors club, bowling etc.

Boise Cascade had an annual picnic with the different divisions and departments having softball teams to compete with each other. The Data Center didn't have enough employees to field a team so we would join the MDW (Minnesota, Dakota and Western) railroad softball team. Boise owned a railroad, a bridge to Canada as well as the water and electric service to International Falls. To some, these softball games were a serious competition but to most of us it was just a good time and free beer with a good excuse to get inebriated. Boise provided free beer as well as a picnic feast with the usual picnic food. There would be games for the kids and free candy bars, soda pop, ice cream, potato chips and other treats all day, as much as you wanted. Our kids would generally make themselves sick but then that wasn't any different than the adults guzzling the free beer and making themselves sick. I thought it was a good opportunity to teach my children that you should use moderation in all things and to learn that you need to use self control.

Then of course there were my bowling buddies and our church had a softball team that played in the city summer softball league. I also did some cross country skiing, only in the winter. I say only in the winter because living in International Falls, MN on the Canadian border, there are times when you probably could ski in most of the seasons. I had my skiing friends, Dan Eineichner and Monty Bokovy. I did some fishing, boating and water skiing, mostly with my family and relatives. Some of my best friends are also my relatives.

These are the type of friends you may not hear from or see for years but when you run into them, it is just as though you saw or spoke to them yesterday. There is never any stress or anxiety and you are comfortable with them because they know you and you know them so you are relaxed with a high comfort level and you are truly glad to see them. We know enough about each other so we're not trying to impress one another and can just be ourselves, no more, no less. I'm sure you all have friends like that and can relate to my feeble attempt to explain it. To all my friends, mentioned or not, thank you for your friendship and loyalty and for putting up with me and my faults which are too numerous to mention and I appreciate that you don't. God Bless each of you and continue to make you a blessing.

13

On the Road – Hitchhiking & Riding the rails in the 1950's

Hitchhiking has become a lost art and most of the younger generation have never heard of it. When I was growing up, it wasn't unusual to see someone along the road with their thumb out trying to hitch a ride. The roads were two lanes, mostly paved with a speed limit of 50 to 60 miles per hour. There was very little danger for either the hitchhiker or for the motorist providing a ride. The greatest danger to the hitchhiker was probably from drunken drivers and many times they would pick you up so you could drive for them and they could sleep it off. We didn't have seat belts or air bags and you could put as many people in the back seat of a car or the back of a pickup as would fit.

Sometimes the ride was only "going down the road a piece" so you might refuse a ride because there was more traffic at this location or you had a better chance of catching a ride at this spot than down the road a piece. If they were going to drop you off in between towns, where the speed limit was 50 or 60 MPH as opposed to standing on the edge of a town or village where the speed limit was 25 or 30 MPH, you were probably better off to stay where you were.

Sometimes hitchhikers printed a sign in large letters on cardboard stating the destination, such as Seattle, WA. Sometimes these signs worked to your advantage and sometimes not. Some people that were only going to the next town would not stop for you because they thought you wanted to catch a longer ride. On the other hand, some salesman or person traveling alone and going to Seattle, may stop for you for some company and to share the driving and you would have a ride all the way to Seattle. We never used any signs, probably because we wanted to catch any ride we could. By doing this we got a lot of short rides and also met many interesting people.

As a teenager, my friends and I would hitchhike to places that were too distant to walk or ride a bike. In modern society it is not considered safe or a wise mode of transportation. For those of you that have never heard of it, it was basically asking for a ride. The mechanics of it were quite simple. We would stand along the shoulder of the highway facing the traffic that was headed in the direction we wished to travel. When a vehicle came down the highway, we would extend the right hand with the thumb pointing in the direction we were headed. The driver of the vehicle would often slow down, drive past you to look you over and if you didn't look too obnoxious, weird or dangerous, would pull over and stop. We would then run up to the stopped vehicle, exchange destination information, and if it suited both parties, get in the car and be on our way. If they were going past our destination, they would drop us off near it but if we were going farther than they were, we would get out when they reached their destination and start the procedure over.

Most of the time we were just going to Lake Bently to go swimming. The lake was about 3 mi. out of town. Sometimes we couldn't get a ride and we would have to walk the 3 mi., uphill both ways. Keep in mind this is ND and sometimes there wasn't a lot of traffic on the road. On occasion we would get a ride with a farmer who had farm animals in the back of the truck. If there was no room in the cab, we would have to ride in the back with the animals and manure. Beggars can't be choosers. When we were done swimming we would have to hitchhike back to town. When there were more than 2 or 3 of us we would either split up into groups of 2 and 3 or if there were only 4 or 5 sometimes, we would have 2 of us stand along the highway to catch a ride while the rest laid down in the ditch where the driver couldn't see them. When the driver would stop, we would all scramble out of the ditch and into the vehicle. There were no seat belts in those days so you could usually get 5 or 6 kids in the back seat. If we split up into groups, the first group to get picked up would ask the driver to pick up the kids in the following group or groups. If a pickup stopped for us, we would all jump in the box of the pickup.

On occasion, Mike Toy, and/or Charles Toy (the Toy boys) and I would want to go to Minot to a Movie, to Underwood to chase skirts or to Williston for the same purpose. I had a sister, Verla in Williston who would feed us and give us a place to sleep and Mike and Charles had a sister, Charlane in Minot and a sister Nellie in Underwood who did the same. Usually we showed up unannounced and just expected to be fed and bed. I can't remember ever being disappointed in the accommodations. When we were hitchhiking 50, 100 or 150 mi. it most always took several rides and most of the day to arrive. We met some interesting, if not scary characters but seldom felt we were in real danger.

On one occasion, one of the "Toy boys" and I hitchhiked to Minot to see Elvis in "Jailhouse Rock". At Velva, which is about halfway to Minot, we got a ride with a guy that wasn't a whole lot older than us. It was obvious he had been drinking. I don't know if he felt intimidated or threatened by us but whatever the reason, he felt it was necessary to open the glove box and show us his handgun. I don't know what kind it was or if it was loaded but if he was trying to impress me and scare me, he was successful. My imagination was running wild with the things he may want to do with that hand gun. I was afraid he might want to try to pull off an armed robbery with us as his accomplices and if we didn't cooperate he would turn the gun on us. There were other scenarios racing through my alleged mind but none of them materialized. He was mostly a braggart and wanted to impress us. We were happy to get to Minot and away from him. There was a

This Dummy Pulls His Own Strings

line about two blocks long at the movie theater but we eventually got in and the movie was worth the wait and the anxiety.

Another time, Mike and I were hitchhiking to Williston. We got a ride at Burlington, which is about 100 miles from Williston, with an older fellow (40 or 50) who was drunk. He was going all the way to 13 mi. from Williston. A few mi. down the road he asked if either of us had a driver's license. I told him I did and he asked me to drive. He crawled in the back seat and said he was going to sleep and we should wake him when we reached the Williston 13 mi. corner. When we arrived we made a feeble attempt to wake him and when we were unsuccessful, drove on to Williston. While trying to wake him, Mike found his wallet on the floor of the backseat. When we got to Williston, we woke him, returned his wallet to him and got out. He was not happy with us for driving the extra 13 miles which would turn into 26 mi. for him. Talk about ungrateful. We probably saved his life by driving for him because as drunk as he was, he probably would have passed out or fallen asleep. In addition, he never thanked us for returning his wallet but regarded us with suspicion. I suppose he thought we probably took money out of his wallet and he wouldn't know it because he had been drunk and didn't know what he had left. We didn't even look in his wallet. No good dude or good deed goes unpunished.

When I was in the Navy and engaged to a girl from Underwood ND that was living with her sister & family in Philadelphia, I would hitchhike from the naval base on the Chesapeake bay in MD to Philly on weekends and holidays. The Navy had shelters like bus stops outside base that were called share a ride stations. Of course once you left the shelter and were dropped off short of your destination, you had to resort to hitchhiking. I always wore my uniform when doing this because it was much easier to get a ride and the police would leave you alone. Once I reached Phily, I could take the subway/elevated train to my girlfriends place. I found, riding the subway alone in uniform was much safer than in civilian clothes. The gang members and hoods didn't bother you if you were in uniform, I guess they didn't want to take on the whole armed forces.

The ultimate hitchhiking experience for me was when I was 16 years old and my very good, lifetime friend, Charles Toy and I hitchhiked from Minot, ND to Tacoma, WA. In case you are unfamiliar with US geography, that is halfway across the United States on roads on the northern edge of the country where there is less traffic than the well traveled southern route. We had a mutual friend, Gary Richards, whose grandparents, (Rieniets) aunts and uncles lived in Drake. He would spend the summers in Drake and we would hang out together, playing cards, listening to music, smoking cigarettes and trying to acquire some beer. He generally stayed with Mike and Charlie Toy rather than his relatives. One summer when he left, he told us we should come out to Tacoma the next summer instead of him coming to Drake. I'm sure he had not cleared this with his parents and I'm sure he thought we would never take him up on it. Charlie and I talked about it and thought it might be an adventure if we would/could hitchhike out to Tacoma for the summer. I never thought I would get permission from my parents to do this but, nothing ventured, nothing gained. I asked my Mom and Charlie asked his. His Mom said if my parents agreed to it, she would also agree. I'm sure she never thought my parents would give me their consent so she was safe. My parents discussed it and tried to talk me out of it but being a Knuth and capable of arguing with a fence post, I couldn't be dissuaded. The thing I didn't know and I'm sure Charlie's Mom didn't know was that my older brother had run away from home several times when he was about my age. I'm sure my parents thought I would also do that if they didn't agree, so finally, they agreed. Better that I go with their blessing than have me run away and probably join the service, may have been their thinking. If I was lucky and survived, I may return home and appreciate it and them.

Here are two sixteen year old kids with very little knowledge of the real world about to go into the real world with little or no money and few skills. We probably had never been hungry or went a day without sustenance. We had little or no fear of the unknown and blindly went forward. Thank God for our mothers' prayers.

Charles and I each packed a little sports duffel bag with a clean change of underwear and clothes and a toothbrush along with a sleeping bag and we were ready for our adventure. By today's standards we traveled light. I don't remember how much money we had but I would guess it was probably less than $20.00 between us. After all we were only going to be gone three months. We both smoked cigarettes and they were 25 cents a pack then. I remember smoking a lot of cigarette butts that other people had thrown away. Being a broke, addicted teenager, I had lots of practice, smoking other smokers' cigarette butts. When I stayed with my sister Verla, she had a friend that would come over for coffee and a cigarette. She usually only smoked about half a cigarette and would leave the rest in the ash tray. I would gather her half smoked cigarettes to smoke later. Verla always accused me of smoking Joyce's butt. I won't tell you my reply but will let your imagination run wild.

Meanwhile, back to hitchhiking to Tacoma. My parents packed a picnic lunch, drove us to Minot and after our picnic, dropped us on the road. As they drove away, I noticed tears in my Mothers eyes. Our first destination was my sister, Verla, at Williston who fed us and gave us a place to sleep the first night. Perhaps we picked up a few of Joyce's cigarette butts also.

I don't know why we chose the route we did from Williston to Tacoma but for some reason we went south from Williston rather than staying on the most northern route, US 2. It's possible we thought there was more traffic on the southern route and therefore a better chance of catching a ride. Whatever the reason, we went south from Williston to US 10 which is now Interstate 94. At that time it was just a 2 lane highway most of the way until you got farther west. This route took us close to the South Dakota border where we then went west through Montana, Idaho and Washington.

I don't remember how far we got the first day out of Williston but I remember sleeping in our sleeping bags along the road more than one night. Usually it was a small town with a gas station close so that we could use the facilities to wash up and brush our teeth. I don't recall spending much on meals. I'm sure we probably

Dwight E. Knuth

survived on candy bars and perhaps a soft drink on occasion. I believe it was the first night that we got stuck in a small town in Montana, probably Glendive. There was a convertible with the top down that repeatedly drove by us. It had 3 or 4 teenage girls in it, as I remember. I'm sure that we hooted or hollered or in some way tried to engage them in a conversation and get them to stop and pick us up. They may even have stopped to talk to us but it must not have been too exciting as I can't remember it. I vaguely recall a carload of guys going by and probably telling us to leave their girls alone. I do remember that we had to spend the night there. There was a box from a dump truck that was turned upside down and sitting on top of four barrels. If my memory serves me, which it seldom does, we slept under that truck box that night to be protected from the rain.

The next day we made it as far as Miles City. Somewhere past Miles City, MT we were sitting at a picnic table in a park along the road and a strange but friendly dude stopped and started talking to us. I would guess he was somewhere in his forties or fifties. He was driving a 1950 Ford and this would have been about 1958. We talked for a spell and learned that he was on his way to Wenatchee, WA and that we could ride along if we would share the driving. I believe he also wanted us to share the expenses for gas, oil, etc. but we told him we didn't have any money which is why we were hitchhiking. He kept telling us that his car was his home and he didn't like it if we took off our shoes and put our feet on the dash. We would buy food and snacks at gas stations and eat in the car. We never stopped at a restaurant to eat. I don't know how many days and nights it took us but we rode with him across most of Montana, all of Idaho and most of Washington. He took a liking to me but didn't really like Charlie for some reason. He seldom let Charlie drive. He had me drive a lot which was fine with me, being a 16 year old. I remember driving through Spokane, WA without having to stop for a red light. There must have been about 20 lights but traffic was light and I could adjust my speed to catch all the lights green. At one point in the mountains of MT he stopped the car along the road, pointed up

This Dummy Pulls His Own Strings

a steep mountain side and said to Charlie, "the last time I was through here I left my hat up there. Would you go up and get it for me?". Charlie just laughed at him and stayed in the car.

I recall another time when we stopped to fill up with gas. He tried to make us feel guilty because he was buying all the gas and we were not contributing anything. The service station had tires stacked beside the gas pumps. He tried to talk Charley and I into throwing a couple of those tires into his trunk while he paid for the gas inside and distracted the attendants. We didn't buy into his scheme and we left without any new tires.

We rode with him almost to Tacoma. Wherever it was that he dropped us off, I believe we made it to Tacoma that same night. When we arrived in Tacoma it was night time and it being a big city and us unfamiliar with it, we hailed a cab and spent the last of our money to go to 1952 South Cushman Street, the address of Dean Richards, the father of Gary and his family.

It was a nice big two story house on a corner lot with a nice fenced yard in a nice part of the city. It was late at night and all the lights were out in the house so we decided not to disturb or wake them. We climbed over the fence, unrolled our sleeping bags, crawled in and went to sleep. Imagine the Richards surprise in the morning when they looked out their kitchen window and saw two bums sleeping in the back yard. Imagine our surprise when they let the dog out and he came running and barking at us. It turned out that the dog wasn't all that vicious and we quickly identified ourselves before they called the police. Now let me remind you these people had no idea that we were coming. Here are two teenage boys visiting their teenage son for who knows how long. Did I mention, they had two other children? Two more teenage mouths to feed. You know how teenagers eat and suck down milk like a young calf. The milk alone could ruin a budget. They were very nice to us and fed us and provided a bed for us to sleep in. Their son, Gary, had stayed at Toys for several summers prior to this so one could claim, turnabout is fair play.

Gary was still attending high school when we arrived. Their schools didn't get out as early as ours did in the spring. Either

ND students are smarter and don't require as much time to learn or they think there is no hope of us ever learning so just let us go. I believe, Gary skipped the first day of school we were there and Charlie and I went with him the next day. It gave us a chance to experience a big city school with the hundreds of kids. I compared this large school with all its kids to the movie "Blackboard Jungle" and imagined at any moment someone would pull a switchblade knife on one of us. Contrary to my imagination, unlike a small town, no one paid any attention to us, almost as if we didn't exist. I don't think the teachers even noticed that there were two extra new students in their class. Gary could take the city buses to his high school, Lincoln high, which was miles across town but most of the time he elected to hitchhike to and from school. He was probably saving the bus money to buy cigarettes. We of course hitchhiked with him. I think we only went with him one day either because it was the last day or one extra day of school was too much.

Gary had several friends of various nationalities. I remember, one was Italian and lots of his friends referred to him as "Wop or Dago". One lived a few houses away and I think we called him "Dewey". Gary was going with Dewey's sister, a very well built, pretty teenager. Most of the time, Gary, his friends, Charlie and I hung out together just enjoying our freedom and skating around the edge of trouble. I would guess there were between 3 to 7 of us wondering the streets of Tacoma at any given time. One evening we were walking down the street when we came across a couple cherry trees with ripe cherries on them, ready to be picked and eaten. Several or all of us climbed the trees and started picking the cherries and eating them. I'm sure we were not too quiet about it and the owner of the home opened his door and hollered at us, "what you all doing in my cherry trees?" One of the guy's, I think it was Charlie, replied, "picking apples". We all promptly left before he could call the police on us. This was before God invented 911. Unless you were in the habit of calling the police, you had to look the phone # up in a phone directory, dial the number and probably wait on hold until they got to you. Even

This Dummy Pulls His Own Strings

if you were successful in connecting with the police, it probably would take them a while to get police to your neighborhood. Even if they did get there fast enough to apprehend you, what would they charge you with, stealing cherries? The proof was gone. We ate them as fast as we picked them. It was a different time.

There was a water reservoir a couple blocks from Gary's house that was used for city drinking water. It was the size of a swimming pool and looked much like one. It had a chain link fence around it with barbed wire on the top, I assume to keep the kids out. We figured we could climb the fence and when we got to the barbed wire use a piece of clothing, like a shirt, to keep the barbs from digging into our hands. This we did. We would climb the fence and use the reservoir for a swimming pool until we got too noisy and one of the neighbors called the police. The reservoir was the only thing on the block and it was 10 to 20 feet above the street, like a mound. This allowed us to see when the police were coming and be quiet and hide in the water with just our heads above water. We would watch them as they drove around the reservoir. I guess they were too lazy or comfortable to get out of the squad car and climb the hill to look in the reservoir. They would shine their spotlight up on the reservoir even though they still couldn't see us because we were submerged in the water on a hill and they were at street level at the base of the hill.

One night we decided that we would all sleep at the reservoir, camping out, party time. A couple of the guys worked at grocery stores as stock boys. The grocery stores in WA sold 3.2 beer. These guys would take a case of beer at the grocery store and set it out behind the store in a hidden location while they were at work. After work they would pick it up and bring it to the reservoir where we would all drink warm 3.2 beer and get a little bit loud until the neighbors would call the police and we would have to vacate the area or as we said back then, "flee the scene".

After a few weeks of lying around thinking of ways to create some excitement, everyone thought It would be fun to hitchhike to the ocean and get some sun and beach time and dig and eat clams. Gary had a paper route so someone would have to stay behind to deliver papers. I think we agreed to draw straws to see who would stay behind or maybe I volunteered because I had experience as a paperboy . I don't remember anymore. Anyway, I learned his paper route and stayed behind while the others headed for the ocean. As it turned out, I was the smart and lucky one. They all came home sunburned to a crisp. Someone stole their clothes from the beach while they were swimming in the ocean and they had to hitchhike home in their bathing suits.

Gary's Dad, Dean was an alcoholic. When he quit drinking he bought himself a 1956 Lincoln. It was a beautiful car, long and sleek, light green. It was the first car I rode in with electric windows. Dean seldom drove it. It sat in the garage almost the whole summer we were there. He took it out once to take us all to his youngest sons ball game and once to take us fishing on the sound.

We did other things in Tacoma beside hitchhike. Because we were all smokers we needed money to buy cigarettes to satisfy our addiction. That was probably the driving force that would cause us to actively look for work. Gary's Mom told us about the berry fields around Tacoma who were always looking for berry pickers. There were Strawberries and Raspberries. My Dad grew berries on the farm which he sold locally, so I was no stranger to picking berries. We didn't even have to hitchhike to get there. The owners would send a big truck around certain neighborhoods where likely berry pickers lived and pick up people to pick. This wasn't for the old or feeble as you had to crawl into the back of the truck. They would get as many pickers as they could into the truck box and take you to the berry field.

At the end of the day, they would pay you for what you had picked and reverse the truck route. Generally you would take your lunch with you or else just eat enough berries to keep you going. I preferred picking raspberries because you didn't have to bend over or crawl on hands and knees like you did for strawberries. The truck picked us up just a few blocks from Gary's. The nice part about it was you could go just when you wanted to, or needed the cash. Most of the pickers were of Mexican descent or kids like us.

This Dummy Pulls His Own Strings

Charlie was kind of a chick magnet, he had that Toy charisma. Like all teenage boys, girls were what was normally on our mind. The girls at the berry fields were friendly and flirtatious and we thrived on that. I guess the ND girls were less flirtatious or perhaps more shy. Some of the guys at these berry fields thought some of the girls were there exclusively for them and resented us flirting with them. I think Charlie ended up in a fist fight once or twice because of it. Charlie was not one to back down from a fist fight, especially if there was a female involved. Charlie was a Golden Glove boxer and quite accomplished at it, going to state a couple years. It was not often Charlie lost a fight, outside the ring. I can't recall ever seeing it happen.

I don't remember all the details or mechanics of the following but I know we met some girls berry picking. It may have been when we were staying with Charlies cousin, Roger. Anyway, they were very religious girls that belonged to a church that we, in our youth, referred to as "Holy Rollers" because they would speak in tongues and dance and clap hands and occasionally roll on the floor. They were serious about their religion. The girls were not above flirting or even necking but couldn't wear makeup and of course wanted to share their religion with us.

There were a couple of these girls that we were interested in and who were interested in us. They asked us to attend their church with them and both Charley and I were raised Baptist, albeit northern Baptist, so how different could it be? We accepted. I remember some of the members speaking in tongues and others interpreting what they were saying. After this went on for a while and we were still there and hadn't run out the door, they asked us all to kneel down on the floor facing the pews we were sitting on as we all prayed. I didn't find this to be such an unusual request because that was how the Baptists did it at Wed. night prayer meetings. Unlike some churches that have kneeling pads that fold down in front of you so you can face forward. Being good Baptist boys we closed our eyes as we knelt and assumed the praying position. I'm not sure that what we were praying for was proper, it probably had something to do with the girls that had brought us here. At any rate, after concluding whatever I was praying for, I opened my eyes to see if Charlie was still there and what to my surprise, not only was Charlie still present, there was no escape available. The entire congregation was gathered around us and was laying hands on us and praying for our salvation. I believe we finally convinced them that we were already saved and we probably had to promise not to touch their young ladies. I don't think we had anything to do with those girls after that or if we did, it wasn't memorable to me. Talk about having the hell scared out of you, literally speaking.

I had a cousin on my Mothers' side, June, who lived in Seattle. Seattle is just a hop and a skip from Tacoma. In fact the two cities share an airport. June was a little older than me by a few years, probably five so if I was 16 she was probably 21. I remember one time as a little tyke probably 5 or 6 years old, I was staying at her parents' house. Her Mother and my Mother were sisters and her Dad was the minister of the Evangelical United Brethren Church in Martin, ND at the time. June was still living at home and was probably 10 or 11 . Her brother, Bill was the same age as I or a year older and we could always find some trouble to get into. Bill and I went to the playground and were playing on the merry-go-round. Another kid that Bill knew showed up but Bill didn't like him because he was a bully. Well, because there were two of us and only one of him, we wouldn't be bullied and we were soon fighting. As I remember it, we were getting the best of him until he threw his cap gun at me and hit me in the head on the right eyebrow. I still have the scar. As head wounds often do, it bled profusely. I started crying and with the blood running down my face ran to Bill's home. My cousin June was there and after we told her what had happened she took off like a wet hen after the kid that hit me with his cap gun. After that she was my hero.

Meanwhile, back in Tacoma, I mentioned to Gary and Charlie that I had a cousin living in Seattle that was an airline stewardess. I had them with stewardess. According to our reasoning, one airline stewardess equaled many of them. So I called June and we set up a time for me to visit her and of course to bring my buddies

This Dummy Pulls His Own Strings

along. Not having any transportation, we hitchhiked. I think June lived with two other stewardesses at the time we visited her. She was a very gracious hostess and even gave us a beer. She asked us if we wanted to go for a ride and of course we accepted and she drove us around showing us the area in her convertible. We had her drop us off on the highway so we could hitchhike home but before we parted she mentioned that she and her two girlfriends were going to Portland for the Rose Parade and asked if we wanted to go along. We, of course, jumped at the chance. What a boost to our ego. Three older girls who happened to be stewardesses and drove a convertible and could buy and drink beer had asked us on a road trip. What a dream come true.

Well the time came for the trip but of course we had to hitchhike to Seattle to catch our ride. When it was time to leave, somehow us three guys ended up in the back seat and the three girls in the front seat. Not quite what we envisioned but oh well, don't push it. June and her friends were planning to stay with another cousin of ours in Portland. When we got to Portland, they asked where we would like to be dropped off. Obviously we hadn't thought this through and had no place to stay so we told them anywhere would be fine. June gave us a phone number to call her, so we could make arrangements to meet to return to Seattle in a couple days.

We got out along the four lane highway and when they were out of sight crossed the median to the lanes going back from whence we came and started hitchhiking back to Tacoma. It wasn't long before the cops went by and told us over their bullhorn that hitchhiking was against the law. Duh, everyone knows that but still does it. We waited until they were out of sight and then resumed hitchhiking. It wasn't too long before the cops were back and this time they stopped and had us get into their squad car. We told them exactly what had happened to us and they said they were taking us into custody but if our story checked out they would let us go.

They assumed we were vagrants that were robbing businesses in the area. They put us all in the same jail cell, locked it and got the phone number to call June and left us to talk amongst ourselves. We imagined they were listening to everything we said with some hidden microphone in the cell. We alternated between cussing them out for picking us up and reiterating our story which was the truth.

After what seemed like forever, they told us that our story checked out but that they were going to release us in to the custody of my cousin that lived in Portland, I believe his name was Wallace Hornberger. He was a really nice guy and did all he could for us. I had never met the guy but he came and got us out of jail and asked us where we would like to go. He said we could stay at his place but he was full up with June and her friends so we told him to just take us back out to the highway and drop us off and we would hitchhike back to Tacoma. We also bummed some cigarettes from him. I even remember what brand he smoked, parliament, with recessed filters.

Well, it turned out that section of road was well patrolled and before long some police came by. By this time it was dark and they told us over the bull horn that it was illegal to hitchhike at night on a freeway. We thought we best not ignore them because we had already been down that road and ended up in jail. Luckily we were experienced at climbing tall chain link fences so we climbed the fence and landed in someone's back yard. We lay down in the grass and tried to get some sleep thinking that we would try hitchhiking when it got light out. It gets very cold at night in Portland and we didn't have any sleeping bags or for that matter even a change of clothes, just what was on our backs which wasn't much.

We did survive the night and climbed back over the fence and resumed hitchhiking. It was a bad location to hitchhike from because cars were going too fast to stop suddenly to pick you up. Being older and wiser (?) we should have walked to an on ramp where traffic was slower and we would have had a better chance of getting a ride. It wasn't long before a sheriff's patrol came by and stopped and had us all get in the car. Again we told them our story, even that we had already been in jail, and again they hauled us into jail but this time the county jail. Again they called June. I am sure she had been out on the town the night before and this was early in the morning so she couldn't have been too happy with us. They made her come down town and buy us all bus tickets back to Tacoma. Again, June is my hero. We didn't see June the rest of the summer. She still speaks to me but I doubt if she would rescue me either from a bully or my own stupidity again.

The year was 1958 and at this point in time, God hadn't invented automatic pin setters for bowling allies. There were racks above where the bowling pins set that someone had to place the bowling pins into and pull a lever that would cause a bar to sweep any pins that were laying down to a pit in the rear and lower the rack with the pins in the proper position. The pins would set where the rack left them and rise up above the ally so the bowlers could throw their ball down the alley and try to knock down the pins. The pinsetter (we) would then pick up the pins and put them in the empty positions in the rack and pick up the bowling ball and place it in the ball return. It was a good source of income for cigarettes. I don't remember what we got paid, it wasn't much but it kept us occupied and it wasn't hard work. Each pin setter could usually handle two lanes at a time and often times, if we did a good job, would get a tip from the bowlers. Sometimes they would even put a dollar bill in one of the finger holes in the bowling ball and roll it down the alley to us. The tip often depended more on how drunk the bowler was than how efficient we were.

After we had been at Gary's for a while, it was obvious to the most casual observer that we were costing them dearly in groceries. These weren't rich folk, even though they had a nearly new Lincoln in their garage. They were working middle class with a Dad that was the bread winner and a stay at home mom, as most moms were at this time in history. We weren't ready to go home yet so Charlie decided to go stay with Gary's friend Dewey. I think Dewey's good looking, well built sister was more of a motivator than budget concerns. Just one man's opinion. Anyway, this lasted for a time until we decided to go to Charlie's Aunt, Uncle & cousin across town in Tacoma. His cousin was about our age or a year or two older and he had a car. I think it was a 1949 Plymouth but I could be wrong about both. His Dad had a Kaiser that was probably about a 1956 if they still made them then. His Mom was a sister to Charlie's Mom and like Charlie's parents, were really nice people. Roger took us around the area in his car sightseeing. We went to Mt. Ranier and climbed farther up than tourists were allowed to. We used our shoes to ski down on the snow. We also went to the Ocean. I don't think we stayed with them long before we decided it was time to start for home again so we would be home in time for school.

It was about 50 years ago so I'm not certain how it all came about but I know that Gary's Dad, Dean, had told us we should catch a freight train when we went home instead of hitchhiking. I think he had ridden the rails when he was younger. I don't remember if that is what we set out to do or if it happened by accident. I believe we started hitchhiking and we were standing along the road, not getting anywhere and we could see the railroad tracks and freight cars from where we were standing and we decided to go check it out. This could all be a figment of my imagination but somehow we got to the railway.

The other bums were very friendly and tried to help us out. This was an acceptable mode of travel for many, especially for the generation that lived through the depression. People were out of work with no money for food or other necessities like coal for heat. Rather than let your family starve and freeze, the men would go to wherever they thought or heard there was some work and then send money home to their family. Because they didn't have any money to buy bus or train tickets to get to their destination, they would hop on an empty box car on a freight train. These were not lazy people looking for a handout. They were down on their luck and willing to work at any job for a meal or some money to send home to their family so their family could also eat. In the autobiography of John Dempsey, the world boxing champion, he tells of riding on the rods underneath the rail cars during the depression. I believe they were brake rods. I would guess this would be a lot more dangerous and uncomfortable than riding in a boxcar.

This Dummy Pulls His Own Strings

Back at the railroad yard, one bum told us to find a wine bottle with a screw on cap and fill it with water at the depot so we wouldn't get dehydrated riding in a boxcar. He said sometimes the freight trains get sidetracked to let the passenger trains go through and you didn't know how long it would be before you got to the next source of water. Also, some towns that the freight trains stopped at had what were referred to as "Bulls" whose job was to clear the freight train of any bums. Some were armed with pistols and would use them if you didn't listen to them and evacuate railroad property. The other bums warned us about the railroad bulls (cops) and where they were friendly and where they would take a shot at you. They gave us tips on how to get on and off a moving train. This was useful knowledge because where and when the bulls were strict, you didn't want to get on the train until it was moving. Periodically the bulls would walk along a stopped train and check all the empty box cars for bums and chase them away. If you got on a stopped train, stay hidden.

Some of the bums had been doing this for a long time and were friendly with the train people (agents) who would tell them where empty boxcars were headed and what the identification numbers were of these box cars. They helped us find a boxcar that was going a long way rather than being sidetracked. The bums said we should find cardboard to put on the floor because many of the boxcars had been used for hauling coal and were very dirty from coal dust. The thing I appreciated most and remember is that they would smoke their cigarettes down about halfway and then give them to us. Like people everywhere, they were kind and compassionate and would look out for us, except for a few bad apples. I guess we were bums in training or intern bums would be a more dignified term. Even bums need to have dignity.

I met quite a few bums and most of them were friendly and helpful. There was only one that I remember that I was leery of and maybe even a little scared of. He was from Chicago and he wanted me to partner up with him and go to Chicago to "roll drunks" for a living. He said you could make a decent living doing that. First of all, in my experience, drunks usually spend all their money on booze and B, isn't that stealing and dishonest? I wasn't convinced that was a good occupation or that he was a good partner, look at his mode of transportation and how he was living. He also had a hand gun which is why I was a bit frightened of him. I explained to him that I already had a partner in crime and we had to get home so we could go back to high school and finish our education. I think perhaps he might have been a little afraid of Charlie because he never approached him with his offer and he let it go after I explained that we were traveling companions.

Wherever it was that we hopped the freight, I know that it was west of the Rockies. I believe it was the first night on the train we went through the mountains. Actually we were side tracked and stopped in the mountains while passenger trains went through. Of course both doors were open on the boxcar we were in and even though we had our sleeping bags to curl up in, it was freezing cold. Our sleeping bags were of the summer time variety, light and not very warm. I had observed some box cars with large sheets of thick steel on the floor and remnants of what appeared to be a camp fire on the steel sheet. I had assumed that bums had used the fire to cook a meal but after a night in the mountains, it was clear to me it was used to keep warm. We survived the night and in the morning it was pleasant to sit in the doorway of the boxcar with your feet dangling and watch the mountain scenery. Freight trains don't seem to go that fast, especially in the mountains. We would get side tracked periodically to let a passenger train pass or even another freight train going the opposite direction.

There wasn't a lot of entertainment in those days before the cell phones, blackberries, I pods, tablets, laptops and internet. We only had conversation and our imaginations. When we were hitchhiking along the road and couldn't get a ride we would throw rocks at telephone poles and have contests. We got pretty good at it by the time we got to our destination. We probably could have conquered an armor clad giant just throwing rocks, unlike David who had a slingshot. In a boxcar, that form of entertainment wasn't available so it was smoke, eat, talk, sing or sleep. We didn't have any cigarettes or food so we mostly talked or slept.

This Dummy Pulls His Own Strings

One morning I woke up and there was an empty peanut butter jar lying where another bum had been. He must have eaten and left while we were sleeping. We'd been on the road for several days with no food so we were pretty hungry. This was probably our first experience with real hunger. I retrieved the peanut butter jar as quietly as I could. Charley was sleeping so peacefully, I didn't want to disturb him. You know how hard it is to clean out a peanut butter jar. There always seems to be a little left. The time of day was dawn and there was very little light. I didn't have any method of cleaning out the peanut butter other than using my finger so I proceeded to clean it out with my finger and lick my finger. The best peanut butter I ever had. Now if I had been devious and didn't want Charlie to discover what I had done, found food and ate it all while I let him sleep, I would have thrown the empty peanut butter jar out and got rid of the evidence. Either I didn't think of it or I thought I was being kind by letting him sleep. When Charlie woke up and discovered the empty peanut butter jar licked clean, he accused me of eating it all and not waking him to share it with him. Of course, I denied it until he pointed out that I had one perfectly clean finger while the rest were totally black. Evidently, the box car we were in was previously used to haul coal at one point, so eventually we also turned black. I really should have been more thoughtful and sharing but I guess my true colors were showing. Charlie swears had the situation been reversed, he would have woken me and shared but he hasn't had the opportunity to prove that. Now, had it been his brother Mike, I have no doubt he would have shared it with me and probably gave me the whole thing and claimed he didn't like peanut butter. He was always giving away our last cigarette, beer or whatever he had that someone else wanted. He was a generous, sharing, caring soul. Not to say that Charlie wasn't generous, sharing and caring, it wasn't quite as obvious as it was with Mike.

I don't remember how many days we were on the freight train but it was long enough to get very hungry and nicotine deprived. We had thought about getting off at Williston, ND and going to my sisters to eat but one of the bums had told us the railroad bulls (cops) were quite aggressive and mean at Williston and you should stay out of sight there. We took that advice, stayed on the train and after a few hours more were in Minot, ND. We got off the train there and walked several miles to Charley's sister, Charlane. I'm sure she didn't want to even let us in the house. We were black from head to toe from the coal dust. She welcomed us and introduced us to her shower and washed our clothes and made us soup to start. After not eating for however many days it was, she cautioned us about taking it slow. We finally satisfied our hunger and were cleaned up. I think we spent the night in Minot and hitchhiked the final 50 miles home the next day. Thus ended our adventure.

We didn't do a lot of hitchhiking or rail riding after this adventure but it was always an option if no other transportation was available. After all we were seasoned hitchhikers and bums. We didn't let the lack of transportation or the price of a bus or train ticket stop us from getting to where we wanted to be. One time I bought a plane ticket to try to make it for a date with my future wife and I hitchhiked the last 50 miles from the airport to home because the bus had already left. I missed that date but a dozen long stem roses did the trick of buying forgiveness.

Hobos

A hobo is a migratory worker or homeless vagabond, especially one who is penniless. By this definition, Charley and I could be considered hobos. We did pick fruit in Washington, however we were not homeless either in Washington or in North Dakota but we were pretty much penniless.

Hobos are itinerant workers, unlike tramps, who work only when they are forced to and bums, who don't work at all. By this definition, I would say we are more qualified as tramps.

It is not known when hobos first appeared on the American railroading scene. It is known that after the Civil War in the 1860s, many discharged veterans returning home began hopping freight trains. In the late 19th century, many followed the railroads west aboard freight trains looking for work or fortune.

The term hobo and how it originated is not clear and there are several language experts who have theories of it's origin. Author Todd DePastino has suggested it may derive from the term hoe-boy meaning farmhand or come from a greeting such as Ho, boy. Bill Bryson in Made In America (1998) suggests it could either come from the railroad greeting, "Ho, beau!" or a syllabic abbreviation of "homeward bound". It could also come from the words "homeless boy".

Life as a hobo, tramp or bum was dangerous. Besides being itinerant, penniless and homeless, there was the hostility of the train crews and the railroad security staff, nicknamed bulls, who often had a reputation for violence against trespassers. Just catching a moving train and riding on a freight train is dangerous. W.H. Davies, author of The Autobiography of a Super-Tramp, lost a foot when he fell under the wheels when trying to jump aboard a train. Having caught a moving train, I can understand how that could easily happen. We were schooled by other tramps to reach for the metal door latch on an open box car. Grab that metal latch while running alongside the slow moving train. Once you had a solid hold on the door latch, use your arms to lift your feet up and swing them into the box car. Once you have your feet and your lower body in the box car, you can release the door latch and roll into the box car fully.

You may wonder why you would try to catch a moving train rather than board when it is setting still. There are several answers to that. If the train is moving when you board, there is less chance a bull will be able to evict you. They can call ahead to the next town or stop and have you evicted but chances are slim of that happening. Another reason for catching and boarding a moving freight train is that sometimes they don't stop but just slow down for the towns. Now when you are traveling with a sports bag, a wine bottle of water, and a sleeping bag as we were, if boarding a moving train, you must throw your belongings into the box car and then be sure to board that car if you don't want to be separated from them. In our case, there were two of us traveling together so we had to make sure we both were able to board the same box car or we would have been separated. Once one of us had successfully boarded, that person could assist the other one in boarding. Also, if there were other tramps already aboard the box car and you were having difficulty, they would assist you. If the train got moving too fast for the second person to board, it was probably moving too fast for the one that had boarded to jump off. We never encountered that problem. The train usually went slow for quite a distance as anybody who has waited for a freight train at a railroad crossing knows.

Sometimes de-training a moving train can also be dangerous. The danger comes more from falling from the forward momentum and breaking bones. We became pretty good at jumping from a moving train with no major injuries. It is also possible to freeze to death in inclement weather aboard a boxcar. Sometimes, there was a sheet of steel that was quite large on the floor of the boxcar and a camp fire could be built on this sheet of steel with wood sticks/logs to keep warm. Of course if the bulls or other railroad officials saw smoke coming out of the boxcar, you would be evicted and the fire put out. This method was not used very much except in dire circumstances, possibly in a storm where the visibility was not good or perhaps in the mountains if you were side tracked for an extended period of time at night. I can tell you it gets very cold in the Rocky Mountains at night, in the fall, even with a sleeping bag. The greatest danger is not from your fellow travelers but from the bulls, accidents or weather.

There are varied reasons for riding the rails. One gentleman I spoke with had a formal education and a college master's degree as well as an extensive vocabulary. He was traveling and riding the rails to write a book about it. Little did I imagine that one day, I would also do that. Many were itinerant workers, following the harvest, from apples in Washington to the plains for the grain harvest. Another was going to visit his family and preferred it, as we did, to hitchhiking. They were all interesting and decent human beings. One tramp shared his knowledge and experience with us.

This Dummy Pulls His Own Strings

He preferred automobile carrier cars. He would find a unlocked car or break into one that was locked and ride in the comfort of soft seats, relatively speaking, and a more comfortable ride and a place to sleep. We never had the chance to try it. We also did not spend much time at hobo jungles where the hobos camp and build fires and cook, exchange stories, share knowledge and experiences. These were the camps the hobo stayed at when looking for work, food and to clean up. We weren't interested in any of that, work, food or cleaning up, we just wanted to get home.

We did spend some time at these jungles while waiting for the next train that could provide us a long haul ride. Some of the hobos were very experienced at riding the rails and knew some of the railroad workers. They knew who they could trust and who to stay away from. They would glean information from them as to which box car was going where and if it was due to be side tracked or was going straight through to its destination. This was very helpful in getting a long ride from point A to point B.

There was also a language and code of ethics in the society of tramps, hobos and bums. There is even an ethical code that was created by Tourist Union #63 during its 1889 National Hobo Convention in St. Louis, Missouri . This code was voted upon as a concrete set of laws to govern the Nation-wide Hobo Body. It read this way:

1. Decide your own life, don't let another person run or rule you.
2. When in town, always respect the local law and officials, and try to be a gentleman at all times.
3. Don't take advantage of someone who is in a vulnerable situation, locals or other hobos.
4. Always try to find work, even if temporary, and always seek out jobs nobody else wants. By doing so you not only help a business along, but ensure employment should you return to that town again.
5. When no employment is available, make your own work by using your added talents at crafts.

6. Do not allow yourself to become stupid drunk and set a bad example for locals' treatment of other hobos.
7. When jungling in town, respect handouts, do not wear them out, another hobo will be coming along who will need them as badly, if not worse than you.
8. Always respect nature, do not leave garbage where you are jungling.
9. If in a community jungle, always pitch in and help.
10. Try to stay clean and boil up wherever possible.
11. When traveling, ride your train respectfully, take no personal chances, cause no problems with the operating crew or host railroad, act like an extra crew member.
12. Do not cause problems in a train yard, another hobo will be coming along who will need passage through that yard.
13. Do not allow other hobos to molest children, expose all molesters to authorities, they are the worst garbage to infest any society.
14. Help all runaway children, and try to induce them to return home.
15. Help your fellow hobos whenever and wherever needed, you may need their help someday.

This code of ethics is good advice for everyone, not only hobos.

Some of the hobo words and the explanations:

Expressions used through 1940s

Hobo term	Explanation
Accommodation car	the caboose of a train
Angellina	a young inexperienced child
Bad Road	a train line rendered useless by some hobo's bad action or crime

Banjo	(1) a small portable frying pan; (2) a short, "D" handled shovel
Barnacle	a person who sticks to one job a year or more
Beachcomber	a hobo who hangs around docks or seaports
Big House	prison
Bindle stick	a collection of belongings wrapped in cloth and tied around a stick
Bindlestiff	a hobo who carries a bindle
Blowed-in-the-glass	a genuine, trustworthy individual
'Bo	the common way one hobo referred to another: "I met that 'Bo on the way to Bangor last spring."
Boil Up	specifically, to boil one's clothes to kill lice and their eggs; generally, to get oneself as clean as possible
Bone polisher	a mean dog
Bone orchard	a graveyard
Bull	a railroad officer
Bullets	beans
Buck	a Catholic priest good for a dollar
Burger	today's lunch
C, H, and D	indicates an individual is Cold, Hungry, and Dry (thirsty)
California blankets	newspapers, intended to be used for bedding on a park bench
Calling in	using another's campfire to warm up or cook
Cannonball	a fast train
Carrying the banner	keeping in constant motion so as to avoid being picked up for loitering or to keep from freezing

Dwight E. Knuth

Catch the Westbound	to die
Chuck a dummy	pretend to faint
Cover with the moon	sleep out in the open
Colt Freese	one who rummages for discarded food at restaurants before his meal
Cow crate	a railroad stock car
Crumbs	lice
Docandoberry	anything that grows on the side of a river that's edible
Doggin' it	traveling by bus, especially on the Greyhound bus line
Easy mark	a hobo sign or mark that identifies a person or place where one can get food and a place to stay overnight
Elevated	under the influence of drugs or alcohol
Flip	to board a moving train
Flop	a place to sleep, by extension, "Flophouse", a cheap hotel
Glad rags	one's best clothes
Graybacks	Lice
Grease the track	to be run over by a train
Gump	a chicken[9]
Honey dipping	working with a shovel in the sewer
Hot	(1) a fugitive hobo; (2) a decent meal: "I could use three hots and a flop"
Hot Shot	a train with priority freight, stops rarely, goes faster; synonym for "Cannonball"
Jungle	an area off a railroad where hobos camp and congregate
Jungle buzzard	a hobo or tramp who preys on his own
Knowledge bus	a school bus used for shelter
Maeve	a young hobo usually a girl
Main drag	the busiest road in a town

Moniker / Monica	a <u>nickname</u>
Mulligan	a type of <u>community stew</u>, created by several hobos combining whatever food they have or can collect
Nickel note	a five-dollar bill
On the fly	jumping a moving train
Padding the hoof	to travel by foot
Possum belly	to ride on the roof of a <u>passenger car</u> (one must lie flat, on his/her stomach, to avoid being blown off)
Pullman	a railroad sleeper car; most were made by George Pullman company
Punk	any young kid
Reefer	a compression of "<u>refrigerator car</u>"
Road kid	a young hobo who apprentices himself to an older hobo in order to learn the ways of the road
Road stake	the small amount of money a hobo may have in case of an emergency
Rum dum	a drunkard
Sky pilot	a preacher or minister
Soup bowl	a place to get soup, bread and drinks
Snipes	cigarette butts "sniped" (e.g., in ashtrays)
Spare biscuits	looking for food in garbage cans (also see "Colt Freese", above)
Stemming	panhandling or begging along the streets
Tokay blanket	drinking alcohol to stay warm
Yegg	a traveling professional thief, or burglar

Dwight E. Knuth

Hobo (sign) code

To cope with the difficulty of hobo life, hobos developed a system of symbols, or a code. Hobos would write this code with chalk or coal to provide directions, information, and warnings to other hobos. Some signs included "turn right here", "beware of hostile railroad police", "dangerous dog", "food available here", and so on. For instance:

- A cross signifies "angel food", that is, food served to the hobos after a sermon.
- A triangle with hands signifies that the homeowner has a gun.[10]
- A horizontal zigzag signifies a barking dog.[11]
- A square missing its top line signifies it is safe to camp in that location.
- A top hat and a triangle signify wealth.
- A spearhead signifies a warning to defend oneself.
- A circle with two parallel arrows means get out fast, as hobos are not welcome in the area.[11]
- Two interlocked circles signify handcuffs (i.e., hobos are hauled off to jail).
- A caduceus symbol signifies the house has a doctor living in it.
- A cross with a smiley face in one of the corners means the doctor at this office will treat hobos free of charge.
- A cat signifies a kind lady lives here.[11]
- A wavy line (signifying water) above an X means fresh water and a campsite.
- Three diagonal lines mean it's not a safe place.
- A square with a slanted roof (signifying a house) with an X through it means that the house has already been "burned" or "tricked" by another hobo and is not a trusting house.
- Two shovels, signifying work was available (shovels, because most hobos performed manual labor).

This Dummy Pulls His Own Strings

As a child, living on the last street on the west side of town and only about two blocks from the railroad tracks and about three to four blocks from the hobo jungle, we often had hobos stop at our house looking for work or a meal. If my father was home, they usually got something to eat at the very least. Sometimes he might even give them a job to do in exchange for a meal. If Dad wasn't home, my mother would turn them away. I can remember them making chalk marks on our steps or foundation to signal other hobos if they were successful or not. Of course, they did this when they thought no one was watching.

I remember my parents talking about the hobos, who they referred to as bums, coming to our farm and stealing eggs from the hen house. They would eat them raw. They would sometimes crawl into a straw pile to stay warm and sleep. Of course when they raided the hen house, they had to do it carefully so they didn't rouse or excite the chickens because then Dad would think there was an animal predator in the hen house and go out with the shotgun to shoot it. I imagine the hobos sometimes stole a chicken and took it back to the jungle to cook and eat. The reality of life is not everyone goes by ethics and codes especially when you are starving. Survival of the fittest.

14
Education

The less I learn the less I have to remember.

The more I learn, the more evident my ignorance is.

Better to remain silent and be thought a fool then to speak up and remove all doubt.

Never have a battle of wits with an unarmed person.

Education is not the learning of facts but the training of the mind to think.
Albert Einstein

All of the above were something I lived by at one time in my life. The first one "The less I learn, the less I have to remember", was my motto in high school and was printed as such in our class year book.

After high school and before, during and after college, the second one, "the more I learn, the more evident my ignorance is" became apparent to me.

The third one, "better to remain silent and be thought a fool then to speak up and remove all doubt", was one I adopted and lived by after witnessing many fools in workplace meetings. Most of them were trying to impress the meeting attendees but only succeeded in the opposite.

The fourth one, "Never have a battle of wits with an unarmed person", is obvious. Neither of you will gain anything and it is part of your life you will never get back.

I documented my education through high school in the chapter, my hometown. I documented my education in the military in the chapter, Army and Navy.

This chapter is more about my college education after high school.

Education is a lifelong pursuit and is never complete as long as we are breathing. In the world we live in, there is a wealth of information and education is at our finger tips via the internet. Our memory is not extensive enough or trained enough to retain all the information we can and do acquire. Now it is a simple matter to access anything that has "slipped" our minds. I've struggled with information overload all my life probably because I didn't train my mind to catalog information and facts. I would keep several physical file cabinets full of data that was printed, in my office, so I didn't need to remember it but could access it, if I could find it. I probably spent more time searching files for information than I spent in productive work. Even using the computer as a file cabinet was inefficient in the early days of computers because the search engines for finding the data had not been written. Now we have Google and Bing and I'm sure more to come on the scene in the near future.

Eventually we may have memory "sticks" or memory add on for our brains that can be accessed just by our thought processes because keying in a word for a search process is too slow and too much work. This should not be too much of a stretch of the imagination when you consider the progress made in recent years.

I guess my age is showing and I'm of the old school where you say what you mean and mean what you say. I'm not fond of the texting craze where you communicate using the first letter of the word (LOL) and abbreviations. If you're too busy to tell me what you mean then perhaps you shouldn't be telling me. BFF can be interpreted in several ways. What do you really mean? Perhaps it means you can't spell what you're thinking. There is enough miss-communication without adding to it. If it isn't important enough to be accurate in communicating, then perhaps it is not important enough to communicate. I don't need to know every action, thought and deed or miss-deed you have or do in the day. I have my own life, you have yours, let's each live ours and share the highs and lows. Communication is a wonderful thing and is the key to understanding but can also lead to miss-understanding if not done properly. It seems that in texting, punctuation is seldom if ever used. Punctuation can change the whole meaning of a sentence, so lack of it is another opportunity for mis-communication. Perhaps it's just me and I'm too lazy or lacking brain function to learn a new language called texting. Someday we may switch the official language from English to Texting. Until then, I will continue to resist change.

On to my formal education. This is where my sister, Verla, entered the picture. She also wanted a better life for me than the day to day struggle of construction work. For you construction workers, this is not a put down to your job or career. It just isn't my cup of tea. I did it long enough to know that I am too lazy for the hard work and suffering in the heat, cold and weather that construction work requires sometimes. Verla was a teacher so valued education. She saw an ad in the local newspaper for computer oriented jobs and thought perhaps this was the way to the future and a good career choice. She called them and set up an appointment with them for me. I was skeptical because I didn't have a college education at this point but agreed to go to the interview. They gave me aptitude tests, the results of which said I had a strong aptitude for computer programming. Basically, I was a logical thinker.

This turned out not to be a job interview as much as a school recruitment for a computer school in Des Moines, Iowa known as The College of Automation. By this time I felt I was ready for college and would probably apply myself and take it seriously. I wanted a decent paying job and work I enjoyed. Because I had scored high on the aptitude tests, they would accept me at this school and teach me all about IBM computers which was the newest occupation. I had decided back in high school that I would probably like to do accounting work. It seemed logical to me that the use of computers would probably be the future of accounting. I decided to give it a try and used some of my construction money along with a loan from my parents to pursue it.

There was a small problem in that I belonged to the North Dakota Army National Guard which required that I attend weekly meetings either in Williston, ND or Harvey, ND. I talked to the Guard officers and learned that I could get a honorable discharge from the North Dakota National Guards to join the Iowa National Guards while I was going to school. When school was finished I could get an honorable discharge from the Iowa National Guards to join the Guards in whatever state I would be going to next. It sounded good to me and I would be getting a paycheck I would need to survive while going to school. I believe the school was either three months or six months, something I thought I could survive and not long enough to waste too much time if it wasn't for me. Also, I shouldn't build up a mountain of debt for such a short period.

My car was not very reliable and the transmission was leaking fluid so I took the train to Iowa. The school had set me up in a rooming house in Des Moines within walking distance of the school. The rooming house was just that, a room with a bed and a desk for studying. No meals were provided so I would have to eat out or buy snacks to survive on. There were a couple of other kids from North Dakota staying there and attending the same school as I was. It didn't take us long to become friends and discuss our living arrangements. As always, everyone seems to want to better their daily living and we began to discuss our options. One of the guys, Art, was a bit older than us and had just been discharged from the Navy so had more life experience than Bob and I. We discussed the option of renting an apartment, splitting the cost and doing our own cooking. Of course we talked about this option with other students going to the same school and found that many of them were doing this already.

Dwight E. Knuth

    Bob had a car so that meant there would be a vehicle to do our grocery shopping. Bob also agreed to let me use his car to attend guard meetings. We decided to look for an apartment and succeeded in finding one within walking distance to school. It was a small one bedroom efficiency apartment with a cot in the living room and a double bed in the bedroom. Having only one bedroom and a cot meant that two of us would have to sleep in the same bed. Art, being the oldest, declared the cot was his. That meant Bob and I had to share the double bed. This didn't bother either of us and we never gave it a second thought. As a teenager I had often slept over at one of my friends home and we would all sleep in the same bed sometimes as many as three or four in one bed. Usually we were so tired we were asleep before our heads hit the mattress. I say the mattress because there weren't always enough pillows. Back then, alternate life styles were not common or talked about. When someone referred to someone as being Gay, they generally meant happy. So, Bob and I didn't have a problem with it. The biggest problem we had with the sleeping arrangement was that directly above our bedroom, in the upstairs apartment, was a young married couple. They sometimes made so much noise in their bedroom that we thought the bed would come through the ceiling. When that would happen, we would get the broom and bang on the ceiling with the handle. That would usually cool their jets and allow us to get to sleep.

    The apartment had a small kitchen with all the appliances. The living room even had a TV set, albeit a black and white TV. I don't believe God had created color TV at this time in history. We had a kitchen table we could use as a desk for studying. Might as well get some use out of the kitchen table. We generally were too broke to eat on it. We ate a lot of potatoes and pancakes. The kitchen table served the purpose quite nicely for studying and we had the advantage of studying together so if one of us was struggling with something, we had our buddies to help us.

    None of us excelled in school but we all accumulated some knowledge and probably were about in the middle of the class.

This Dummy Pulls His Own Strings

We all graduated and were confident in our knowledge that we could be gainfully employed.

Upon graduation we headed back to our respective homes to pursue employment in our new field. North Dakota in the 1960's was not a hub of employment especially in the area of computers or automation. I applied with the state job service and read the want ads in the newspapers. After having no luck in my new field of employment, I lowered my expectations to any job in any field available. I would get some interviews but I was still in the National Guards and it seemed to me that whenever they learned that I was a member of the Guards, they lost interest and the interview was pretty much over. If you were in the Guards, your employer had to let you take two weeks off every summer for Guard camp. There were a lot of crisis that the Guard units were called to active duty for, such as The Berlin Crises and others. It was against the law to refuse employment or terminate an employee because of their membership in the Guards but they could always find another reason.

A guy can only drink so much beer and sleep until noon everyday before you run out of money. Some of my friends who were also unemployed and seeking beer money thought it might be an interesting experience to talk to a Navy Recruiter. These friends were Charles and Mike Toy, Emery Suckert and Bruce Bruner. We all headed to Minot and talked to the Navy recruiter. We learned that my four friends could all join the Navy under the Buddy plan and go through Boot Camp together. Because I was already a member of the National Guard and had gone through Basic Training in the Army and served six months of active duty, I was considered "Prior Service" and would go to a special Boot Camp that focused on the difference between the other services and the Navy. It was a much easier Boot Camp because I had already had my share of hollering at, degradation, insults, raging drill instructors and brain washing.

Navy also gave us aptitude and intelligence tests and determined that we could be trained as military fighting machines. My desire was to go into the computer accounting field and the

Navy guaranteed that if I would give them four years of my life, they in turn would train me as a machine accountant, providing I could be cleared for a secret clearance. We all honored their offer and signed on the dotted line. Of course we all had to pass a physical to be accepted.

We all partied hearty with going away parties over and over but didn't have a solid date for leaving. Finally we learned there was some hold up with Mike Toy's enlistment. It was decided that Charles, Emery and Bruce would go on ahead under the buddy plan and I would wait for Mike to be cleared. Mike and I would not be together in Boot Camp because I would be in a prior service company and Mike would be in regular Boot Camp. Mike was OK with this. He easily made friends and wasn't nervous about being alone. I was used to the military and knew the procedures and what to expect so was not nervous about it either.

After many more parties and much more beer consumed we finally learned that Mike did not pass his physical because of a punctured ear drum. This gave me the go ahead to leave for Boot Camp. Compared to the Army, Boot Camp was a breeze and I was again receiving a pay check.

At the conclusion of Boot Camp, when I was familiar with all the Navy knots, language, history, pride and service, I was assigned to PAMI CONUS (Personal Accounting Machine Installation Continental United States), Bainbridge, MD. There, I attended machine accountant school and graduated number one in my class with the highest grades ever to that point. It might have had something to do with the fact I had already been trained in machine accounting at the College of Automation in Iowa. I guess I did learn and retain something there. Sometimes while sitting in class, I felt like I could be teaching it. There was a time or two that the instructor was struggling with something or was not explaining it clearly that I tried to help out by adding my "two cents". I could have gotten that training free in the Navy instead of paying for it. However, I am not disappointed that I chose that path because without the prior school, I may not have been guaranteed it by the Navy. Always stack the deck in your favor.

This Dummy Pulls His Own Strings

The Navy gave me a well rounded education in computers and practical experience with computers so when I was discharged I felt I was ready for the civilian world of computers and all it had to offer.

North Dakota was still not a bastion of computer using businesses but I was offered a job at First National Bank of Grand Forks as a computer programmer. The bank used different computers than the Navy did but they were willing to train me in the language these computers communicated in. I eagerly accepted even though the pay was less than desirable. In fact it was nearly poverty level. Being a single person with a new car and not a lot of debt, I could survive with a room at the YMCA and eating my meals there.

When I went to work for Boise, I was going home to IBM computers. My Navy buddy, who got me the job interview, taught me the IBM Report Program Generator (RPG) language and then refreshed me in IBM Assembler Language. During my employment at Boise I learned Cobol language and PL1 (Program Language 1) which was a combination of Fortran and Cobol. After Jim left International Falls, I was the sole programmer who could write and read Assembler language. Being the only employee with a job skill gives you some measure of job security. You can't become too comfortable or demanding because they can always hire someone new to replace you. Assembler language was close to machine language (binary code of 1 and 0's) and could be broken down to machine language so the code could be tweaked in the testing process for varied results.

At one time, we were converting to Honeywell computers so we attended classes teaching us the language of the Honeywell computers, mainly Cobol. Cobol, like RPG is a business language whereas Fortran is a scientific language. Being the sole Assembler programmer, I was responsible for rewriting all the Assembler programs to Cobol. The Honeywell computer proved to be too slow compared to the IBM so we had to reverse the conversion of all programs and go back to the IBM languages.

When personal computers became available and most everyone in the office had one, the IT staff needed to be trained in the software that resided on them. In our case this was Microsoft and their schools. I was in charge of security so obviously attended their security software classes. Most of the schools I attended were in Minneapolis but I attended one class in New York City for a week.

Education is an ongoing lifelong journey. As long as there is change, education is mandatory. The only thing constant is change so education will never end.

While working at Boise, now Office Max, I attended our local Junior College, Rainy River Junior College, under the GI bill. I was working full time, sometimes overtime, married with young children, and taking a full load of college classes. I also was the treasurer for our church and for the Northland Activity center, a non-profit for mentally challenged children. I was on the Dean's list several quarters while attending junior college, so I was also spending time hitting the books. Some of the classes were difficult and others very enjoyable. I especially liked the literature classes and English classes. Creative Writing was one of my favorites. However, I was burning the candle on both ends and when the GI bill ran out for me, I stopped my formal education before graduation.

For my descendants that are looking for advice on pursuing your education, any education you pursue, however you pursue it can only be helpful to you. Knowledge is something no one can take from you unless you become a drug addict and kill your brain cells. Education can be obtained by different methods. There is the formal education that is force fed to you. Not everyone learns well by this method but if you can learn by this method and have the resources for it, I say go for it. There are different ways of force feeding formal education. One is the traditional method by which you learn several subjects during the same time period. Another is the method where you study one subject at a time for a specified time and upon completion of that subject start a different one. My daughter, Kimberly, chose this method at Cornell College and got her degree and did well with her education. Another form of formal education is trade school where you learn about a trade you have an interest in. I attended the College of Automation which was a trade school that taught IBM unit record equipment and computers and computer programming. My son, Eric, chose this route also, graduating from an aviation mechanics trade school as an aircraft mechanic.

Other options are the military, all branches of the service have excellent schools in about anything that interests you. You can also get a formal college degree in the military at one of their academy's or in Officer Candidate School. As an enlisted person, you are eligible to receive tuition payments at the end of your enlistment to attend college.

On the job training is an excellent method to learn an occupation. Often times you are learning from someone with years of "real life" experience who can teach you far more about the occupation than any professor or school.

You can pursue knowledge on your own about anything that interests you. With computers and the internet, there is practically no end to the opportunities that exist for learning. You can do this independent of schools or use online schools.

Every day of life is an opportunity to learn and no day goes by that you don't learn something. Just remember to listen. When you're talking, you're not learning anything. Learning is enjoyable. Knowledge is exciting and amazing.

15

Retirement

I retired at the age of 58 because I could and because I wanted to. I was somewhat burned out at work and found it was more politics than the actual creative work I enjoyed. There were endless meetings on endless topics that went on for ever and ever and accomplished little or nothing. One example was an employee satisfaction survey conducted by an outside consulting firm. The survey was done by an outside consultant so the employees could answer honestly without anyone knowing how they viewed the organization so there wouldn't be any repercussions for stating their opinions.

It all sounds good on paper and in theory is probably a lofty goal to make employees happy and create a better work place and friendly environment. The problem was, when there was an area that was unfavorable in the survey, the employees would be called together to discuss it and try to correct it. Now any time you get two people together, chances are they are going to disagree on something. This was many more than two people and there was much disagreement. It would be discussed and then discussed some more until a committee would be assigned to analyze it and come up with a solution. More meetings of the committee and then the committee would submit their findings and recommendations to the employees and the discussions would start all over again.

It appeared to me that some employees just wanted to continue these discussions so they wouldn't have to go back to work. I got so exhausted and tired of these discussions that I learned when these surveys were taken to answer them as though I was 100% satisfied with the work place and environment so I could at least get some work done and hopefully avoid these endless and seemingly pointless meetings. It seems other employees felt the same as I did because future surveys had a much higher percentage of satisfaction and I don't think it was because of the solutions being implemented to make it a better work place. There was still just as much grumbling and as many disgruntled employees as before so the proof is in the pudding.

You are never going to please everyone all the time and just as there are employees that can not be managed, there are employees who seemingly are predisposed to be unhappy in their work just because that is their mindset. I used to be better able to tolerate some of these things but I suppose after 25 years, one does burn out.

I had often said and believed that if you don't like working for your boss, you should find a new boss rather than complain about it and make everyone else unhappy. Of course, just because you have a bad day or disagree with your assigned tasks, you shouldn't quit your job. If after trying to work out your differences, you find you are incompatible, pursue other interests. This I did and my new boss was my beautiful, smiling wife. A much improved work environment with great benefits. We still didn't always agree but it was much more enjoyable working out our differences.

I could have probably found employment, even at that age, but I didn't have the energy or inclination to pursue it and move to another location and start over so I chose retirement. I also could have stayed in my current position but I didn't have my heart in my work and as my parents taught me, any job worth doing, is worth doing well. If your heart is not in it, you will not do your job well.

After 16 years of retirement, I am satisfied with my decision and happy in my retirement. The sailing has not always been smooth or pleasant but that is the way life is. There are many things that we have no control over. We both had cancer. I was diagnosed first and it was prostate cancer. I was told it was slow growing and there were several options for treatment. My Father also had prostate cancer so I had some familiarity with it. I opted to take the bull by the horns, so to speak, and have it removed surgically. My hope was that by doing this, it would be gone and not have a chance to spread to other parts of my body.

On the very day Mayo Clinic called to tell me they considered me cancer free, my wife received a call from her Dr. telling her she had breast cancer. I guess God thought we could deal with one cancer at a time. She went through all the tests, biopsies, poking, prodding, pain and discomfort that you get with a treatment plan. She had a port surgically implanted so she could have the chemotherapy without an IV each time. They did chemotherapy, which was difficult both emotionally and physically but I thought she tolerated it quite well. The hardest part emotionally for her was losing her hair and going bald. She purchased some wigs and did well, I thought, making jokes and keeping a positive attitude through it all. She then had a mastectomy to remove the breast and elected not to have surgery to replace it.

After that surgery healed she had radiation daily, 5 days a week for months. For the radiation we had to drive 200 miles daily so our week days were consumed with just getting to and returning from radiation treatments in all kinds of winter weather. We had weekends off and they gave her a break at Christmas for two days. After radiation she was prescribed hormone therapy for five years. After five years they declared her cancer free and took her off of the hormone therapy.

Three years later she died of cancer. They diagnosed it as the return of her breast cancer which had invaded her liver and bones. It was at stage IV when they found it in July, 2014. She died in Sept. just a couple months after the diagnoses. When diagnosed she initially told her health care people she didn't want to fight it and go through all the tests, biopsies and false hope when the result was death anyway. They convinced her that by doing all those things they could give her up to two years more of life as opposed to six months if she did nothing.

They were wrong about the six months. They also promised her she would feel better and have a better quality of life. I told her I would support her in whatever she chose, that I selfishly would like to have her as long as possible but didn't want her to go through a lot of suffering. She chose to have the treatments to give her a better quality of life and extend it. That didn't happen as her body rejected the chemotherapy and made her very sick, uncomfortable and caused her much suffering. She was a person who believed in the power of prayer and I believe she was praying for her suffering to end.

She was a courageous person and was not afraid of death and I believe at the end she welcomed it. There was such peace in her face at death, a peace I had not seen in such a long time. Even in death, she was beautiful and as in life, she died with dignity and grace. I miss her beyond words.

Prior to Kathy being diagnosed with cancer, my daughter, Kimberly was living with us and was a big help both emotionally and physically. She thought she should have a place of her own and she looked for and found a house and purchased it. It was located right across the street from the house we first moved into and she lived in her first three years of her life. It was an older house that needed some repair which I said I could do. We remodeled the kitchen and I did some other repairs, painting and landscaping to make it more presentable, livable and modern. When Kathy was diagnosed with cancer it was a way for me to escape from reality and give myself a chance to restore my resolve and keep going. I felt guilty about leaving Kathy and escaping reality when there was no escape for her but she would insist that I do it and that it was good for me. Eventually, I completed the projects at the house enough so Kim could move in. I was still working on landscaping projects and painting the outside of the house.

Our son, Eric was having marital problems and went through a divorce. He had three children that it was very difficult for. The children always seem to be the ones that suffer greatest in a divorce but they are resilient and recover. Eric lost his job in the process and moved back home. I put him to work helping me with Kim's house. I should say, I helped him with Kim's house. There is nothing he couldn't do and do well and always could come up with a solution to the most difficult problem. We cleaned, scraped, primed and painted the siding. Eric installed some crown molding and we installed gutters and drainage as well as other projects. It was a joy going to work and spending the day working with Eric. Eventually Eric got a job as a guard at the Boise paper mill. That ended our working together but he was still living at home which was nice for his mother and I. Living so far from his kids, he naturally got lonesome and eventually returned to Minneapolis to be nearer his children.

Meanwhile our daughter, Kimberly had her own home and a very good job working from home and doing quite a lot of traveling. She had several boyfriends from time to time but I must have set the standard too high because none of them seemed good enough or right for her. I happened to agree with her. If you aren't going to be happy with any one of them, why put up with the hassle. She is smart enough to know the only person you can change is yourself. Her biological clock was running out on her and she wanted to have a baby. She looked into adoption but the process was long, uncertain and expensive so she started to look at other options. In our modern society, it doesn't take two people present to have a baby. They have things like sperm banks where you can purchase sperm from the father of your choosing who has the qualities you would like to see in your children. She made a choice and had her Dr. implant the sperm and yup, became pregnant. Kathy and I gave her our support for this undertaking and told her we would help her with the raising of the child.

As you are aware, pregnancy and childbirth is an emotional as well as physical roller coaster. For Kimberly the physical piece was the piece that created much emotional stress in the form of fear, not to mention the physical pain associated with her condition. Uterine fibroids are a noncancerous growth that can cause pelvic pressure, backache or leg pains. With a baby growing in your body competing for space, you don't need unnecessary growths.

This Dummy Pulls His Own Strings

They were discovered during an ultrasound and there were multiple fibroids. Other than taking up space, applying pressure and causing pain, they normally aren't associated with risk to the baby or mother. They do cause much discomfort and can be extremely painful. This being her first pregnancy, Kim had nothing to compare it to so she didn't know if a symptom was normal or not. She did have her mother and Dr. to glean information from.

Kim had chosen to have the birth in Duluth at St, Mary's hospital which is about a four hour drive from International Falls. This made me a little nervous as I did not relish the thought of her giving birth on the way to the hospital in the car. Sometimes these babies just appear when they want to. They may perceive birth as a hide and seek game, here I come, ready or not. In preparation of this happening, I packed the trunk of the car with cloth towels, paper towels, newspapers, bottled water and a good first aid kit. My boy scout training surfacing, be prepared.

When the due date came and passed, I wasn't all that concerned because her mother went a month past her due date for both her pregnancies. The Dr. said for some females, a ten month pregnancy is not uncommon. Nine months is just an average. Also the date of conception is not an exact science in most cases. I was sleeping with one ear on alert, waiting for the sound of the phone.

As it turned out, I was getting ready for bed somewhere around ten PM the evening of Feb. 19th, 2009 when the phone rang. It was Kim who informed me she thought the baby was on his way because her water broke and she was having contractions. Eric was still living with us and he informed us he was coming with us. I had been keeping the car gassed up and ready to go so it was just a matter of getting my medications, insulin, glucose meter etc. together and throwing a few things in a bag and off to Kim's house about 10 minutes away. We decided to have Eric drive because my night vision was not that good and my vision varies with my blood sugar level. We got Kim packed into the front seat, Kathy and I in the back and Eric behind the wheel and away we go. Kim had called St. Mary's and conferred with them and they confirmed that we definitely should come, post haste.

The trip to Duluth was uneventful but in spite of the hour no one was getting any sleep. Eric didn't drive fast enough to endanger anyone but he wasn't exactly following the speed limit and no one complained. I would imagine we arrived sometime between two and three AM. The contractions were still not that close together. Eric and I camped out in the lounge area while Kathy and Kim did what they could to speed the process along. I dozed on a very uncomfortable couch the rest of the night. There was no dozing for Kim and Kathy who were walking the halls and were much more uncomfortable than dozing on a couch. The process didn't seem to be progressing as it should be so they tried to induce labor which also didn't seem to help. Morning passed into afternoon and Jack was still refusing to make his entrance. He evidently has that independent stubborn Knuth gene that says, I pull my own strings, even if I'm not a dummy. When I'm ready, I'll make my appearance, until then back off.

Kim was in hard labor for what seemed to me hours. At one point, it appeared that the whole medical staff was in her room with her and Kathy. They wouldn't let Eric and I in the room and the Drs. and nurses would go in and out. I was standing in the hall right outside her room and would inquire of them to find out what was happening and if everything was OK. They assured me everything was fine but it was a difficult labor and birth. I could pretty much tell that from all the activity. It turns out that Jack had inherited the large Hoffman head that his grandmother, her siblings and their father had. This seemed to make it difficult for him to exit the womb despite all the help from the medical staff and his mother. I was concerned that they would have to do a C-section which could be risky with the fibroids. Finally at 5:33 PM on Feb. 20, 2009 Jack made his appearance into our world, a healthy baby weighing 9 lbs., 10 oz., 23 inches long with blue eyes and brown hair.

His grandmother, Kathy, was concerned that no one was paying attention to Jack so she stayed with him and kept him company while the medical staff helped Kim finish the process.

This Dummy Pulls His Own Strings

When I first saw Jack I was a little concerned because his head was somewhat odd shaped like a cone. What sort of alien did the sperm come from? Obviously, the head was too large to emerge so it had to be compressed to exit and thus the cone shape. This was a temporary thing and over time it reverted to the original round shape heads normally are. It obviously didn't affect Jack or do any damage to the brain. He is a remarkably intelligent little boy who absorbs knowledge like a sponge and shares that knowledge with me every day. He was reading at the ripe old age of five and doing math like simple addition, subtraction, multiplication and division. Of course, that shouldn't be a surprise to me because my other grandchildren were also cute and smart. I think God is making children smarter than when I was a child. Proof positive is my children and grandchildren.

After we returned home with Jack, Kim took some time off from work to be with Jack and to adjust to their new lifestyle. All of our lives were changed in that our focus was all about Jack as it is when a baby comes into your life. When Kim returned to work, she found a day care for Jack and we split the day up where he went to the day care in the AM and came to Grandpa and Grandmas in the PM. It was a pleasure and privilege to have the little guy and watch him grow and develop. Our other grandkids lived in different cities so we only got the privilege of being with them when we visited them or they visited us.

Every summer they would come to spend a couple weeks with us while their parents went back home to work. We could enjoy their presence, get reacquainted and build memories with them. They always had a long list of things we should do while they were here such as the Littlefork fair, swimming and picnicking at the beach, ice cream in Ranier, feeding the chipmunks at Sha Sha, building things in Grandpa's shop, playing hide and go seek, Frisbee, Bocce ball, crazy days, kick off, books and the list goes on. Usually we would accomplish most, if not all and would be happily exhausted when they left. They would also come with their parents for a few days to a week at Christmas, depending on their parents work schedules and again whenever they could.

We would visit them in their home whenever we could, so they were not strangers to us.

Sometime after Jack was eating real food and had graduated from baby food, we noticed he would get hives and rashes after eating. He sometimes would have difficulty breathing and would have to be taken to emergency where they would give him medication with a nebulizer. After a few of these trips, Kim took him to an allergy specialist in Duluth and found he was allergic to eggs, peanuts and mustard. He got his own nebulizer and was started on daily nebulizer treatments and more often when needed. This changed the way we did everything as far as preparing food and eating was concerned. We had to be aware and prevent cross contamination. If you buttered a piece of bread that had egg in it, you couldn't use the same knife or butter to butter Jack's bread which did not have egg in it. As a toddler we had to be sure he didn't pick up crumbs and put them in his mouth or accidently get a peanut or other candy or food that had been cross contaminated in the factory with eggs, peanuts or mustard.

It was a privilege and a joy to have Jack in our home daily and to care for him, share time, space and love with him. He was a very good child except when he had allergic reactions to something. I think much of the bad behavior we witness in children is the result of something physical that is just not right with them which causes them to act out. There are some spoiled brats but I believe they are the exception.

It was especially great for me to care for Jack because I didn't get to do that with my own children. I was off to work and often missed the firsts of their infancy and childhood such as their discoveries in this new world of theirs and their wonder and awe of life and God's creation. This sharing of life and the little discoveries is what life is all about. I refer to it as the sharing of Love. What prompted me to get married was that I wanted to share all these moments with the one I loved. When we were married I had a hard time leaving Kathy to go to work because I wanted to spend the whole day together with her and share space and time. It was

This Dummy Pulls His Own Strings

the same when my children were born. I had a hard time leaving them to go to work. I didn't want to miss all the fun. It was a little like my son Eric, when he was a toddler and wouldn't take a nap even though he was exhausted and would fall asleep pushing a car on the floor. We asked him why he didn't want to take a nap when he was so tired. He told us that he didn't want someone else to use up all the fun while he was sleeping. Now I could stay home with Jack and be the one using up all the fun.

When you are retired, people who are not, ask you what you do all day and how you keep busy and keep from getting bored or stay out of your spouse's way. Other spouses of newly retired, sometimes complain because the spouse is always around and underfoot. I tell people I do whatever I want and have never had a problem being bored. As for being underfoot, Kathy sometimes complained that she saw less of me after I retired than when I was working. I like to putz which in my definition is just go do something and in the process of doing that something, something else shows up that needs doing. So it goes, from one something to another something until the day is gone and you need to start making a list of somethings that need doing. I have lists of winter somethings, summer somethings, inside somethings, outside somethings, emergency somethings, a round tuit somethings, deadline somethings and new lists appear daily. I seldom look at these lists in fact most of the time, I can't even find them. Kathy would ask what my plans for the day were and I would tell her I plan to putz. She would respond with, "you old putz". So it goes.

So in response to those wondering what I do all day in retirement, I do something. The possibilities are endless. I do find that I have to balance my activities to control my blood sugar. Too much sitting, for example, writing my book, will cause elevated blood sugars, due to lack of exercise. Too much exercise will cause my blood sugar to drop and an insulin reaction. So it is a balancing struggle as is life in general. Balancing work, social activity, pleasure, exercise, education and other mental and physical activities is what we all do on a daily basis. Retirement is no different. My mantra is, all things in moderation.

After Kathy died, I regret that I did too much something and not enough nothing. I should have spent more time on the deck with her just drinking in her beauty, physical and intellectual and just enjoying time together. It's one of my few regrets in life. I do not now or have I ever regretted retiring at the young age of 58. If you can, I would recommend retirement as early as you can so you can spend more time with those you love.

We enjoyed some travel in our retirement. We took several trips to Hawaii which we both loved. A trip to Italy that I write about in the chapter, Closer to the Tuscan Sun. A trip to Mesa, AZ to see Kathy's sister and brother who wintered there. A trip to Philadelphia, PA, Atlantic City, NJ and Delaware for Kathy's nephews, Lee's wedding. A trip to Boise, ID to stay with our good friends, Dan and Joyce Einiechner. We took many trips to ND and MT to visit relatives in both states.

Many of these trips we flew Northwest airlines on standby because our son, Eric was an aircraft mechanic for them which gave us the opportunity to fly free with them anywhere they went. The catch was we had to fly standby which meant that if the plane wasn't full and there were seats available and the flight wasn't overweight, we could board and fly. Sometimes that meant sitting in the airport all day and sometimes we would even have to stay in the airport for two or three days before we got on a flight. It also meant that we flew according to the status of the employee. If a pilots parents wanted on the same flight as us, they would get the seats before we would. There was also a dress code that we had to adhere to. If you didn't have a schedule and had time to kill and didn't mind airport food, it was a cheap mode of travel. After spending a couple nights at a hotel, it might have been cheaper to buy a ticket.

When my aunt Elsie who lived in Drake, ND died, we elected to fly to Minot, standby, rent a car and drive to Drake for the funeral. From International Falls there is not a direct flight to Minot, ND. You must fly to Minneapolis and then to Minot. To get to Minneapolis, you sometimes have to take a flight that stops at Hibbing or Brainerd. We didn't have any difficulty getting on a flight in the Falls but when we got to Brainerd, we got bumped off the flight and sat around the airport most of the day until another flight later in the day came in which had seats for us.

However, the weather had gotten really foggy and they couldn't give that flight clearance to land until the fog lifted which it finally did, enough to land the plane. By the time they got the plane ready for takeoff again, the fog had returned so they wouldn't let it take off. I was looking into renting a car to drive to ND from Brainerd, MN but people that were coming into the airport said there were cars in the ditch all the way to the airport. It seems that the fog was also making the roads slippery so not only could you not see, you couldn't stay on the road. I gave that idea up pretty quickly.

We finally got clearance to take off and made it to Minneapolis. We caught a flight out of Minneapolis to Minot with no trouble. This was before the oil boom and how many people want to go to Minot in mid-winter. When we got to Minot, they wouldn't let us land because they also had fog. They talked about landing at Bismarck and busing us to Minot but for some reason that never materialized. Instead we circled Minot until we had just enough fuel left to get back to Minneapolis so that is where they took us. By this time it was the middle of the night and we didn't have enough time to get to Minot for the funeral so we just returned home.

I could bore you with many more standby flight stories as well as scary flying stories but will spare you the boring standby flight ones and only bore you with the scary ones. While I was still working, I spent a summer on a task force that required me to fly every weekend. I would fly out of the Falls on Sunday afternoon or Monday morning and return to the Falls on Friday evening or Saturday morning. Sometimes I was flying to the west coast and sometimes to the east coast. On one flight coming into Denver, we were coming in for a landing and were almost on the runway when the pilot put the pedal to the metal and took us back up. He got on the intercom and told us he aborted the landing because the tower told him the landing gear didn't come down on one side. We circled while they tried to get the landing gear down which they did prior to us running out of fuel and we landed with no problems.

On a flight coming into the Falls in the winter, we had a buildup of ice on the wings and props. The pilot changed altitudes to try to get rid of the ice which worked. The problem with that strategy was that the ice would fly off the props and hit the fuselage. It sounded like they were big chunks of ice that would come right through the fuselage when they would hit. Fortunately that didn't happen but I wasn't the only one thinking it might. When we landed at the airport in the Falls the whole plane erupted in a mighty cheer.

On several flights I witnessed fire coming out of the jet engines. I guess that may not be an unusual occurrence but it got my attention. On one flight in a thunderstorm, I swear I saw lighting strike the wing right outside my window. Nothing happened so maybe it was just close.

Retirement after Kathy died is not the retirement I signed up for. I robbed the cradle, in part, because I thought she would outlive me. Not the case. My love of my life deserted me and left me to my own devices. She tried to teach me things I would need to know to survive on my own but I was a distracted and absent minded learner. My daughter Kimberly, took over the household responsibilities such as laundry, house cleaning and cooking as well as keeping me from getting depressed after Kathy died. Eventually I realized that Kim should have a life of her own and not be senior sitting me. I relearned much of what Kathy had tried to teach me and took over the responsibility of the household chores like cleaning and laundry. Kim still does the majority of the cooking but I contribute on occasion. My standards for cleaning and laundry are not even close to those of Kathy or Kim but it doesn't bother me. Things are reasonably clean and in order and the dust balls just have to tolerate me in their space. Even when Kathy was living, we shared the evening meal with Kim either at our place or at Kim's. We still do that and we get to see each other at least once a day and catch up.

Not only do I miss Kathy's talents for household chores, I especially miss her presence. I'm the guy that wanted to share everything in life with her. Something happens and I want to tell her about it. Someone tells me something and I want to share it with her. Making plans together, even if they are as simple as grocery shopping or who I ran into at the store or post office. When you've done that and shared a life with someone for nearly fifty years, it is difficult when that changes and is no longer possible. It's part of the process of grieving. Grieving is a difficult assignment and one I would skip if possible. It appears without warning and when you least expect it for no apparent reason. It doesn't appear that you have any control over when, what or how it shows itself. I compare it to boxing in that you need to roll with the punches and find ways to counter punch. Sometimes all you can do is put up your guard, cover up and wait for it to subside. For those of you that say grief is the price of love, you are correct. However, to my simple mind, that is a price I would pay over and over to experience sharing love, especially the love Kathy and I shared. The epitaph on our tombstone says "To Share Love is the Meaning of Life".

16
I Believe

I Believe...
That anyone, given the right circumstances,
Is capable of anything, be it good or evil.

I Believe:
If you never make a mistake,
You aren't doing anything.

I Believe...
That debate, disagreements, arguments or whatever the politically correct current choice of naming them is, are a means to learning and sharing knowledge and should not be avoided. Neither should they be done disrespectfully but with learning as the primary target remembering that to learn is more to your benefit than to be right is. Would you rather be right or happy?

I Believe...
That we all grow and change by our experiences and knowledge acquired and that we can only change ourselves. The only change we can have on anyone else is by the experiences and knowledge we share with them.

I Believe....
That most people are not purposely trying to hurt you.
They just speak before engaging their thought processes.

This Dummy Pulls His Own Strings

I Believe…
That friendship and Love grow proportionately
To the amount of effort you put into the relationship.

I Believe…
That you can do something in an instant
That will give you heartache for life.

I Believe….
That it's taking me a long time
To become the person I want to be.
Perhaps I'm a slow learner.

I Believe…
That you should always leave loved ones with
Loving words. It may be the last time you see them.

I Believe….
That you can keep going long after you think you can't.

I Believe….
That we are responsible for what
we do and say, no matter how we feel.

I Believe…
That either you control your attitude or it controls you.

I Believe…
That heroes are the people who do what has to be done when it needs to be done, regardless of the consequences.

I Believe…
That sometimes when I'm angry
I have the right to be angry,
But that doesn't give me the right to be cruel.

Dwight E. Knuth

I Believe....
That maturity has more to do with what types of experiences you've had and what you've learned from them and less to do with how many Birthdays you've celebrated.

I Believe.....
That it isn't always enough,
to be forgiven by others.
Sometimes, you have to learn to forgive yourself.

I Believe...
That no matter how bad your heart is broken
The world doesn't stop for your grief.

I Believe...
That Love, not time, heals all wounds.

I Believe....
That our background and circumstances
may have influenced who we are,
but, we are responsible for who we become.

I Believe...
That you shouldn't be so eager to find
out a secret. It could change your life forever.

I Believe....
Two people can look at the exact same
thing and see something totally different.

I Believe...
That your life can be changed in a matter of
hours by people who don't even know you.

I Believe....
That even when you think you have no more to give,
when someone cries out to you,

you will find the strength to help.

I Believe...
That credentials on the wall
do not make you a decent human being.

I Believe...
That the people you care about most in life
are taken from you too soon.

I Believe
The happiest of people don't necessarily
have the best of everything;
They just make the most of everything they have.

I Believe...
In one God, the Holy Trinity, Father, Son & Holy Spirit

I Believe...
In A loving, forgiving, caring and compassionate God.

I Believe...
That God is Love.
That the absence of Love is the absence of God.

I Believe...
That hell is the absence of God and Love.

I Believe...
That religion is all about Love as it says in the Bible
    The first command I give you is:
    Love the Lord your God with all your heart and with all your
    soul and with all your mind and with all your strength.
    The second is this:
    Love your neighbor as yourself.
There is no commandment greater than these.

Dwight E. Knuth

I Believe...
That Jesus was sent to allow forgiveness of sins and eternal life, through Faith and Grace.

I Believe...
In the Bible, written by humans, interpreted by humans and that the human equation leads to differences of opinions and religions. Those differences allow us to choose the one we "like" or "fits" us best, not necessarily the right one.

I Believe...
In freedom of religion and the right to choose.

I Believe:
In the Church
- As a place to Worship and Praise God
- As a community of like believers in the interpretation of the Bible and Religion
- As a community of celebration of religion
  - As a safe place of loving guidance but not as a place of judgement

I Believe...
In Prayer
- In quiet communication with God
  - Taking everything to God in prayer (as taught by my parents)
    - It allows for quiet reflection and good decision making
- In private prayer as opposed to public prayer
  - In my opinion, public prayer is more about impressing the public than talking and sharing with God. Many times it doesn't seem that we are humbling ourselves before God. Maybe, it is just my ego and not the way everyone prays in public.
- In community prayer
  - Where we pray for the same thing such as healing of an individual, leaders of the world/country etc. but do it individually as in prayer circles, chains or groups.

I Believe...
That we are doing a disservice to our children by lying to them and proclaiming fantasies and fairy tales to be true, especially the Santa Claus one. We are setting them up for heartbreak when they discover the truth, which is minor to the reality that we are teaching them to lie and that lying is OK. Mommy and Daddy do it so it must be OK. It starts with this approved lying and expands as the child builds life experiences. Expanding into lying to make someone feel good, to spare someone's feelings and then for selfish reasons. Soon it is a way of life and you are lying to the ones you love such as your spouse and your children. The greatest disservice is that we are taking the focus away from the birth of Jesus and putting it on a fictional character. We are changing the focus of Christmas from the birth of Christ and his life to our selfish desire for gifts from Santa Claus. When the children are exposed to the truth, does it put doubt in their mind about Jesus. Is his birth real or just fictional like Santa Claus? Is all of Christmas fictional and what can I believe, if anything. After all it was my parents that lied to me and proclaimed Santa to be real. Are they also lying about Jesus? How does this bolster our children's faith in religion, specifically, Jesus? I believe we are planting seeds of doubt. I am just as guilty as everyone else in perpetuating this myth. I even bought a Santa suit and played Santa for my children as well as friends children and at some village children's Christmas parties. I remember some children being scared to death of Santa, this loud, fat, strange dressed stranger that kept saying HO, HO, HO. They would cry and run to their parents who would lie some more to get their kid to sit on this awful persons lap so they could take a picture. Some of the older children would not be scared but would be awe struck and dumb founded. They were old enough to suspect that this was all a lie, yet they wanted so much for it to be true. Is this actually the real Santa Claus? He knows my name, he knows my parents. He knows things about me. They would sit on my lap and look into my face with admiration and put their hands on my face to see if it was real.

I remember one little boy in particular that was dying of cancer. He didn't have long to live and of course his parents just wanted to bring some joy and happiness to him. I visited him in his home where we thought he would be most comfortable and accepting. I, in the form of Santa was not the happiness they wanted him to have. I refrained from the loud boisterous Santa and tried a quiet restrained Santa with love and comfort. I must not be a good actor because he was still scared of Santa. I thought at the time, I should not be masquerading as a jolly fat man but should come telling bible stories about Jesus and his love for children. How Jesus expressed that he wanted the little children to come to him and that he loved little children. That he would soon meet this Jesus and Jesus loved him and would hold him and take care of him until his parents joined him. It broke my heart to see this poor child in his suffering and me not able to lesson it but adding to his already stressful life.

My own children reacted differently to Santa. The older of the two, my son Eric, suddenly became very honest with Santa. Santa had brought him a long wooden toboggan, something he had asked for and wanted very much. He was sitting on Santa's lap looking at the toboggan when Santa asked him if he had been a good boy. His reply was, "Not that good". My daughter, Kimberly, was the younger and more perceptive and probably less believing. I think she was only three. She was sitting on Santa's lap and would trace the veins on my hands with her little fingers, deep in thought. When Santa left she told her mother that Santa's hands looked just like Daddies. She also wondered why Daddy was never home when Santa came. Of course we lied some more by telling her daddy had to work.

Then there is the Easter Bunny, another religious holiday where the focus is taken away from religion to place it on a fictional character. Why do we do this? Is it so the non-believers, non-Christians have a reason to celebrate the holiday, so the retailers can make more money? You don't see the Jewish religion creating a fictional character to deliver the gifts for Hanukah or creating a reason for the non-Jewish to celebrate.

The Stork is another lie which seems to be fading away. We didn't think our children could handle the truth of conception or child birth so we had a bird drop the kid down the chimney. This is as unbelievable as Santa coming down the chimney.

Then there is the tooth fairy, the boogey man and who knows what other fairy tales are perpetuated in other cultures. Is this not the case of crying wolf too often. If they lie to me about these things, just what can I believe? Is the birth and crucifixion of Jesus not reason enough to celebrate Christmas and Easter? It seems to this confused human that the truth is always the best route to take. Don't sugar coat life.

I Believe...
In honesty & integrity

17
Religion

All I have seen teaches me to trust the creator for all I have not seen.
Ralph Waldo Emerson

Whoever does not Love does not know God, because God is Love.
1 John 4:8 NIV

Laughter is the closest thing to the grace of God.
Karl Barth

He will keep us in perfect peace, all those who trust in him, whose thoughts turn often to the Lord.
Isaiah 26:3

I know the previous verse to be true from my own life. I learned it from my parents who were the perfect example of it.

Religion is a personal choice but is influenced by your family and friends. Much of what you learn as a child is carried into adult life. If you are born into a specific religion (your parents' beliefs) many times you will continue in that religion as an adult. It's what we are familiar with and comfortable with and we all like our comfort. Some other influences on your religion choice are your life partner who may believe differently than your parents did. If you marry someone with a different religion, you may learn and accept that religion. Also friends, relatives and peers

This Dummy Pulls His Own Strings

may influence you. I am not an expert on religion or even very knowledgeable about religion in general or my own religion. It could be said that I am not very religious but I am spiritual.

What I am writing about is from observation not a result of study or research. My Father was a student of religion and I'm sure I learned much from him and my Mother who was raised as a Pennsylvania Dutch, much like the Quakers of early America. I regret that I didn't pay more attention as a youth and learn more from them. They lived their religion, they walked their talk and I learned much from their lifestyle. They also taught me tolerance of others and others' beliefs'.

My Father attended and graduated from Northwest Bible College in Minneapolis, MN, so he had a fair formal education in religion. He never went to high school but had an eighth grade education before going to college. That seemed remarkable to me. He was studying to become a minister but God had other plans for him. He had some medical problems that prevented him from his chosen profession as a minister. He was also as he put it, hard of hearing which made it difficult for him to communicate with others. However, he did get his preachers license which is in my possession but probably not transferable, so if I start preaching, just ignore it.

Dad was a respected deacon in our church and filled the pulpit, preaching for the ministers when they were absent for whatever reason. His preacher's license was issued by the North Dakota conference of the Evangelical Church on May 15, 1926. His parents belonged to this Church and helped organize and build a country church of this denomination. His Dad's brother, the Rev. Fred Knuth was the first minister of this country church. When the surrounding towns and villages started churches and the roads were built and improved and the motor car came into existence and use by the settlers and farmers, people started attending the town churches and the country churches were abandoned. They sold the country church building to the Lutherans in Butte, ND and it was moved there and stands there yet today. It may still be an active church and was a few years back but I am not sure of the status today. My wife's brother Michael Hoffman and his wife Pamela Federanko were married in this church.

On Dad's preaching license it states that as long as the license is not revoked by the church, he maintains his preacher's license. The Evangelical church, later became the EUB (Evangelical United Brethren) Church which later merged with the Methodist Church.

When they sold and moved the country church, my Grandparents attended church in Guthrie which was close to the homestead. This was a Baptist Church and my Dad's brother, Herman was the preacher there at one time. My Mother's baptism certificate shows that she was baptized by Rev. Herman Knuth at the Guthrie Baptist church. I'm sure that everyone that was previously a member of the Evangelical Church had to be baptized by immersion when they joined the Baptist Church, even if they had been previously baptized in another congregation as a baby.

The Baptist's are kind of a stickler when it comes to Baptism. They believe it has to be as an adult by immersion. The very word baptism means immersion or so they say in their literature concerning baptism. They believe we should follow in the example of Christ who was baptized by immersion. When I joined the Lutheran church, I was told I would not have to be baptized in the Lutheran church but that they would accept my baptism in the Baptist church. However, had my wife elected to become a Baptist, she would have had to be baptized by immersion because the Baptists would not accept her Lutheran baptism.

When the Baptist church in Guthrie closed its' doors most members went to the Drake Baptist Church. My Grandparents and several of my Aunts and Uncles went back to the Evangelical church in Drake. My parents, for whatever reason, chose to stay with the Baptist church. About the only difference in the two churches of any significance was their belief in baptism. Also, the Evangelical church seemed to be more tolerant of things like dancing, playing cards and drinking of alcohol, than the Baptists or at least not quite as judgmental about them. I would surmise that is one reason most of my relatives went back to the Evangelical church. My Dad told me of his youth on the homestead and how his Dad would make his own beer and keep it in the cellar. My grandparents, having immigrated from Germany, probably were fond of beer. In Germany, beer is to Germans what vodka is to Russians or wine is to Italians. Dad also said, as a child, they played cards and on occasion would have neighbors over and clear the living room of furniture so they could dance. So it doesn't surprise me that my relatives preferred the Evangelical church.

As an example of my Fathers integrity and how his peers regarded him, on one occasion when there was a disagreement among members of the church about a church members' lifestyle and this person was being judged by other members, this person said he would abide by whatever my father said but no one else. He chose my father as his judge, not a role my father wanted. He respected my Father's honesty, integrity and fairness. I don't know the result of what took place because my Father was not one to divulge a confidence but I know from living and growing up with my Father, he was a forgiving man, a patient man, a God fearing and God loving man and an honest and fair person.

I was born and baptized a Baptist of the northern variety as opposed to Southern Baptist. At an early age, the age of reason, I accepted Jesus Christ as my personal savior and was baptized, Baptist, immersion style at Camp Bently in Lake Bently west of Drake, ND. Some of my friends of my age were also baptized at the same time. My baptismal certificate says I was 8 years old. The Baptists don't baptize you as a baby or infant but rather when you, as a person who can make your own decisions, decide to become a Christian and follow the Baptist faith.

In retrospect, I think 8 years old is not really that age, the age of reason. What was I going to do, tell my parents I wanted to follow the Jewish faith? It's more a parents and peers influence than a personal informed decision. Also, it was an emotional decision because your family and church family was so happy that you had reached your decision to accept Jesus as your personal savior. I'm sure just knowing that you were making those you loved happy, helped you make this decision at the ripe old age of eight years. There also was pressure, mostly from peers. When are you going to do it? Not, are you going to do it but when? It was kind of a forgone conclusion that everyone was going to be baptized. I remember my Mother telling me I could make that decision whenever I chose but it was obvious that they had strong beliefs and practiced their faith and religion daily so the seed had been planted and was just waiting for fruition. I knew it would make my parents very happy.

I have no regrets of my decision and am appreciative of my parents' strong faith and teaching it to me. I still believe most of what I was taught as a child concerning the Baptist faith. It concerns me that many children are not raised with a religious background in our modern society and that later in life they will not have that early childhood religious education and faith to fall back on. I know it has been a great comfort to me throughout my life. I'm not advocating one religion or denomination over another, just a religion and a belief philosophy with faith in God.

There are so many disagreements about what the Bible actually says, how it should be interpreted and if these human men that wrote the Bible were actually inspired by God or were promoting their own agenda. That is why we have so many different denominations. The Bible did not suddenly appear by some miracle as the Ten Commandments did. The Bible was written over a period of 1500 years by some forty different men, who were moved by the Holy Spirit to give us the word of God. Who was the judge that verified that they were moved by the Holy Spirit? These 40 men were supposedly all good men, but yet, they were men, imperfect human beings and sinners as we all are. Many of these men were Holy men and indeed influenced by the Holy Spirit. How many of them believed they were inspired by God in their own alleged mind but had their own agenda?

In recent times, we hear stories of self-proclaimed men of God that have taken advantage of their followers, even convincing them to commit suicide as a group by drinking cool aid. Some of the biblical "men of God" were quite selfish and may have been looking to present themselves favorably for history. King David was a good man but none the less a lustful man. Was he inspired by the Holy Spirit when he bedded down with his best friends wife and sent his best friend off to the battlefield where he certainly would be killed, giving David free access to his widow? I think not. It just shows that we are all human and therefore are subject to selfishness, egos and other not so desirable influences.

Before the Bible was written, it was handed down for 2000 years, creation to B.C. 2000, from generation to generation, orally. I'm sure in these 2000 years there were changes to the stories as we witness when we tell a story and it passes from person to person. There can be as many versions of a story as there are people who witnessed it. I found this to be true in my research of my family history for this book, even in written records, differences exist.

Not only is there room for error in the recording of the history of the Bible stories and life as it was then but in the translation from one language to another. We've had Hebrew, Greek, Aramaic, Canaanite, Phoenician, Arabic, Yiddish and Latin and who knows all the different versions and translations. Some of the early Bibles had many more books that were eliminated as the Bible was changed to its' current version and even the current version differs on the books that are included.

I'm not the first one to question the creation or interpretation of the Bible which is why there are different denominations in the Christian religion. Few of us can agree and if we don't agree, we form our own denomination. Of course we all are aware of Martin Luther, breaking away from the Catholic Church and forming the Lutheran Church and possibly for good reason, at least he thought so.

The Baptists broke away from the Mennonites or maybe it was the other way around and the Mennonites broke away from the Baptists. Then you have the Evangelicals and Methodists who somehow found common ground and merged but prior to the common ground they found it necessary to be separate denominations. Did they merge for religious reasons or was it about finances, survival and the money? These examples are just in the Christian religions. Do these differences of opinions, beliefs and interpretation of the Bible matter. To my way of thinking, in the scheme of eternity, probably not.

In my alleged mind, I have made religion simple, because I am simple minded. It is all about Faith and Love. God is Love. Heaven is the presence of God and his Love. Hell is the absence of God and therefore the absence of Love. My mind can not imagine the absence of Love nor do I ever want to experience it. I try to make my religion about Love, Prayer and Faith. Love your neighbor, Love your enemy, pray for those that wish or do evil to you. Prayer is just a communication with your God. Sometimes it feels like a one way communication but that is ideal for most of us who just want to talk and not listen anyway. So there you go, pray.

When I married, we were married in the Lutheran church. It seemed, that was the way things were done. It was the brides day and she should be married in her home church in front of her friends and family where she was at home and comfortable. It was kind of a passage from her current life and family to joining her husband and his life and family. Much like in the old testament, Wither thou goest, I will go. It made sense to me.

When we attended church, after we were wed, it was the Lutheran church. We decided that when we had children we should attend church as a family and all attend and belong to the same denomination and church. It just seemed it would be more "family" oriented if we all believed and practiced the same version of religion. I grew to like and respect the Lutheran church and they seemed to believe basically the same way the Baptists believed, except for baptism and confirmation. I liked the formality in the Lutheran religion as opposed to the informality of the Baptist church. Isn't part of church, the worship and honor of God? Should we not do that formally? I'm not saying informal worship is wrong, just not the way I envision it.

In the Baptist worship, the ministers don't wear robes. During the service, it isn't unusual for a member of the congregation to give a "amen brother" during the sermon. When someone who was a stranger appeared in the pews, the minister would ask them to stand so everyone could see them and introduce themselves.

This Dummy Pulls His Own Strings

If you brought a guest to church, the minister, from the pulpit, would ask you and your guest to stand and introduce them. My wife Kathy, as a teenager and young lady was very shy and reserved. When I took her to the Baptist church as my girlfriend, she was mortified when she had to stand and have me introduce her. I was very proud, because she was extraordinarily beautiful and I might add sexy, even fully clothed. She didn't have that opinion of herself which made her all the more attractive. Lucky for me, she was a humble person or she would have found a better mate.

The Baptism of infants, appealed to me and the confirmation of your faith as a child. My sister, Verla, had married a Lutheran and joined the Lutheran church which was another factor that carried a lot of weight for me. I always had a lot of respect for Verla and the decisions she made. It seemed to me the Lutheran church was much friendlier and preached love and forgiveness as opposed to the Baptists who literally tried to scare the hell out of you, especially when they had revival services.

I believe they had revival services because they knew no one could live up to their rules and expectations so they had revival services for the backsliders and sinners like me, to give us a chance to redeem ourselves publicly and come back into the fold. It may be parallel to the Catholics confession. The Baptists or Lutherans don't have confession like the Catholics but the revival seemed like a blanket confession where you say, "my bad, please forgive me". As a lad, it seemed to me, some people would sin repeatedly, then go to the revival meetings and be saved, yet again. Then repeat the process the next year. How many times can you or should you be "saved"? The evangelist would refer to them as backsliders and appeal to them to come forward and be saved from their backsliding. They seemed to be either insincere or slow learners because they always repeated every year. I guess the evangelist was good at scaring the hell out of them but just for a short time, that evening.

This may have been the evangelists' method of boosting the results of his preaching and saving the masses. We all are backsliders to some extent, being sinners. It looks much better for the evangelist if he has more people coming forward to be saved. It also helps the unsaved to come forward to be saved if they aren't standing alone. These were good people and were sincere at the time but somehow God had short changed them when it came to follow through. Perhaps they should have focused more on, lead us not into temptation when they prayed the Lords' prayer. This is just my Baptist judgmental training coming to the foreground. I guess I should not limit the judgmental side of religion to Baptists. As Humans we like to gossip and be informed and in that endeavor we generally declare our judgement. Perhaps the fear of the judgement part of gossip is the part that strives to keep us on the straight and narrow path, our moral compass.

It seemed to me, strictly my opinion, the Baptists or I should say the Baptist religion, was very judgmental and if you didn't live in a certain manner, according to the prescribed standards, you were bound for hell. Judgment day was a daily occurrence. Yet they believed you were saved by grace and not your works and preached it but you better live according to the rules which were more don'ts than do's. Don't drink alcohol, smoke, dance, go to movies or have or even think about sex until you are married. These all may be good rules to live by but on occasion I think I would like to enjoy life and by their standards, sin a little. Sometimes a little temptation is good for you, if for no other reason than to chalk it up to experience and maybe something, perhaps, you should avoid. But remember, some mistakes are too much fun to make only once. My Mother used to say about certain people that they were so heavenly minded, they were no earthly good. I have known many people like that.

The Lutherans drank alcohol, even the pastors, with their parishioners, not even attempting to hide the fact. Some pastors smoked, danced, went to movies and I'm pretty sure had sex before marriage or at the very least, thought about it. I know of some Catholic Priests who were not so celibate. One, I knew, was sleeping with a member's wife and I heard she was not the only one. I would have liked to hear some of those confessions.

The confessions were probably his first clue that there was some action available.

All the things I wanted to do as a teen ager but had to feel guilty for if I did, the Baptists forbid. Many of the Baptists did them anyway but wouldn't admit it, which was a good source of gossip. Early in my life I decided, guilt was a useless emotion. If you are going to feel guilty about something, just don't do it.

By becoming a Lutheran, I could do all those things and not take the guilt trip. What a great religion. I didn't have to take a guilt trip or go to confession. Of course it was too late for the sex before marriage as I was already married when I became Lutheran. I strongly believe that if you value your marriage and love your partner, you should not have sex outside the marriage weather you are Lutheran, Baptist, Catholic or any religion.

Even Mormons don't believe in sex outside marriage. If they want sex with someone that isn't their wife, they just marry her, thus the many wives. I'm not judging them, it might be the answer to the adultery problem. Rather ideal for the man of the house, if one wife is angry with you just go to one that isn't. I'm a little confused how that lifestyle promotes love between a man and a woman or many women. Seems to me there would be jealousy, competition, gossip, slander and many unhealthy emotions that have nothing to do with love. It is kind of a step backwards in society where females are more like property than equals. Again, it is not promoting shared love, I don't believe.

Shortly after we were married, I started going to classes to join the Lutheran church in Grand Forks, ND which is where I was employed and we lived. We were planning to join the Lutheran church there and I had not been confirmed in the Lutheran faith. They would accept my Baptism by immersion from the Baptist church which I thought was a confirmation of my faith in God but this church wanted me to be confirmed in the Lutheran practices and teachings. They probably thought I was going to be doing the "Amen Brother" during the service. I wasn't opposed to the classes, because I was interested in the Lutheran faith and wanted to learn about it and the differences from other religions and faiths. I have always been interested in different beliefs and practices of religion. As a young lad, in the Navy, I took a course on comparative religion. I found it quite interesting, especially the history of the different religions.

I was fired from my job in Grand Forks (see the chapter on Work) and we moved to International Falls. My Navy buddy, Jim Gulbranson, who got me the job in International Falls, was a member of First Lutheran Church along with his wife and her parents. We attended church with them and decided to join. The minister was Rev. Virgil Anderson, a very kind and loving Swedish man. He told me I didn't need to take confirmation classes to join the Lutheran church but just transfer my membership from the Drake Baptist church to First Lutheran and go through the formalities.

This I did and thus became a full-fledged, non amen saying, hymn singing, pot luck Lutheran. I am still a member of First Lutheran Church and while our children were growing up attended regularly. I taught Sunday School, served as treasurer for many years and served on the church board several times under two different ministers. Rev. Anderson is one of the people I grew to admire and respect most in my life. He was a very charitable man and a wonderful speaker even though he was at times very emotional which is why he was such a good speaker. He was sincere and put feeling into his sermons. I don't think I ever slept through one of his sermons. He was respected, not only as a minister but as a human, a man, community member, family man and friend.

We attended church regularly and were active in the church family until my health started to fail, the kids were grown up and left home and I couldn't learn to say no without feeling guilty about it. I suppose it was my guilt indoctrination in my youth coming out. I was told by my Drs. at Mayo clinic that perhaps I was burning my candle on both ends and that may be why I was getting migraines. In actuality, after the fact, I think it was because I was not getting enough sleep. I also have chrons disease and type 1 diabetes. Both diseases can be difficult to manage, especially when you are sleep deprived. Stress also affects both of those diseases and guilt can exacerbate or cause stress.

Church is a lot like many other organizations, clubs or social activities, they have projects that they want you to participate in, all which take time and effort. Not only do they want you to participate in projects, they want you to be an active member and if at all possible an officer or board member. Sometimes these projects or activities gave me pause as to why we were doing them. Was it for the greater good of humanity and the community and spreading the "good news" of Christ and for his glory or was it a selfish social activity that was for our own pleasure and enjoyment. I imagine you need to balance the two.

While I was healthy, I enjoyed all these activities and did them willingly but when not feeling well, it was a real chore and detrimental not only to me but to my family. I wasn't good at saying no and took the easy way out by just not participating or attending church anymore. I also quit going to diabetes monthly meetings for basically the same reason. They wanted me to be president. From my education at Mayo clinic, I had a lot of knowledge about the disease and gave presentations at the meetings. I've even had some of my Drs. tell me I knew more about diabetes then they did. I knew being president required more energy than I had to devote to it because I filled in for the president on occasion, so I quit. The cowards and easy way out or I prefer to call it self-preservation. I also gave up my service to our local Credit Union on the Supervisory Committee for the same reason. If you are going to belong to any social, professional, religious, business or any organization you should participate in it and be active, I feel. If other members can't count on you for your participation, then perhaps you should bow out. This I did.

There are other reasons (excuses) that attending church was not in my best health interest. One was the amount of perfume some of the ladies wear. In an open seating theater, if someone with strong perfume sits next to you, it is a simple matter to get up and move away. In church, at least in our church, we knew everyone and didn't want to hurt anyone's feelings by getting up and moving if the smell of perfume was overpowering. Not only did I know these ladies, many of them were friends of ours. I would start to get a migraine almost immediately when exposed to strong perfume. Strong soap or scented candles or deodorants sometimes have the same effect.

My Dr. at Mayo clinic also told me that anyone with a weak immune system, as he assumed I did, because of my chronic diseases, should avoid crowds for obvious reasons of picking up cold and flu germs. This was before God invented flu vaccines. The Dr. said church, with all the crowds, closeness, handshaking, passing the peace and pot luck meals was a prime area for picking up germs. I guess if your immune system is working properly, it only makes you stronger but if you are constantly fighting chronic diseases or on chemotherapy, you might want to lower your risk by avoiding large crowds. We all find our excuses to do what we want to do or to avoid what we don't want to do. Sometimes they are legitimate and sometimes just excuses. We pick and choose, whatever suits us at the time.

When we quit attending church on a regular basis, no one seemed to notice for a long time. Then some of our friends and church members would mention that they hadn't seen us in church for quite a while. I would reply that I hadn't seen them in church either and often times that would end that conversation. How could I see them in church, I wasn't in attendance? The persistent ones would pursue it further and I sometimes would explain the situation and sometimes just say we were taking a break, depending on how close they were and how much information I felt comfortable sharing. At no time did we receive a call or visit from a pastor or member of the congregation concerning our absence from the church community. The only visit we received was one year for the annual pledging when we were visited and encouraged to submit a pledge of giving for the year. I'm talking about a period of 20 to 30 years. For a few years, they would mail us the monthly church news and our envelopes for giving. I would submit by mail a contribution from time to time but at some point we decided to select other charities

This Dummy Pulls His Own Strings

to give to and quit contributing to the church. Eventually the newsletters quit coming and the envelopes for giving stopped also. Maybe it's just the mode of operation of the Lutheran religion, live and let live.

I'm quite sure if someone in the Baptist church I grew up in, quit going to church, the pastor would be knocking on their door encouraging them to return to the flock. I know from time to time some of the Baptists would have a falling out with some members of the congregation and would quit going to that particular Baptist church and start attending a different Baptist church. If they quit attending church completely, there definitely would be a member visit if not a pastor visit.

When I was active and on the board of our local Lutheran church we decided to computerize our membership. This was long before the advent of laptop computers or even home computers. I got permission from my employer, Boise Cascade, to keep our church membership on their mainframe computer and to write the programs to analyze the membership. This allowed the pastor to see what age groups we had and where he needed to concentrate his efforts. The minister at this time was pastor Virgil Anderson. If members were inactive in the church, our database would tell him who they were and how long it had been since they were active. He would visit the member and try to bring them back into the flock. If a member didn't attend services for a period of time, didn't make a contribution or didn't commune for a certain period of time, they were put on the inactive list.

After pastor Anderson left, this membership database wasn't used anymore and eventually when Boise Cascade upgraded their mainframe computer, the database and programs were not converted to the new platform. Pastor Anderson was the last pastor, I'm aware of, that made house calls, sometimes with his wife and sometimes alone, with or without an invitation. While I was an active member I made monthly house calls to all our pastors because I was the parish treasurer and delivered their paychecks. I don't know why the practice of ministerial house calls stopped but I suspect it was at the members request.

Growing up as a young Baptist lad, our ministers made house calls with or without an invitation to active and inactive members and sometimes to families that were known not to attend church or be members of any church. Sometimes these Baptist ministers would visit members of other denominations to invite their children to Sunday School or Bible school. My wife, as a Lutheran child, was visited by a Baptist minister and given bible story books she was very grateful for. She attended their Bible school just to get more bible story books.

While I was growing up, I had three ministers in our family, a paternal uncle, a maternal uncle and a cousin. I know they all did house calls. When my wife died, I did not have one minister visit me at my home. Neither did any local minister call on the telephone. We met to plan the memorial service at the church office. The only minister that called on the phone and prayed with me over the phone was a Mennonite minister who lived in California. He previously lived here and ran a construction company on the side. We hired him to do some work for us and became friends with him.

At the time, Kathy was going through her first cancer diagnoses and treatment. He would pray with her and help her in her struggles and she expressed that it was helpful and important to her that he took the time from his busy schedule to pray with and for her. She very much appreciated his compassion, care and prayers. He is a very wise, kind and caring person that is very non-judgmental. Had he still been living in town, I know he would have been here to pray with me. As it was, he called and we visited and he prayed with me over the phone which gave me comfort.

I guess it should come as no surprise that the ministers house calls have gone the way of the Drs. house calls. I'm sure many of you do not even know that Drs. used to come to your home when you were too sick to go to their office. They did this at the end of the day after the office closed. At least that was how it worked in my hometown. I even had the good Dr. stop by to check up on me without a request to do so, in my hometown, when I was a child, just to see how I was doing. There was an advantage to doing this

This Dummy Pulls His Own Strings

for the Dr. or pastor. They could get a glimpse of the home life and environment the person was living in which sometimes has an affect on the healing process both health and spiritual.

Picking and choosing is what we do when we decide what religion and denomination we will follow if we don't follow in the path of our parents. Most Christian religions are based on the Bible and God but vary to some degree because they interpret the Bible and Gods' rules differently. Many times we choose the interpretation that best fits our lifestyle or how we want to live. I want to drink alcohol. The Baptists don't think you should, so rather than sneak around doing it or do it and be criticized or judged for drinking alcohol, I will leave the Baptist church. The irony of this is later in my life, I gave up alcohol because of the diseases I have acquired and the effect it has on them. Go figger. Some of you might say that is my punishment from God for leaving the Baptist church to follow my selfish sinful ways. I don't subscribe to that theory. The point is, you can find a religion or denomination that pretty much fits how you want to believe and live. Most religions have rules or commandments for living in society that we all try to adhere to such as the 10 commandments and the Golden Rule.

One thing I am curious about, why are protestant churches so competitive? I belonged to the First Baptist church and then joined the First Lutheran church. There is also a First Assembly of God church. You never see a Second Baptist, Lutheran or Assembly of God church. Why do they all need to be First? Perhaps a better question is why do we and I in particular feel the need to join a church that is First? The answer to that is beyond my education or thought process or as we used to say, above my pay grade. Perhaps the government should fund a study on this, they somehow come up with the answers to all non-essential studies. To even confuse the issue more, you never see a Catholic church that is First. All the Catholic churches are named after Saints, it appears and there are a whole mass of them. As you can probably tell, I am being facetious. I really don't care. I just wanted an excuse to use the word facetious because I really like that word and it is under used.

It is one of the few words that use all the vowels in order. We need more facetiousness in our daily lives. Don't you agree?

Organized religion is a group of like believers who believe and practice religion in a prescribed fashion. They support one another and validate each other's beliefs. It is more than a social organization but it is often treated much like a social organization by its members. In the Lutheran church, food is an important part of the church. I don't think I ever attended a meeting of any sort where coffee and something sweet wasn't served. That's really healthy for diabetics with a sweet tooth and no will power or for that matter, over eaters with no will power. Lead us not into temptation, but deliver us from evil.

Every Sunday after church we had coffee and sweets and of course the Lutherans are famous for their pot luck meals. Have you ever eaten pot luck and found cat hair in it? Makes you stop and wonder if the cat was eating out of the dish while it sat on the counter. If the cat had access to it, what else? At least there shouldn't be any mice around. But what about the casseroles that didn't have cat hair? Did the mice have access to that one? That opens up a whole new can of worms. I guess what doesn't kill you makes you stronger. Humans are a social animal and thrive on social networks. Much more can be accomplished by joining forces than can be accomplished by each individual separately. They even made up a new word for it, "synergy". It's derived from the word "sinergy" which means sinning as a group, which provides more enjoyment as opposed to sinning by yourself.

Most religions were formed to honor and worship God. There are as many ways of doing that as there are religions. The Holy Bible is the basis for many religions. The Bible is interpreted differently and therefore there is disagreement in the meaning of it and thus different religions. Even in the same religion there is disagreement about certain aspects of the religion and different branches or sects are created. It seems as though religion is more about disagreement than agreement. You can bring up most any part of a belief in a religion and there will be disagreement about it which is generally referred to as a discussion. There probably

This Dummy Pulls His Own Strings

wouldn't be a discussion about it if everyone agreed. Why is this? Because we are all free thinking human beings. Was this part of God's master plan and what was the purpose? I think, in my alleged free thinking mind, that God does have a purpose for it but it escapes me and confuses me. Many times we take our own best interest into our free thinking and our natural selfishness and ego enters into how we believe.

Just to confuse the issue and do a little pot stirring, what exactly is heaven? A physical place or a spirit world. The Bible suggests physical when it speaks of streets paved with Gold. Those of us who have accepted Jesus as our savior and believe in God and the trinity, according to the Christian religion, will inherit eternal life and just as Christ rose from the dead, so also will we ascend into heaven. At the second coming when we arise from our graves, is it our physical bodies or a spiritual body as an angel? Are we resting in peace (RIP) until the second coming or are we with our loved ones that have died before us? People say to you when you have lost a loved one to death that now they are with their former spouse or child or parents or whomever has gone before. Are they really or just resting in peace waiting for the second coming? I'm confused. This is not unusual for me or for many others. There are two different believes about this both in the Baptist religion and in the Lutheran religion.

This heaven will not have grieving or sadness or tears we are told. If all our friends and family that we love so dearly, did not believe as we did and are not in heaven with us, will not that cause sadness and grieving? Are we all so selfish that all we care about is that we made it? I can't imagine eternal life without others I love unless there are no emotions in heaven. Do your emotions die when your body and brain dies even if you are resurrected? Maybe, as on earth, our memory is the first to go and we have no memory of our earthly life. Eternal Alzheimer's? When you die, your brain dies. Your memory is a function of your brain. Is your brain resurrected with your body or is your memory excluded from resurrection. If your memory is also resurrected and you remember your earthly life and the people you love, how can you not have sadness in heaven if some have gone missing? I am probably wrong about all of it. I'm sure God has it taken care of, I just need to have faith. If we're eternally happy, who cares?

Another question that causes my alleged mind to over analyze is how did all the different races come about? The Bible doesn't seem to address this or in my limited knowledge, I haven't found the answer. We are all descendants of Adam and Eve, which I don't fully understand either. There must have been some inbreeding there. Maybe there is no rule in the Bible concerning inbreeding.

Then came the flood and everyone was eliminated except for Noah and his family. Again, some kissing cousins. But that still doesn't answer the races and how they evolved. Japanese, Chinese, Indian, Native American Indian, Negro, Spanish, Mexican, Caucasian and many others. There is some scientific evidence that the skin coloration was an evolution process caused by sun exposure, etc. We all know that different face and body features evolve, so I am not too surprised that we don't all look alike even though we are all descendants of Noah. Again, religion is about Faith, Hope and Love.

Love is an emotion and the Bible says God is Love. If God IS Love, then is heaven, Gods' presence? If Gods' presence is heaven, then doesn't it follow that hell would be the absence of God? If that is true, then would eternity be spiritual rather than physical? Will there only be those in heaven that guessed the correct religion and followed it or will it be all who believe in God and the trinity? What about God's chosen people, the Jews, who do not believe that Jesus is the Son of God? Will God forsake them and deny them heaven? These questions and more will be answered when we are no longer looking through a dark glass that confuses the mind and we are face to face with Jesus. Until then, it is all about Faith and believing.

To my simple mind, Faith doesn't mean there are no questions. Faith is believing, in spite of the questions. If all my questions are answered satisfactory and God and the Bible are proven, without a doubt, where is the need for Faith? I guess it is natural for us as humans to seek the truth and prove everything, including our

This Dummy Pulls His Own Strings

religion. To me, that is not what my religion is about. Having Faith, Hope and Love is what my religion is about to me so I need to ask questions but have Faith, as taught by my parents, that God is in control and has or will handle it.

In heaven, where there is no sadness or hopefully other negative emotions, such as anger, disappointment, frustration, unacceptance, jealousy etc. how is that handled? We can't get along on earth but in heaven the lamb will lie down with the lion. Well maybe that's a bad example, the lion is no longer hungry.

What about our petty selfishness and egos. Do we lose our egos and our selfishness? Kind of like when we are inebriated and happy go lucky, not a care in the world or in this case, not a care in heaven. I recently experienced what I believe to be a case of ego and arrogance.

I stopped my car in an area where there was no parking except for the designated parking spaces which were all occupied. I was going fishing with my grandkids so had a lot of gear to unload. I had just witnessed a young couple take the designated handicap spot for their pickup. They parked the pickup and took off in their kayak, obviously not disabled. However, they had a wheelchair on their license plate signifying they could park in the disabled spot. Before they parked there, I had considered pulling in, unloading, then parking elsewhere. I decided against doing that because if a disabled person came along and saw the space occupied, they would probably leave and I would have denied that disabled person their right to a parking space.

So rather than lugging all my gear from a long distance, I stopped, right in front of a no parking sign to unload the gear and then go park in another designated area. I justified stopping there because I was not parking, only stopping which was evident because I didn't even shut off the motor while unloading. Parking would be turning off the car and leaving it there for an extended period of time, not just the few minutes it takes to unload. In life as in religion, we tend to justify whatever actions we take to ease our conscience. There was still plenty of room for other vehicles to get by me. While stopped here with my trunk open while unloading the gear, a vehicle came driving up from the opposite direction with a boat and trailer, not slowing down at all or so it appeared to me. My thoughts at seeing this were they must believe they have plenty of room and at the speed they are traveling, I wouldn't have time to move my car anyway but in case their judgement is impaired I better keep a close watch on them.

I had anticipated this could happen because it was used as a turnaround for people pulling boats so they could back down the boat ramp, so I left enough room for them to get by me. I expected they would slow down and carefully negotiate passing me and I could always move my car if they had difficulty. I was standing at the back of my car when I saw them coming so stopped crossing the road with my gear to allow them clear passage. Lucky for me I did, as they were not planning on slowing down or stopping. They appeared to be in a big hurry to launch the boat and begin the fun. The vehicle made it by with no trouble but either the driver had been imbibing or was not that good at towing a trailer because he didn't allow for the trailer to get by me before he cut over. The wheel of the trailer scraped my back fender and bumper and actually moved the car over. He just kept driving, never looking back or stopping. Even after I hollered, you hit me, he ignored me and kept going. His window was open so he should have heard me because he was a short distance from me at this point. I thought when he stopped in front of the ramp, he would walk back to exchange information and acknowledge that he hit me. That never happened.

He backed down the ramp, stopped, got out of the vehicle and into the boat and proceeded to launch. I knew the person and knew him to be an intelligent, well respected, business person in the community. I had done business with him. I hollered again that he had hit me and he hollered something unintelligible from his boat, never stopping what he was doing. His attitude seemed to be, I don't have time to be bothered with you or your problems. Egotistical and arrogant was my perception. This angered me and I proceeded to walk down to where he was launching. I asked him if he had said something to me and if he would repeat it. He said he had and it was something about if I had not been parked in a no parking zone, he would not have hit me.

Well duh, obvious to the most casual observer, tell me something I don't already know. If I had stayed in bed that morning, I wouldn't be talking to an idiot. I apologize to the idiots because they had no choice in the intelligence they were born with. This person actually had intelligence but chose not to use it. I asked him if I could get his insurance information and he replied, when I'm done here, if you have a piece of paper. I started looking through my wallet for a piece of paper and my insurance information, all the while being ignored by him as he went about the process of launching. He was the only one launching and there was another launch adjacent to him that was unoccupied so he wouldn't have been holding anyone up if he stopped what he was doing and gave me his information. I started to do a slow burn and was getting very angry at being ignored and realized I had to get my emotions under control or I would be jumping in his boat with him and introducing him to the deck. The result of that would more than likely have been an assault charge against me. I acted on my boxing training and rather than attacking him while angry, I put away my wallet and walked away. If he can ignore me, I will do likewise. I learned in boxing it is not smart to attack while angry because you are not thinking clearly and often times will get the snot literally pounded out of you.

I went back to my car and moved it to a parking area after one of his passengers took pictures of the crime scene and admonished me for parking in a no parking area. This person appeared to think they had the right to hit me because of where I was parked. It appeared to be a boat load of arrogant, egotistical, narcissists.

By fleeing the scene, it gave me time to calm down, even go for a walk and think about what to do. I realized that perhaps he was in a hurry to launch because he had been drinking and was trying to get out of there before anyone had a chance to talk to him face to face or question his sobriety. I had never known this person to be other than friendly and a gentleman.

Dwight E. Knuth

Under the right circumstances, anyone is capable of anything. His behavior in this instance sure appeared to be egotistical and arrogant and not at all friendly. I determined on my walk, I best not talk to him or I might lose it and end up in jail. It wasn't worth ruining my time with my grandchildren because this individual had an ego problem. It also would not be a good example for my grandchildren although it might make an interesting story at family gatherings. Do you remember Grandpa, the time you were jailed for punching out that guy that hit your car? I resolved to let it go and forget about it, which I did.

For my friends and relatives that want to know who this person was, don't bother asking me because I will not tell you. I don't wish to slander his name all over the place, he can do that himself by his actions, I just want to step on his blue suede shoes.

My perception of this individual is that he failed sandbox 101 in kindergarten where we learn to share and get along with one another. Another point I would like to make is that it is important that we set a good example for our children and grandchildren. If we act arrogant and egotistical in our life, our children and grandchildren will probably act accordingly. It's probably his parents fault, most things are. It can be a learned trait handed down from generation to generation. Children learn what they live. The same thing applies to losing your temper and resorting to physical violence.

The question that came to my mind is when we are in heaven and we experience these types of differences, how will anger or other emotions be controlled and these types of situations avoided. As my Mother used to say, if we can't get along on earth, how do we expect to get along in heaven? If we are the same individuals in heaven we were on earth and our enemies that we prayed for are also there, how will our differences be dissolved? Is it the Love factor? Because God is Love, are we infused with his love and these situations therefore never arise. I like to think that is the case.

As modern day society changes, religions also change. A small example. As a young Baptist boy, I was not allowed to go to movies. I can't imagine where in the Bible it says, "Thou shalt not attend the cinema", especially since God hadn't invented it, at that time. But yet it was generally accepted that it was wrong to go to movies and possibly even a sin. This was before God invented television, at least in North Dakota. Now, I don't know a single Baptist who doesn't go to movies or watch them on TV. Many are very selective in what they watch but do not believe it to be sinful anymore, just a personal choice.

Even the 10 commandments seem to have changed to 10 suggestions. One in particular, "Remember the Sabbath, to keep it Holy", seems to have taken on new meaning. When I was a boy we attended church a minimum of four hours on Sunday. No work was done other than sustaining life such as feeding the farm animals and ourselves. My maternal grandmother wouldn't even allow us to play games. When I was in the Navy, I had buddies that were Catholic who always attended church on Sunday. We could be laying on the beach in Atlantic City, NJ, bikini watching, and they would go get dressed, go to church and then come back to continue the bikini watching. I'm almost positive there was lusting involved. Well, the 10 commandments don't mention bikinis or the watching of them.

Today, in the town where I live, there is a paper mill that makes paper 24 hours a day, seven days a week. This requires workers on Sunday. No religion is exempt from working on Sunday. However, I understand, there are ways to avoid Sunday shifts by trading shifts or other means. Everyone takes their turn without any time off for attending church. We live in a paradise with many lakes, some in remote areas. Many residents have cabins on these lakes and go to the cabin for the weekend. Many, I would guess the majority, don't return on Sunday to attend church. It seems like we view the Sabbath as just another week day and oops, we forgot to keep it Holy or we justify it with we are enjoying God's creation and keeping it Holy in that way. Who is the one that defines Holy? I guess you could call me old school because I disagree with some of the modern definitions of Holy. Even in our church services where we used to dress up to worship God and show respect as opposed to the modern casual dress and sometimes barely dressed.

Then there is the worship itself where seldom if ever do we sing the old standard hymns that were important to our parents and sung by them not only on Sundays but daily as they went about their work. I Guess I'm becoming an old fuddy duddy. Then we have the modern communion where we don't even go to the alter and kneel but grab a wafer on our way by, dip it in wine and devour it on our way back to our seat. Seems kind of like someone is saying, keep it moving, we have other places to go and things to do and oh by the way, God, thanks for sending us your Son for our salvation. I can't imagine there are many prayers offered or confessions said or forgiveness requested in this hurry up commune with God. I say, why even bother? So we pick and choose, even the commandments and we justify to ourselves what fits our life styles. After all, it doesn't say Thou shall or Thou shalt not, it says Remember the Sabbath. Is it just a suggestion? Something you should do if you're not inconvenienced.

So it goes with many other moral values that have changed, eroded or been ignored. It used to be and some of you can remember, when no one, or very few, lived together and had sex together until they were married. In many states, if you did live together out of matrimony for a specified time, the state considered you "common law" wed. At least most didn't broadcast their sexual activity. Now just about everyone lives together before they get married, if in fact they ever marry. I'm pretty sure there is sex involved. I've heard members of the opposite sex, the kinder, fairer, gentler sex, argue that everyone should have sex before marriage to insure they are compatible in that department. Where were these feminists when I was on the prowl? Has the Bible changed? I don't think so. Our society and moral fiber and mores have changed.

Some of our morals in the good old US of A have strayed from Biblical teachings for the better such as women's rights and slavery. We sometimes justify this behavior by saying the Bible was written during a different time and culture and what applied then doesn't apply anymore.

This Dummy Pulls His Own Strings

Going way back to biblical times, females were treated almost like a possession or at least a person that didn't control their own destiny. Fathers chose their daughters husbands and accepted goods as a dowry from the chosen husband. Is that not selling your daughter? Sounds like property to me. Some fathers were the ones that had to have the dowry to get a husband for their daughters. Still, trading of humans. Some religions allowed many wives for one man but not the reverse. Kind of like the animal kingdom where one male breeds many females. The man was the head of the household and ruled. Over time, society has righted some of the female inequalities and eliminated or at least frowned on slavery for the most part. Inequalities still exist and probably always will in society.

One that still exists is the right of gays and lesbians to marry the same sex in some states. There is progress in this, from the days of the Bible but many who are against "gay rights" use the argument that the Bible says marriage should include a man and woman. Not being a Bible scholar, I wonder does it also say, one man and one woman or one man and many women? Also, the Bible speaks to how you should treat your slaves, so does that mean the Bible and the teachings of God condone slavery and we should not have eliminated it, in the US of A? If we are using the Bible as an instruction book on living in the modern world and it is God's instructions to us, should we not be following all of it instead of picking and choosing which ones apply in modern society? It's natural for humans, being all unique, to interpret the Bible differently and pick and choose what we want to believe and how we should live, worship God and practice religion. Freedom of religion is part of the freedoms we enjoy in this country that our founding fathers insured we have. These problems are not going to be solved or resolved in this book, I'm writing. In fact, the answers to many of my questions will not be known until we meet our Savior, face to face.

I choose to believe that some things in our modern society are better today than in Bible times. Two of them are slavery and women's rights. I lean also towards Gay rights when it comes to marriage. Now don't try to read between the lines and think I am gay, unless you mean happy. Because of the way I was brought up and our social values, I have a hard time watching two guys kissing. Watching two girls kissing doesn't have the same effect on me. Why is that? I think I should be more tolerant of the gay lifestyle including gay marriage. Anytime there is Love, it should not be discouraged, even between two people of the same sex. What the world needs more of is Love, sweet Love.

Of course, there are many who disagree with me. Just like the ones that disagree with me on women's rights and there are more than most realize, I don't condemn them for their opinions or beliefs. Some of you who are reading this will condemn my beliefs, which is your right. Some of you will even stop communicating with me, which is also your right. Some religions teach, you should associate with like-minded people and separate yourself from people that don't believe as you do. If you do this, how do you broaden your thinking or become more open minded to different opinions than yours? As Ruth Graham once said when she was being interviewed and asked if she and Billy ever disagreed. She answered, of course we disagree, if we agreed on everything, one of us would be unnecessary. If you agree with everything I am writing, than one of us is unnecessary and I would guess, in your opinion, the unnecessary one would be me. So that is one thing we disagree on and therefore we both are necessary.

I have sat in churches and listened to preachers proclaim the word of God and tell women to be submissive to their husband and to obey their husbands, which he says is the word of God. I happen to like the idea of a partnership between two people in marriage and thus no domination by one over the other. It worked out well for us in our marriage but then I married an extraordinary, intelligent, reasonable woman.

Was the Bible written as a guide for the time or for all time? Should women be denied equal rights or education and be dominated by men? I believe that was kind of how they were treated when the Bible was written. If I give myself the liberty of straying from the word of God by allowing them equal rights and education, then I feel it would be hypocritical of me to not allow others to stray from the word of God in the marriage of one man and woman. This is just one man's stupid opinion and being a dummy, I do pull my own strings.

So what does it all mean? We have disagreement over the Bible and it's interpretation, how we should live and what we should believe. In my humble opinion, I believe religion is personal and only you can decide what you choose to believe. Someone else can not give you Faith, Hope or Love. These come from within yourself. My personal belief is that you need Faith, Hope and Love but the greatest of these is Love. If God had answered all the questions I have, I would not need faith or hope. He gives us a way to eternal life through his son, Jesus by forgiving our sins. We need to believe and have faith.

Random thoughts, rambling or stirring the pot.

Those of you that are single parents, consider yourself in good company. God is also a single parent.

If I could sit down with God and have a conversation with him over a cup of coffee, one question of many, I would ask is, why is there not a Mrs. God. Why are you a single parent? There is the trinity, Father, Son and Holy Ghost but no Mrs. God, or for that matter, no daughter. We were created in God's image. To a simple mind like mine, it would follow that there would be a Mrs. God and God the daughter. The Holy family, not just the trinity. On earth, woman was created as a help mate. Someone to share love and life with. I'm pretty sure God doesn't need a help mate and he loves us all and probably isn't lonesome but shouldn't he have someone to complain to about the mess we're making down here on his creation? God the Son, in the form of Jesus, didn't come on the scene until we, as humans, needed a method for salvation and a way to obtain eternal life. Perhaps, God the daughter is waiting in the wings for the next chapter in humanity. God didn't reveal his Son to humanity until the proper time. What else does he have to reveal to us? For the Catholics reading this, as Christians we do have Mary the mother of Jesus and I don't mean to diminish her role in the Holy family. However, she is not part of the trinity, God the Father, God the Son and God the Holy Spirit.

Meanwhile, we see through a glass darkly, but then face to face. This is just a sample of the "deep thinking" or "pot stirring", call it as you see it, that flows through my alleged simple mind. I'm sure my heavenly Father gets just as exasperated with me as my earthly parents did and probably still do.

18
Last Chapter

1993, Kathleen and Dwight Knuth

Dwight E. Knuth

My sweet, funny, valentine, you make my heart smile.

Last week Kathy and I were told that her breast cancer has returned, possibly to her liver and bones. She had a liver biopsy Monday but we haven't received the results of that test. Her Dr. told us it looks bad.

This may be the last chapter of her life and as always, she is thinking how this news affects the ones she loves. She is hesitant to tell them because she doesn't want to ruin their day or she will wait until morning so it won't ruin their nights' rest. She'll wait to tell some until she is strong enough for her to help them through the news. As always, she is a deeply caring, unselfish, loving person.

God blessed me and allowed me to spend 47 years with this wonderful person who helped make me who I am, at least the good in me, if any exits. I hope and pray that he will allow me more pain free time with her. Not my will but God's will. I am truly grateful that God had it in his plan for us to spend our lives together and to share our Love. Love is what life is all about and it has been a wonderful life, poverty and abundance, sickness and health, sadness and happiness, all of it. Because I had someone that was so special to me to share all of life's moments with. God blessed us.

They did further tests to try to pinpoint the source of the cancer because different sources mean different treatments. The cancer is in her liver and bones. They did a MRI brain scan and found one brain but did not find brain cancer. I'm afraid if they did that on me they would have a hard time locating the brain, being a human with little brain. They did find that the bone cancer is in the skull in addition to ribs and other areas. They did a CT scan of the lungs and found them to be clear of cancer but found blood clots in the lungs which triggered a phone call from the health care facility urging us to get to the emergency room immediately. Why, all of a sudden is it an emergency when she has told them for weeks she is coughing up blood, doesn't quite make sense but

This Dummy Pulls His Own Strings

I'm sure they had her best interests in mind. They are very caring health professionals and do the best they can and we value their care and caring.

With this information, the oncologist, Dr. Friday, believes the source of the liver and bone cancer is the previous breast cancer. Therefore, they will tailor the treatment to the source breast cancer cells. This means she can take her chemotherapy in pill form rather than with an IV. She is extremely grateful for that. They also want her to take an injection a day of a blood thinner, indefinitely, to avoid blood clots. I have been giving her these injections and she is doing well with them. Probably better than I am doing at giving them to her. I don't mind giving myself injections but don't like giving them to her. She doesn't have the fat reserve, I have. In fact, there is very little skin and meat to inject, forget the fat. She hates these daily injections but again she is trying to make my job easier by being strong and not showing her emotions. You can see the resolve build in her face as she prepares herself for her injection. She will also receive an injection once a month to strengthen her bones.

She is taking a plethora of pills for pain, nausea, constipation, diarrhea and anxiety. Some are twelve hour pills, some eight hour, some six hours all with medical names that are impossible to read or pronounce. Just balancing the pills and keeping them straight, is enough to give you anxiety. Kim and I try to help her with keeping everything recorded and administered but it is a full time job for three people. Some pills need to be taken with food which is very difficult when you don't have an appetite. It seems she is just eating to get her pills down.

She has a lot of pain and struggles with fatigue and sleeps a lot. She gets frustrated because the smallest task wears her out and inhibits her breathing. Despite the pain, anxiety and frustration she maintains a sense of humor and fights to keep a positive attitude. She is one tough lady. Sometimes I wish she wouldn't be so tough so I could cry with her and try to comfort her but this is her call and she has to handle it the way she needs to, not the way that I would prefer. I'm the weak one and the one that lacks the strength to deal with it. Rather than share my weakness and grief with her, I go to the shower and let the tears flow.

It is very difficult to watch the struggles she has but I am so proud of her and her ability to fight on and the strength and resolve she exhibits every day. I am grateful she has chosen to prolong her life because it means I get to hug her, hold her, hold hands with her, have conversations, laugh and cry with her and share space and time with her. I feel guilty for selfishly wanting her presence with me, when it is causing her suffering.

Initially, when she was diagnosed, she told them she didn't want to go through all the tests and treatments that are required for prolonging life when death is certain. When they told her she would live six months without treatment and possibly two years with treatment, she decided to go with the tests and treatments. Her oncologist told us that she would feel so much better and have more energy and a much better quality of life with the treatments. It turned out he was wrong about that and when she could still speak, she expressed how angry she was with him for promising her a more comfortable and longer life that never happened.

Of course, when her siblings and mine, heard her diagnoses and prognosis, they all wanted to come and see her. She kept putting them off, waiting for when she had more energy and felt better. She was worried about how hard it would be for them when they saw her in the condition she was in. She was a lady with dignity and didn't want to lose that dignity in front of the people she loved and those that loved her.

She started the chemotherapy treatments Sept. 3, 2014, the day after our wedding anniversary. We went out to dinner on our anniversary with Kim, Jack and Eric. Kathy ate very little and seemed fatigued to me but was trying not to ruin it for the rest of us. She seemed glad to get home. Fifteen days later she died.

She started the treatments and within four days she was having many adverse reactions to them. I would call the cancer treatment hotline daily for her because she was on pain medications and had a hard time understanding directions they would give and even explaining how she was feeling. She constantly fought constipation and diarrhea. She had a hard time eating anything, throwing up a lot which made it impossible for her pills to do their job and not knowing how much of the medication was still in her or how much came up, she would have to wait for the prescribed time before taking them again so she wouldn't overdose.

I had asked the oncologist to give her pain patches because one of our friends had recommended them for her because they had worked so well for her. The Dr. wouldn't prescribe them because he said in his experience; they didn't work well for patients like Kathy who were quite thin. I argued that the lady who recommended them was quite thin and they worked for her but he said he wanted to try other pain medications that he was sure worked better. Kathy, even sided with him and said it had been a long time since we saw this friend and perhaps she had gained weight because of medications she was taking so that was the reason they worked for her. I could see, I was not going to win this argument and I'm sure Kathy was afraid they wouldn't do the job and she would be in a lot of pain. I on the other hand, thought they were worth a try and if they didn't work, it would be obvious and we could go back to the pills. I, however, was not going through the pain and Kathy didn't complain about it so I was not fully aware of the degree of pain she was having.

I tried another approach and asked the Dr. about marijuana. He said if you know where and how to get it, go for it. Minnesota had just passed the medical marijuana approval, which I had voted for, and I was under the impression it was in effect. That was not the case. The Drs. could not prescribe it until the first of the year. I had never used any but had access to it when I was in the Navy, just never wanted to try it. I thought if it was available fifty years ago, I should be able to acquire some in this day and age. So we were left with the pills that may or may not do the job, depending on if Kathy could keep them down.

In addition to not being able to keep down her pills, Kathy's mouth was getting very sore and bloody so she couldn't eat and sometimes had difficulty speaking. Besides being painful, it was very frustrating to her. She had medication to apply inside her mouth with a swab which was also very painful. Because she couldn't take pills anymore, she was in more pain and she couldn't take her allergy pill which exacerbated her allergies and she was constantly throwing up and spitting out bloody mucous. The cancer hotline nurse finally told us to stop the chemotherapy pills and to see a Dr. either at home or to travel 100 miles to see her oncologist. I wanted to go see her oncologist because I was afraid the local Drs. would not be adequate to give her the relief I wanted her to have but I was afraid the 200 mile round trip would be too hard on her. I asked her what her preference was and she agreed it was best to see her oncologist. She was so weak, in pain and miserable, she just wanted some relief.

This was a lady with a lot of pride, inner strength, dignity and grace. I wanted to use a wheelchair for her at the medical facility but she insisted she could walk OK and didn't need one. She even joked that she was safer walking because I was not the best wheel chair driver as I had hit a few obstacles in the past with her wheelchair. I couldn't argue with that but finally convinced her to use a wheelchair. I think she didn't want to draw attention to herself or have people feeling sorry for her.

When we saw the oncologist, he took one look at her and said, "that looks painful". She was having difficulty speaking and just nodded her head. He prescribed some medication for her to be injected to help with the sore mouth which he said was thrush. The shot was in excess of three thousand dollars and I didn't notice that it did all that much good. He also prescribed the pain patches I had been asking for without me even bringing it up. It was obvious she could not ingest pills. He also told her he didn't know what he was going to do about the cancer. That really lifted her spirits and I wanted to relieve him of some of his teeth. It seemed to me he could have simply said he would look into alternative treatments. He probably didn't because he didn't want to subject her to more false hope. I think it was at this point that she lost the will to fight and perhaps wanted the end to be expedited.

This Dummy Pulls His Own Strings

At one point, much earlier, when she was diagnosed with terminal cancer, she asked if I would be willing to help her end her life when it made no sense to prolong it. I told her I was too selfish and could not do that. I was beginning to reconsider that because, still being selfish, I couldn't stand to watch her suffering. I didn't bring it up again and neither did she. I'm sure she still believed I wouldn't consider helping her with it.

Her siblings were expressing a desire to come see her and Kathy finally relented and said it was OK. Her two oldest brothers from Montana, Lynn and Larry, twins, immediately made plans to come and her only sister, Vivian, said she would come to help with cooking, cleaning and any other work that needed to be done. Kathy agreed to this and plans moved forward. She also agreed to have her two younger brothers come after her older ones left but she was concerned that it was going to be really hard on them, especially her youngest brother, Mike, whom she grew up with and was probably closest to. My sister also wanted to come visit to say final goodbyes and Kathy agreed to that also but of course wanted to see her siblings first.

The pain patches were working to some degree and occasionally she could supplement them with a pain pill. Her two oldest brothers and sister arrived and Kathy was able to speak to them and even share a laugh or two with them. The last evening of their visit, she had a really good visit with them and seemed to enjoy it and had a few laughs.

Lynn and Larry left and we were preparing and making plans for her two remaining brothers to visit. Her mouth was so sore at this point that she was not eating anything and couldn't even stand ice chips in her mouth. She would rub a popsicle on her lips for the soothing effect but was getting little or no liquid in her body. She had insisted earlier that she wanted to die at home and not in the hospital. However, she was down to under 100 pounds and was getting dehydrated so I suggested we go into emergency and have them put in a IV to get her hydrated and the possibility of some nourishment and better pain medications. She agreed to this without any protesting but you could see this was not something she wanted to do. I thought perhaps she was suffering from nicotine withdrawal because she wasn't able to smoke because her mouth was so sore she couldn't suck on the cigarette to inhale the smoke. I asked her if she wanted a cigarette before we left and she shook her head no. I then asked if she wanted a nicotine patch and again she shook her head no.

I imagine she anticipated they would admit her to the hospital and she would never see her home again, which is exactly what happened. I noticed as we were preparing to go to the emergency, she was looking around her home, taking it all in, as if this would be the last time she would see the home she created and loved. It broke my heart.

In the emergency room, they put in an IV but first put her through the pain of making her take a few pills. She was very brave about it and when I would argue with them that she couldn't take the pills because of her sore mouth, she would tell me it was OK and she would attempt it. They had some reason they couldn't give them by IV but I was in protection mode. Eventually they said she needed to be admitted to the hospital which she agreed to. They said it would be for a few days to get her hydrated and some nutrition in her. I also agreed to it after Kathy said it was OK.

I stayed with her around the clock, except for about one hour the second day she was there to go home and check everything, shower and change clothes. They had her in a double room by the nurses' station so it was easier for them to monitor her. The second bed in her room was unoccupied so the nurses would tell me I could sleep in it at night and they would bring me warm blankets. I asked if it would be OK to move my bed next to her bed so I could hold her hand at night. They said it would be fine and even helped me arrange it. They had her so pumped full of pain drugs that it was like she was unconscious. However, I believe she knew what was happening and could hear what we were saying. The nurse would come to swab her mouth with medication and tell her to open her mouth and she would. When it would get too painful, she would clamp her teeth together on the swab until the nurse would promise her she would stop if Kathy would

This Dummy Pulls His Own Strings

let go of the swab. Kathy would open her mouth and release the swab. I would tell Kathy what was happening and when people would come to see her and leave. There was no acknowledgement from her that she understood but I believe she did. I think she was in a drug, dream like world where she was aware of what was happening to her and could hear what was taking place. Her Grandchildren came after work from the twin cities, a 5 hour drive one way. They sat with their "Nana" for several hours and then drove back to the cities so they could be there in time for work and school.

After a day or two, her youngest brother, Mike and his wife, Pam arrived from Bismarck and her sister, Vivian returned from Kettle River. Her other brother, Roger and his wife, Arlene were on their way from Billings, Montana.

The Dr. wanted to move Kathy to the hospital in Virginia, MN. I expressed my concern that the trip in the car would be too hard on her and that I wasn't sure I could get her in and out of the car without hurting her even though she weighed next to nothing. We were having this conversation in her room with the Dr. on one side of her bed and I on the other. He suggested we transport her by ambulance. I asked him why we would take her from this hospital to another. He said she could get better care there and would live longer. I asked how much longer. He said probably a couple days which really irked me, knowing that the end was very near. I said "what is the point"? I also told him that she wanted to die at home so if they couldn't keep her in the hospital, we should take her home to die, not Virginia, MN. He said she could stay in the hospital there or we could take her home and have hospice help us with her care. I said, let's take her home.

Kathy had me promise if she was near death that I would not let them prolong her life. She warned me that they would try to do this and she had experience with this when her Dad was dying and the nurse wanted to take measures to keep him alive. Kathy told me she threatened to do physical harm to the nurse if she proceeded. Evidently she was convincing because the nurse stopped what she was doing. Kathy told her to make him as comfortable as possible but not to do anything to prolong his life. She made me promise I would do the same for her because she anticipated this happening.

While making arrangements for hospice care, they informed me that hospice could not help out until a day after she was home because no one was available. One of the nurses lived just across the street from my home and up the street a couple houses. She is a very compassionate, caring and giving person. I set out to find her and talk to her and see if I could hire her to help care for Kathy until hospice could come. She has a family of little kids and a husband and works full time at the hospital. I thought with her living so close, if we had difficulties or problems, I could call her and she could probably help over the phone or run over for a while. She came to see how Kathy was doing and I approached the subject of hiring her. She said she would not think of doing it for pay but she would do it without pay. She said I could call her anytime, night or day and she would help any way she could. I wanted to pay her but she insisted that she would not accept any pay. I thought there are ways around it and I could give her and her husband a Christmas gift of money, gift cards for dinners at local resorts or some other way to show my appreciation for her kindness. I think that her and Kathy had bonded and were already friends. That was the way with Kathy, she often made friends with people she met. She could read people and tell if they were good people or as she would describe it, creeps. I, on the other hand, was clueless. I would immediately like someone and she would say he/she gives me the creeps. Her instincts were right on, most of the time and I often sought her opinion when it came to people. I didn't necessarily reject or accept the person, based on her opinion but I would proceed with caution if she had an unfavorable opinion of them. If I proceeded to associate with people she wasn't fond of, she would tolerate them for my sake but remain distant. She did this on several occasions. It didn't surprise me that she had formed a bond with her nurse in the few months she knew her.

This Dummy Pulls His Own Strings

I was trying to make arrangements to take Kathy home the next day. I may not have been thinking clearly and I was verbalizing my plans in Kathy's room to someone, that my plans were to put Kathy's hospital bed in the living room, where she could look out the picture window and see the sunshine in her favorite spot. That way she wouldn't be isolated from the activity at home by being stuck away in her bedroom and I would sleep on the couch beside her where I could continue to hold her hand during the night. This would free up our bed for one of her brothers and his wife. I believe Kathy heard me expressing my plans and didn't really agree with them or like them. I base that on the fact that she died before I had a chance to implement them. Knowing her determination, resolve, dignity and wish not to be the center of attention and her wish to die with dignity, I can imagine her thinking, this is not going to happen, even if I can't express my wishes. I also think she was thinking she wanted to spare me, her siblings, children and grandchildren from witnessing what she would probably refer to as a "production" or a "circus". The mind can think and form opinions when you are under the influence of drugs in a hospital setting. You may not be able to express your thoughts but it doesn't stop your mind from working. I know this from past experience in a hospital setting after a heart attack and triple bypass operation. Again, I believe it was her desire to spare me and the rest of her loved ones with the difficult task of caring for her and watching her suffer, only to die. I think she was praying for it to end and she simply put her hand in the hand of the man from Galilee and entered into eternity with him. She was a strong believer in prayer and the power of prayer. I remember her telling our five year old grandson to pray to God when he was scared of the dark at night if he woke up in the middle of the night and God would take care of him. I also believe in prayer and the power of prayer and I am absolutely sure she and God had many conversations, many of them on my behalf. Kathy and I both witnessed and were taught the power of prayer from our respective parents, growing up. My mother often told me, pray without ceasing and it was something she practiced.

In the early moments of the morning before Kathy died, while holding her hand and lying in my bed next to hers, I put my head next to hers and asked her if when she arrived in heaven, if she would greet her parents and siblings for me. I reminded her that they would be there to greet her. I also told her to greet my parents and siblings for me. I told her I loved her and would join her when God chose and said goodbye. There was no acknowledgement that she heard me or comprehended. A few short hours later, I got up, made my bed, moved it away from hers, kissed her on the forehead, told her I loved her and that I was taking her home today. They brought me my breakfast. I checked my blood sugar, took my insulin and sat down to eat breakfast. The nurse came in to check on Kathy and said, "Dwight, you better come here". I went over to her bed and the nurse said, "She's gone, Dwight". I looked at Kathy's face and there was such peace and contentment in her face, I knew her suffering was over. She was still beautiful, even in death. I lost it, all the emotions and tears flowed freely for I don't know how long. A complete melt down. They brought me a chair and I sat by her body and hugged her and cried until they pulled me away so the Dr. could pronounce her time of death. Even after that, I went back to hold her and cry over her still warm body. When her siblings and our children arrived, I left Kathy to hug and cry with them. The nurse called our pastor, who we found out was out of town and the pastor that was filling in came to pray with us over Kathy's body. I knelt by her bed, held her hand one last time and prayed for my soul mate, the love of my life, my best friend and companion for forty seven years of marriage and the five years prior to marriage when I first met her. The happiness she brought to me made the sadness so intense, It is impossible to describe it. This is the price or cost of Love. I would do it all over again and pay the price again, if only I could.

Her brother from Billings, Montana and his wife had not arrived yet and I was concerned that he would need to see her before she was cremated. I also told the hospital staff that she was an organ donor. It was important to her that I remember that. She reminded me several weeks before she died and made me promise to do what was necessary to allow her organs that could be used to be harvested. The hospital staff informed the donor people and said it would not be a problem if her brother wanted to view the body before it was cremated.

They told me the donor people could only harvest the eyes and they had to fly to International Falls to do that so they would keep the body in the hospital morgue until that happened and longer if need be. Our son, Eric, took care of talking to the donor people over the phone and answering the multitude of questions that needed to be answered. It was not an easy task and I am so grateful to him for doing that and helping me fulfill his mother's wishes and my promise to her. Days later, I received a thank you letter and certificate from the Lions in appreciation of the organ donation. If Kathy would have known her eyes could be useful after her death, it would have made her very happy. She was a voracious reader and always had several books in the process of being read either on her kindle or hard and soft cover. I had converted one of our bedrooms into a library for her. It was filled with books and they overflowed to the living room and the TV room as well as kitchen and dining room and our bedroom. Even the bathrooms had books in them.

She also liked to play scrabble and played on her kindle. Because of her reading, she was well versed and had a very extensive vocabulary. My vocabulary was not always what it should be and at times I would talk like the sailor I had been. Kathy also said I spoke like some of the people of the community I grew up in, Drake. It was a German settlement and German was spoken in the homes of many of my friends. Sometimes the translation from German to English was not the proper English. For example, you may hear someone say, "throw me down the stairs, my hat" or "throw the bull over the fence, some hay". Kathy referred to this, when I would talk this way, as me reverting to "Drakeonian", after the name of the village I grew up in, Drake, ND. She meant no disrespect for the fine people of Drake or the people of German heritage, she just thought I should speak properly, as I had been taught.

Kathy's brother from Billings, Roger and his wife, Arlene arrived and they said they did not need to view the body for closure so I informed the hospital staff so the funeral home could proceed with the cremation.

Our children, Kimberly, Eric and I met with the funeral home people and proceeded with plans for Kathy's memorial service and obituary. Kathy had requested of me that I write her obituary and that it be accurate. I did the best I could while grieving and I believe it was accurate but I left out that she had been an Avon representative, had done daycare for many children and in the early days of our marriage had taken in ironing, which she was very good at and loved doing.

In my alleged mind, her most important task was raising our children, which she put her heart and soul into and did a stellar job of. I have often heard compliments of our children and what wonderful people they are. That was Kathy's influence on them and the way she raised them and taught them our values. Values passed down from our parents. Many people have told me they wished their children had turned out like ours. Kathy made a conscious decision to be a stay at home Mom and raise her children and be a homemaker.

This was her choice. I told her she could go to work outside the home if that was her desire or she could stay home. Either way she would be contributing to the income of our family. If she stayed at home, the income was not as visible but was still there. It was there in the savings she realized by shopping the bargains and rummage sales. In fact she was so good at finding bargains and saving money, at one point, I told her we couldn't afford to save any more money. The savings was there by the money she saved in the expense of going to work, driving a second car, insurance on it and repair not to mention the initial cost. It was there in the savings of the cost for dressing for work as well as hair dressers, lunches and things associated with working at a job. It was there in the savings of day care expenses and baby sitters. It was there in the valuable research she did in stock market investments to build a nest egg.

However, if she needed to work outside the home, the income she made would be evident and contribute to our needs. Only she could decide what was best for her. She decided to stay at home and raise the children and be a homemaker but to sell Avon products for some added spending money and as a self-esteem booster. It was also a way to meet people and make friends. She excelled in both.

After meeting with the funeral home people, there were tasks to get ready for the memorial service. We, Kim, Eric and I, went to the florist to order flowers for the service. Kim put together two memory boards of pictures with Eric's help, digging through a foot locker trunk and scouring the house looking for specific pictures. I spent an afternoon listening to funeral hymns on the internet trying to decide which ones to use. One of Kathy's favorites was "Put your hand in the hand of the man from Galilee" so we chose that one. One of my favorites is "Take my hand precious Lord" so we chose that one also and elected to have the soloist, Joe Belanger, sing them.

We selected, "Stand up, Stand up for Jesus" as the congregational hymn. The story behind that choice is; Kathy was pregnant for ten months with each of our children. The Dr. said that this is normal for some women. The 10th month was very uncomfortable for Kathy. She said that when she lay down, she was like a beached whale and couldn't get up by herself. I would have to help her get up. In the morning before I left for work, I would have to help her get out of bed or she would be stuck there until I came home for lunch. She was still doing all the house work and cooking and laundry.

She was a very happy pregnant lady and actually glowed her entire pregnancy with both children. The last month was sometimes difficult getting around or being on her feet too long. We had gone to church during the last month and we were about to sing, "Stand up, Stand up for Jesus" and the pastor said he thought it would be appropriate for us to stand while singing this hymn. We were all standing but Kathy was in some discomfort so I told her she should sit down, which she did. The music started and the congregation burst forth with "Stand up, Stand up for Jesus" and Kathy popped right up beside me. I guess she thought they were demanding she stand up. Either that or the baby kicked her hard enough to make her jump up. Eric did kick her hard enough to break what the Dr. said was the breast bone.

We met with the minister of Zion Lutheran church, pastor Steve Olson and with the musician, Joe Belanger. We learned that Steve had served his internship at the Balfour and Butte, ND Lutheran churches and knew many of the people in the area, especially the Lutherans. Balfour is the village that my grandparents came to, by immigrant train, when they homesteaded in the area. The Lutheran church in Butte was built by my grandfather as a country EUB church on highway 14 just north of Balfour. The first minister was my grandfather's brother, Rev. Fred Knuth. When they closed the church they sold it to the Lutherans in Butte and moved it to Butte. Kathy's brother, Mike, married Pam Federanko who lived next door to and attended that church all the while she was growing up and she was married in that church. This gave us some common ground with the minister that we had just met and made us feel comfortable with him. As my Mother was so fond of saying, "God works in mysterious ways".

Vivian, Kathy's sister, was here prior to Kathy's death and was planning to stay when I brought Kathy home to help me care for her. Mike, Kathy's brother and his wife Pam were here before Kathy died and Pam just made herself familiar with Kathy's kitchen and took over the cooking of meals. Roger, Kathy's brother from Billings and his wife Arlene arrived and they pitched in and helped any way they could doing whatever was needed. This freed Kim, Eric and I to take care of the arrangements for the memorial service.

I sat down to write Kathy's obituary as I had promised her I would. It appears later in this chapter with her burial service.

I forgot to mention in her obituary that she was an Avon representative for several years, going house to house to sell the Avon products. Even after she had her first child, she would walk around the neighborhood, pushing the baby carriage and later the stroller, and call on her customers. She also did day care for working mothers both in Grand Forks and in International Falls. The kids she cared for remained special to her always. She would follow their activities in school and often attend concerts and plays they were in. She also loved to Iron clothes and would take in ironing for extra income. These things should have been included in her obituary but I dropped the ball.

Grief is a strange emotion. As my granddaughter, Katelyn described it, it sneaks up on you and attacks without any warning, sometimes in the middle of a conversation or other activity. It can make you speechless and a weeping, slobbering fool to others around you. It is all consuming. It is, of course, different for just about everyone but has some elements that are common. For this unpredictable quality, many people avoid grieving people. I have experienced people see me and avoid me, some practically running to get away. Even when I would advance toward them, they would retreat. I may have been guilty of this behavior myself, on occasion, when seeing an acquaintance that has recently lost a loved one. I suppose it is a control issue. We are afraid that we may lose control in public and create a scene by crying so we avoid the situation. When one of your friends or acquaintances avoids you, initially, before thinking about it, it is a bit off putting until you engage the thought processes and realize what is going on.

Sometimes, the reality of grieving deserts your mind and you revert to the reality before your loved one died. I have come home, weeks after Kathy died, entered the house and called out, "honey, I'm home" before realizing, she is no longer here. I have come home to an empty house and had the thought that perhaps Kathy will call me this evening because when she was away from home and me, she would often call me in the evening because she knew I would be home then. It is only a fleeting thought but it makes you pause and ask yourself if you're losing your sanity. I justify it by convincing myself that I want my reality to be what it was before Kathy died, so bad, that my mind is ignoring the reality as it is now. Perhaps that is part of the grieving and healing process. The other reality I may be ignoring is that I have finally gone over the edge and lost my alleged mind, in which case, it would be proof positive that indeed I did have a mind and it is not alleged.

I have been doing some organizing of my household and making some changes to it. Kathy was obsessed with cleanliness. I'm not so much. I like things organized, orderly and pleasant looking but don't mind a dust ball here or there as long as they stay put and don't invade my food or drink. Before Kathy died and before I knew she was dying, when she was low on energy but still wanted a clean house, I would sometimes, with a lot of prodding, do some dusting or vacuuming for her. I can recall thinking, if we didn't have so much stuff setting about especially non-essential stuff, it would be much easier cleaning. I recall my Aunt Elsie saying to my Dad one time when they were visiting our home and thought we had gone someplace, their home is really nice but I wouldn't want to have to clean it. She was referring to the non-essentials setting around making the home look nice, inviting and homey.

I, in my infinite wisdom, decided to rid my home of some of these non-essentials and make my job of cleaning much easier. I would look at something and say to myself, I really don't need that setting there cluttering up the place. If it wasn't there, I wouldn't have to dust it or move it to clean around it so I think I will get rid of it. I would remove it and later walk into the room and the room wouldn't feel or look right so I would retrieve it . Not only did I not get rid of things that were non-essential, I added a few.

Kathy must have had about two dozen pair of reading glasses. She had them placed strategically around the house so they were handy whenever she needed a pair for reading a grocery list, a recipe, a magazine, book, kindle or whatever. I tried to convince her that she should wear her reading glasses on a chain around her neck like I do with my glasses. In my case, I need to remove my glasses when I am reading. She didn't like them hanging around her neck so she dismissed that idea and strategically placed them around the house. When I dust, not only do I pick them up to dust under them but I also dust them. I thought I would gather them

This Dummy Pulls His Own Strings

up and give them all away. I had the gathering all done but was sad not to see them lying around the house anymore. I thought I would compromise and just put a few pair back where they usually resided. That helped somewhat but this alleged mind of mine that can't remember the name of a face I have known almost all my life, when I see it in the grocery store, remembers every place a pair of Kathy's reading glasses should be and aren't anymore. I keep putting more reading glasses back where they belong and I imagine soon all twenty four pair will be back in place.

In going through Kathy's things, I've come across things she put away probably because she was tired of dusting them. I say to myself, I really liked that and it reminds me of Kathy so I'm going to put it back where she had it. Every day the clutter increases. You would think that things that remind me of Kathy would cause me pain and prolong the grieving. I find there are conflicting emotions. I want to be reminded of Kathy and when I am it makes me happy for the memories and simultaneously sad because they are only memories now. Again, I imagine this is a phase of grieving that will fade and eventually I can put her reading glasses away. I will cherish and hold on to the memories of her as long as my alleged mind is capable.

For many people in the grieving process, firsts are very hard. The first holiday that your loved one is gone, the first time you eat out alone, the first visit with mutual friends, the first family reunion, the first trip alone, the first vacation alone, etc. I've found for me, it is no harder than the normal every day procedures. Holidays, generally find me surrounded by my loving family and other firsts are just extensions of the everyday new normal. There are times when I want to say, did you hear that or did you see that and quickly realize the reality that Kathy is not here to share the moment or experience with me. At those times, it makes my heart ache because we shared everything, either in the moment or after the fact. Even reading the newspaper or social media, we would share and say did you know or did you read or did you hear? Often times now, I catch myself wanting to share something with Kathy. When the need is overwhelming, I talk to her picture. Of course, it's not the same because there is no reply or disagreement or conversation but sometimes I try to imagine her side of the conversation or her reply. In these imaginary conversations, I win all the arguments which brings me back to reality because generally Kathy was right, especially when it came to decorating our home.

I read on social media, that "The real power of a man is in the size of the smile of the woman sitting next to him". No one was given credit for saying it. I know this to be true from experience and I now know why I feel so powerless, because that smile is no longer sitting next to me. Oh how I miss that smile.

I took the ashes of my beloved life partner, my teenage sweetheart and the Love of my life back to the North Dakota prairies for burial in the Balfour, ND cemetery. Her siblings and spouses and children were in attendance as was my surviving sibling and children of my siblings. My children and their children were there. Four of the Toy family came with roses, my childhood and life long friend and brother, Charles and his wife Sharon and his two sisters and my life long friends and sisters, Charlane Bertsch and Sharon Bullard were there sharing their love and memories of Kathy. Classmates of mine and friends in attendance were Arlo Blumhagen, David & Suzie Traiser, Della Volmer, wife of my deceased classmate, Allen Volmer, Dennis Jans and also some of the local people were in attendance to honor, remember and celebrate Kathy's life.

It was good to be home and have the love and support of family and friends. I feel so lost but not alone. I suppose that is because half of me is missing and it was the best half of me. It feels more like three fourths of me is missing and a big heart-ache has replaced it.

I recall that most burial services I have attended were rather impersonal and not at all comforting. I thought I could do a better job of conducting a burial service than a clergy person that didn't know Kathy or I and just did the one size fits all service. For that reason, I wrote and conducted the burial service myself, which for me was more meaningful and even comforting, speaking words that came from the life and love we shared. Following is the burial service I prepared and delivered.

Kathy's Burial Service

Thank you for coming and sharing with me our goodbye to a special lady.
I will begin with a prayer.

In the name of the Father, Son and Holy Spirit, Amen

Dear Heavenly Father,
We gather here today to remember the life of Kathleen Edith Hoffman Knuth. We also gather to say goodbye one last time and celebrate the life that she enjoyed here on earth. Thank you for each precious moment and memory that we shared with her. Her life has touched many in so many different ways. We pray that your peace and presence will be with us during this time and always.
In the name of the Father, Son and Holy Spirit, Amen

Kathy often referred to me as an absent minded professor with more emphasis on the absent mind than the professor. In preparing the service for today, I have written it down and will read from what I have written. I did this because my memory is not what I would like it to be and sometimes I forget what I was saying but I still keep talking until I finally remember it. So to spare you that, I will read from a script.

Obituary of Kathleen Edith (Hoffman) Knuth

Kathleen Edith (Hoffman) Knuth died September 18th, 2014. She was born in Minot, ND August 26, 1947. Her parents, Edith (Larson) Hoffman and Sylvestor Hoffman brought the baby girl to their farm home in Ryder, ND to join her siblings who were, Vivian and Vincent (twins), Lynn and Larry (twins), and Roger. Three years after her arrival, Kathy's family was blessed with the arrival of her brother Michael. When Kathy was about 5, the family moved to a farm they purchased southeast of Kief, ND. Kathy enjoyed the ND prairie and farm life, attending a one room country school through the eighth grade and then graduating from Drake High School in Drake, ND.

In her teen years, she was pursued by many but she was slightly partial to a sailor from Drake, ND that dated her when he was on leave and finally convinced her to become his life partner on September 2, 1967. They lived in Grand Forks, ND for 2 years and then moved to International Falls, MN.

Kathy was a voracious reader and educated herself through the hundreds of books she read. She always had a book she was reading and sometimes more than one. She was also an obsessed Scrabble player, either as a board game or on her kindle, she was a gracious hostess, loved decorating her home and keeping it spotlessly clean. On occasion, one of their military friends would do a white glove military inspection checking her cleaning ability. She always passed his inspection except when they would plant some dirt as a joke. She had a wonderful sense of humor and wore a beautiful smile that lit up whatever room she was in. She liked to travel to distant lands that she read about, especially Hawaii, her favorite and Italy. She was a good listener and complete strangers would tell her their life story and problems. She was compassionate, understanding and easy to talk to as well as being interested in what you were saying as opposed to talking about herself.

Kathy had many qualities, too numerous to mention and they do not adequately describe or explain her personality. Like her Mother, she was a classy lady with dignity. Her smile won your heart immediately and as you spoke with her and got to know her, your emotional ties grew.

Surviving Kathleen are her husband of 47 years, Dwight Knuth and Children, Eric Knuth, Duluth, MN and Kimberly Knuth, International Falls, MN. Her Grandchildren, children of Eric, Michael Knuth of Brooklyn Center, MN, Katelyn Knuth of Fargo, ND and

Nicholas Knuth of Andover, MN; child of Kimberly, Jack Knuth of International Falls, MN.

Kathleen is also survived by five of her siblings. Sister, Vivian (Lavern, deceased) Larson of Kettle River, MN, Brothers, Lynn (Ellen) Hoffman, Park City, MT, Laurence (Dawn) Hoffman, Polson, MT, Roger, (Arlene) Hoffman, Billings, MT, Michael (Pamela) Hoffman, Bismarck, ND. She is also survived by a sister-in-law, Constance Hoffman of Minot, ND.

She was predeceased by her parents, Edith (Larson) Hoffman and Sylvester Hoffman, an infant sister, Elaine Faith Hoffman, and brother Vincent Delano Hoffman.

End of obituary.

I'm sure Kathy is much too busy cavorting around heaven, settling into eternity, probably cleaning heaven, redecorating it, adding her special touches, spreading her love and smile, to pay any attention to what we are doing here. That is as it should be. In fact when I asked her what kind of service she would like, she replied, that is for you and the rest of our families and friends that are living. Do what you need to do. I won't be in attendance. I didn't disagree with her at the time because it was an emotional conversation but I beg to differ with her. I see Kathy all around me today. I see her in her children and grandchildren. I see her in all of you and the love and admiration you had for her. I see her in myself and the influence she had on my life.

If I could have one last conversation with Kathy, my end of it would go something like this. Thank you for sharing your life and love with me. For your devotion, caring and compassion. For tolerating me for those many years, usually with a beautiful smile. Thank you most of all for our beautiful children. It was a very good life, filled with love and blessings. I thank God for bringing you into my life and I thank Him for your parents and siblings that helped shape you into the beautiful person you are. My prayer is that you are spreading your happiness and peace and sharing your love in your new home. God Bless you, My Love.

Now I would like to give my voice a rest and exercise my ears by letting any of you that wish to say anything, speak your thoughts. As Kathy said, this service is for us. So if you would like to share a story, thoughts, emotions, laugh, cry, sing a song, whatever you wish. As you can see, this is informal, so whatever you wish to share will be fine. On the other hand, don't feel pressure to say anything. If no one speaks, that is also fine. In the words of Kathy, "Do what you want". Anyone?
Thank you for your presence and for sharing your love.

For our scripture today I would like to share with you what is often referred to as "The Love Chapter". First Corinthians, where Paul is writing to the people of the church at Corinth. He was explaining that without Love everything else is meaningless. I couldn't agree more with him.
As you can see, the epitaph on our tombstone says, "To Share Love Is The Meaning Of Life". In the mid 80s, the Dalai Lama visited the United States and Santa Fe, New Mexico was one of the cities he visited. He was fascinated with the mountains and the ski area and asked if he could go to the top of a mountain and observe skiing. He and the rest of the monks, all in their normal dress of robes got on the ski lift and rode to the top of the mountain. They were wondering around, watching the skiers in wonder at this unfamiliar sport and they stopped in front of the lift. Someone shouted too late, "Don't walk in front of the lift". Four teenage girls came off the quad chair and ran into the Dalai Lama and his group of monks. Girls and monks all collapsed into a tangle of legs, skis, and poles. The Dalai Lama was lying in the snow with his face distorted and of course everyone thought he was hurt with broken bones, possibly a broken back. They soon realized that he was not injured but was helpless with laughter. "At ski area, you keep eye open always!" he said. They went down the ski lift to the lodge for cookies and hot chocolate. As they finished, a young waitress began clearing the table. She stopped to listen to the conversation and finally sat down. After a bit, there was a pause in the conversation and she spoke to the Dalai Lama.

She said, "Can I, um, ask a question?" She spoke with complete seriousness and said, "What is the meaning of Life?" There was a stunned silence at the table. The Dalai Lama answered. "The meaning of life is happiness." He raised his finger, leaning forward, focusing on her. "Hard question is not 'what is meaning of life?' That is easy question to answer! No, hard question is what make happiness? Money? Big house? Accomplishment? Friends? or..." He paused. "Compassion and good heart? This is question all human beings must try to answer: What make true happiness?" He fell silent, gazing at her with a warm smile. "Thank you," she said. "Thank you." She got up and finished clearing the table.

For me, what make true happiness, was sharing Love with Kathy. It is also sharing Love with my children, grandchildren and all of you so to me, the meaning of life is sharing Love.

Back to our scripture for today. I chose the King James Version because I think it is more poetic than the newer versions although the newer versions make it clearer.

1 Corinthians 13:1-13

Though I speak with the tongues of men and of angels, and have not Love, I am become as sounding brass, or a tinkling cymbal. And though I have the gift of prophecy, and understand all mysteries, and all knowledge; and though I have all faith, so that I could remove mountains, and have not Love, I am nothing. And though I bestow all my goods to feed the poor, and though I give my body to be burned, and have not Love, it profiteth me nothing.

Love suffereth long, and is kind; Love envieth not; Love vaunteth not itself, is not puffed up, Doth not behave itself unseemly, seeketh not her own, is not easily provoked, thinketh no evil; Rejoiceth not in iniquity, but rejoiceth in the truth; Beareth all things, believeth all things, hopeth all things, endureth all things.

Love never faileth: but whether there be prophecies, they shall fail; whether there be tongues, they shall cease; whether there be knowledge, it shall vanish away.

For we know in part, and we prophesy in part.

But when that which is perfect is come, then that which is in part shall be done away.

When I was a child, I spake as a child, I understood as a child, I thought as a child: but when I became a man, I put away childish things.

For now we see through a glass, darkly; but then face to face: now I know in part; but then shall I know even as also I am known.

And now abideth faith, hope, Love, these three; but the greatest of these is Love. (KJV)

To me, this is the most relevant scripture in the Bible because it is the foundation for life. For God so loved the world that he gave his one and only son, that whoever believes in him shall not perish but have eternal life. John 3: 16

For the service today, I will use "The Service at the Grave" from the Lutheran Service Book and Hymnal. From Service Book and Hymnal copyright © 1958 admin. Augsburg Fortress. Reproduced by permission.

Blessed are the dead which die in the Lord from henceforth; Yea, saith the Spirit, that they may rest from their labors. I am the Resurrection and the Life, saith the Lord; he that believeth in me, though he were dead, yet shall he live; and whosoever liveth and believeth in me shall never die.

Forasmuch as it hath pleased Almighty God in his wise providence to call out of this world the soul of our sister, Kathleen Edith Hoffman Knuth, we therefore commit her body to the ground. Dust thou art, to dust thou shalt return. Jesus Christ our Saviour, shall at the latter day raise thee from the dead.

Almighty God, who by the death of thy Son, Jesus Christ, hast destroyed death, and by his rest in the tomb hast sanctified the graves of thy saints, and by his glorious resurrection hast brought life and immortality to light, so that all who die in him abide in peace and hope: Receive, we beseech thee, our unfeigned thanks for the victory over death and the grave which he hath obtained for us, and for all who sleep in him; and keep us, who are still in the body, in everlasting fellowship with all that wait for thee on earth, and with all around thee in heaven, in union with him who is the Resurrection and the Life, even Jesus Christ our Lord. Amen

Now the God of peace, that brought again from the dead our Lord Jesus, the great Shepherd of the sheep, through the blood of the everlasting covenant: Make you perfect in every good work to do his will; working in you that which is well pleasing in his sight; through Jesus Christ, to whom be glory for ever and ever. Amen

The Lord Bless thee and keep thee. The Lord make his face shine upon thee, and be gracious unto thee. The Lord lift up his countenance upon thee, and give thee peace. Amen
In the name of the Father, Son and the Holy Spirit. Amen

This concludes the service. There will be a catered meal this evening in Bismarck at the Seratoma park at site # 6. This park is next to Dakota Zoo, if anyone needs assistance finding it, I'm not your person. Someone from Bismarck, I'm sure, can help you or my son who can find anything on the internet, if he can get service here, may be able to help you. Dinner is at 6:00pm and will be grilled prime rib and roast turkey.

Everyone is welcome, Kathy is buying. We will celebrate Kathy's life with a dinner and time with family and friends. This is the family reunion Kathy and I talked about having but never accomplished about a year ago. It is for my family and her family, OUR family and OUR friends. If you have people that couldn't be here today but who can attend this evening, please bring them. All are welcome.

Thank you and safe travels. See you in Bismarck.

This concludes the burial service.

I told Kathy before she died that I more than likely would not marry again. I think it came up when she was lamenting the fact that she had never quit smoking and now it was too late. She mentioned that my sister, Verla, in trying to convince her to quit had told her that smoking would probably kill her and then I would probably marry some bimbo that would be spending all the money that Kathy had worked so hard for and saved. Kathy told me to be cautious about whom I chose to marry and spend her money. I told her that she had spoiled me and that no one could take her place so I would stay single and spend all her money myself.

That part is true but it is also true that in sharing a life, history is a big part of it and if I married again, the history would not be there. Forty seven years of history is more than most are allotted. Part of that history gives you the comfort of knowing one another, our likes and dislikes and our idiot-syncracies (idio-syncracies). That part would be missing and at this advanced age, I valued that comfort part of knowing what the other is thinking and their feelings. I didn't find it boring but rather comforting. I can always find something to do so I am never bored. As you can tell, I value my own opinion and find myself good company and even like myself.

Just as Kathy is "Unforgettable" as in the song by that name that Nat King Cole sang, Kathy is also "Irreplaceable". Right now that is what I would be trying to do and that would be unfair for anyone.

Falling in love again, would be a new experience but one, at least at this point and time, I am not ready for. Grief is an emotional passage that never ends. Perhaps someday, I will be far enough in that passage to consider alternative life styles, as they say now days but marriage probably won't be one of them. As my father said after my mother died and some of his female friends were coming to visit him, "I had a good marriage and good life and one marriage is enough for me". That was back before people were living together without marriage so I'm sure he never even considered that possibility. I kind of feel the same way as he did, at least right now. As the song goes, "Times, they are a changing". So, never say never.

Epilogue
One Dummy pulling his own strings

I titled the book as I did because I am somewhat of a non-conformist. My Mother and many of my relatives would probably say I am just ornery. I prefer to think of myself as an independent thinker. Whatever you choose to label me is fine with me because I will still pull my own strings and I am still a dummy.

Even as a child, I pulled my own strings. I would play with girls and even play dolls with the girls. My male friends would tease me and even sometimes make fun of me but that wouldn't stop me. I would often tell them I liked girls and enjoyed playing with them. I also liked to play with boys toys such as cars and trucks and play with guys when we were playing basketball and boys games.

The girls were not fond of playing basketball in the yard where there were chickens because of the chicken waste you could step in or even bounce the ball in which then transferred to your hand. Guys would just rub it off and continue the game. I noticed that after a while some of my friends were also playing with girls and enjoying both the playing and the girls. Soon the girls were welcome and even sought to play softball, anti-i-over, kick the can, moonlight- starlight, cowboys and Indians and even winter games like king on the hill. I'm not claiming I was responsible for this. I believe it was a natural progression. I'm just saying I naturally progressed before many of my friends and didn't allow them to pull my strings.

As a teenager, I was a rebel without a clue. I smoked and drank and rebelled against rules especially those rules enforced in the school. I wasn't as much of a rebel as some of my friends that would actually get in a fist fight with a teacher but I would push the envelope and think outside the box before it became popular. I did not use drugs or smoke marijuana, ever. Still haven't. I never found that to be a problem or a temptation, even as a young adult. None of my friends as a teenager did either. I'm not sure if it was because of the lack of availability or personal choices. Latter in my young adult life while in the Navy, the availability was not a problem. For me it was a personal choice. There was never any pressure from my peers to use or smoke because they didn't want to share and I was too broke or cheap to buy my own. I also valued my life and honestly was afraid of the addiction.

As a teenager and beyond, I was exposed to a lot of infidelity of friends and acquaintances with girlfriends and wives. To most of my peers, if the chance came along for sex, It was an opportunity you shouldn't pass up. I mostly agreed with them but when it came right down to it, didn't want the heartbreak to occur that often comes to others, especially if one of my friends would be the injured party. Also, If sex was too available, I was very suspicious and thought it might be a trap and I might be forced into marrying a pregnant girl. While watching all the unfaithfulness that goes on and being tempted to participate in it, I noticed that most of the time, it involved alcohol. Not always but most of the time. Especially for those that normally wouldn't be involved in this behavior and who would have feelings of guilt and regret after participating in it. As a single person, I resolved that if a girl was married, she was off limits to me. Not only because of the possible heartache it could cause but because jealousy is unpredictable. I wanted to keep breathing. Single girls were fair game but be careful of traps.

Later, after I became a husband, everyone but my wife was off limits. I soon realized after I was married that many opportunities could and did arise to be unfaithful and there were those that didn't let the fact that they were married, slow down the pursuit.

I felt the best way to deal with this, especially when alcohol was involved, was to eliminate the opportunity. I tried never to go out for a night to drink without my wife. I won't say I never went drinking without my wife but it never happened without my wife's knowledge and ok. If the guys went out for a few drinks after work, I would suggest we call our wives and invite them. If my wife couldn't or didn't want to join us, I would have a drink or two and go home. Sometimes, situations would be such so the wives wouldn't be included such as bowling night or softball games or supervisors club. On these occasions, sometimes the participants wanted to continue the fun after the activity had ended. I would suggest we call our wives to join us. Sometimes I would be accused of being pussy whipped. I would admit I was and tell them I was happy being in that circumstance. Usually, the wives were called or I just went home. I believe that anyone given the right circumstances is capable of anything, good or evil. Alcohol is one of the circumstances that makes that true. So you see, it was myself I couldn't trust so I tried to avoid the situations where I could be tempted. I had many acquaintances who would go out drinking without their spouse. Then the spouse would be upset and say if you can do that, so can I. They would get their friends together and go out drinking. This would lead to disagreements, jealousies, fights and in many cases divorce. In fact, just about all the people that practiced that type of lifestyle, that I can think of, ended up divorced. I valued my marriage and family more than that. So, I pulled my own strings.

Another way I pulled my own strings and didn't follow society was the new vehicle. It seemed to me everyone wanted a new shiny vehicle and would go above their heads into debt to acquire one. This often led to financial struggles which led to family arguments of finances and how to spend them. I had one new car in my life which I acquired when I was single and in the Navy. After that, I always bought used vehicles, generally about ten years old. They were generally vehicles that were previously owned by friends, relatives or local people. People I knew or knew of and knew their character and if they took care of their things or abused them. This is easier to do in a small town where you know everyone or know of them. Usually I paid cash for them so eliminated the monthly car payment and interest on them.

Ten year old vehicles are generally not that expensive, especially relative to a new one. I usually drove them for about ten years or until they were twenty years old. My reasoning was I could spend a lot of money in monthly repairs and still be spending less than the car payment on a new car.

I am not mechanically inclined. In fact my father-in-law often got a good laugh at my expense and my lack of mechanical knowledge. Like the time I was going to do my brother-in-law a favor by changing oil for him when he was dying of cancer and could no longer do it himself. I drained the transmission instead of the oil pan. The car doesn't run well with no transmission fluid and an oversupply of oil. Everyone got a good laugh out of that one, exposing my ignorance. However, because of my ignorance of mechanics, I took my vehicles to mechanics that knew what they were doing and my father-in-law often said, "Dwight takes good care of his cars". If I try to do the repairs myself, I generally end up taking it to a mechanic and pay more for him fixing what was wrong in the first place plus correcting what I screwed up. I was willing to pay a mechanic to keep my car in good running order and reliable just as you pay any other professional for doing what they are trained to do.

The trick is to find a honest reliable mechanic and stick with that one. He gets to know your car and is familiar with the quirks. It's kind of like a hair dresser you become comfortable with and don't want anyone else. I would go to the garage and make an appointment for the one mechanic I wanted and be clear I didn't want anyone else working on the car. Sometimes I would have to wait days for that mechanic because he had built a reputation and was in demand.

I once had a GMC pickup that was the laughing stock of the town because it was so rusted out there was not much left of it. I had to take it to an auto body repair shop to have a new floor welded in because the mud, dirt and snow would come into the

cab driving down the street. It was
because of the mechanic that took care
would start in the winter when it was way
other vehicles that were not garaged would no
driving to work and parking in the parking lot there
could do no harm to its appearance.

At the Boise Cascade paper mill where I worked, they would have a vehicle roaming the parking lot in the winter when it got below zero at shift change times. This was so if anyone's vehicle didn't start they could give you a jump start. I don't remember ever needing to get a jump start at the mill, even when it was forty below. So if it got covered with pollution from the mill smokestacks or got bumped or scratched from another vehicle, you had a hard time telling. Many times when I would take it around town and park in a parking lot of a business, when I would come out of the business, there may be several young men or boys standing by it pointing and laughing. I would laugh with them and point something else out to them.

When this would happen and my mother-in-law was with, she would get upset and defend it. She loved that truck. I generally used it for pulling the boat, going to work and hauling things. I had a second vehicle my wife used that was probably as old but not so rusted out. Sometimes in the mill parking lot there would be nice new vehicles, even corvettes and I would say to myself, why would you drive an expensive vehicle like that to work? I believe I saved tens of thousands of dollars by doing this. Instead of spending that savings on other things I didn't need, I invested it in my 401K retirement plan that allowed me to either invest in the stock market or fixed interest accounts.

I never was very concerned with how I looked because I didn't have to look at myself except if I happened by a mirror. My wife tried to dress me so I was presentable but even that didn't always work. One example was wearing a proper head cover when it is below zero. In the Navy we had wool watch hats that were warm and covered your whole head including your ears. I loved my watch hat and had several and when winter arrived would start wear it as soon as it turned a little on the cold side. It didn't matter if there was snow on the ground or not. Comfort above appearance. I also noticed that I would be the first one to start wearing a knit wool hat but once some of the others noticed I was wearing it, they would also start wearing one. You could say I was a trend setter. I would sometimes get sarcastic comments like isn't it a little early for the headgear or it isn't that cold out. I would simply reply that it did the job for me and it is your choice to wear what you want. Some of the macho guys would not wear any head cover all winter and some would wear baseball caps all winter. To each his own. The knit hat did not enhance your hair style especially if you had long hair. Oh well, again, comfort over appearance.

    The point is, don't pull your own strings to go against society or be a rebel or be different. Pull your own strings because you are a thinking individual that makes your own choices in life and makes them because you have thought about them and it is the best choice for you and your life. Don't let others dictate your life for you. Just because something is popular or is done by everyone else, doesn't make it right for you. On the other hand, if you are a shy person and don't want to stand out or be different, that is a choice you have made because it is best for you. Go with it. Sometimes the best choice for you is to go along with the crowd to live at peace with the crowd and those you love and don't want to hurt or embarrass. Just think about your choices and the consequences of them to you and those you love.

Afterword

Whatever you do, put romance and enthusiasm into the life of our children.
Margaret Ramsey Macdonald (1870-1911)

This book is written for the benefit of my Children and Grandchildren. Hopefully they can get an idea of what life was like while we occupied space on this planet. By recording the escapades of my ill spent youth as well as the everyday struggles, failures and successes, I hope you will find the romance in life and create your own enthusiasm for life. It would be my hope that you will come away with the knowledge that life is to be lived, enjoyed, embraced and you need to roll with the punches life throws your way.

Define your own life. Don't let other people write your life's story for you. Pull your own strings.

You need not search for happiness because happiness is an attitude. As Abraham Lincoln said, "you are as happy as you make up your mind to be". To quote another wise person, David Steindl-Rast, "Gratefulness is not the result of happiness, it is the cause of happiness". Live gratefully and you will live happily. Which is just another way of saying, have a positive attitude, look on the bright side of life. There is always something to be grateful for.

As you go through life making and learning from your mistakes, remember that some mistakes are too much fun to only make once. Also know that if you never make a mistake, you aren't doing anything.

My prayer for you is that your life will be filled with Love, laughter, hope, dreams, kindness and faith in yourselves, others and our creator. That in your life you will experience pleasure and enough pain to enhance the pleasure. Joy and a lessor amount of sorrow but enough to insure the joy is appreciated. That you do not fear or shy away from living life and all the emotions and you embrace and celebrate life. God bless you and make you a blessing.

About the Author

Dwight is an author that writes about life and the emotions experienced. His telling of his life story is not always a happy story but he tries to sprinkle even the sad moments with a little humor or irony and he is not above sarcasm.

As the title suggests, he is a bit of a non-conformist or as his wife called him, "A Rebel Without A Clue". As a child when his Mother was at her wits end with him she would say, "I hope you live long enough to have children and that they turn out exactly like you". She also told him not to ever worry about being kidnapped because they would bring him back in a short time. Even his Dr. at the Mayo Clinic told him he would live long enough to make everyone he loved miserable.

He never got in any serious trouble but he liked to skate around the edge of it and occasionally his skates slipped and he fell into it.

He was a golden glove boxer in high school without much success. His strategy as a boxer was to bleed all over his opponent. At the age of 16, his friend and he hitchhiked half way across the US and on the return trip hopped a freight train and learned how to be a successful bum. At the age of 17 he joined the ND Army National Guard and continued his boxing career. In the Army he gave up the strategy of bleeding on his boxing opponent and won the NDANG championship. The local constable was so fond of him, rather than jail him he tried to render him unconscious with his Billy club.

After high school he joined the Navy, pursued a career as a computer programmer, married, worked for a major US Corp. as a computer programmer, system analyst and Mgr. of IT. He retired at 58, beat cancer, cared for his wife as she died of cancer and lives alone in the icebox of the nation, International Falls, MN

CPSIA information can be obtained
at www.ICGtesting.com
Printed in the USA
FFOW02n1121051216
29846FF